FEDERALISM AND POLITICAL RESTRUCTURING IN NIGERIA

Federalism and Political Restructuring in Nigeria

Edited by
'Kunle Amuwo
Adigun A.B. Agbaje
Rotimi T. Suberu
Georges Hérault

Spectrum Books Limited
Ibadan
Benin-City • Kaduna • Lagos • Owerri

and
IFRA
Ibadan

Published by
Spectrum Books Limited
Spectrum House
Ring Road
PMB 5612
Ibadan, Nigeria

in association with
Safari Books (Export) Limited
1st Floor
17 Bond Street
St Helier
Jersey JE2 3NP
Channel Islands
United Kingdom

Europe and USA Distributor
African Books Collective Ltd.,
The Jam Factory,
27 Park End Street,
Oxford OX1, 1HU, UK

© 'Kunle Amuwo, Adigun Agbaje, Rotimi Suberu and Georges Hérault, 1998

First published, 1998

Reprinted 1999

All rights reserved. This book is copyright and so no part of it may be reproduced, stored in a retrieval system, or transmitted, in any form or by any means, electronic, mechanical, electrostatic, magnetic tape, photocopying, recording or otherwise, without the prior written permission of the copyright owners.

ISBN: 978-029-009-5

Printmarks Ventures, Ososami.

Dedicated to

Claude Eleme Ake (1939-1996)
Africa's foremost political economist

Contents

Dedication	*v*
Acknowledgements	*xi*
Contributors	*xiii*

INTRODUCTION:	ON THE NOTION OF POLITICAL RESTRUCTURING IN A FEDERAL SYSTEM K. Amuwo and G. Hérault.	1
SECTION ONE:	FEDERALISM AND POLITICAL RESTRUCTURING IN HISTORICAL PERSPECTIVE	11
Chapter 1	Nigerian Federalism in Historical Perspective. Tekena N. Tamuno.	13
Chapter 2	The Development of the Federal Idea and the Federal Framework, 1914-1960 Osarhieme Benson Osadolor.	34
Chapter 3	Federalism, Inter-ethnic Conflicts and the Northernisation Policy of the 1950s and 1960s Olawale Albert.	50
Chapter 4	Political Restructuring as Militarisation: Fragments of Evidence from Civil Society Sanya Osha.	64
Chapter 5	Beyond the Orthodoxy of Political Restructuring: The Abacha Junta and the Political Economy of Force `Kunle Amuwo.	71
SECTION TWO:	FEDERAL CHARACTER AND POWER SHARING.	99
Chapter 6	The Federal Character Principle and the Search for National Integration J.A.A. Ayoade.	101
Chapter 7	The Ideology of Power Sharing: An Analysis of Content, Context and Intent Adigun Agbaje.	121

Chapter 8	Rotational Presidency and State-Building in Nigeria. `Wale Are Olaitan.	137
Chapter 9	The Constitutional Conference, Political Restructuring and Women's Access to Power I. Bola Udegbe.	147
Chapter 10	The Federal Character Principle, Consociationalism and Democratic Stability in Nigeria. Dauda Abubakar.	164
Chapter 11	Federal Character Principle and National Integration. C.C. Agbodike.	177
Chapter 12	On the Ethics of Ethnic Balancing in Nigeria: Federal Character Reconsidered. Chris O. Uroh.	191
Chapter 13	Federal Character as an Equity Principle. David A. Utume.	201

SECTION THREE: POLITICAL RESTRUCTURING AND THE ECONOMICS OF FEDERALISM — 211

Chapter 14	Revenue Allocation in Nigeria: Derivation Principle Revisited. Gini A. Mbanefoh and Festus O. Egwaikhide.	213
Chapter 15	Revenue Allocation Commissions and the Contradictions in Nigeria's Federalism. Olutayo C. Adesina.	232
Chapter 16	Revenue Allocation and Economics of Federalism. G.D. Olowononi.	247
Chapter 17	The Impact of Oil on Nigeria's Revenue Allocation System: Problems and Prospects for National Reconstruction. Cyril I. Obi	261

Chapter 18	States' Creation and the Political Economy of Nigerian Federalism. Rotimi T. Suberu	276

SECTION FOUR: THE EXECUTIVE IN COMPARATIVE PERSPECTIVE. 297

Chapter 19	The Executive Under the Nigerian Constitutions, 1960-1995. J.D. Ojo	299
Chapter 20	Prognosis for the Organisation of the Executive Arm of Government in Nigeria's Fourth Republic. Bolade M. Eyinla	316

CONCLUSION 333

The Future of Nigeria's Federalism R.T. Suberu and A. Agbaje	335

Index 351

Acknowledgements

Several individuals and groups have contributed to the preparation of this volume. The idea of a conference and/or volume on political restructuring in contemporary Nigeria was initially conceived by *Institut Francais de Recherche en Afrique* (IFRA) in conjunction with the French Embassy in Lagos as a follow-up to the 1996 EEC-sponsored Conference in Bordeaux on the European Union and the Nigerian democratisation process. We would like to thank Professor Daniel Bach of *Centre d'etudes d'Afrique Noire* (C.E.A.N.) Bordeaux, Professor Alex Gboyega of the University of Ibadan, Professor Georges Hérault of IFRA and Jean-Claude Piet of the French Embassy in Lagos for their vital contributions at that initial stage of the project's conception. The editors would also like to thank Drs. Jibrin Ibrahim, Nnamdi Obasi and H. Gusau who were members of the initial working team set up to facilitate the project. The editors are grateful to the various contributors for responding to our invitations to submit papers for consideration for inclusion in this volume and, in a number of cases, for revising their contributions for publication. The editors are especially grateful to Professors John Ayoade, Gini Mbanefoh, J.D. Ojo and Tekena Tamuno who, in spite of their very tight schedules, responded to our invitation to contribute 'lead' papers to this volume.

The editors are grateful to the staff of the IFRA Secretariat, University of Ibadan, for logistics support. We would also want to thank Spectrum Books for their prompt and competent execution of this project. We are particularly grateful to the Company's Publishing Director, Mr. Tony Igboekwe, for his enthusiasm and professionalism.

Finally, this volume is appropriately dedicated to the late Professor Claude Eleme Ake who, but for his tragic death on November 7, 1996, we had planned to involve in this project. May his gentle soul rest in perfect peace.

Contributors

Abubakar Dauda is of the Department of Political Science, University of Maiduguri, Borno State.
Adesina, C. Olutayo is a Lecturer in History, University of Ibadan.
Agbaje, A.A.B. is Senior Lecturer, Department of Political Science, University of Ibadan.
Agbodike, C.C. is of the Department of Arts, Nnamdi Azikiwe University, Awka, Anambra State.
Albert Olawale is of the Institute of African Studies, University of Ibadan.
Amuwo 'Kunle is Senior Lecturer and Head, Department of Political Science, University of Ibadan.
Ayoade, John, A.A., Professor of Political Science, is the current Dean, Faculty of The Social Sciences, University of Ibadan.
Eghwakide, Festus is Senior Lecturer in Economics, University of Ibadan.
Eyinla, Bolanle M. teaches History at the University of Ilorin, Kwara State.
Hérault, Georges is a Professor of Linguistics and Director of IFRA (1992-1997)
Mbanefoh, Gini is a Professor of Economics at the University of Ibadan and Acting Vice-Chancellor, University of Nigeria, Nsukka (UNN).
Obi, Cyril I. is a Research Fellow at the Nigerian Institute of International Affairs, Lagos.
Ojo, J.D., a Professor of Constitutional Law, is presently the Dean, Faculty of Law, University of Ibadan.
Olaitan, 'Wale, a Political Science teacher, is the current Sub-dean, Faculty of Social and Management Sciences, Ogun State University, Ago-Iwoye.
Olowononi, G.D. teaches Economics at the Ahmadu Bello University, Zaria.
Osadolor, B.O. until recently of the Department of History, University of Ibadan, is currently at the Universitat Hamburg, Germany.
Osha, Sanya teaches Philosophy in the General Studies Department of the Ladoke Akintola University of Technology, Ogbomoso, Oyo State.
Suberu, R.T. is a Senior Lecturer in the Department of Political Science, University of Ibadan.
Tamuno, T.N. Professor of History and a former Vice-Chancellor of the University of Ibadan is the Chairman, Presidential Panel on Nigeria's History Project.
Udegbe, I.B. is Senior Lecturer and Head, Department of Pyschology, University of Ibadan.
Uroh, C.O. teaches Philosophy at the University of Ibadan.
Utume, D.A. is of the Department of Political Science, Benue State University, Makurdi.

INTRODUCTION

INTRODUCTION

'Kunle Amuwo and Georges Hérault

On the Notion of Political Restructuring in Federal Systems

It is becoming increasingly clear in the wake of the new globalism that ensued after the cold war that federal systems, no less than non-federal ones, are faced with two key demands — namely those of nationalism and democracy. Whilst it is true that it has hardly been easy to manage federal systems, including the so-called classic ones built, according to Max Frankel, from below, even those ethnically-segmented federations like Nigeria that lack both democracy and development are often at great pains not to disintegrate.

In 1979, the editors of an important work published in Nigeria, *Readings on Federalism* that brought together in one volume views of some of the leading scholars in Comparative Federalism worldwide claimed, in their preface, that

> one of the things which was stressed by several participants from other countries (aside Nigeria)... was the fact that several federal states are either engaged in, or about to begin, the process of reviewing their federal systems in order to retain their relevance to their societies.

They also added, perhaps for effect, that "the need to review each federal system was not seen as a sign of weakness or as something to apologise for". (A.B. Akinyemi *et al* (eds), 1979:ix). This is because, whereas federalism "promises... that federal institutions may be designed to meet the particular needs of the communities establishing them" (S.S Ramphal, 1979:xvii), the promise is often honoured more in its breach than in its delivery. In general, federalism's minimalist promissory note to permit nations and peoples forming the union, their own nationalism and self-determination is more easily endangered in a non-democratic federal system than in a democratic federal polity. This is fundamentally so because absent in the former is a civic culture which is more or less entrenched in the latter. The civic culture is germane to the thriving of the working conceptual phraseologies in a federal system such as `unity in diversity'; `existence of relatively independent centres of power', `local people deciding on local priorities', etc.

In 1996, M. Kesselman, J. Kriger and W.A. Joseph, general editors of, amongst others, *Democracies at the Crossroads* arguing that many countries in the North at different levels of consolidation of both industralisation and democracy, express the hope, *inter alia*, that the post-war democratic experience of Germany and Japan will "provide lessons in how formerly authoritarian regimes can consolidate democracy". The editors also underline the significance of the typologies of India and Brazil, third world countries that are struggling, the one fairly successfully for over half a century, the other for less than two decades, to implant and consolidate democracy.

It is instructive that aside from Japan, all the states aforementioned are federal polities. It would therefore appear that K.C. Wheare (in L.A. Jinadu, 1979:21) was, afterall, right to have posited that democracy is a condition of federalism. In his words "federalism demands forms of government which have the characteristics usually associated with democratic or free government". The major attributes of federalism include territorially-based, though centrally enforced power and resource distribution, `a centre with limited responsibilities', shared rule and self-rule; pragmatic and flexible leadership and rules of the game etc. It is hardly possible to maintain, let alone consolidate, a legitimated federal system without due and strict observance of the foregoing attributes.

Indeed, if we define governance as involving a struggle of competing interests in a given polity and we agree that in the post-cold war era, federal systems cannot but grapple with the issue of collective identity, federalism and democracy necessarily come into sharp focus as mutually reinforcing conceptual, theoretical and processual categories that are locked up in the dynamics of a dialectical relationship. In other words, there is the notion of the "democratic idea" which is all about "the challenges often posed by citizens' demands for greater control and participation even in countries generally regarded as highly democratic" (Kesselman, Krigger, Joseph, 1996:9). When this finds copious and robust expression on ground as democratic practice in the form of the politics of collective identities in terms of "the political consequences of race, ethnicity, gender, religion and nationality and their complex interplay with class-based politics", the federal polity is likely to be less acrimonious than when the democratic idea is little more than a putative or theoretical construct.

On the German experience since the Berlin wall fell in 1989, Christopher S. Allen (1996:215) has this to say:

> The challenge for German politics is to maintain a system of democratic participation that encompasses both extra-institutional groups and specific organised political institutions in a way that enhances democracy rather than destroys it.

The Notion of Political Restructuring in Political Systems

In general terms, one of the several variables apart from a civic political culture that draws the linkage between the democratic idea and democratic practice is political restructuring. This is one concept or notion that means different things to different political leaders in contemporary federal systems more so in those where (as in post-June 12, 1993 Nigeria) most nationalities seek a "radically restructured federation in which the power of the federal state is reduced" (A.O. Olukoshi and O. Agbu, 1996:87). Political restructuring seems to be informed by the poor praxis of an admittedly formal federal system. In other words, the clamour for restructuring is more stringent in countries with a federal form of government — and perhaps also a federal constitution — but with a unitary practice. As William Riker (cited in A. Stepan, 1997:24) has noted, "what counts is not the rather trivial constitutional structure, but rather the political and economical culture".

The political and economic culture of a federal system in terms of the aggregate premises — both value and factual - of governance can, to varying degrees, depending on the nature and character of the federal state, be antithetical to the wishes, aspirations and goals of individuals and nationalities. Thus, the argument of J.J. Linz (1997a:21), that "federalism can only assure that nobody could be fully unahppy but certainly not that everybody will be happy with the solution". However, when a neopatrimonial federal logic makes happy only state officials and their acolytes, even if the latter cut across ethnic, religious, regional, class and gender cleavages, pockets of dissent, dissidence and contestations will naturally emerge. Olukoshi and Agbu (1996:97) have, on this score, contended, rightly in our view, that

> it is ... necessary to recognise that the crisis of Nigerian federalism is not just about bickering `tribes' but also about social injustices that are rooted in cross-national class and gender conflicts.

Expressed differently, whilst federalism has brought several nations within the Nigerian polity together, actual federal practice has hardly been able to keep them together happily.

Similarly, whilst the Indian Constitution directs the Indian government to promote social and economic equality and justice - and that country is generally regarded as a fairly successful federal democracy — clear indications of repression still subsist; hence the argument that "Indian democracy has accommodated many new power challenges while successfully repressing the most difficult ones" (Atul Kohli, 1996:309).

Essence of Political Restructuring

Notwithstanding the existence of other forms of logic, the main drive towards institutional reforms in a federal system is the recognition, however arrived at, that existing state institutions, particularly at the centre, are inadequate to apprehend, comprehend and resolve immediate and new challenges. Citing governability as one of the three major contemporary political tensions in India, Kohli identifies the attendant dilemma as consisting of ``how to create effective political institutions that can both accommodate diverse interests and provide effective government'' (Kohli, 1996:325).

To all appearances, political restructuring in a federal polity is intended to achieve certain specific objectives. One, restructuring is meant to serve as a steering mechanism to properly give focus and locus to atttempts at collective identity and distributive politics. The aim is to correct perceived structural defects and institutional deformities. To tinker with political structures is perhaps suggestive that whilst democratic practice may not yet have firm roots, the democratic idea has some form of expression. The importance of the latter ideal in a federal system can hardly be over-emphasised, particularly where there are not only actually existing irredentist movements but also nationalities being driven to agitate for separatist identities.

Two, political restructuring is intended to lay an institutional foundation for a more just and a more equitable sharing of the political space by multinational groups cohabiting in a federal polity. The strategic objective seems to be the solidifying — or perhaps merely engendering — of a sense of national community. Within this context, political restructuring is an indication that some spirit of political bargaining, however circumscribed, does exist, notwithstanding whether or not the decision to restructure the polity by the ruling class or clique was voluntary or otherwise.

Furthermore, part of the *raison d'etre* of political restructuring is a better appreciation of the need for tolerance and respect for civil and civic rights of both aggrieved ethnic majorities and marginalised ethnic minorities. In underdeveloped and poor federal polities where, as in Nigeria, the federal structure is perceived as a device for the elite to take advantage of state largesse (W.D Graf, 1988:15), this `civic rationality' comes into sharp focus. Whenever it is given free rein, the federal system as well as the nation-state or, as the case may be, the state-nation become legitimated, in one and the same breath, in the eyes of the civil society and the multinational groups. Where, on the contrary, civic rationality or logic is conspicuous by its absence, disintegration of the wretchedly-wedged federal polity will sooner or later loom large on the political horizon.

The Nigerian Example

Nigeria's political restructuring efforts under the Abacha military junta (November 1993 till date) has been informed mainly by elite factionalism as well as by the persistent demand by pro-democracy and human rights groups (as in the twilight years of the Babangida military presidency (1985-1993) for a Sovereign National Conference. The latter was conceptualised by these groups as the only viable forum to reinvent the Nigerian federal system with a view to correcting perceived structural lopsidedness and functional inequities.

The clamour for a Sovereign National Conference exacerbated in the aftermath of the annulment of the presidential election held on June 12 1993. Given the fact that the election was historic to the extent that a `Southerner' (Chief M.K.O. Abiola) was elected the country's president for the first time in its annals and the fact that its annulment was effected by a `Northern' military president, the impression was created, rightly or wrongly, that the North did not want a transfer of power to the South. Old wounds were opened so much so that in the midst of the high-wired politics, in the now re-jigged political market — as gleaned through the massive political manoeuvrings from the Babaginda regime through the lame-duck Interim National Government to the seizure of power by the Abacha junta — Africa's most populous country was gradually snowballing into a state of anarchy and non-governability.

The annulment merely worsened the decline in the capacity of the Nigerian state to govern and to deliver. The Constitutional Conference, the Abacha junta's only response to the generalised disorder and discontentment in the land, was itself heavily regimented and massively flawed from the beginning. As detailed in some of the chapters in this volume, an appreciable number of members nominated into the Constitutional Conference Commission (the body charged with organising the conference) and the Conference proper were known to have spoken against the propriety of the Conference before their appointment. The junta would later appoint a good number of its advisers and ministers from members of the Constitutional Conference.

Since the Conference ended in June 1995, the Abacha regime has demonstrated, both in words and in action, that the Conference was only a plank for inter-nationality relations amongst the country's multinational groups. It has also sent unmistakable signs that only those politicians, particularly from aggrieved nationalities such as the Yoruba, the Ogoni, the Ijaw etc, who stood up to be counted on its side in the critical period of the early months of its *coup de force* would benefit from state patronage. To the well-known neo-patrimonial logic of the Nigerian federal state has been added a monist and non-accommodationist perspective of politics.

In other words, if the inauguration of the constitutional conference in June 1994 was preceded as in the post-military civilian restoration regime in Brazil in the 1980s by calls for ``deeper institutional ruptures with the authoritarian past'' (M.de Carmo Campello de Souza, 1996:348), it was largely because not only the country's economy and polity, but also its self-identity, were in crisis. Things have, since 1993, not been the same again in Nigeria. In the place of a seeming inclusive model of politics that the Babangida regime was putting in place through its costly transition-to-civil rule programme — a programme that was deliberately aborted at photofinish by the regime's principal *dramatis personae* is an apparent exclusive model of politics being systematically played by the Abacha junta and its politico-military acolytes. In the process, several social classes, political and nationality groups have been denied both their self-identity and self-expression. The consequence has been monumentally negative. *Primo*, more doubts are being raised and more open discussions, both within and outside Nigeria, are going on a *propos* the increasing possibility of the country's disintegration. In this context, the Yoruba people in the diaspora have suggested two options as a way out of the political impasse. One, a breakup of the Nigerian federation, as presently constituted, so that the Yoruba, perceived by their leaders in the diaspora as a target of economic and political persecutions by the Abacha junta, could seek their own national destiny outside Nigeria. Two, a return to the regional autonomy of the First Republic. In the latter context, the organisers of the 5th National Yoruba Convention held in Houston, Texas in April 1997, ``expressed their readiness to work for a constitutional arrangement and political restructuring in which the Yoruba nation, along with other nationalities in Nigeria has an unfettered autonomy that will foster their civilisation'' (``Drumbeats of Secession'', *The News* 26 May 1997:12-19).

Secondo, there is a further deterioration in the phenomenon of the `retrenchment of the Nigerian State', first advertised by Professor Sam Egite Oyovbaire in his presidential address to the Nigerian Political Science Association (NPSA) in Ilorin in May 1985. In a fundamental sense, to the extent that the Nigerian State does not cease to deny Nigerians their civic rights as citizens, many Nigerians take refuge in the ethnic right to recover their citizenship. Yet, as the state continues to lose touch with the reality of the misery index of Nigerians, and acquires the character of a recluse evacuated from the public domain, even the ethnic right is being violated and assaulted by a state that hardly has any other viable instrument of relationship with multinational groups and civil society aside structural force and violence.

The sum-total of the foregoing behavioural characteristics of a military junta involved in putative political restructuring is fairly clear: political restructuring without a committed political will, anchored on openness, transparency, tolerance and accommodation, will abbreviate the underlining philosophy of political restructuring and reforms. The result will be an empty shell — a *form* of restructured federal system with seemingly new centres of power, territorially and functionally, but with little or no *substance* capable of placing the federal state on a more or less even keel.

Whilst it is true that democracy, both as "a way to govern a state" and as "a complex system of institutions, rules and patterned incentives and disincentives" (Linz, 1997b:10,13) is difficult to operate in a poor ethnically-segmented federation that has largely been run by military juntas as a unitary system, it is not altogether impossible. What is required to take the first step in this direction is for the Nigerian State to open up the political space a little; to begin the process of healing the political and economic wounds through frank and sincere dialogue with concerned multinational groups. Some of the chapters that follow have addressed this extremely important issue with the candour and fortrightness it deserves. Current history — namely the reality of the post-cold war era — seems to be on the side of an eventual democratic political restructuring. A sovietologist's verdict on Russia in the aftermath of post-Gorbachev reforms is relevant to the Nigerian typology, more so within the context of fairly well-articulated sundry international sanctions: "the global nature of politics and economy has made impossible the type of isolation that provided a bulwark for the legitimacy of the Soviet State for many decades" (Joan De Bardeleben, 1996:90).

References

Akinyemi, B.A. P.D. Cole, W. Ofonagoro (eds.) (1979) *Readings on Federalism*. Lagos: Nigerian Institute of International Affairs.

Allen, C.S (1996) "Germany" in M. Kesselman, J. Kriegger, W.A. Joseph (gen. eds.) (1996) *Democracies at the Crossroads*. Lexington, M.A. Toronto: D.C. Heath and Company.

Bardeleben, J. de (1996) "Russia" in M. Kesselman *et. al Communist and Post Communist Politics at the Crossroads*. Lexington; M.A. Toronto: DC Heath and Company.

De Souza M. de Carmo Campello (1996) "Brazil" in M. Kesselman *et. al.* (gen. eds.) (1996) *Democracies at the Crossroads*. Lexington, M.A. Toronto: D.C. Heath and Company.

Graf, W.D. (1988) *The Nigerian State: Political Economy, State Class and Political System in the Post-Colonial Era*. London and Portsmouth: J. Currey and Heinemann.

Jinadu, A.L. (1979), "A Note on the Theory of Federalism" in Akinyemi *et. al,* (eds.) (1979) *Readings on Federalism.* Lagos: Nigerian Institute of International Affairs.

Kesselman, M., J. Kriegger, W.A. Joseph (1996a) *Democracies at the Crossroads.* Lexington, M.A. Toronto: D.C. Heath and Company.

Kesselman *et. al* (1996b) *Communist and Post-communist Politics at the Crossroads.*

Kohli, Atul (1996) "India" in Kesselman *et. al* (1996a), p. 285-327.

Linz, J.J. (1997a) "Democracy, Multinationalism and Federalism" Background paper for the Conference on "Democracy and Federalism", All Souls College, Oxford University, June 5-8.

Linz, J.J. (1997b) "Democratization and Types of Democracies: New Tasks for Comparativists", Background paper (as above) 58pp.

Olukoshi, A.O. and O. Agbu (1996) "The Deepening Crisis of Nigerian Federalism and the Future of the Nation-State" in A.O. Olukoshi and Lisa Laakso (eds.) *Challenges to the Nation-State in Africa.* Uppsala: Nordiska Afrikainstitutet.

Ramphal, S.S. (1979) "Keynote Address in Akinyemi *et. al, Readings on Federalism.* Lagos: Nigerian Institute of International Affairs.

Stephan, A. (1997) "Towards a New Comparative Analysis of Democracy and Federalism", Paper read at the Conference on "Democracy and Federalism" (as cited earlier)

SECTION ONE

Federalism and Political Restructuring in Historical Perspective

CHAPTER 1

Tekena N. Tamuno

Nigerian Federalism in Historical Perspective

Overarching Issues

Neither history nor politics nor economics has given the cause of ``federalism'' in Nigeria a smooth ride. However, a lot depends on what one means by the far from plain word ``federalism''.

Federalism, as I understand it, is that form of government where the component units of a political organisation participate in sharing powers and functions in a cooperative manner though the combined forces of ethnic pluralism and cultural diversity, among others, tend to pull their people apart. Delicate arrangements of this kind, where carefully worked out, provide sufficient room for the co-existence of centre-seeking and centre-fleeing forces. Peace, for lucky communities which achieve and sustain measures of this, under these arrangements, is not necessarily that of the grave. Where people agree sometimes, and disagree sometimes, concerning the goals and means of cooperative governments of this kind, friction and conflicts do occur. Where also their systems work, as planned, conflict-resolution is quite possible: through the timely and effective intervention of accredited authorities and organs of government.

Readers already familiar with the works of K.C. Wheare[1] and other pundits in the field of federalist studies will no longer fight over definitions and descriptions. Other issues remain to provoke controversy. Of course, types of federalism differ. Just as there are ``strong'' and ``weak'' forms of federalism, there are also periodic variations which permit ``strength'' or ``weakness'' within the same system to be measured differently. So it was with Nigeria and the USA during their respective phases of secessionist threats and civil wars. Moreover, theory and practice within the same system, as that of Switzerland since her 1848 Constitution, encourage observers to call what they saw either federation or confederation[2]. Similarly, India's Republican Constitution (1949) defies strict classification.

Reliance on academic authorities, perhaps, had impacts beyond reasonable expectations on the theorists themselves. For example, Honourable Justice Atanda Fatayi-Williams, later Chief Justice of

Nigeria, 1979-83, during an international conference in May 1976, spoke of the influence of K.C. Wheare on Nigerian federalism thus:[3]

> Unlike most of the older federations, what we did in Nigeria was like unscrambling scrambled eggs. We started as a unitary state and then opted for a federation afterwards. The problem of Nigeria originally in 1951-52 was one of devolution of powers, but when the constitution which was given us by Macpherson broke down we opted for a federal constitution. Very little was known by most of us about the theory of federation at the time. They were always quoting Wheare at every constitutional conference. It may well be that if we knew more about the theory at the time, we would have emerged in our effort to provide our people with a federal constitution that took account of all the peculiar circumstances of our country and our peoples. When things began to fall apart, those of us in the know quickly realised that ours was the tragedy of assumptions. We assumed everybody, both federal and regional governments, the opposition, the electorates, the courts, the civil servants, the generality of the people and even the boy (sic) academician would play the game according to generally accepted rules. Well, because of the interplay of political forces which were beyond their control, they did not; the result was emergency (sic) of military rule. It became clear to us all thereafter, that all the time there was no total commitment to the concept of federalism.

Let us examine further Fatayi-Williams's account of the origins of Nigeria's phase of federalism. Often, theorists speak of building federal structures from the top or bottom of a given socio-political organisation[4]. Sometimes, Nigerian critics specifically asked whether the units federated were ``territories'' or ``nationalities''[5]

In Nigeria's type of federalism (from 1954), territories rather than nationalities (ethnic groups) were the focal-points of the arrangements in place. These arrangements had a long and chequered history and were so complex as to confuse concepts concerning building a federal structure from the top or bottom of a given socio-political ladder.

Again, Nigeria's example gives credence to the general (though not absolute) rule that emphasis on economics constituted the ``first concern'' of a federalist or quasi-federalist arrangement while political considerations came later[6]. Thus, matters concerning trade and industry and finances (revenue and expenditure) tend to be front-runners under a list of common interests where others of a strict political nature seem to divide heterogeneous communities which seek separate as well as common identities in forms of limited co-operative governments.

In other lands, these constituted the basis of a ``Customs Union''. In Nigeria, as earlier studies had shown, trade and politics were also closely linked not only in the nineteenth century but also in the twentieth.

In the latter century, Nigerian politics became, more and more, one of barter for economic and social benefits. For hardened practitioners, the gains of politics proved more decisive than altruistic considerations.

Indeed, "Amalgamation" theories of the 1898-1914 type were not necessarily the first to hit the political horizon in the territories that later became Nigeria. Mechanisms for British control here, from the middle of the nineteenth century, took various forms. Towards the end of that century, Britain had in place a Colony and Protectorate of Lagos, an Oil Rivers (later Niger Coast) Protectorate and Niger Territories (administered by the Royal Niger Company with a royal charter). Funds for their administration came from different sources (local and imperial). British tax-payers were reluctant to hear a heavy burden for the administration of these British holdings. Not everyone of these could balance its budget from local sources of revenue. Nor were their actual and potential resources equal. British policy-makers, therefore, explored new ways of doing old things (to optimise colonial control with minimum resources). Pragmatic, economy-based, considerations, such as these provided the *raison d'etre* of the 1898-1914 schemes concerning amalgamation in Nigeria. Local public opinion, for or against these schemes, was neither sought nor given. The prime-movers were British; their own interests, no matter how strictly defined and applied, mattered most to them. Their prime consideration (that of the 1898 Selborne Committee) was to use the funds available from the richer "South" to offset the adverse financial standing of the less prosperous "North" and so reduce fiscal dependence on scarce imperial grants-in-aid. These I have amply demonstrated elsewhere.[7]

The 1898 Niger Committee, headed by Lord Selborne, also recommended that amalgamation of the "Niger Territories" be carried out in instalments. The Colonial Office agreed. Hence, the first and second instalments of amalgamation in Nigeria. The first (1906) phase brought under a common administrative head the two segments in the "South" (the Colony and Protectorate of Lagos; the Protectorate of Southern Nigeria). The second (1914) phase culminated in a large combination (the Protectorate of Northern Nigeria with the Colony and Protectorate of Southern Nigeria). The British architects of that amalgamation left, till the end of World WAR II, a clarification of Nigeria's political future: whether or not this would lie in unity or require another (federal) answer.[8]

Changes in imperial policy, after World War II, and increased agitation by Nigerian spokesmen for self-government and independence led to concessions by British officials from the 1950s. The era of "dyarchy" in Nigeria, that of shared responsibility between British and Nigerian officials, during the 1950s, brought about a significant change from reliance on representative institutions to granting doses of responsible government at regional levels and the centre. The constitutions that followed embodied the results of deliberations involving Nigerian representatives and British officials during several constitutional conferences inside and outside Nigeria. One of these was the General Conference at Ibadan in 1950 which preceded a major constitutional change in 1951. Other constitutional conferences followed, in Lagos and London, between 1953 and 1958, to sort out critical issues before independence was granted in October 1960.

Thus, the growth and development of federalism, from 1954, took into consideration elite points of view as expressed by Nigeria's party political leaders of that era. Whether or not the bulk of the population, the masses at the so-called grassroots level, felt the same way is a moot point. In practice, both the elite and the masses allowed Nigerian federalism to encounter severe crises during its ``formative years''. That Nigerian federalism, in particular, and the Nigerian multi-nation state, in general, did not experience sudden death in its formative years is not merely through good luck but also from increasing public awareness of the balance of advantage between issues that unite and those that divide.

The centre-seeking factors with increasing cogency, since the 1898-1914 Amalgamation arrangements, included market-related aspects of a large population, the Apapa-Lagos harbour and large revenues from expanding crude-oil exports from the 1970s. These same considerations strengthened the federal case in its bloody struggle with the Biafra Movement and eventually lessened the potency of confederalism since the 1950s.

The Constitutions of the 1922-54 era (Clifford, Richards, Macpherson, Lyttleton) were less controversial than those since independence (1960, 1963, 1979, 1989). Those in the latter group were also more difficult to classify. It was not always clear what name to call them: whether or not truly federal, quasi-federal, pseudo-federal, centralist, militarist or otherwise.

During an international conference in May 1976, an eminent Nigerian scholar (Professor J. Isawa Elaigwu) presented a paper [9] on `The Military and State Building: Federal-State Relations in Nigeria's ``Military Federalism'' 1966-1976'. Surely, ``military federalism'' was not one of the conventional species known to K.C. Wheare and Co. in their seminal studies. Even so, one can concede that, during the era of military rule, there existed a unique type of federalism: an invention with a Nigerian accent.

Moreover, Nigeria's Constitutions since independence encountered another problem shared, this time, with some of their predecessors.

For long or short periods, attempted confederal infusions into Nigeria's body-politic met with tough resistance from her severally tested immune-system. The periods of confederal crises and calls for restructuring of the existing basis of co-operative governments spanned colonial and post-colonial periods: 1953-54, 1966, 1983-5, 1993-95. Agitated public debates, for and against confederalism in Nigeria then, tended to rock basic assumptions about the prospects of lasting federalism in an intense environment of serious doubts and fears concerning a common political identity.[10] These agitations led to increasing calls for a ``National Conference'' to redress perceived wrongs.

When compared with India's Republican Constitution (which allowed a quasi-federal set-up from 1950), Nigeria's, from 1963, revealed some unique features. One of these aspects of constitutional development in Nigeria demonstrated the limits of radical restructuring in a land colonially famous for its own concept and practice of ``Indirect Rule'' (a misnomer for Indirect Administration before and since the era of Sir Frederick, later, Lord Lugard). Nigerian leaders, from 1963, failed to go as far as their Indian counterparts went. The latter decided, quite early, that a power-sharing role in government and politics would be inappropriate to traditional rulers in a post-colonial setting.

At independence, Nigeria's traditional rulers maintained a status allowed them since formal federalism in 1954. Under the 1960 (Independence) Constitution[11], that recognition did not seem anomalous. However, in 1963,[12] what the new dispensation, after the exit of the British Crown as Head of Nigeria, permitted was the ``Federal Republic of Nigeria''. This change was confirmed by the next Constitution in 1979[13]. The 1989 Constitution, aborted in 1993, contained the same appellation for the same federation.

The question thus arises: How republican is, or has been, the ``Federal Republic of Nigeria''? No matter what the Constitutions, since 1963, implied, Nigeria (as of 1997) has been a multi-nation state with several monarchies (big and small) throughout a ``Federal Republic''. Particularly, at vital ``traditional'' levels, several royalties and majesties continue to claim public attention and national recognition far in excess of what one will expect under a truly republican setting (even at the so-called local government level). Deposition or de-recognition by relevant authorities of offending chieftains (high and low) did not end zones of friction and conflict in parts of the so-called ``Federal Republic''.

In practice, neither the 1960 Constitution nor the Republican variant in 1963 ended previous (colonial) practice of setting up ``Houses of Chiefs'' at the regional level. Hence, no far-reaching attempts were made in Nigeria to do what India did before powerful and wealthy maharajahs, rival claimants for power and authority, compromised the new political order after independence.

Rather than interpret restructuring as post-independence leaders did in India, those of Nigeria preferred, under the 1995 Draft Constitution, to return to familiar old (colonial) ways of establishing and maintaining close links with hierarchies of chiefs. Thus, the 1995 Draft Constitution provided for a Federal Council of Traditional Rulers with advisory functions over a wide range of matters of national interest.[14] Under this, each State House of Assembly was allowed to establish not only its own council of chiefs but also a traditional council for a local government area or group of local government areas for advisory duties appropriate to its area of jurisdiction.[15] That institutions such as these were far from republican, in theory and practice, was not a factor seriously considered by the architects of Nigeria's 1995 Draft Constitution.

Furthermore, under a new constitution, as was done under its immediate predecessors, notions concerning ``sovereignty'' of the people need to be closely examined. Elsewhere,[16] I had carefully examined notions of ``sovereignty'' in terms of ``*owners* or *donors* of any jurisdiction conferred in any instrument of government, civilian or military''. My conclusion in November 1991 was that, despite familiar passages such as ``We, the People...'' in the preambles of Nigeria's Constitutions (1963, 1979 and 1989), the elite rather than the masses of the poor and marginalised in society were the ones who played key roles in the making of these instruments. So far, nothing dramatic has happened to enable me change the basis of that conclusion. Indeed, the 1995 Draft Constitution was the handiwork of selected and elected persons: quite a number of whom with doubtful credibility among a wide range of unrepresented interests during the period (1994-95) of its formulation and revision. Moreover, before some of these instruments (1963-1979) became effective, no plebiscites, no referenda, took place. Despite initial attempts to repeat the procedure adopted for the 1979 Constitution, in the making of another in 1989, the latter attempt, like its predecessor, ended with military revisions and conclusions. The 1995 Draft Constitution did not appear to adopt a different path and conclusion. Put simply, the old (colonial) phenomenon of command constitutions, federal or not, for Nigerians did not end quickly since independence. Clearly, the first in that group, the Independence Constitution, came as an Order-in-Council of the British Crown[17]

A consideration of these overarching issues will continue, and end, with a few more matters of considerable significance. We shall begin with the close connection between the letter and spirit of Nigeria's post-independence Constitutions and the series of coups d'etat since Nigeria's first in January 1966. Why these extra-constitutional methods of changing what is normally the "supreme law" of the land occur and how to prevent them through constitutional provisions alone are matters not to be explored further here. We can, however, meaningfully examine some salient matters arising from coups d'etat and counter coups. Among these is the vulnerability of the general concept of the "rule of law", as properly understood and applied in a liberal democracy of the kind favoured by the Willink Commissioners (1957-58). Moreover, the incidence of these extra-legal sources of conflict with a written constitution has also changed radically conventional ideas concerning the interpretation and application of Nigeria's body of laws throughout the federation. Before the era of coups d'etat in Nigeria, the law (including the constitution) was what judges said it was. With coups d'etat, the law (any law) was what a long line of decrees and edicts and their makers said it was. Justice, in a federation, constantly governed by these decrees and edicts, became less certain and legitimacy more suspect.

Besides, federalism, as interpreted and applied by a succession of military rulers at the federal and state levels in Nigeria, engendered fears of overrobust centralism. In turn, advocates of confederal alternatives had a field day in Nigeria when conflicts could not be resolved with the consent of the governed. Nigeria's long link-up with coups d'etat and counter-coups, since January 1966, indicated that these, like the proverbial bad penny, always turned up. Developments such as these helped to give Nigeria's succession of federal arrangements an unstable base during the first four decades of independence.

Next, with increasing public disillusionment over lasting gains from frequent reviews of constitutions in Nigeria since independence, their *raison d'etre* has also become suspect. Similarly suspect, in the public mind, is the overall usefulness of federalism (besides basic economic considerations) in a land suffused with two of its most potent threats: absence of liberal democracy and pervasive poverty and misery. Legions in doubt ask the familiar question: *Cui bono*? (To whom is it an advantage?). Who, indeed, gains what, how, why, from Nigeria's unique species of federalism?

Answers, to be meaningful and convincing, will seek to cover the relevant areas of goals and means in the public domain. At issue, then, will be a clear understanding of the appropriate and sufficient relationship between objects of public policy on one hand and ways and means on the other. In this context, federalism (like constitutionalism) is more a means to an end than an end in itself. That end, for a majority of Nigerians, lies in their sustainable welfare. To secure sustainable levels of welfare will also require effective measures on the part of rulers, to pass, at least, two standard tests of legitimacy: those of participation and performance. To pass these tests requires people: as leaders and followers, as object and means of credible governance. Dry bones, such as federalism and constitutionalism, by themselves, cannot attain these goals of reasonable public policy unless under a liberal democracy governed by the basic rules of legitimacy.

Thirdly, and finally, in this sub-section of overarching issues, there is need for a sober reflection on the wider implications and significance of another relevant and key question. This is the one raised by the famous English poet, Alexander Pope (1688-1744):[18]

> For forms of Government let fools contest;
> Whatever is best administer'd is best.

In these aspects of governance (or management), the pragmatic test as Pope suggests, is most compelling. His persuasive argument can be extended, from a system of administration that works best, to administrators themselves: particularly, those at a system's top Indeed, concerning rulers and leaders in societies (at home and abroad), history constantly reveals characters of differential abilities. For example, there are some who resemble the famous first Duke of Wellington (victor over Emperor Napoleon I at the battle of Waterloo in 1815). Of Wellington, later Tory Prime Minister of Britain, 1828-30, the candid verdict of historians was that he would have died with a reputation for administration if only he had not administered. On the other hand, Emperor Bonaparte, a successful general in his own right, fared much better in administration though his end was disastrous.

Some nations, multi-ethnic or not, have produced their own crop of top leaders like Wellington or Bonaparte at one time or another. Of course, Nigeria, too, has done so since independence. In her era of military rule, Nigeria brought out the likes of Wellington among a long line of generals-in-government. Civilian politicians who also behaved like Wellington made matters worse for Nigeria since independence.

Alexander Pope, therefore, ended his analysis of forms of government prematurely. History, over a long span of time and space, helps one to conclude (though not necessarily as a general rule) that a decisive factor, in the conduct of nation-states, multi-ethnic or not, federally governed or not, is the human element: particularly, at the level of leadership. Compared with this primary factor, all other elements associated with the instrument or system of government assume secondary or complementary roles.

Brief Comments on Related Themes

It is now time to reflect also on the themes examined by the other chapters in this book. It is my wish to take a little bite at one big apple in each of the themes. Thus, there will be enough apples left for those, with more space, to bite and chew.

(i) The Zoning System and Power-Sharing in Government:
Initially, the need for power-sharing (with implied zoning) took the form of demands for the creation of more states in the federation. Further economic justification for an obviously political demand led to arguments concerning intensive and extensive development at grassroots levels (local government areas). In a country with well-known ethnic pluralism and cultural diversity, loud cries were frequently heard over discrimination, domination and neglect. The era of dyarchy in the 1950s and the approach of Independence intensified the fears and anxieties of several ethnic minorities in the former Northern, Western and Eastern Regions of the federation. These led to the establishment of the Willink Commission in 1957. Its report, in 1958, sought to allay these fears through two cardinal measures: liberal democracy of the Westminster model with fundamental human rights guaranteed, the federalisation of one police organisation (The Nigeria Police Force) plus the disbandment of Native Authority and Local Government Police elsewhere. Steadily, disillusionment followed the dreams of the Willink Commissioners over early realisation of liberal democracy. Other dreamers and complex circumstances encouraged the creation of more states in instalments: the Mid-West Region (1963), twelve states (1967), nineteen (1976), twenty-one (1987), thirty (1991), thirty-six (1996). Remarkably, former critics of the ethnic minorities in the era of the Willink Commission became avid beneficiaries of state creation from 1967.

When state creation, by itself, failed to correct perceived problems of marginalisation and domination, among other complaints, a new "zoning" remedy became part of the standard agenda of socio-political reformers in the early 1990s. The National Constitutional Conference, 1994-5, however, rejected requests to re-group existing states into six zones: North-Eastern, North-Western, Central, Eastern, Western and Southern.[19] On the other hand, Professor Onigu Otite, in a scholarly 1995 study[20], also advocated six zones ("for the purpose of rotatory Presidency"). His list was more specific in some aspects of zoning: North-West, North-East, North-Central (Middle Belt), South-West, South-East, and Deltaic South (Delta, Edo and Rivers States).

Any new zoning system — two, six, or more in number – would seriously impair existing intra-state and inter-state relations within the federation. Besides, none of the states of the federation is completely "homogeneous" (i.e., without fierce sub-group differences as often revealed, in some states, during assets-sharing exercises, the delineation of local government areas, or public-sector employment activities). At a zonal level, issues like these would be more complex.

Moreover, those who, at present, are reluctant to share political power, on a free and fair basis, may not change for the better if the focus of attention changes from small states to big zones. Furthermore, the components of power to be shared may not be the same for zones, states, local government areas and individuals. All in all, this is a mirage not worth pursuing through constitutional provisions.

(ii) The Federal Character Principle and National Integration

Here, too, the critical areas for problem-hunting and problem-solving seem to lie in ethnicism, nepotism and relatively low levels of loyalty (not to self or group but to a higher order of things). A country, with over 374 ethnic groups, over 400 distinct languages (as against dialects), at least three groups of belief-systems (Christians, Muslims, Adherents of African Traditional Religions), as well as a large variety of customs, does have sufficient reasons for concern over issues of pluralism and complexity. Small wonder, then, that the National Constitutional Conference made elaborate provisions[21] concerning the meaning and application of that difficult term ``Federal Character''.

Professor Otite, a recognised specialist in this area, considered ethnicity and religion as the ``most devastating features of our contemporary Nigeria''[22]. To alleviate these problem-areas in national integration, Otite recommended enlightened leadership, rotation of high political offices (including the Presidency), ``democratisation of development'', education, among others[23]

Another scholar, in the area of ethnic politics in Nigeria, Professor Okwudiba Nnoli, agreed with the views of Dr. Bala Usman, historian, pro-reform activist, on practical problems in implementing, thoroughly, any given policy or directive on ``Federal Character''. To establish ``indigeneity'', both Nnoli and Usman agreed, would require thorough genealogies which few in Nigeria, if required to do so for public-sector appointments, could provide[24]. To achieve what Nnoli termed ``inter-ethnic harmony'', he advocated radical (far-Left) measures to bring together an alliance of what he called a ``progressive or revolutionary regime'' with the ``rural and urban poor majority''. Concerning the role of that type of alliance, Nnoli said[25]:

> It should divert funds and energy from the creation and consolidation of states to the formation of viable associations of poor peasants, workers, petty traders and the underemployed and unemployed. This should be done through the instrumentality of a political movement motivated by their interests, dominated and guided by their organisations, devoted to the implementation of progressive policies, and protected by an army that would have transformed itself from an inherited colonial institution designed to protect foreign capital to a veritable people's defence force.

> The peasants, workers, petty-traders and artisans, and the underemployed and unemployed are the only true and dependable ally in the struggle against ethnic sectionalism and the inherited colonial system... But the drums of their silence are beating louder than ever.

In plain terms, and well beyond radical frontiers of thought, I consider this conclusion inescapable: that ``Federal Character'' will begin and end as an artificial principle for as long as the concept of Nigeria, as a common motherland or fatherland, remains largely a dream among the ranks of the elite and the masses. Realities on the ground, nicknamed ``Nigerian factor'', tend to be effective dream-killers.

On the other hand, in a published statement (1993), a former president of Nigeria optimistically said[26] (in an address on ``Federalism and Nation-Building in Nigeria''):

> If, in the pursuit of their interest, the British created Nigeria, today, Nigeria has come to have a different meaning for us. If Nigeria used to be a mere geographical expression, it is now an organic state.

If the above statement represented the truth, the whole truth, and nothing but the truth, groans and pains before and since the nullification crisis over the ``June 12'' (1993) exercise, contemporary terror and fire in Nigerian towns and cities, overwhelming hunger and disease in rural areas, mass rush to new-fangled religious homes as well as traditional herbal/ritual centres, and the like, would not have featured prominently, as they have done, in Nigeria's recent print and electronic media. Indeed, ``under an organic state'' (if properly understood), peace, security, stability, prosperity would have been achieved at lesser cost.

(iii) Revenue Allocation and the Economics of Federalism

As indicated much earlier, finance tends to underpin a lot of things in life (as this affects individuals, nation-states, as well as the rules and regulations governing them). This is more so as individuals, in their private capacities, and the people of a given geo-political area have unequal opportunities and resources (natural, human, otherwise).

Government too is a costly enterprise no matter the type of constitution under which it is carried out. Where national resources are limited and public-sector services needed increase, politics and economics tend to play games many sufferers seem not to enjoy. In the evolution of Nigeria's multi-nation state, particularly after the 1914 Amalgamation, many of such games were played over and over.

To set rules for the proper regulation of these games, and ensure "fiscal equity" under prevailing constitutions, as these changed from time to time, government appointed known experts to head commissions and committees for thorough investigations and recommendations.[27] Among the earliest in the series were: Phillipson (1946), Hicks-Phillipson (1951), Chick (1954), Raisman (1958), Binn (1964), Dina (1969), Aboyade (1977), Okigbo (1980). Between 1988 and 1989, government regularised the composition, powers and functions of a National Revenue Mobilisation, Allocation and Fiscal Commission. This body, however, did not, could not, provide sustainable solutions to several complex and vexatious problems at all three levels of the federation[28].

Quite often, the roles of these bodies suffered adversely from a combination of factors. These included rapid changes in the personnel of federal, state, and local governments, the creation of new states, changes in the division of powers and functions under federalism, external factors (particularly, as these affected crude oil exports), wage policies and structures for public functionaries at the federal, state and local government levels, among others. Moreover, Nigerian interest-groups were more interested in revenue-sharing than in revenue-generation.

Thus, the Federation Account and allocations from it easily became the target of national politics without appropriate and sufficient regard for the logic of economics and fair play in the management of limited resources. Corruption and abuse of office on the part of federal, state and local government functionaries made matters worse. The management of special funds (from the Federation Account) for perennially distressed areas, pollution-control, public works, among others, intensified inter-state rivalries as well as friction and conflicts between the Federal (Central) government and interested states. OMPADEC, for example, established in 1992, for proper development of Oil-Mineral Producing Areas, created more problems than it could solve[29].

Clearly, before and since the era of formal federalism in Nigeria, from 1954, the fiscal relationship between the centre and the periphery resembled the roles of a householder and housekeeper. In turn, it was also one of the paymaster of the piper dictating the tune.

Indeed, despite constant variations in the percentages allocated from the Federation Account to the states and local government areas, the centre always had the largest share. The image of "God-Father", thus, stuck to the centre with the "lion's share". Not even a policy change (in the 1997 Budget) allowing differential wages and salaries for public servants at the federal, state and local government levels seemed promising enough to improve, substantially, the plight of the periphery. *Vanguard* (20 January 1997) saw matters thus:

Unless states and local government councils intensify their drive for internally-generated revenue, the perennial trip to Aso Rock to solicit for funds will continue... In fairness to state military administrators and local government councils, they have been driven to imposing "illegal" levies and taxes because of inequitable sharing of the funds accruing to the nation and because a Federal Republic is now governed as a unitary state.

As controversies over these complex matters raged, it became clear to vigilant observers that few states (other than Lagos, Rivers and Kano) did or could pass standard "viability" tests of their creators[30].

On this, the *Daily Times* (18 November, 1995) did not mince words:

In our view, the problem of economic non-viability cannot be solved by the states seeking increased financial supplements from the federal government. Rather, the long-term and lasting solution lies in making economic viability a principal condition for the separate (sic) existence of constituent states. And also to rectify the warps in our federalism occasioned by the centrepetalist (sic) ethos of military rule. Towards the attainment of this objective, individual states must be made to match their budget proposals with internally-generated revenue. A situation in which state budgets are tied to allocations from the federation account is neither realistic nor healthy for the growth of federalism. It encourages inexcusable complacency on the part of the state governments, most of which no longer fully maximise opportunities for internal revenue generation, because of entrenched mentality of dependence on the federal government. The decentralisation of salary structures to reflect differential endowments and capabilities of individual states and local governments must also be contemplated at this point in time if we are truly to confront the realities of our complex federal polity.

Considerations like the above apart, neither the "derivation" principle (at the centre of controversies) nor any other combination of revenue-allocation formulae can provide a sustainable solution under present arrangements concerning "fiscal equity". Rather, the existing powers to tax and spend (throughout the federation) need to be radically reviewed to enable either the survival of the fittest at any level or the deliberate development of "small" government at the centre. The latter will, in turn, involve granting of increased reserve powers and functions at the periphery of the federation. This will also be in keeping with the logic of an apt Chinese proverb: distant hoses do not put out local fires.

(iv) **Proportional Composition of the Executive and Government Stability**

Comments already made under the sub-section of power sharing extend to this. In addition, some basic assumptions and recommendations by the

National Constitutional Conference, 1994-5, like those of their predecessors, may require further review. For example, the basic ingredients of legitimacy (as previously indicated here) are at the heart of measures to ensure political stability. Without these fundamentals, any other approach seems to dodge key issues concerning the proper development of a multi-nation state in peace and security.

First, the National Constitutional Conference, 1994-5, favoured a rotational presidency (between ``North'' and ``South'') multiple vice-presidencies (three from designated areas), proportional representation in the federal cabinet (for parties scoring 10 per cent or more of total votes), membership in the federal cabinet by recognised experts, retention of parliamentary seats by serving ministers and the appointment of special advisers. Similar arrangements were allowed also at the state level[31].

The new basis of rotation is not clear and can confuse lots of interest-groups. The definition of ``North'' and ``South'' in the 1995 Draft Constitution did not differ, remarkably, from what these meant under the 1914 Amalgamation. This categorisation of ``North'' and ``South'' implied the recognition of two geo-political ``Zones'' under a new constitution. However, this approach seems a retrograde step not worthy of repetition in the light of the far-reaching changes in attitudes and values associated with an old (Colonial) state of affairs.

Next, the above approach ignored other key aspects of the problem of executive government in Nigeria. Professor J.D. Ojo, of the Faculty of Law, University of Ibadan, in examining problems of the executive in Nigeria, 1960-81, drew necessary attention to discernible lessons one could learn from experience then. Among these, he emphasised the need for implanting the doctrine of ``Cabinet Responsibility'' in a constitution to avoid separate action by members with different party ideologies in a coalition government. He also drew attention to the dangers of ``Presidential dictatorship'' as well as abuse of public trust among functionaries[33]. Ojo further observed[34].

> Most Nigerians waited silently during the 1st Republic when politicians abused their sacred trust by systematically destroying (a) great fabric of constitutional government. Some even applauded the wreckers when perpetrating heinous crimes against fellow Nigerians. This is why people must oppose any abuse of power however caused. To wait patiently until a Messiah comes to deliver us from our own abuse might be a forlorn hope.
>
> Democracy is not safe in a country where a large majority of the population is illiterate. Their inability to understand the problems of government is readily visible. Worse still, they become very strange bedfellows to politicians who make extravagant promises.

How, then, could the majority of the people make themselves important to their rulers? Here, too, the same National Constitutional Conference did less than justice to a matter of critical importance: the issue of Proportional Representation (PR) as a possible aspect of Nigeria's future electoral system. It merely listed[35] PR as one of the systems it considered. Its preference was for the British-type "First-pass-the post" (or simple majority) system.[36] On the other hand, one did expect the same conference to indicate why it rejected PR in favour of a less representative system, though one much simpler to operate. That PR, no matter how complex to manage in a largely illiterate and technologically disabled society has some pluses on the side of justice for several disadvantaged (marginalised) groups is well-known[37]. In spite of its familiar minuses, it is quite possible to work out and apply aspects of PR suited to meet Nigerian needs (as other societies troubled by the key issues of electoral representation and participation in governance in the Middle East, Western and Eastern Europe had done). The rear-guard (back-door) injection of PR into federal and state cabinets in Nigeria, under the 1995 Draft Constitution, is an attempted short-cut neither appropriate nor sufficient for the large issues involved in nation-building. These do require measures to ensure legitimacy, through adequate participation and performance, from the electoral process to the executive stage of governance. These basic ingredients of legitimacy do provide credible buttresses of political stability under a liberal democracy.

(v) **Models of Organisation of the Executive Arm of Government: Comparative International Experience.**

In addressing relevant issues under this sub-section, it is pertinent to recognise, at once, that every constitution, federal or otherwise, is a product of, at least, three cardinal factors: time, circumstance and leadership. Thus, it will not be advisable for one country to copy, without due care, the instruments of another to solve problems considered unique to its own milieu. Besides, even where seeming similarities in situations tend to exist, a careful analyst has to take into cognisance differences in interpretation and application of known constitutions, federal or otherwise, as these relate to their letter and spirit. Quite often, differences, largely determined by the cognate factors of time, circumstance and leadership, are as significant as similarities, if not more so. With this necessary *caveat*, one can compare or contrast the predicament or experiences of one country with those of another.

As is well-known, Nigeria copied, between 1960 and 1962, aspects of the Westminster (Parliamentary) model of government in the U.K. and later (under her 1979 Constitution) the Presidential System in the

USA. Nigeria did so without reflecting the spirit of the institutions she tried to copy. Other observers, impressed by minimal government at the centre, had often cited the example of post-1848 Switzerland[38]. But Nigeria did not go the Swiss way. The French Model (of an active partnership between President and Prime Minister) hit Nigerian headlines[39] briefly during a consideration of the recommendations in the 1995 Draft Constitution. Despite obvious similarities with those of post-Gaullist France, arrangements under India's Republican Constitution did not appear to impress Nigerians. Neither the French nor the Indian model made a strong impact on Nigeria.

On the other hand, the familiar turmoil in post-Tito Yugoslavia, post-1989 breakdown of old-style federalist permutations and combinations in the former USSR and Czechoslovakia, plus renewed separatist agitations in Canada, in the early 1990s, did catch the attention of Nigerians equally engaged in the sensitive and complex modalities of restructuring liberal democracy and government in multi-ethnic settings.[40] The street-side of politics and official reactions to them in those lands of serious troubles over major aspects of nation-building in multi-cultural circumstances hit headlines in print and electronic media worldwide.

With due caution, and on the quiet side of multi-lateral relationships, one could also try to ascertain what lessons, if any, Nigeria could draw from the theory and practice of ``cooperative federalism'' as developed in the USA and the Federal Republic of Germany. Professor Fred Morrison, University of Bonn, had, in a paper presented in Lagos in 1976, thrown sufficient light on these aspects of ``cooperative federalism''[41] This term, he explained, meant ``harmony, mutual assistance, common endeavour'' in administrative (executive) relations between national and state authorities under these two federal systems.[42] Under these mutually advantageous arrangements, it was possible for the national government in either country to require the administrative (executive) assistance of its state authorities for projects of common interest. In these matters, the national government made grants-in-aid (with or without a matching contribution by a state) for purposes of execution or administration. In doing so, the national government avoided associated problems in establishing appropriate, but costly, bureaucracies at the state level.

The notion of ``cooperative federalism'' seems quite attractive though its elaborate modalities to ensure accountability, cost-effectiveness, efficiency as well as the timely resolution of conflicts deserve more detailed study in Nigeria before any precipitate attempts are made to copy these as they were in other lands. Looking before one leaps is still sane guidance in private and public affairs.

(vi) Additional Areas of Concern

The first of these concerns appropriate constitutional requirements for political parties in the Federal Republic of Nigeria. Under the 1960 and 1963 Constitutions, decisions favoured multi-party arrangements. However, through the process of registration, party members were restricted, though five or six passed the prescribed tests between 1979 and 1983. Under the 1989-1993 arrangements, two state-recognised parties emerged. Critics called these ``parastatals''. Eleven out of thirteen political associations failed to meet government approval (*Third Eye*, 17 July 1995). Government, under a military presidency, proceeded to build secretariats for its approved two parties, drafted their constitutions and liberally granted them funds for basic operations. Under the 1995 Draft Constitution, five parties were recognised in late 1996. These too expected government funding without visible concern over freedom of action.

Under a system of liberal democracy, and for the needs of PR, an alternative policy would have been to allow parties free access to the electoral arena. Voters would then make their choice freely and fairly: preferably, through a system of secret ballot.

More important would be sacrosanctity of the electoral verdict. Experience at federal elections in December 1964 and June 1993 demonstrated how tinkering with the electoral process and verdict could be political dynamite. Indeed, the notorious pattern of electoral rigging and violence during the 1950s, 1960s, 1983, resulted in considerable political instability in Nigeria. A crisis-prone sequence like that needs to be carefully watched and prevented.

Next, the issue of an official language in Nigeria's setting of multi-culturalism is clearly one with difficult solutions. Here, again, great care needs to be exercised. What lessons can Nigeria learn from others with similar experience? Malaysia, India, USA, for example, preferred a *lingua franca* most widely spoken. On the other hand, Indonesia carefully sought out and adopted the language of one of its smallest ethnic groups. Inventing a new language of compromise (WAZOBIA) need not be the way out.

Third, and final, in this sub-group, one needs to consider the issue of the division of powers and functions in a federation. A close examination of the Legislative Lists, in Nigeria's Constitutions since 1960, reveals the contraction of powers assigned the periphery whereas those of the centre regularly increased with every review. But, it is at the periphery that 70 per cent or more of Nigeria's population live. It is their empowerment that will make important difference between the lots of the very rich and the ``poorest of the poor'' in Nigerian society. It is the peace and prosperity of the rural dwellers that will provide a lasting bedrock of political stability for Nigeria, large in size and complex in culture.

Concluding Comments

In all these respects and more, Nigeria deserves to examine the far-reaching implications and significance of serious threats to nation-building and political stability in the West African sub-region, in particular, and elsewhere in Africa. Though some of these strife-torn countries in contemporary Africa do not operate federal constitutions, their problems exemplify common anxieties and fears over goals and means in governance. Surely, Nigeria has had her own share of tough problems in nation-building. In this miscellaneous group were well-publicised secession threats, coups d'etat and counter-coups, civil war, repeated and repeatable agitations over electoral processes (including a serious nullification crisis), vexatious transition arrangements, controversial constitutional reviews and reforms, threats to public security and safety, among others. She can therefore teach others, and learn from others, useful lessons in all these respects and more.

One is, however, deeply aware that countries in other continents and sub-continents, worldwide, have had their own share of problems over nation-building – some centuries old, some less. Revolutions, counter-revolutions, secession threats, civil wars, regicide, among others, are part of a global menu of problems and experiences.

In circumstances such as these and more, Nigeria's proper development, in the twenty-first century, needs to take into an appropriate and sufficient account the correct significance of relevant events in Africa and elsewhere in an obviously troubled world. This is more so as the early glow of independence in Africa recedes and more problems over its consolidation emerge to confound previous optimists concerning this continent's political future. That some of these troubled countries have been bogged down with repeated and repeatable problems since independence underlines their severity and unwelcome durability. That troubled countries in Africa invite interventions from outside make the current situation more regrettable. That the group of troubled nations gets wider and wider is no comfort to millions of Africans: men, women and children.

Nearer Nigeria are neighbours (as in 1997) still in deep trouble: Cameroun, Chad, Niger, Togo, Liberia, Senegal, The Gambia, Sierra Leone. Not too far are others in constant trouble: Mauritania, Algeria, Sudan, Ethiopia, Central African Republic, Equatorial Guinea, Somalia, Uganda, Rwanda, Burundi, Zaire, Angola. One can also recall that the OAU, a friend in need during Nigeria's bloody encounter with the Biafran Movement, could not protect Ethiopia's territorial integrity before the successful secession of Eritrea after more than a decade of bloody warfare. Besides, Sudan, since 1983, has not yet brought to a successful end incessant thunder and lightning from freedom-fighters in her southern flank (as of 1997). Nor did Britain save her former federation in East Africa from breaking up in the era of de-colonisation.

Moreover, global communication satellites and breath-taking information technology have made the world smaller and brought home to vigilant observers anywhere, on fast lanes, copy-able tactics of governments and people in distress over nation-building far far away. The list of such events in Africa and beyond tended to increase rather than decrease between the 1980s and 1990s.

Developments like these, in Africa and elsewhere, do help to recall the aptness of that familiar saying: "A stitch in time saves nine". In the final analysis, federalism, constitutionalism, restructuring, national integration and every conceivable aspect of governance are about people, as object and means of reform, about effective strategies for their welfare; not otherwise.

Select References

1. K.C. Wheare, *Federal Government*. Oxford, 1963.
2. A.B. Akinyemi, P.D. Cole, Walter Ofonagoro, eds., *Reading on Federalism*. Lagos 1980, *passim*.
3. *Ibid.*, pp. 73-74.
4. *Ibid., passim.*
5. *Ibid.,* p. 68
6. *Ibid.*, p. 246.
7. For details, see T.N. Tamuno, *The Evolution of the Nigerian State: The Southern Phase, 1898-1914*. London, 1972, 1978.
8. See also T.N. Tamuno, *Nigeria: Its People and Its Problems*. 1989, Lagos, pp. 11-12, 46.
   T.N. Tamuno, *Peace and Violence in Nigeria*. Lagos, 1991, pp. 400-401.
9. Akinyemi, *et al., op. cit.*, pp. 155-181.
10. Tamuno, *Peace and Violence in Nigeria*. pp. 400-437. Also, *A.M. News*, 28 December 1995, *The Guardian*, 21 December 1993, *Daily Times*, 10 December 1993, *The Guardian*, 7 November 1993, *The Guardian*, 28 October 1993, *The Guardian*, 1 May 1994, *The Guardian*, 12 April 1994, *Third*

10. ... *Eye*, 12 July 1995, and A.H.M. Kirk-Greene, *Crisis and Conflict in Nigeria.* Vol. 1, pp. 60-311.

11. The Nigeria (Constitution) Order in Council, 1960: West Africa, Statutory Instrument, No. 1652, 1960.

12. The Constitution of the Federal Republic of Nigeria, Lagos, 1963.

13. The Constitution of the Federal Republic of Nigeria, Lagos, 1979.

14. *Report of the Constitutional Conference containing the Draft Constitution* (1995), Volume 1, p. 174.

15. *Ibid.*, pp. 9, 168-9, 184-5.

16. Tamuno, *Peace and Violence in Nigeria.* pp. 239-257.

17. See also Footnote 11 above.

18. Tamuno, *Nigeria: Its People and Its Problems*, p. 83.

19. *Report of the Constitutional Conference containing the Resolutions and Recommendations*, Vol. 11, 1995, p.62.

20. Onigu Otite, *Nigeria: Towards Salvaging a Ravaged Society*, Post-Graduate School Inter-Disciplinary Research Discourse, University of Ibadan, 18 July 1995, p. 22.

21. *Report of the Constitutional Conference...*, Vol.II, 1995, pp.14, 146-7.

22. Otite, *op. cit.*, pp. 11-12.

23. *Ibid.*, pp. 19-31.

24. Okwudiba Nnoli, *Ethnic Politics in Nigeria*, Enugu, 1980, pp. 268-277.

25. *Ibid.*, p. 289.

26. Ibrahim Badamasi Babangida, *Federalism and Nation Building in Nigeria.* Abuja, 1993, p. 1.

27. T.Y. Danjuma, "Revenue Sharing and the Political Economy of Federalism", Paper presented at the National Conference on Federalism and Nation Building in Nigeria: The Challenges of the Twenty-First Century, Abuja, 14-18 December 1992, pp. 7-17.
See also, Akinyemi, *et al.*, *op. cit.*, pp. 109-125.

28. *Ibid.*, pp. 18-39

29. *The Guardian*, 22 January 1997.

30. *Daily Times*, 18 November 1995.
31. *Report of the Constitutional Conference...*, Vol. II, 1995, pp. 64-68.
32. *Report of the Constitutional Conference...*, Vol. I, p. 98.
33. J.D. Ojo, *The Development of the Executive under the Nigerian Constitutions*, 1960-81, Ibadan, 1985, p. 168.
34. *Ibid.*, p. 169.
35. *Report of the Constitutional Conference...*, Vol. II, p. 161.
36. *Ibid.*
37. For aspects of PR, see Akinyemi *et al.*, *op. cit.*, pp. 352-371.
38. Akinyemi, *et al.*, *op. cit.*, pp. 260-4, 430-32.
39. *Newswatch*, 14 August 1995, p. 20.
40. *Daily Times*, 9 November 1995.
    See also Tamuno, *Peace and Violence in Nigeria*. pp. 565-66 Babangida, *op. cit.*, p. 3
41. Akinyemi, *et al.*, *op. cit.*, pp. 241-59.
42. *Ibid.*, p. 241.

CHAPTER 2

Osarhieme Benson Osadolor

The Development of the Federal Idea and the Federal Framework, 1914-1960

Introduction

This chapter examines the development of the federal idea during the colonial period as a driving force in the evolution of the federal framework in Nigeria. The time focus is primarily on the period from 1914 to 1960, in which the thinking about federalism as a means for a more effective political order and national integration became a crucial factor in the political restructuring which led to the adoption of an integrated federal structure in the Constitution of 1954 and subsequent post-independence constitutions. The issue of integration whereby the various ethnic groups would achieve higher levels of mutual trust, national identity and consciousness, was the thrust of the arguments of the advocates of federalism in Nigeria.

Previous studies of Nigerian federalism[1] have tended to neglect the history of the development of the federal idea before 1960. The aim of this chapter, then, is to focus on this area of neglect while exploring the following thesis: that political restructuring can usefully be regarded as an instrument for promoting national integration at different epochs in the history of a country when political problems threaten national unity and stability. In line with this thesis, federalism is perceived in this chapter as a dynamic instrument for political organisation which can take on different forms over time and witness further changes in the future.

From this standpoint, it is possible to draw appropriate lessons on how a well organised federal state can boost national unity while preserving the peculiarities of cleavages within the federal arrangement in the overall interest of stability and socio-economic development. The point of emphasis is that political restructuring should lead to the establishment of a national identity even as the range of inter-group relations are enlarged, leading progressively to the evolution of national character in spite of the existence of an ethnically plural society as is the case in Nigeria. To cope with the problems of national integration, alternative strategies and long-term solutions are often pursued by political leaders and decision makers, but in the post-independence political situation in Nigeria, imbalances in the federal structure have over the years been allowed to generate and aggravate crises, while proffered solutions have tended to be of an adhoc nature, leading often to debates on the national question.

For the purpose of analysis, this chapter is divided into four subsections which examine trends in the federal idea, 1914 to 1949, the crisis of transition, 1950-1952; federal solution to political crises, 1953-1960, and the problems of the present. The concluding part seeks to show that the history of the development of the federal idea in Nigeria from 1914 up to the present time has been a struggle against disintegration and a campaign for national integration and survival.

Trends of Thought, 1914-1949

Before 1914, colonial conquest had altered the pattern of inter-group relations in the Nigerian geographical area, but it was the strength of the existing integrative factors which made it possible for Sir Frederick Lugard to contemplate a proposal in 1913 for the amalgamation of Northern Nigeria and Southern Nigeria which could have developed as two separate countries. The decision of Lugard to create a unified Nigeria on 1 January 1914 did not result from the pressure of local political groups; it derived from considerations of administrative convenience as interpreted by a colonial power. Lugard considered it unnecessary to carve up a territory undivided by natural boundaries, moreso since one portion (the South) was wealthy enough to commit resources to even "unimportant" programmes while the other portion (the North), could not balance its budget, necessitating the British taxpayer being called upon to bear the larger share of even the cost of its administration. This partly explains the amalgamation, an act which provoked bitter controversy at the time, arousing the resentment of educated elites and of some British administrators. It, nevertheless, saddled the country with an issue – the relationship between North and South – that has dominated its politics to this day.

The act of amalgamation was not a federal idea; Lugard did not conceive the idea of a federal state for Nigeria even though there were strong integrative factors of inter-group relations and the trend of opinion before 1914 favoured the division of the territory into a number of units which could develop into component units of a future federation. Between 1861 and 1914, the different peoples had been brought together under British colonial authority as a result of conquest, and not necessarily as a result of the desire to develop existing linkages of precolonial inter-group relations. It was, however, felt that a federal system would enhance national unity and integration of the component parts of the country. Sir Walter Egerton, holding the dual posts of Governor of Lagos and High Commissioner of the Protectorate of Southern Nigeria, recommended a form of federation; another British official, E.D. Morel, advocated splitting the territory into four provinces; and C.L. Temple, acting Governor of Northern Nigeria, also advocated that the territory be split into more political units than the existing two.[3]

Temple, who anticipated the plan of Lugard for amalgamation, had advised that the large territories of Northern and Southern Nigeria be broken into smaller units to ensure effective administration, better service to the people, and the development of an efficient bureaucracy; but regretted that "matters have so changed that the excessive centralisation which at present exists is a real disadvantage".[4] Lugard ignored or rather rejected all the proposals of a federal state, and insisted on a unified system of administration, apparently because of his training and profession as a military man. Of course, he advanced his argument for the decision: postponement of amalgamation for many years; cost of providing new secretariat and staff; unification of the laws, general orders and policy; territorial re-division which transferred portions of one administration to the other, or included portions of each in a new administration, would have been productive of chaos and interminable appeals for `rulings'. In spite of these reasons, at the time of amalgamation, Northern Nigeria had twelve provinces and the South had nine, with the colony of Lagos as the tenth province. The political structure, albeit tentative, was already in existence for a federal framework.

The political restructuring of Lugard in 1914 would seem to suggest that the exercise was designed to involve as little dislocation of existing conditions as possible, while providing for the introduction later of such changes as were either foreseen, but not immediately necessary, or might be suggested by future experience. This was also the thinking of the Colonial Office when Lugard submitted his proposals on 9 May 1913:

> Sir F. Lugard's proposals contemplate a state which is impossible to classify. It is not a unitary state with local government areas but with one central Executive and one Legislature. It is not a personal union of separate colonies under the same Governor like the Windwards, it is not a confederation of states. If adopted his proposals can hardly be a permanent solution and I gather that Sir. F. Lugard only regard them as temporary – at any rate in part...[5]

The main issue was that the restructuring was temporary and after the transition period, "the answer to the problem – unitary state v. federal state – will probably have become clear".[6]

Partly on account of the above facts, and also due to opposition to British rule, early Nigerian nationalists began to advocate the concept of a single Nigerian nation. The official policy was hostile towards those nationalists whose ideas of self-government were in terms of a single and unified Nigerian nation. Sir Hugh Clifford who succeeded Lugard as Governor of Nigeria dismissed such an idea.[7] To him the idea of a Nigerian nation was inconceivable; and this can be interpreted to mean that the colonial government was determined to oppose its development. This was why Northern Nigeria was excluded from the authority of the Nigerian Legislative Council established by Governor Clifford in 1923.

The constitutional arrangement which came into effect in 1947,[8] however, sought to provide a framework for greater interaction between Nigerian peoples. For the first time, the North was brought into the same legislative authority with the South. Unfortunately, developments from within the Legislative Council were indicative of the fact that legislators from the Northern Provinces were not prepared to accept the demands of the nationalists in the South, who were clamouring for immediate self-government.[9]

In spite of the problem of North-South dichotomy in the Legislative Council, the general trend of thought was that of a bias for a federal system which became an interesting theme of debate. Mallam Tafawa Balewa expressed the opinion of the North when he said:

> I am beginning to think, Sir, that Nigeria's political future may only lie in a federation, because so far as the rate of regional progress is concerned, some of the Regions appear to be more developed than others...[10]

In 1947 he had expressed the view that since amalgamation of the Southern and Northern Provinces in 1914,

> Nigeria has existed as one country only on paper, and that it was "still far from being considered as one country, much less to think of it as being united."[11]

However, the two main objectives of Nigerian nationalism, namely self-government and the attainment of national unity, explain the background to the development of the federal idea. Because of the differences among Nigerian peoples in terms of language, religion, custom and tradition, historical background and the different stages of their development, majority of Nigerian legislators, in contributing to debates, favoured a federal system that would give the regions or provinces the possibility of maintaining their identity while remaining part of a unified state. For them, the federal state was extremely productive of unity, and hence also promotive of culture.

This feeling was given formal expression in a motion introduced by Mr. Adeleke Adedoyin that the Legislative Council "approves of the unity of Nigeria by federation of the regions which should become autonomous in due course, and that the whole country develop towards self-government on this federal basis".[12] The argument for the motion was that each level of government should be limited to its own sphere which should also be autonomous and independent as may be defined in a constitution and as in a federal system in which some powers are constitutionally reserved for the states. According to him, federalism should be the foundation of the superstructure of the country's government to enhance nation-building. The motion was deferred on the advice of the Chief Secretary,[13] but re-introduced on August 21, 1948 after the arrival of Sir John Macpherson as Governor. It was, however, withdrawn by leave of council as it was an important constitutional matter, with assurance given that the issue of federalism would be considered during the review of the Richards Constitution.

In 1949, the colonial government took the initiative in launching constitutional discussions. The method adopted was one which allowed Nigerians at every level to participate in putting forward suggestions for the country's constitution, through a series of discussions held first at village, then district, followed by provincial, regional and national conferences. The specific task of each of the conferences was to find answers to a whole series of fourteen complex questions, each of which demanded the most careful examination. The first three of the questions focused specifically on the issue of federalism and it is important to quote them in full because of their political implications:

1. Do we wish to see a fully centralised system with all legislative and executive powers concentrated at the centre or do we wish to develop a federal system under which each different region of the country would exercise a measure of internal autonomy?
2. If we favour a federal system should we retain the existing regions with some modification of existing regional boundaries or should we form regions on some new basis such as the many linguistic groups which exist in Nigeria?
3. Should the regional legislatures be granted legislative and financial powers instead of being advisory as at present?[14]

It is pertinent to note that these questions on federalism were of interest to the advocates of the federal system in Nigeria. In the Legislative Council, the debates had shown that the argument for federalism was hinged on its utility, with Dr Nnamdi Azikiwe in one such debate pointing to what he called the pragmatic utilitarianism of federalism.

The works of Nnamdi Azikiwe and Obafemi Awolowo, together with the remarkable contributions of Nigerian students in the United Kingdom, had given an entirely unique fillip to the federal idea. As far back as 1943, Azikiwe envisaged a federal commonwealth of Nigeria, made up of eight ``protectorates" based on ethnic affiliation.[15] In 1947, Awolowo said that since the existing three regions were established merely for the purpose of administrative convenience, only a truly federal system would suit Nigeria's political conditions.[16] Before the review of the Arthur Richards Constitution, Nigerian students in the United Kingdom held a conference in Edinburgh and part of the statement they issued was a declaration for federalism: ``The Constitution of Nigeria should be based on some form of federation which would permit all the nationalities of Nigeria to develop to full political and national cultural maturity..."[17]

Before the General Constitutional Conference of 1950 in Ibadan, a number of issues had emerged from the trend of thought on federalism: first, that the foundation of the federal state should be a national act based upon a constitution; second, that federalism and decentralisation should not be taken as meaning the same thing; third, that federalism would be a test of the administrative expediency of distributing authority between the centre and member states; fourth, that the acceptance of the federal idea in political restructuring would affect the evolving legal order and constitution; and finally, that the existing framework for political participation since 1914 had proved inadequate for national unity and integration.

Crisis of Transition: For and Against Federalism, 1950-1952

From the time of the Constitutional Conference in 1950 and up to 1952, the development of the federal idea had to contend with British divide and rule strategies and attendant official opposition to the idea of federation.

In the making of the 1951 Constitution, series of conferences at various levels were held before the General Constitutional Conference which met in Ibadan on January 9, 1950. During the period, eight provinces (five and three respectively in the East and West) were in favour of the federal system; ten provinces (six in the North, three in the West and one in the East) suggested modification of present boundaries to tackle more effectively the problems of balkanisation; while six provinces (five in the North and one in the East) condemned the federal idea outright.[18]

At the Ibadan General Conference, no serious thought was given in the majority report to the posers on federalism. Rather, the emphasis was on regionalism. This was in spite of the fact that in the countdown to the making of the constitution, it was felt that the solution to the difficult problem of regional representation in the central legislature might be found by following the example provided in federal constitutions.[19]

There were four minority reports attached to the recommendations of the General Conference. The reports were signed by conference members who were opposed to the majority recommendations of the conference. The minority report signed by Mbonu Ojike and Eyo Ita favoured a federal system in opposition to regionalisation. In the report, they stated: Regionalisation is opposed because it divides the country "... what we want is a strong federated Nigeria..."[20] The three elected Lagos members of the council – Dr. I. Olorun-Nimbe, Dr. Nnamdi Azikiwe, and Mr. Adeleke Adedoyin – who were also leaders of the National Council of Nigeria and the Cameroons (NCNC) also submitted a minority report which, *inter alia*, favoured a federal system. One of the Lagos members, Dr. Azikiwe, in expressing his views on the reports of the select committee on the recommendations of the Ibadan General Conference, reminded the legislators that "the trend of public opinion in Nigeria was towards the creation of a federal system of government based on ethnic grouping".[21]

During the period of transition, the main political parties became associated with a distinctive attitude on the subject of a desirable constitutional framework for Nigeria. The Action Group insisted on federalism, and advocated for the creation of three new states or regions out of the existing three regions in order to accommodate cultural diversity. The NCNC was in support of a federal state and also advocated for more regions, in which political power would be divided between the central government and the regions. It was stated in the freedom charter of the NCNC in April 1948 that the country should be organised into "states on national and linguistic bases, enjoying legal equality within the framework of a federal commonwealth". The Northern Peoples Congress advocated for decentralisation, insisting on wide powers for the regions as the basis for any form of government and, if necessary, for a federal state. The *Egbe Omo Oduduwa* also advocated "the grouping of Nigeria into various autonomous states or regions, purely on ethnic basis", with smaller ethnic groups being free to decide with which larger groups they would be willing to be temporarily amalgamated.[22] This same view was shared by the Nigerian Youth Movement which campaigned in the 1940s that the guiding principles in the division of the country into regions must be ethnic classification, cultural affinity, common problems and, perhaps, administrative convenience.[23]

It was expected that through constitutional reforms and the granting of concessions, the British would demonstrate their willingness not only to decolonise but also to adopt a federal framework. During the transition period, the process of gradual control of power was a central issue within Nigerian political practice at least from 1945. The advocates of federalism shared a common apprehension of the dangers of concentrated powers, especially when representatives from Northern Provinces at the Ibadan General Conference in 1950 threatened to pull out of Nigeria unless they were guaranteed exactly one half of the seats in the House of Representatives.[24] The British granted their request. "That arrangement and other political developments since independence", argues Ikime, "have created a political culture in which a particular group considers that control of Nigeria's central government is its birthright".[25]

"The federal state" was the prime value for the nationalists who advocated for it in what became known as the Macpherson Constitution of 1951. In spite of the trend of thought that self-government should be attained on federal basis, the 1951 Constitution did not reflect the federal system. It may be argued here that the constitution was something of a paradox. While it involved Nigerians in colonial administration, it emphasised existing differences through regionalisation. Obaro Ikime also points out that it is not difficult to reach the conclusion that the British, who were the umpires at the constitutional conferences, had some stake in ensuring that the conservative North dominated the central legislature.[26]

The drawing up of the constitution was a remarkable undertaking; the events, followed by threats of disintegration, were reflections of the crisis of transition. The crisis was difficult and challenging: the nationalists demanded for a federal constitution, but the British were against federalism. In fact, just as it became impossible to find meaning in the evolving process, it also became doubtful whether the constitution would endure the period of transformation from one era to the next. Dr. Nnamdi Azikiwe, an advocate of federalism, was not optimistic about the success of the constitution. He said:

> "it is my sincere belief that, like all makeshifts, it will flounder and necessitate early revision" since "no constitution which fails to measure up to highest standards of democratic living can have lasting benefit for the people..."[27]

It was unlikely that the 1951 constitutional framework would encourage greater interaction between the North and South; it was to encourage the regionalisation of nationalism in Nigeria, as the political parties became increasingly regional based, which further encouraged a solidification of the North-South dichotomy during the decolonisation process from 1952 to 1960, and the intensification of rivalries and mutual distrust. This was an evidence of the structural weakness and manifest deficiencies of the new constitution which failed to address the problems of national integration in an evolving nation-state.

Federal Solution to Political Crises, 1953-1960

The year 1952 was of relative calm in the political history of Nigeria as ethnic or inter-party strife was avoided; the impression was given by Nigerians that they were giving the 1951 Constitution a fair trial. From 1953 onwards, the House of Representatives witnessed turbulent sessions as the tempo and intensity of political agitation sharply increased, leading to a succession of dramatic events within and outside the central legislature.

The constitution was unsuitable to the prevalent conditions in the country because it was ``basically a Unitary Constitution with extensive authority of the central government with its powers of control over the regions''.[28] It proved unworkable one year after it came into effect. Besides its structural weakness and manifest deficiencies, Nigerian nationalists were determined to drastically revise the constitution, or, in the alternative, accept it grudgingly as the last colonial constitution prescribing a dependent status for Nigeria.

However, it was the ``Motion of Destiny'' moved by Anthony Enahoro of the Action Group on March 31, 1953 in which he requested the House of Representatives to accept as a primary political objective the attainment of self-government in 1956 that triggered off political crisis and the threat of disintegration. The Northern members opposed the motion. Ahmadu Bello, the Sardauna of Sokoto and leader of the Northern Peoples Congress moved the adoption of an amendment on the substantive motion, changing ``in 1956'' to ``as soon as practicable''.[29] The debate on the amendment motion was bitter and tempestuous; it ended only when the NCNC and AG members walked out of Parliament.

The Northern members were subjected to insults and abuse by Lagos crowds, and during the ensuing weeks they were ridiculed and strongly criticised by the Southern press. The crisis was to culminate in a series of riots in Kano which lasted four days resulting in the death of fifty persons with over two hundred wounded.[30] Shortly after the riots, the Northern House of Chiefs and the Northern House of Assembly passed an eight-point programme which in effect demanded the dissolution of the Nigerian state.

Since the 1951 Constitution did not give the regions the possibility of maintaining their identity as part of a unified state, the political crisis was the inevitable consequences of the surface manifestation of deep and unresolved tension in two inter-related areas, that is, Northern fear of Southern domination in a self-governing Nigeria, and Southern dissatisfaction with the 1951 Constitution in particular and frustration over the slow rate of advance towards self-government in general. In any case, the twenty-five year period of separate political development had deepened lack of understanding between the two parts of the country, and tended to breed divergence in political outlook, mutual contempt and suspicion.

To find solution to the political crisis, the Colonial Secretary, Oliver Lyttleton, convened a Constitutional Conference in London from July 30 to August 22, 1953 to revise the 1951 Constitution, originally expected to expire in five years. At the conference, a federal constitution was accepted by the leaders of the main political parties. This solution was not reached easily but it was the only feasible answer to the problems of national integration. The work of the conference was completed by a further conference in Lagos in January and February, 1954.

The political restructuring leading to the 1954 Constitution established a federal framework for Nigeria.[31] The constitution provided for greater regional autonomy and for the removal of powers of intervention by the central government. However, it carried the concept of regional administration much further by declaring Nigeria to be a federation, recognising to a limited extent the autonomy of regional governments for their internal administration.

Its limitation notwithstanding, the advocates of federalism were determined to ensure the success of the constitution. Dr. Nnamdi Azikiwe, who became a member of the Federal House of Representatives in 1954, declared: "As for me and those who think like me politically, we are determined to make the revised constitution an avenue for holding the country together through a strong federal government".[32] Although the constitution provided for increased regional autonomy, he was of the view that this should give the impetus "to build up and to strengthen the central government for the unification of the country and for the integration of the diversities in outlook, tradition and culture".[33]

A consequence of the new political arrangement was structural imbalance of Nigeria's federal framework, which became the most potent source of fear of domination among various groups. Although the federal idea was appropriate to the socio-political situation, the form of federation was not an appropriate framework capable of protecting the groups from internal strife. Regionalism in Nigeria had given rise to federalism, which in effect meant that the main political parties were to recognise their regional bases as their only and proper sphere of political action.

From this analysis, it is evidently clear that the federal framework of 1954 did not attempt to prevent the dominance of one group over the other, which also meant that competitive federalism followed logically. Competitive federalism assumes that relations between nation and state must be competitive as each vies for dominance. K.S.Y. Momoh had pointed out in the House of Representatives that in any true federation, ``there should be no region that should be so large as to be able to override the wishes of any two or more regions put together''.[34] Perhaps, this explains why the nationalist struggle ceased to be an effort to generate national consciousness for nation-building and became a movement to reconcile conflicting aspirations of the political class at the level of inter-ethnic, inter-regional and inter-party relations. In other words, competitive federalism in the 1950s encouraged fully regional loyalties of the main political parties and made the task of national integration difficult.

It is also pertinent to note that an important feature of the federal framework of 1954 was the three-regional structure, for which the country was bedevilled by problems arising from fears of domination as already pointed out. The nature of competitive federalism before 1960 made it impossible to satisfy the increasing demands for local autonomy by minority groups within the existing three regions. For example, the minorities in Eastern Region formed the Calabar-Ogoja-Rivers (COR) state movement and demanded a separate state. In the Northern Region, minority groups formed various associations to demand for the creation of a Middle-Belt state. In the Western Region, the Mid-West State Movement demanded the creation of Mid-West State. The pressures from these movements led to the establishment of the Willink Commission to investigate the fears of minorities and the means of allaying them. The report of the commission confirmed that there was convincing evidence of fears among the minorities but insisted that the creation of new states would delay the proposed granting of Nigeria's independence.[35]

The minorities did not seem to agree. When the question of independence was debated on August 5, 1958 by the central legislature, Mr. U.O. Ndem from Calabar constituency expressed the sentiments of the minority groups when he said he had read books on constitutions and had ``not found any state running a federal constitution with the same population, diversity and the same size as Nigeria with only three regions''.[36] He stated: ``if we say we have adopted a federal constitution we must go the whole length. We must make a real and ideal constitution as obtaining in other countries.''[37]

As it were, competitive federalism intensified the politics of ``winner takes all'' as political competition was no longer lively but rather intensified inter-ethnic suspicion, hostility and rivalries and, after 1960, made separatist tendencies very attractive. It was only because the issue of self-government was crucial that the political class had to agree to deal with it as a matter of mutual concern. Woven into the fabric of an evolving national political culture, competitive federalism began to affect the attitudes of the political class toward the political system generally and toward its component parts, affecting also their attitudes toward the role and place of individuals in the political system.

The federal structure of the 1950s and the nature of competitive federalism during the period, no doubt, produced a weak national political culture. Changes were inevitable for sustainable political development and, of course, political restructuring in the past would appear to support the conservative line of thought viewing states in the Nigerian federation as administrative units rather than political units with separate powers. A movement towards a new direction in the political sphere is torn between two antagonistic forces: the forces of progress and the conservative forces. The question is: which way, Nigeria?

The Problems of the Present

Explanation for the present Nigerian problems lies in the course of the country's historical development. Along this course since 1914, the situation has been that of political intrigue and bloodshed – nationalist aspirations turned into inter-regional, inter-ethnic and inter-party antagonism and mutual distrust; collapse of the First Republic; coup and counter-coup; a bitter civil war; collapse of the Second Republic; unending barrack revolts or coup d'etat; the aborted Third Republic; confused political direction – of which there have been obvious signs of reverses in some, if not all aspects of, national development.

The difficulties and dangers of the present require long-term solutions; but as a precondition, there must be a concerted effort in restoring lasting peace, law and order, confidence in leadership and good governance. Then, of course, the will and determination to address all the issues relating to and arising from the national question. Thereafter, there would be the need to evolve a coherent policy and ideology of national integration and nation-building instead of ad hoc solutions to national problems such as the `cake-sharing' syndrome which made Nigerian leaders to ignore the problems of national integration.

It is also reasonable to point out that there is need for improved or true federalism which will take into account the way the fabric of the society is constituted and how power is perceived in such a culture. This means the adoption of a new form of federalism that would fulfil the aspirations of the people. In fact, a true federal system which promotes co-operation also enhances the democratic process and gives it greater vitality.

While it is plausible to argue that the socio-political conditions in which the federal system was introduced in the 1950s had built-in mechanism for failure, which led the country to drift from one crisis to another after independence, the Nigerian political class must be judged a failure in terms of social engineering and nation-building since 1945. In the present situation, it would be difficult for new institutions to induce appropriate changes unless the political culture of the society, with reference to the political system, is internalised by the population. This will undoubtedly enhance future political development.

Nonetheless, the problems of the present also originate from the fact that the structure of power is such that government rarely operates in accord with the federal principle even though Nigeria's post-independence constitutions can be described as federal. The states must not be mere administrative units but political units with separate powers properly defined in the constitution. The constitutional assignment of powers and functions between the central government and component states can take several forms but the distribution of powers remains an essential element. There is therefore, the need to reformulate the constitution of Nigeria on a truly federal basis which takes full account of Nigeria's social diversity.[38] Such a construction would provide the legal framework for monitoring intergovernmental relations, enabling the society, through its representatives or monitoring agents, to focus attention on the problems and future of the federal system. During the colonial period, the British administrators lacked the will and determination[39] to effect meaningful political change. This is the challenge to the present generation of Nigerians.

Conclusion

Federalism, like other systems of government, is dynamic. In spite of the colonial experience and the character of the Nigerian state from 1960 till today, federalism remains a viable system for the allocation of power between governments and as an instrument for national integration.

Political restructuring in Nigeria should provide the opportunity for a new form of federalism in which each of the states should have a constitution which must be consistent with the national constitution and legal order. This may be able to resolve the national question which still persists because federalism has been operated essentially as a unitary system where central government dominates. Nigeria has been presented with several opportunities to utilise the process of political restructuring to identify its major integrative problems and tackle them. Now, in the last few years of the twentieth century, the country cannot afford to allow the opportunity to reinvent its federal system and tackle problems of integration go unutilised.

Notes and References

1. The main works include: A.B. Akinyemi *et al* (eds.) *Readings on Federalism.* Lagos: Nigerian Institute of International Affairs, 1979; U.O. Eleazu, *Federalism and Nation Building – The Nigerian Experience 1954-1964.* Infracombe: Stockwell, 1977; S.E. Oyovbaire, *Federalism in Nigeria: A Study in the Nigerian State.* London: Macmillan, 1985; B. Dudley, ``Federalism and the Balance of Political Power in Nigeria''. *Journal of Commonwealth Comparative Political Studies.* Vol. IV, 1966.

2. National Archives Ibadan (hereinafter referred to as NAI) A4/K2. Sir Frederick Lugard's ``Confidential'' proposals on the amalgamation of Nigeria, May 1913, in A.H.M. Kirk – Greene (ed.) *Lugard and the Amalgamation of Nigeria – A Documentary Record.* London, 1968, p.224. See also Cmd 468 of 1920.

3. *Ibid.* See Introduction to the Democracy Record, and C.L. Temple's ``Confidential Minute'' to Lugard dated 1 February, 1913 and published as Document II.

4. *Ibid.* See Document II

5. Colonial Office, 583. Minute by C. Strachey, 21 June 1913. Quoted in I.F. Nicolson, *The Administration of Nigeria 1900 to 1960: Men, Methods, and Myths.* Oxford: Clarendon Press, 1969, pp.209-210.

6. Ibid p.210.

7. NAI, NL/D. See Governor Clifford's address to the Nigerian Council, December 29, 1920.

8. NAI, CSO 5/5/43 2/8/1946. The Nigeria (Legislative Council) Order-in-Council 1946 making other provision for the constitution and powers of a Legislative Council for Nigeria.

9. From the time the Arthur Richards' Constitution came into effect, wartime developments have affected the nationalist struggle in Nigeria. The nationalist movement had become a powerful force, with a broader basis of popular support, a more coherent programme, and a more militant strategy than in pre-war years. The movement was capable of questioning, in action as well as in words the constitutional, administrative and economic assumptions of British authority.

10. NAI, NL/F2. *Legislative Council Debates.* Second Session, March 10, 1948, p.453.

11. NAI, NL/F2 *Legislative Council Debates.* First Session, March 24, 1947, p.208.
12. NAI, NL/F2 *Legislative Council Debates.* Second Session. March 12, 1948, pp. 550-551.
13. NAI, NL/F2 *Legislative Council Debates.* March 24, 1948, pp 720-721.
14. O.B. Osadolor ``Nigerians in the Colonial Central Legislature: A Study of Their Contribution to the Nationalist Struggle, 1923-1960'', M.A. Dissertation, University of Ibadan, 1988, p.92. See also, NAI NL/F5C ``Legislative Council at Work.'' 1948-1949.
15. N. Azikiwe, Political *Blueprint of Nigeria.* Lagos, 1943.
16. O. Awolowo, *Path to Nigerian Freedom.* London, 1947, pp. 47 ff.
17. Cited in *Legislative Council Debates.* Fourth Session, April 3, 1950 p.510.
18. Evidence from *Legislative Council Debates.* Fourth Session, April 3, 1950 p. 509.
19. NAI, NC/B7 *Constitution Review and the New Budget* (Proceedings of the Meeting of the Legislative Council held at Enugu in March/April, 1950) p.57.
20. NAI, NL/F5 *Proceedings of the General Conference on Review of the Constitution, January, 1950.* Lagos, 1950, p.244.
21. NAI, NL/F2 *Legislative Council Debates.* Fourth Session, April 3, 1950, p.509.
22. *Ibid.,* p.511
23. *Ibid*
24. B.J. Dudley, ``A Coalition Theoretic Analysis of Nigerian Politics, 1950-66''. *The African Review.* Vol. 2 No. 4, 1974, p.532.
25. Obaro Ikime, ``In search of Nigerians: changing patterns of inter-group relations in an evolving nation state'', Presidential Inaugural Lecture delivered at the 30th Congress of the Historical Society of Nigeria, at the University of Nigeria, Nsukka, on 1 May, 1985, pp.21-22.
26. *Ibid.,* p.21
27. NAI, NL/F2 *Legislative Council Debates.* Fifth session, March 7, 1951, p.255.

28. I.A. Ayua, ``Constitutional Developments in Nigeria since the Colonial Era'', in J.A. Atanda and A.Y. Aliyu (eds.) *Political Development* (Proceedings of the National Conference on Nigeria since Independence, Zaria, March 1983, Vol. 1). Zaria, 1985 p.411.

29. See NAI, NL/H2 *Nigeria, House of Representatives Debates.* Second Session, March 31, 1953, pp.985-996.

30. For details, see *Report on the Kano Disturbances.* Kaduna, 1951.

31. NAI, CSO 5/5/48A *Nigeria (Constitution) Order in Council,* 1954.

32. NAI, NL/H2 *Nigeria, House of Representatives Debates.* Third Session, March 8, 1954, p.37

33. *Ibid.,* p.36

34. NAI, NL/H2 *Nigeria, House of Representatives Debates.* Third Session. March 9, 1954, p.92

35. See Nigeria, *Report of the Commission appointed to enquire into the Fears of Minorities and the Means of Allaying Them.* London, HMSO, 1958.

36. NAI, NL/H2 *Nigeria, House of Representatives Debates.* Official Report Vol. III, August 5, 1958, p.155.

37. *Ibid*

38. See for example, William Riker, *Federalism: Origin Operation, Significance.* Boston, 1964. See also, Geoffrey Sawer, *Modern Federalism.* London, 1969.

39. See, NAI MN/B4A. Sir Bernard Bourdillon, *Memorandum on the Future Political Development of Nigeria.* Lagos, 1939.

CHAPTER 3

Olawale Albert

Federalism, Inter-ethnic Conflicts and the Northernisation Policy of the 1950s and 1960s

> There are Europeans, but, undoubtedly, it is the Southerners who have the power in the North. They have control over the railway stations; of the Post Offices; of Government Hospitals; of canteens; the majority employed in the Kaduna Secretariat and in the Public Works Department are all Southerners; in all the different departments of Government it is the Southerners who have the power. (FN 1957:728).

Introduction

In one of his works, Afigbo [1989:6] divided the evolution of Nigerian federalism into three epochs: the period of ``informal federation'' [1900-1946]; the first phase of ``formal federation'' [1946-1966]; and; the second phase of ``formal federation'' [1967-date]. These three periods, unlike the pre-colonial epoch, have been marked by intense rivalries among the three major ethnic groups in Nigeria, namely, the Hausa-Fulani, Yoruba and Igbo. This chapter focuses on the conflicts between these ethnic groups during the first formal phase of the Nigerian federalism [i.e. 1946-1966]. We are most particularly interested in the frustrations that made the Hausa-Fulani to embrace the ``Northernisation policy'' between the 1950s and 1960s. As a result of this policy several southern Nigerians employed in the North were retrenched from their jobs and replaced with Northerners. This chapter discusses, in details, the remote and immediate causes of this ``Northernisation Policy''; how the policy was implemented and its further consequences on ethnic conflicts between the southern Nigerian immigrants in the North and their Hausa-Fulani hosts most especially in Kano on the one hand and between the northern Nigerian Fulani oligarchies who swore to unite the north by all means and the christian-dominated Middle-belt politicians who resisted being used by the NPC to further its ethnocentric and religious interests.

Antecedents of the Northernisation Policy

The colonisation of Nigeria by the British, which could be said to have started in 1850 in Lagos, was completed in 1903 with the military expeditions that crushed the invincibility of the former Sokoto Caliphate. The management of the emergent political system was however done under two protectorate systems: the Northern and Southern Protectorates. The two protectorates were politically amalgamated in 1914 thus giving rise to the formation of the modern Nigerian state. The country was further divided into three regions – North, West and East – in 1947 when the Richards Constitution came into effect [see Ezera 1960; Coleman 1958 for details].

The Richards Constitution compounded the ethnic conflicts in Nigeria owing to the fact that before it came into effect the country was managed under two separate and contradictory systems. In the North, the political system was controlled by traditional rulers [Emirs] in line with the pledge of Lord Lugard to the *Lamido* of Adamawa and the Sultan of Sokoto in 1901 and 1903 respectively that he would not tamper with the existing religious and political systems in northern Nigeria [Albert 1994:58-9]. It was around this promise that the policy of indirect rule [see Ikime 1970], which was very popular in colonial northern Nigeria, was woven. On the other hand, southern Nigerians had representatives in the National Legislative Assembly and so were more sophisticated politically than their northern counterparts. Western education was also not as successful in the North as it was in the South [Graham 1966]. The disadvantaged position of the Northerners, compared to their counterparts in the South became evidently clear with the advent of the Richard's Constitution which made it necessary for the two groups to work together. The constitution thus compounded the mutual suspicion among the different ethnic groups in Nigeria and marked the beginning of acrimonious ethnic politics in the country. The three political parties that were established around this time took steps to entrench themselves in their predominant cultural regions – the Northern Peoples Congress for the Hausa-Fulani northerners, Action Group for the Yoruba-dominated western Nigeria and the NCNC for the Igbo-dominated eastern region. Each of the parties became the instruments for protecting the narrow interests of some particular ethnic groups (Sklar 1963:474; Williams 1980:35].

Each of the three main ethnic groups feared the domination of one another. The Yoruba feared the Igbo, the Igbo feared the Yoruba, the Yoruba and Igbo who constituted the Southerners were feared by the Northerners and vice versa. The political statements of the leaders of these political parties before and after the formation of their parties helped to further inflame the fear of domination. The statements sometimes betrayed the intentions of these political leaders and also confirmed what the other groups feared about them. For example Dr. Nnamdi Azikiwe who started as a pan-Africanist soon started to confuse his roles in African politics for the superiority of the Igbo over other Nigerian groups. He noted in 1948;

> It would appear that the God of Africa has created the Ibo nation to lead the children of Africa from the bondage of the ages... The martial prowess of the Ibo nation at all ages of human history has enabled them not only to conquer others but also to adapt themselves to the role of preserver... The Ibo nation cannot shirk its responsibility from its manifest destiny [*West African Pilot*, July 8, 1948].

Reacting against the various attempts made by Dr. Azikiwe to present the Igbo as the most superior ethnic group in Nigeria, Chief Awolowo noted in 1960:

> It seemed clear to me that [Azikiwe's] policy was to corrode the self-respect of the Yoruba people as a group: to build up the Ibo as a "master-race" [Awolowo 1960:135].

The North was conscious of its shortcomings under this first phase of the Nigerian federalism. It readily acknowledged the superiority of the South in terms of an early start in western education and hence political sophistication. But this formed the basis of the northern fear of southern domination. Mallam Tafawa Balewa expressed this fear in a speech delivered in 1957:

> ...the British entered the country from the sea, the areas we now call the Northern, the Eastern and Western Regions of Nigeria came under the British administration at different times. By virtue of their being geographically situated near the sea coast, the Western and the Eastern Regions came under the British influence earlier than the Northern Region. For this...the rate of progress and developments in the Western European civilisation has been uneven with the vast Northern Region dragging behind...Man at times...is by nature suspicious, and it is therefore natural for the people of the North, though greater than the South, in numerical strength, to fear domination. I am sorry to say...that those fears still exist and they can only be erased from our minds by the most sincere practical demonstration of goodwill and by the unselfish co-operation of the South. By this I mean that the South should have sympathy for our shortcomings and that they should not be too hasty to condemn our actions...take the question of staff in our public services. The South with its many schools and colleges, is producing hundreds of academically and technically qualified people for the public services. The common cry now is Nigerianisation of the public services. It is most important in a federation that the federal service shall be fully representative of all units which make up the federation. Now, what do we find in Nigeria today? There are 46,000 men and women in the Federal Public Services. I have not been able to obtain the figures of the number of Northerners in the service but I very much doubt if they even amount to one per cent..unless some solution is found it will continue to be a cause of dissatisfaction and friction [FN 1957:728-741]

The Southerners were unsparing in their criticism of their counterparts from the North. The latter were presented as very lazy and unprogressive people for whom the Southerners were not ready to wait. If Nigeria was to progress the Northerners must be ignored. The Southerners most especially the Yoruba thought it would be an abnormality for them to be equated with or asked to serve under the Hausa-Fulani. Therefore one of the popular songs composed by the Yoruba-dominated Action Group in the 1950s states that it is: "Better to die than to pay homage to a *gambari*[Hausa person]". It was therefore not too difficult for the Hausa-Fulani to realise that if they have to survive under the Nigerian federalism they had to devise different strategies, whether decent or otherwise, for ensuring the unity of northern Nigerians using the platform of the NPC. They exploited religious symbolism and sentiments to promote their political interests. The simple strategy was to present the Southerners to the Northerners as christians who should not be rated better than infidels [*kafiri*]. Of course, it had been argued as early as 1824 by the Hausa that the intelligence of an infidel should not be rated more than that of an ass [Denham and Oudney 1826:75]. Committed Muslims, which most Northerners are, were therefore encouraged not to have anything to do with such "unbelievers".

Just as the Southerners did not hide their contempt for the Hausa-Fulani the latter did not hide its demonisation agenda from anybody. One of the northern political leaders openly told Dent [1971:452] in the late 1960s: "We had to teach the people to hate the Southerners; to look at them as people depriving them of their rights, in order to win them over". Those Northerners who deviantly tried at this period to associate themselves with the southern Nigerian political parties were seen and treated as religious outcasts. Commenting on the logic behind this, Professor Dudley noted *inter alia:*

> Islamic influence in winning mass support can hardly be underestimated. The identification of the party and its leaders [the patron of the Northern Peoples Congress is the Sultan of Sokoto, the Sarkin Musulumi] with the religion of Islam is such as to suggest that the party represents the consensus of the society —*Ijma'* — and not to accept the consensus of the society is to be heretical — *Bid'a* — a rebel from the community, but as the Prophet said: "The hand of God is upon the community [*al-jama'ah*]; and he who sets himself apart from it will be set apart in Hell-fire. He who departs from the community by a handspan ceases to be Muslim" [Dudley 1968:143]

To win the support of the non-muslim northern Nigerians, most especially those from the Middle-Belt, the NPC professed a policy of unity in diversity by developing the slogan "One North One People, irrespective of religion, Rank or Tribe". Consequently, the Northerners, most especially at the initial stage, began to see themselves as belonging to the same cultural world and should therefore pursue common political goals. The major enemy to be fought were the Southerners.

The Last Straw

The issues discussed above reflect what could be described as the remote causes of the Northernisation Policy. The events that immediately led to it started to gather immediate storm in 1953 though it was actually in the 1960s that it became official policy. Chief Anthony Enahoro, an Action Group member moved a motion on the floor of the House of Representatives in Lagos asking that the British should disengage from their colonial enterprise in Nigeria by granting the country her independence in 1956. This motion was opposed by the northern Nigerian members of the NPC who felt Nigeria was not ripe for independence [Bello 1962:110-148]. They therefore moved the motion that the independence should be granted ``as soon as practicable'' instead of 1956. The Sardauna of Sokoto, Sir Ahmadu Bello explained the opposition of the Northerners against the 1956 date in the following terms:

> The North does not intend to accept the invitation to commit suicide... As representatives of the people, we from the North feel that in all major issues such as this one, we are duty bound to consult those we represent... If the Honourable members from the West and East speak to this motion unamended, for their people I must say here and now, Sir, that we from the North have been given no such mandate by our people... We were late in assimilating western education yet within a short time we will catch up with the other Regions, and share their lot... We want to be realistic and consolidate our gains. It is our resolute intention to build our development on sound and lasting foundations so that they would be lasting [House of Representatives' Debates, March 31, 1953 p. 992 quoted in Nkemdirim 1975:68-9].

The obviously angered southern Nigerian members of the AG and NCNC resorted to calling the Northerners ``Ministers'', ``Slaves of the white man'', ``His master's voice'', ``stooge'', ``Kolanut men'', ``Kolanut chiefs'' etc. [[NRG 1953:4]. The humiliation the Northerners suffered in the parliament was nothing to be compared to what later happened to them after the proceedings of the day:

> Groups of Ibo and Yoruba surrounded them and called them ``thieves'' and ``slaves of the white man'', ``stupid Hausas'', ``the men who have no minds of their own''. At one shop, the shop boys refused to attend to one minister's servant. In the evening when the electric light was lit Emirs in upstairs' flats who could be observed had similar insults shouted up on them. Over and above all this the members felt very deeply that it should be necessary for them to be protected by police guards at all the stations in the Western Provinces [NRG 1953:4].

Federalism, Inter-ethnic Conflicts and the Northernisation Policy.   55

In the North, the people saw the Lagos incident by the Igbo-Yoruba southern Nigerian coalition as an open hostility against the Northerners. As the Sardauna of Sokoto, Sir Ahmadu Bello later commented:

> We were not only angry at our treatment, but indignant that people who were full of fine phrases about the unity of Nigeria should have set their people against the chosen representatives of another Region while passing through their territories [Bello *op.cit* p.135]

Back to their northern Nigerian constituency, the leaders of the NPC went round to educate the people on why they objected to the self-government motion of the AG. It was at this same moment that the leaders of the AG too decided to carry their 1956 independence campaign to Kano, a city which Paden [p.361] described as "the primary repository of northern values and indentites". Members of the NPC decided immediately to use all possible options to prevent the AG visit from taking place. Acting on the instructions of the NPC leaders, Honourable Mallam Inuwa Wada, the Information Officer, Kano Native Administration addressed some battle-ready youths in Kano on the 14th May 1953 in the following terms:

> We have come here this morning to speak to you as members of the Northern Peoples Congress because we understand that delegates of the Action Group will arrive in Kano by air on Saturday, the 16th instant... Having abused us in the South these very Southerners have decided to come over to the North to abuse us, but we have determined to retaliate the treatment given us in the South. We have therefore organised 1,000 men ready in the city to meet force with force... To show the Southerners that we represent the common men in the North, the Northern Peoples Congress has declared a strike in all Native Administration offices for Saturday, 16-5-53... We wish to state finally that we have not been sent by the Native Authorities, we have come to speak to you as members of the Northern Peoples Congress and we are prepared to face anything that comes out of this business. We are not like the Southerners who brew trouble and allow their followers to go to prison or suffer what they have done; we are prepared to go to prison or die. [Cited in NRG 1953].

While the politicians in the North were battle-ready and their AG members were packing their baggages ready for the visit to Kano, the southern Nigerian press took up the "nationalist" struggle. Referring to the speech of Mallam Inuwa Wada, *The Daily Service* 15th May, 1953 reported that:

> The proposed tour of the Northern Region by the Action Group to educate the masses *has scared officialdom and the stooges,* the Sardauna group; both of them are now organising N.A. officials to demonstrate against the delegates [emphasis mine]

The next day the newspaper reported in another article entitled

Reactionaries are Scared

> The Northern tour of the Action Group which begins today *has put reactionary elements on the run*. The Sardauna group, the *dutiful allies of British imperialism,* are reported to be campaigning against the tour and are sparing nothing to precipitate a strike by the N.A. officials today. We sympathise with these *reactionaries who have told so many lies to the Northern people* that they are scared by the possibility of the people being given an opportunity of hearing the truth. But we can assure them that no amount of threats can deter Action Group from meeting the people of the Northern Region... [emphasis mine].

This report must have further reinforced the resolve of the Northerners to prevent the AG from successfully visiting Kano. As early as 8.30 a.m. on Friday, May 15 1953 about 3,000 demonstrators, largely consisting of Native Administration Staff; assembled at Fagge armed with bows and arrows. From there, the crowd led by hundreds of cyclists and horsemen moved to Sabon Gari in the process of which more demonstrators were recruited. As they moved, they were shouting: "We do not want the Yoruba here". Then the rioters descended on the Sabon Gari market and closed it down. In the process, many of the traders got wounded [Nkemdirim:72-3]. Between this first day and May 18th, 1953, violence was a daily ritual in Kano. At the end of the civil-disorder, thirty-six people were officially declared killed [NRG:1]. Two hundred and forty-six others were wounded. Most of them were treated for gunshots.

The 1953 riots led to greater mutual distrust between Northern and Southern Nigerians. Shortly after the riot, the Northern House of Chiefs and House of Assembly passed a motion which in effect would have led to the dissolution of the Nigerian Federation [Bello:143-4]. The two Houses asked for strong regional governments linked together by a non-political central agency whose mandate would be to deal with whatever matters the regional governments passed to it from time to time. Reacting to this motion, the Colonial Secretary Mr Oliver Lyttleton announced his plan to introduce such constitutional reforms that would enhance greater regional autonomy in Nigeria. This led to the July-August 1953 London Conference which representatives of the different Nigerian regions attended [Olusanya 1980:536-7; Coleman 1965; Ezera 1964]. The Lyttleton Constitution of 1954 was produced out of the deliberation at this important conference. The new constitution which still supported federalism provided for the regionalisation of the civil service, judiciary and law-making bodies so that each region became freer to run its government as it deemed fit.

The Northernisation Policy: "Enough is Enough: Every Baby unto its Mother's Breast"

In pursuance of the opportunities offered by the new constitution, the governments in the Western and Eastern parts of Nigeria pursued aggressive policies of educational and economic advancement [Nkemdirim:103]. They established more schools and offered scholarship to students. Their civil service became more Nigerianised as a result of which many expatriates were retired. In the North, the people also introduced some social and educational reforms in their bid to catch up with the level of development in the South. To achieve the much desired autonomy, the Northerners began an aggressive "Northernisation" Policy as a result of which many southern Nigerians lost their jobs in the northern public service and were replaced by Northerners. Between January 1954 and August 1958, a total of 2,148 Southerners were dismissed from the Northern Public Service [Daily Service, August 5, 1958] and encouraged to seek employment in the South where they belong. Up till 1954, there was no single northern Nigerian in the administrative cadre of the northern public service. Immediately after the commencement of the "Northernisation" Policy five Northerners were appointed. By 1958, there were five Northerners in the top echelon of the service, sixty-nine in the administrative and professional cadre and 237 in the executive and higher technical cadre [Dudley 1968:219-220].

In 1958, an attempt was made to define the "Northernisation" Policy by the Regional Public Service Commission: "if a qualified Northerner is available, he is given priority in recruitment; if no Northerner is available, an expatriate may be recruited or a non-Northerner on contract terms" [Report 1958]. During the same year, Sir Ahmadu Bello the leader of the NPC and the Premier of Northern Region noted that the aim of the policy was to make "Northerners gain control of everything in this country" [HNC Debates 1958 col. 36]. "Non-Northern Nigerian" as used in the above quotation would normally be taken to mean all "strangers" in northern Nigeria. Of course, this would naturally have been expected to include "expatriate". But this was not the case. Therefore, Non-Northern Nigerians here referred specifically to southern Nigerians. Northernisation had so many components that one of its critics from the North, Alhaji Abdul Rasaq noted: "Northernisation, in its psychological effects, is turning the North and Northerners into introverts such that nothing is good for the North which is not Northern" [cited in Dudley 1968:225].

A circular [CON/4] dated 14 November 1960 from the Ministry of Local Government Northern Region espoused the government's stand on some political aspects of the policy. It insisted that only Northerners may be employed by native authorities as daily paid labourers or to pensionable posts. Native authorities were advised to take disciplinary action against any employee who deliberately employed non-Northerners into the Northern civil service. Towards ensuring that the government's instructions were not violated, it was decided that a copy of all native authority advertisements for appointment to pensionable posts must be sent to the Secretary, Northernisation Implementation Committee of the Premier's Office, Kaduna for his advice on whether Northerners were available for such posts or not.

The Northernisation Policy was initially limited to the civil service. To facilitate its extension to the informal economic sphere, some indigenous northern Nigerian businessmen formed various pressure groups which were affiliated to the NPC: The Northern Transporters and Contractors Company, the Northern Nigerian Contractors Association, the Northern Transport Owners Union and the Northern Amalgamated Union. As a result of the pressure from these various groups, the procedure for awarding contracts by the Provincial Tender Boards in Northern Nigeria was reassessed and Southerners were carefully edged out [Dudley 1968:232]. In desperation, some southern Nigerian contractors and big businessmen had to become members of the NPC by taking the membership cards. Some of them complained that they had no places to work or obtain contracts in the South and therefore pledged to vote for the NPC as a way of earning their living [Okafor 1961:143]. Statutory corporations and some private commercial firms having businesses with the government were also under pressure to turn their establishments into instruments of political patronage. One of the "credentials" for getting employed or advanced in such establishments was to be a member of the NPC. A particular firm in Kano, NICCO, owned by a naturalised Nigerian [formerly Sudanese] had to dismiss some of its staff who refused to join the party [Dudley 1968:193-4]. On 18th November 1960, the NPC Administrative Secretary to the Administrator of Kaduna Capital Territory issued a circular that all land leases in Kaduna must first be cleared with the NPC. Only card-carrying members of the party were expected to own land in the city.

The "Northern Amalgamated Merchants Union" was particularly formed by some influential businessmen from Kano. The main objective of the union was to serve as the medium through which businessmen of northern Nigerian origin could be provided with the enabling environment to effectively compete with the southern Nigerians (who dominated the northern economies). The position of the union was expressed on the floor of the Northern House of Assembly by its spokesman, Alhaji Ahmadu Dantata, a member of the House representing Kano. In 1957, Alhaji Dantata urged the House to formally extend the

Northernisation Policy to the economic sphere [See House of Assembly Debates, Official Report Feb.-March 1957 pp. 77-8, 361-6 and 387]. The government responded to this request by establishing loan corporations which granted generous loans to deserving northern Nigerian businessmen. Many of these businessmen still had to depend on educated southern Nigerians for the management of their businesses. For example, the name of Alhaji Dantata himself appeared in the study conducted by Martin Dent as one of those that used the southern Nigerians. He ``employed Ibos to man his petrol stations and in the clerical aspects of his business in preference to Northerners because they gave better value for money'' [Martin Dent 1971:391]. The European firms in northern Nigeria who were also out to make their own private profits rather than playing politics depended on southern Nigerian staff for their operations. Therefore, Yusuf Bayero who was representative of Sumaila District in Kano noted in 1963: ``There is no firm [in Kano] where you can find a Northerner in a responsible post. If you see a Northerner in it, he must be a labourer and not an important person'' [Northern House of Assembly, *Debates,* March 13 1963:292]. Muhtar Bello Yola representing Dawakin Tofa East District, Kano suggested how such firms could be dealt with:

> As most of the commercial firms seem to have no regard to the Northernisation Policy of the government of Northern Nigeria would the Honourable Premier cause the system of employment in commercial firms [to be] investigated and necessary action taken to make them change their attitude towards Northernisation Policy? [*Debates* p.204]

According to John Paden, the Northernisation policy was designed by the Premier of Northern Region, Sir Ahmadu Bello with the support of the indigenous Kano trading community [Paden 325]. Sir Ahmadu Bello blamed the British for the unchecked migration of Southerners into the North, but expected the Southerners themselves to have voluntarily left with the Europeans immediately after Nigerian independence. This suggests that Sir Ahmadu Bello did not recognise the right of the southern Nigerians to live in the north as espoused in the constitution of the Nigerian federation. He consequently noted during one of the debates on the floor of the Northern House of Chiefs in 1965:

> The person who brings a stranger into the house (should expect that) when the owner of the house has gone, the stranger too should pack up and go [Northern House of Chiefs, Debates, March 19, 1965:55]

On the extent of the Northernisation Policy he said,

> The Northernisation Policy does not only apply to clerks, administrative officers, doctors and others. We do not want to go to Chad and meet strangers catching our fish in the water, and

taking them away to leave us with nothing. We do not want to go to Sokoto and find a carpenter who is a stranger nailing our houses. I do not want to go to the Sabon Gari Kano and find strangers making the body of a lorry, or to go to the market and see butchers who are not Northerners [*Ibid.*].

The paradox however is that whereas it was easy for the political leaders in northern Nigeria to relieve the Southerners in their midst of their jobs in the formal sector of the economy, it was rather difficult to get rid of those in the informal sector. Apart from the fact that the Northerners depended on sea ports in the southern part of Nigeria for the supply of their needed manufactured goods from overseas they derived the bulk of their revenues from the custom duties paid by the petty southern Nigerian traders [Geary 1927:213]. The Southerners engaged in private businesses in Kano therefore increased as some of them formerly in the formal sector were retired or dismissed. Rather than travelling back to their home towns, the discharged Southerners [especially the Igbo-speaking among them] in Kano chose to remain behind in the city investing their retirement entitlements or savings on private businesses. Their economic successes and refusal to accept Islam despite their long stay in Kano later produced other kinds of violent encounters between the Hausa-Fulani Kano population and their southern Nigerian hosts [see Albert 1993 and 1994].

A Critique of the Policy

Even under the present political dispensation in Nigeria, there is no specific law or policy which makes it mandatory for any state of the Nigerian federation to employ ``strangers'' from other states. In the North, southern Nigerians are still given contract employment where they are at all needed. It is also quite unusual to see a Northerner employed in any of the southern Nigerian civil services. This probably explains why the Southerners could not do anything about their sack from the North between the 1950s and 1960s.

The Northernisation Policy led to the take-over of the Northern civil service by political party members and the subordination of the career civil servants. A major implication of this is the politicisation of the civil service. There were twelve permanent secretaries in Northern Nigeria in 1963. Most of them were professional politicians. For example, Ibrahim Dasuki who was in charge of local government and Ibrahim Argungu in charge of establishment and training were both NPC members of the Northern Regional Assembly. Yahaya Gusau who acted as a permanent secretary was also a law maker in the regional legislature. So also were other prominent figures in the Northern civil service as Ali Akilu, Abubakar Imam, Dan Buram Jada etc. Most of these people were offspring of the traditional northern ruling oligarchies – mostly sons of Emirs and Chiefs. Of the twelve permanent secretaries in the North at this time, only two of them were university graduates. Most of the top civil servants with the native administration had no secondary school education. These people were resented by the different categories of graduates recruited to work with them.

The educational qualifications of the northern civil servants and the kind of jobs each category was entitled to had some centrifugal ethnic correlations. Writing on this Dudley [1968:224] noted:

> While the `far North' have so far tended to predominate in the top-ranks, the new crop of administrative grade civil servants are more likely to come from the `lower North'. Thus of the thirty-nine students who entered Ahmadu Bello University in 1962 to read for degrees in administration and law – and most of these would make the civil service their career – 66.6% are from the lower North. The percentage intake from this area in 1963 is higher, this being 84.0%. In other words, northernisation is creating a situation in which the upper reaches of the administrative class are dominated by N.A-type men largely from the far North with relatively poor education but long administrative experience, while the bottom ranks of that class may soon be filled by younger graduates from the lower North. The position is made no less easier by being complicated by what one might very loosely term ``class'' divisions in that while those from the far North tend to be associated with the families of the traditional ruling oligarchy, chiefs, district heads and so on, those from the lower North have more humble social antecedents being sons of farmers, traders and artisans of varying skills.

But of more concern to other northern Nigerians was the fact that most of these big weights in the Northern civil service came from a section of the North: Sokoto and Bornu. This made critics from within Northern Nigeria to dismiss the Northernisation policy as a policy of ``Sokotonisation'' and ``Bornu-isation'' [*West Africa* 6th May 1961]. The policy was therefore interpreted as another form of political patronage rather than a policy of political emancipation from the domination of southern Nigerians. This later explains the separatist politics of the Tiv-led UMBC. The better educated peoples of the Middle-belt [``lower North''] could see their interests to be at stake under the ``aristocratic feudalism'' championed by the NPC. NPC loyalists were appointed to head the various Tiv N.As, all tax collectors suspected to be UMBC members were sacked and replaced with NPC members, some UMBC members were tried on trumped-up charges and sent to prison, many were prevented from enjoying the benefits of the Northernisation Policy by being denied government contracts like the Southerners, they were also discriminated against in the award of scholarships and refused job placement even when they had good certificates needed for such jobs.

Some Tiv market places were closed down by the N.A. police as a way of causing economic hardship for them and so on [Anifowose 1982:142-4]. They therefore tried to redress their problems of alienation sometimes allying with the forces of AG, NCNC or the Aminu-Kano led NEPU in Kano. The attempt of the NPC oligarchy to suppress UMBC members was violently resisted in 1960 and 1964 respectively and since then the North – most especially the policy of ``One north one people'' professed by the Hausa-Fulani – has not been the same again.

Bibliography

Albert, I.O. [1993] *Inter-ethnic Relations in a Nigerian City: The Historical Perspective of the Hausa-Igbo Conflict in Kano, 1953-1991.* Ibadan: Institut Francais de Recherche en Afrique.

————[1994] "Urban Migrant Settlements in Nigeria: A Historical Comparison of the Sabon Garis in Kano and Ibadan, 1893-1991", Ph.D thesis University of Ibadan, Nigeria.

Afigbo, A.E. [1989] "Federal Character: Its meaning and history", P.P. Ekeh and E.E. Osaghae [eds.], *Federal Character and Federalism in Nigeria.* Ibadan: Heinemann.

Anifowose, R. [1982] *Violence and Politics in Nigeria: The Tiv and Yoruba Experience.* New York: Nok Publishers International.

Awolowo, A. [1960] *Awo.* Cambridge University Press.

Bello, A. [1962] *My Life.* London.

Coleman, James [1958] *Nigeria: Background to Nationalism.* Berkeley, and Los Angeles.

———— [1965], *Nigeria: Background to Nationalism.* Berkeley.

Dent, M.J. [1971] ``Tarka and the Tiv: A Perspective on Nigerian Federation", in R. Melson and H. Wolpe [eds.], *Nigeria: Modernisation and the Politics of Communalism.* East Lansing: Michigan State University Press.

———— [1971] ``The military and politics: A study of the relations between the army and the political process in Nigeria", In R. Melson and H. Wolpe (eds.) *Nigeria Modernisation and the Politics of Communalism.* East Lansing: Michigan State University Press.

Dudley, B.J. [1968] *Parties and Politics in Northern Nigeria.* London: Frank Cass and Co. Ltd.

——— [1973] *Instability and Political Order: Politics and Crisis in Nigeria.* Ibadan University Press.

Ezera, Kalu [1960] *Constitutional Developments in Nigeria.* London.

——— [1964] *Constitutional Developments in Nigeria.* London.

Federation of Nigeria [1948] *Legislative Council Debates [Official Report],* March 16.

Federation of Nigeria [1958] *House of Representatives Debates [Official Report],* Vol. ii session 1957-58.

Geary, W.N. [1927] *Nigeria Under British Rule.* London: Methuen and Co. Ltd.

Graham, S.F. [1966] *Government and Mission Education in Northern Nigeria 1900-1919.* Ibadan University Press.

House of Representatives' Debates, March 31, 1953 p. 992 quoted in Bernard Nkemdirim, *Social Change and Political Violence in Colonial Nigeria.* Elms Court, Arthur H. Stockwell Ltd, 1975, pp. 68-9.

Ikime, O. [1970] "The Establishment of Indirect Rule in Northern Nigeria". *Tarikh* Vol. 3 No. 3., 1970.

National Archives Kaduna, CON/4, "The position of Non-Northerners in the service of Northern Regional Government [2] Claim to Northern Nigerian Status II.

Northern Regional Government, *Report on the Kano Disturbances 16th, 17th and 19th May, 1953.* Lagos: Government Printers, 1953.

Okafor, R.B.K., Parliamentary Secretary, N.C.N.C., [1961] *Report on the recent north regional elections.* This is a Confidential report to F.S. McEwen, N.A. National Secretary, N.C.N.C. 6 May

Olusanya, G.O. [1980] "Constitutional Development in Nigeria 1861-1960", in O. Ikime (ed.) *Groundwork of Nigerian History.* Heinemann Books.

Sklar, Richard L. [1963] *Nigerian Political Parties: Power in an Emergent African Nation.* New York, Enugu: Nok Publishers.

Williams, Gavin [1980] *State and Society in Nigeria.* Idanre: Afrografika.

CHAPTER 4

Sanya Osha

Political Restructuring as Militarisation: Fragments of Evidence from Civil Society

What happens to civil society and the search for a democratic and peaceful order when political restructuring utilises militaristic methods and points in the undeclared direction of the goal of militarisation of civil society? This chapter proceeds from the assumption that much of what has passed as attempts at political tinkering and engineering, especially since the Babangida era and even more so in the succeeding Abacha years, has involved the use of typically military strategies of surprise, subterfuge, ambush, subjugation, cooptation and control for a single purpose. This purpose has been to fashion a more docile and predictable civil society not only in the image of the military but also one whose strategic sections, if not its entire province, is turned into a strong prop for military and other forms of autocratic and pseudodemocratic rule.

In making this assumption, it is conceded that it is not all experiences of military rule that necessarily pursue as an article of faith the militarisation of the structures and ethos of civil society, seeking to conquer society and remould it in the interests of military generals who govern. Even in the context of Nigeria's post-indepedence political history up to the Babangida era, attempts by military governments to militarise and subject civil society to military logic were either inchoate (as in much of the Gowon era) or successfully checked and rebuffed by civil society acting alone or (often unknowingly) with opposition groups from within the military itself (as in the Ironsi, Gowon and Buhari years).

It is also conceded that non-military forms of rule can also contain seeds of militarisation if by militarisation we refer to the consequences for society of increasingly dictatorial rule. This process was witnessed in Nigeria's political terrain in the latter part of the First (from 1962) and the Second (from 1981) Republics.

Nevertheless, it is suggested in this chapter that the period from 1985 when Babangida shot himself to power up to date has witnessed a continuity in the project of militarisation of civil society. The rest of the chapter deploys fragments of evidence from civil society to illustrate the point.

The Fragments of Evidence

Given that civil society is that section of society which engages the state and its governing regime "for the purpose of constructing, defining and institutionalising values, norms, rules and principles by which society is governed as well as the terms of such governance"[1], it is not surprising that the terrain of civil society is a contested terrain even in the best of times and a slippery, treacherous terrain in circumstances such as the one in which Nigeria has found itself in recent years. What remains beyond doubts is that much of the struggle between pro-regime forces and those of the prodemocratic opposition in that country would have been etched into the fabric of civil society.

Thus, one hardly needs to look anywhere else for the agitated footprints of such contestation in the forms of the drive for and resistance to the regime's militaristic instruments and goals of surprise, subterfuge, ambush, subjugation, cooptation and control of civil society.

Perhaps, the most dramatic of surprises was the annulment of the June 12, 1993 election, an election in which civil society had participated enthusiastically and peacefully by channelling its energies and preferences through a party system created by the military regime itself. No less dramatic, and perhaps even more regrettable but definitely revealing of the nature of military oligarchs in power since 1985, was the hanging of the Ogoni nine, including Ken Saro-Wiwa in 1995. The hanging was ordered by government in defiance of Nigerian and international civil society and global opinion which had mobilised to appeal to the military regime to spare the Ogoni nine charged in military courts for murder arising from a quest for minority rights and campaigns for the environment.

Moreover, in the period since 1985, unheralded changes have been made in previously announced official timetables for political transition, while such surprising developments have been combined with subterfuge and ambush by military autocrats to turn unpredictability into an art of statecraft. Thus, political chicanery and an undisguised lack of sincerity by military autocrats have led to the traumatisation of civil society as well as the evolving political society comprising the party and electoral system.

To worsen the situation, the concept of ambush was equally and lavishly applied on the socio-political landscape by the governing regimes and their supporters. For instance, not only have Babangida and Abacha perfected the system of setting impossible conditions for those aspiring to public office under their political transition timetables; they have equally and freely, often without notice or credible reason, banned, unbanned, and reimposed bans on aspirants for elective political office, some after election results were already known!

Moreover, the entire socio-political landscape has been suffused by the imperative of subjugation of oppositional and not-so-oppositional forces by the military. For instance, several notable Nigerians, including General Alani Akinrinade, former Chief of Defence Staff, Africa's first Nobel prize winner for literature, Wole Soyinka, Anthony Enahoro, the elder statesman who moved the motion for independence in 1953, John Oyegun, the former governor of Edo State, Bolaji Akinyemi, former Minister for External Affairs, Bola Tinubu, a Senator in the aborted Third Republic and Cornelius Adebayo, a former governor of Kwara State, have gone into exile for reasons of personal safety in the last few years in the context of what officials insist is a democratic transition programme.

Even at the level of states, military administrators have routinely behaved as if the Nigerian civil society is just one vast military barrack that has to be policed into line using the harshest possible means. They have tended to behave like royalty, with the civil populace in the states over which they govern living virtually at their mercy. For instance, former Lagos State Administrator Olagunsoye Oyinlola had a penchant for setting up adhoc task forces for sundry problems in transportation, health care, crime, among others, whose members acted in total disregard of the rule of law. Civilians were terrorised, markets shut down at will, though normal bureaucratic agencies existed for the problems for which the task forces were created.

Several other administrators also flagrantly dismissed civilians who served under them without careful recourse to labour laws. Group Captain Baba Iyam who governed Kwara State, in one fell swoop dismissed over 7000 civil servants in 1995. And even in the month he was redeployed to Edo state, he laid off another 1500 workers. Furthermore, on March 4, 1996, Group Captain Iyam closed down three private Christian Colleges namely UMTC Chapel Secondary School, Baptist High School, and Union Baptist Grammar School because they had not complied with his order to ``give room for the teaching of Islamic Religious Knowledge'' in their curricula. This was after the proprietors of the schools had received court rulings stating that the schools be re-opened. The government of Kwara State ignored the law courts. In 1997, the Kaduna State administrator sacked the entire 30,000 strong civil service whose members had gone on strike to press their demand for long-standing fringe benefits.

In Ondo State, Colonel Ahmed Usman at one point threatened to close down courts that granted bail to or acquitted people alleged to be associated with secret cults. The same charge can be levelled against his counterpart, Lt. Colonel Dauda Musa Komo, who held sway in Rivers State. He presided over the charade that led to the judicial murder of

Ken Saro-Wiwa. Komo also prevented Chief Gani Fawehinmi from entering Port Harcourt, the capital of Rivers State, to make legal representations for Saro-Wiwa during his trial. His entire tenure was marked by terror in which elaborate `wasting operations' were carried out in Ogoniland.

Wanton abuse of office has not been restricted to administrators alone. Military officers who serve as ministers have also contributed immensely in disrupting civil order and the rule of law. Major-General Abdulkareem Adisa, the Minister for Works and Housing, for instance, carried out a massive demolition exercise in Lagos under the guise of protecting the city's road network. His colleague at the Ministry of Communications, Major-General T. Olanrewaju ordered similar punitive acts against commercial operators of telephone booths.

So pervasive has this militarisation been that even civilians entrusted a measure of authority or governmental power under the military also began to act with the arbitrariness that characterises the actions of military functionaries. A particularly distressing case is the one in which Dr. Olu Ogundimu, one-time Commissioner for Health in Lagos State, expelled the entire 230 students of the government-owned School of Nursing because they had some disagreement with the management of the school.

Another unfortunate but recurring development is that soldiers frequently leave their barracks to torment the civilian populace. They go about inflicting all manners of physical punishment on people, from motorists to street vendors. The military uniform has, hence, become a symbol of terror.

As this chapter is being written, many prominent trade union leaders, politicians, senior journalists and serving and retired military officers, who have been identified with oppositional views and or groups, languish in detention or jail, some without trial, others, after appearing in military courts notorious for disregarding due process.

Beyond this wielding of the clobbering stick, however, the process of militarisation has involved the complementary use of the juicy carrot to ensure cooptation, erode and call to question the credibility of leading lights in civil and political society, and, in the process, enhance the possibility of making the military appear much more credible and preferable by default.

This drive for control has been further powered by a battery of decrees, largesse selectively dispensed to reward loyalty and secure the breaking of ranks among the opposition, government creation and funding of political parties as well as the placing under the watchful eyes of the military presidency of such key agencies of democratic rebirth such as the electoral commission, whose officials are subjected routinely to orders and declarations from operatives of the military regime. In addition, the State Security Service (SSS) has been given extended mandate including the vetting of all those aspiring to elective and appointive offices at all levels of governmental and party affairs. Given that a clean bill from the SSS is a prerequisite for nominations for such offices, the implication of this for governmental effort to control civil and political society is not in doubt.

Thus, militarism as practised by the Abacha junta has left the Nigerian civil populace in a prostrate state. Virtually all spheres of civil existence have been adversely affected. The university, that customary citadel of freedom, culture and learning has been invaded by the cancer of militarism. Where all the attributes of knowledge, development and tolerance ought to prevail, there have been the worst forms of violence, decline and mental heamorrhage.

Sole administrators have been appointed for the Ahmadu Bello University, Zaria, the University of Nigeria, Nsukka, the Ladoke Akintola University, Ogbomoso, the Federal University of Technology, Minna and the Edo State University, Ekpoma. Of these troubling cases, Ahmadu Bello University stands out because a retired army general, Mamman Kontagora, was appointed sole administrator.

Conclusion

The preceding notes are perhaps enough evidence in support of the need for political restructuring and rebirth in Nigeria. Unfortunately, however, the same evidence reminds us all that political restructuring under unrepentant military rule committed in theory to democratic transition cannot in fact fail to erode from democratic precepts and deepen those processes seeking to turn society into the image of the military itself.

In essence, it is clear that years of authoritarianism cannot be cancelled and reversed in favour of democratisation by mere pledges and declarations. Actual political reform has to be preceded by democratic practice and the popularisation of democratic ethos. In addition, political reform has to be informed by the reality that the implanting of democratic culture is a multi-stage process that cannot be initiated in an environment deliberately placed under siege by generals who govern.

Despite all this, the need for political reform supportive of democracy and genuine federalism has never been as important and as urgent as it is now for Nigeria. In a thought-provoking paper[2], Larry Diamond emphasises this point when he states that there is every need now to develop ways of anticipating political crises around the world before they degenerate into the type of genocidal conflicts that have plagued Bosnia, Somalia, Rwanda and Liberia. As Diamond warns, it is now imperative "to learn to recognise the early warning signs of state collapse and to establish a framework for preventive action on the part of the international community". Indeed, countries do not crumble all of a sudden without prior tell-tale signals. As he goes on to add[3].

> The process is anticipated by numerous signals of decay. Political institutions lose capacity, flexibility, and legitimacy. Social and economic problems mount in the face of state corruption and ineptitude. Crime and violence flourish and fear proliferates. Some authority withers and people retreat into informal arenas. Political power and national wealth become monopolised by an increasingly narrow elite, which substitutes force for dialogue, bargaining, and legitimate authority. Mass constituencies become more and more alienated, angry, and embittered. Contending elites manipulate ethnic, regional, and religious cleavages in the struggle for power, and incidents of deadly conflict escalate in number and scale. Political and social conflicts are increasingly depicted as a struggle for domination by one ethnic group over another. Excluded groups – effectively most of the population–feel increasingly desperate and victimised. Civil society fragments and recedes. Every type of institutional glue that binds diverse cultures, regions, classes and factions together into a common national framework gradually disintegrates.

This, in full, is what characterises a society that is about to undergo socio-political and economic collapse. Unfortunately, all the warning signals enumerated above are evidently present within the Nigerian polity. Moreover, on Nigeria, Diamond also agrees that "the military is destroying the country". So grave is the situation that, he states in unequivocal terms[4],

> If Nigeria's descent into anarchy, state collapse, or civil war is to be averted, the military must be induced to withdraw from power, and a civilian process of political reconstruction must be initiated.

Diamond goes on to list a number of face-saving measures that the Nigerian military can adopt in its bid to withdraw from power but it is doubtful whether it would comply.

At this juncture, however, it must be pointed out that civil society itself must undertake the all important task of fashioning the tools to rebuild itself. As it is now, those tools are extremely rudimentary where not totally absent. We do not need to endure the revolutionary throes that tore apart most of Latin America and several parts of Africa. Indeed, history can eventually turn Nigeria into a safe haven if we choose to learn from it. Democracy, in spite of all its numerous seductions, is also a painful process of learning and development. If it is to assume its full worth, it must be stripped of its abstract quality and its romantic appeal;

in other words, it has to be fashioned painstakingly with the tools of a nation's labour. These tools need not necessarily be those fabricated by western liberal democracies, but the first steps in the direction of a democratic, federalist future would definitely involve rolling back the ethos of militarisation in civil and political society, constructing democratic fora at the grassroots, and encouraging the growth of an autonomous press and critical thinking among the mass of the people.

Endnotes

1. Adigun Agbaje, ``Party Systems and Civil Society'', in Crawford Young and Paul Beckett (eds.); *Dilemmas of Democracy in Nigeria* (University of Rochester Press, 1997) and Adigun Agbaje, ``Knock, Knock Totalitarianism?: Transitional Politics, Democratic Collapse and the Future of Governance in Nigeria'' (Forthcoming).

2. Larry Diamond, ``Preventive Diplomacy for Nigeria: Imperative for US and International Policy'', Paper presented to the House International Relations Committee, US Congress, Washington, D.C., 28 November, 1995, p.1.

3. *Ibid.*

4. *Ibid.*

CHAPTER 5

'Kunle Amuwo

Beyond the Orthodoxy of Political Restructuring: The Abacha Junta and the Political Economy of Force

Introductory Notes and Problematic

There is perhaps no other time in the political history of modern Nigeria than under the Abacha military junta that the country's arrested development can, without excess of language be described as at once deliberate and programmed. There is little doubt that the Abacha regime inherited a political economy that, by the palace coup date of November 17, 1993, was both unviable and unenviable to the extent that it was crisis-ridden.

Whatever may have been General Sani Abacha's politico-military antecedent – in particular his informal *numerodeux* position in the people-unfriendly regime of General Babangida (1985-1993) who was virtually humiliated out of power only three months earlier – a section of the so-called progressive politicians who allegedly invited him to seize power erroneously believed he would right the wrong of the June 12, 1993 annulment. The `progressive politicians' have been proved wrong. Many of them who thought the General was a democratiser, if not a democrat, are today either in jail or undergoing trial in Nigeria or in forced exile in Europe and North America on account of a political economy of force that, like Bashorun M.K.O. Abiola, the President-elect, has found them on the wrong side of the political divide.

Contested from day one, General Abacha and his government have been concerned not so much to effect national reconciliation and re-invent the country's federal system as, more wittingly than unwittingly, exacerbating notions of `believed oppositions' and `competitive mistrust' (R.A. Jospeh, 1991: 50-51) that have undermined national integration and national unity in Nigeria since juridical independence. The way the Abacha junta has handled the national question – by refusing to address it – has, since 1994, spawned a network of communal groupings and sub-national forums (*Afenifere, Ohan'Eze*, Northern Elements Coa-

Coalition, Eastern Mandate Union, etc) as well as strengthened minority and marginalised groups (J.O. Ihonvbere, 1996: 215ff). The result has been the widening of the gap between the Nigerian state, at once militarist and North-driven, and the constituent parts of the diverse, polyglot, federation. There is equally a distancing, at the level of organising principles and values of the State-system, between the Nigerian state and the Nigerian civil society.

The gap is, effectively, between the dominant ideas of a barely literate junta bent on a studied pursuit of Northern primacy, as a generic canopy for other interests, including General Abacha's vaulting ambition to self-perpetuate in power, and Antonio Gramsci's ``common sense'' of the citizenry. The continued persecution of mass organisations, essentially based in the Western part of the country, is meant to empty the otherwise vibrant civil society, including the mass media and other cultural infrastructures, in particular the universities and intellectuals/academics, of their `knowledge power'. The war of the `few' (state-system) against the `many' (civil society, particularly its most effective spokespersons), also aims at vitiating the feeling power' of the masses (C. Boggs, 1993: 56-58). The ultimate objective is to collapse the two notions – `common sense' and `feeling power' – into the political expediential sense of the junta – a sense that is both practical and pragmatic. The political rendition of the foregoing is that either the Abacha junta, initially self-styled as `a child of necessity' is allowed to rule, or there will be chaos in the country.

The major problematic this chapter seeks to elaborate is that the Abacha junta, not unlike the other North-dominated civilian and military governments before it, is pursuing an active, sectionalist agenda.

The agenda has several parts: personal, clannish, religious and regional; and it finds expression in the construction of a Northern hegemony in the country's political landscape. Unlike its predecessors, however, the Abacha junta is pursuing its agenda with such single-mindedness that brooks no dissent and that also appears unconcerned about the future health of the country's federal system. Yet, the junta, following the footsteps of the Balewa, Gowon, Shagari, Buhari and Babangida governments, furnishes a political discourse that provides a veneer of nationalism and patriotism, that seeks to shield away a sectionalist agenda. This is not a novel federal political praxis in Nigeria. This suggests that the Abacha junta did not inaugurate the praxis, but has skilfully, albeit largely negatively, manipulated and exploited it for self-regarding and group-related interests.

There is popular resistance to the politics of hegemony construction, however. Whilst the platform of resistance has hardly been national in outlook, the existing one has seemingly been further diminished in stature in the aftermath of the events surrounding the aborted presidential election of June 12, 1993. The vibrancy of the existing culture of resistance is consequent upon the assault done to the strength and capability of the state by a copious policy of official force and coercion on popular and pro-democracy forces. Indeed, corporate force renders the state weak and vulnerable. It is, in the final analysis, this complex nature of the relations between the state and civil society in Nigeria which emboldens some students of Nigerian politics to argue that the Nigerian crisis is not fatalistic.

There are limits, both within the state-ruling clique and the civil society, which tend to dent otherwise sharp and rough edges of a Northern, militarist state. This is a paradox of sorts. The reality on ground is that there is a routinisation of popular culture, that lies beneath the layer of a perceived docility and resignation of Nigerians since the brutal crushing of labour in 1994; the infiltration and division of the Campaign for Democracy (CD) in 1995 and the seeming stultification of the combative power of the Academic Staff Union of Universities (ASUU) in 1996. This popular culture is, to my mind, increasingly, and perhaps also, robustly, suspicious of institutional authority, electoral politics and official claims to nationalism. This popular resistance has largely been located in the West of the country – plus, to be sure, nationality agitations by the so-called minorities in, amongst others, Ogoni and Ijaw lands. But this merely conforms to a historical reality: when the West- and the East- began nationalist agitations to free Nigeria from British colonialism and imperialism in the pre-1960 era, the North said it was not ready for independence. Yet, it is the North that has not only largely appropriated the gains of independence, but has also rebuffed attempts, since 1960, to re-negotiate a more just, equal and equitable federal system.

There are, in consequence, two levels of analysis in this piece, those of domination and empowerment. "One of the chief claims of critical social science", Brian Fay (1987:130) has argued, "is that power is not only domination but also empowerment; that it has both a positive as well as a negative side; that power, like all social interactions of active beings, is rooted, in part, in the reflections and will of those interacting, both the powerless and the powerful". This claim also finds expression in a salient thesis of the sociology of Knowledge, namely, "we are conscious of the world as consisting of multiple realities" (P.L. Berger and T. Lukmann, 1966:21).

Expressed in the language of a lay man, in the concrete Nigerian political context, there are two faces of Nigeria, corresponding to our two levels of analysis which, I argue, are germane to apprehending and comprehending the contemporary Nigerian dilemma in nationhood. Bola Ige (1994:20) gives a rather poetic rendition of these two faces:

On the radiant but anxious face, you can read quite clearly that the various peoples of Nigeria can and do want to stay together and move forward together in unity, peace and progress if they are allowed to take decisions about their future calmly and without being harassed; the other face is squirming frantically, and the bloodshot eyes which stare so fearfully from that face seem to say that those eyes would rather bleak and scatter the peoples of Nigeria than allow them to decide their own future.

In clearer language, Ige adds that:

One face is that of local colonialism of the military in cahoots with a small but closely-knit tribe of conservative and selfish hegemonists; the other face is of freedom, democracy, the rule of law and well-being.

Thus, whilst John Rapley (1994:504) is correct to have argued that authoritarian regimes are not immune to societal pressure, that is, ``they may be able to resist popular pressure, but the result may not be an interest-free state, but one in which a single interest monopolises power'', in Nigeria the reality is slightly different. In the duel between democratic and anti-democratic forces, to be sure the latter has been ascendant, but that does not mean that Nigeria is a `principality with one head', to paraphrase the expression of the French jurist, Bertrand de Jouvenel. Rather, whilst anti-democratic forces (mainly in the State) *assault* their pro-democracy counterparts (which reside essentially in the Civil Society); the latter also *assail* the former, thereby wrenching critical compromises and ensuring vital policy detours, even though the nature and character of the Nigerian state – people-unfriendly in the extreme – is yet to be altered in any meaningful way.

Theoretical and Historical Perspectives

I have earlier argued that to understand Nigerian politics, one needs to go beyond sheer formalism. One has to search for those seemingly intangible building blocks that give meaning and intelligibility to real process and structure of politics. The dialectical framework of analysis articulated by Marx and Hegel is apposite here. Their philosophy's basic assumption is that critical thinking begins with a refusal to accept `reality' as it is constituted in the observable world. As summarised by Boggs (1993:155), the task of intellectual work ``was to probe beneath the exterior level of objective reality in order to unravel the discrete elements of historical process and meaning''.

Antonio Gramsci (1971:124) talks about the `modern Prince' holding together, in a dialectical unity, the two levels ``of force and of consent, authority and hegemony, violence and civilisation, of agitations and of propaganda of tactics and of strategy''.

Now, in the present context of ascendancy of anti-democratic forces in the form of ethno-regional hegemony, the people hardly count. This is because hegemonists seek to punish perceived irredentist communities, forgetting that they only punish the people they swore on oath to protect and serve. In other words, hegemonists who run a neo-patrimonial political system can hardly act morally. As Emile Durkheim (1993:45) puts it, ``to act morally is to act in terms of the collective interest.'' He contends further that ``ethics is a matter of the whole'' (p.110), but concedes that only a few `exceptional minds' have ever attained that goal. For the rest, the average or ordinary rulers, ``they only act with a view to the most immediate goals, their vision hardly extends past the little worlds in which they live'' (Durkheim 1993:111).

In view of the foregoing, the need arises, in the Nigerian state-system, to re-examine the utility of certain concepts and frameworks of analysis. For example, noting the virtual capture of the Nigerian state by President Shehu Shagari's cohorts and stalwarts in the National Party of Nigeria (NPN), Joseph (1991: 187) contends following Whitaker, that:

> clearly, the advance of democracy and the consolidation of public authority must be reconceptualised in Nigeria so that progress in the former does not entail the enfeeblement of the latter.

This type of analysis misses the point precisely because there has hardly been any progress in the democratic agenda in Nigeria. What goes on in its name in the form of a rather permanent transition to civilian rule hardly extends the public or political space. Thus, it is a farce. Indeed, it is the failure to put democracy on the public agenda, let alone talk of any advance, that reinforces sectional, as against public, authority. And the consolidation of sectional authority, in the name of national authority, is little more than an anti-democratic agenda *simpliciter*.

Thus, whilst Joseph and other scholars like him are right describing the Nigerian polity as prebend-or rent-driven, there is the need to rework the attendant clientelist thesis in their paradigm somewhat differently, even though in a manner not altogether incongruous with the rendition of the thesis in extant literature, as a hierarchy of patrons and clients, cutting across horizontal regional, ethnic, religious, etc.) and vertical (class) cleavages, in which the North is `divinely' chosen to lead and the others destined to follow.

Maitama Sule, a scion of the conservative northern political oligarchy articulated this imaginary hierarchy of anointed and non-anointed `majority' ethno-regional groups as follows:

> The Northerners are endowed ... with leadership qualities. The Yoruba man knows how to earn a living and has diplomatic qualities.

The Igbo is gifted in commerce, trade ... God so created us individually for a purpose. Others are created as kings, servants ... We all need each other. If there are no followers, a king will not exist (cited in Ige, 1994:16).

The power for hegemony construction by the North (really a Hausa-Fulani aristocracy, more concretely an array of cliques, amongst which the `Kaduna Mafia' is perhaps chief) is derived from different sources. Bola Ige (1994:23-24) indicates three of such, namely, the retreating colonial power; the military as well as ``a ruling elite of a particular nationality (and active collaboration of some others) to oppress and terrorise the other nationalities''.

The power the hegemonists have possessed since 1960 is used to prey on the Nigerian state whose resources are perceived as finite. It is around the state that they also weave similar interests, clients and acolytes who are attracted to them nationwide. Patrons or leaders from other nationalities in the country who do not subscribe to this crude despoliation of the state, as if the offices of the latter are no more than spoils of war, are marked out for political humiliation, if not annihilation. Historically, such patrons were to be found both within the so-called monolithic North and the South. Over the years, regions, nationalities and leaders that have been seen by the Northern hegemonists as posing a threat to their domination have been dealt with in either of two ways: the carrot, via corporatism and entryism, to be sure, as junior partners in the widening patron-client network; or the stick, through a systematic policy of withdrawal of rents or development subsidies. There is an additional point to note on the latter, however. The hegemonists, using both civilian and military governments, even though they are more comfortable with the latter given their similar anti-popular and anti-democratic orientation, create a set of stooges who are inappropriately called leaders of thought with whom to do business.

The North has always had a hegemonic construction plan, even before the formation of the so-called Kaduna mafia as an informal forum in 1966. Indeed, using the need to combat the perceived threat of southern domination as well as the `protection of the unity and integrity of the North' as a rallying cry, the Sardauna of Sokoto who doubled as the Northern Regional Premier, Sir Ahmadu Bello used senior Northern bureaucrats and technocrats in Kaduna and, to a lesser extent, in Lagos, the federal capital, to, *inter alia*, ensure that `backward' North was not colonised internally by the `developed' South. As part of the overall strategy to contain the South, a major thrust of Bello's Northernisation Policy in the 1960s was the preference shown to expatriates in employment placements above Southerners.

The 'Kaduna Mafia' had its humble beginnings in the North's somewhat deliberate and robust reaction to General Ironsi's Unification Decree Number 34 of May 1966, that was largely perceived as biased against the North. As Adebayo Olukoshi (1995:245-278) has shown, from the core of northern bureaucrats, the Mafia soon attracted members from the growing class of northern professionals; senior military officers, and intellectuals, notably academics from the Ahmadu Bello University (ABU), Zaria – and, by extension, Bayero University, Kano (BUK), Othman dan Fodio University, Sokoto and University of Maiduguri. Olukoshi also makes the important point that weaned in crisis, the Mafia-and similar groups – has, over the years, thrived most in crisis. Its activities and those of its allied groups become more manifest during crisis situations.

The 1967-70 civil war period gave the Mafia and its allies a certain character; an essentially sectionalist one. The other period of crisis, the contemporary one, 1993 till date, perhaps more dangerous than a civil war situation, has equally propelled the hegemonist powerplay of the North to the front burner in a manner capable, *a la longue,* in creating a Rwandan or Zairean phenomenon in Nigeria.

The contexts of the two eras are different, however. Whilst "the Mafia grew in strength as the northern Nigerian bureaucracy emerged as a strong centre of political power in the country" (Olukoshi, 1995:254), the Mafia and its allies nationwide are powerful today on account of an admixture of political, military and bureaucratic powers at their disposal. I will argue later that General Abacha, like General Gowon, though a northern minority is happy to be appropriated by northern hegemonists principally because the appropriation may also help him to attain his own personal agenda of hanging on to power for as long as possible, either as a military head of state or as a 'civilianised' president.

In playing out his dual role of purveyor of both a sectionalist and personal agenda, General Abacha has an array of historical parallels he can cite as precedents.

First, the Northern Peoples Congress (NPC) that controlled not only the North, but also the centre in the First Republic (1960-1966) has generally been described as 'over-bearing' and 'short-sighted'. These political behavioural traits were very much evident in the relations between the Balewa-led federal government and any region(s) that failed to play national politics according to the norms, values and principles dear to the NPC and the then federal government. It has been argued, for example, that the take-over of the Western Regional government in 1962 was prompted by two factors, to wit, "to destroy Obafemi Awolowo politically and force the Yoruba to *salaam* the North" (Ige, 1994:11). Well over thirty years after, the Abacha junta, short of declaring a state of emergency in the Western states or taking over their governments, is gradually isolating these states, treating their people as third-class citizens — to the extent that the more generally pliant Igbo leadership has happily and eagerly filled the vacuum left by its Yoruba counterpart. The ultimate objective seems to be to, at best, force the Yoruba leadership into the country's `main-stream" politics – meaning, playing a perennial second fiddle, according to the schemata furnished by Maitama Sule or, at worst, pushing the Yoruba to war in order to destroy their civilisation and kill their leading intellectuals and politicians.

Two, the NPC, Bello and the senior northern civil servants of the first republic suppressed the Northern Elements Progressive Union (NEPU), the United Middle Belt Congress (UMBC) and the Borno Youth Movement (BYM) in the North and were also `'an important part of the elaborate effort to stifle pluralism, open dissent, freedom of expression and the rights of the minorities in the region" (Olukoshi, 1995:265). This pattern has been sustained over the years. The successors of the NPC and Bello – civilian and military governments alike – have consistently sought to vitiate principled resistance against perceived northernisation, Islamisation and de-secularisation of the country by the South in general and the so-called `Lagos-Ibadan' press and academia in particular.

Three, the claim of the `Mafia' and its allies to represent the North has no basis, neither in logic nor in representation. It has been contended that `'the membership of the `'Kaduna Mafia' hardly reflected any democratic coalition of social forces ... Workers and their unions, students organisations, youth movements, minority nationalities and women were hardly represented in the `Mafia' grouping but were rather seen as forces to be mobilised, even manipulated, not on a democratic platform, but through parochial, religious and regionalist sentiments for objectives that, at best, were hardly democratic and, at worst, were patently anti-democratic" (Olukoshi, 1995:264). In the post-June 12 military-driven politics, officer-politicians and their clients in and out of power who make the most strident nationalist pronouncements are also the most sectionalist in character and behaviour.

Finally, having foreclosed an open debate on what the so-called `Northern' interest they claim to champion is all about, they are resolute to do the same thing nationally. The northern hegemonists have never supported, let alone championed, calls for an All-Nigerian nationalities conference to thrash out the national question in the ethnically-segmented Nigerian federal system. Similarly, since the Mohammed-Obasanjo regime (1975-79) when the first occasion for constitutional talks came up, the North has consistently queried the need to discuss salient issues such as the imbalance of a federal system with an over-bearing centre; alienation of the Igbo people and the minorities from the mainstream of

Beyond the Orthodoxy of Political Restructuring. 79

national politics; and, in the post-1979 period, complaints about the systematic negation of the federal character principle. As an example, they resisted the proposal for the adoption of an executive president in the Second Republic. They did so only because they feared a Southerner could become president. Once they lost out, the Mafia and its allies went to work to ensure that a Northerner became president (Joseph, 1991:133ff).

We will show later that the same behaviour was observable *a propos* the Constitutional Conference in 1994-95. Yet, the events that provoked the calls for the conference which compelled the Abacha junta to give in, albeit in a truncated form, were such that a spirit of give-and-take and principled compromise were much needed. The hegemonists floundered miserably; they failed to rise above sub-national interests.

The Logic of Political Restructuring

Students of political structures and military-driven constitutionalism in Africa often take for granted the paradox inherent in a military junta organising constitutional talks and superintending the writing of a new constitution. For Eboe Hutchful (1991:183), however, the paradox is real only at the level of organisation, not at the level of the use to which a new constitution will be put. This is so, according to Hutchful, because

> the objective of most military-sponsored constitutions has been to legitimise and civilianise military rule, rather than restore constitutional life as such.

Furthermore, Hutchful contends that a new military junta tends to have some charismatic appeal, in the sense of restoring political order as quickly as possible. This explains why, except for the most discerning political groups, all others acquiesce to the notion that the new junta will act "to redefine the formal context and space within which politics may be practised and to infuse the state with reserves of legitimation" (p.184). Hutchful also argues that in the course of their transition programmes, whatever their rhetorical commitment to non-partisanship, their subjective interests and preferences are discernible beneath the layers of formal and general rules of political procedures (p.185).

Two other salient points about military-driven political restructuring and constitutionalism are worth mentioning. One, in the process of re-jigging the groundnorms of politics and political structures, hitherto dispossessed nationalities and other groups are hardly favoured. Hutchful (p.185) deserves to be quoted at some length here:

> The overriding political objective has been state preservation and the reconstruction or reinforcement of modes of political dominance. The intention is less the liberation of national politics than to limit

the space of politics, either as a form of activity or as a structural level within the social formation.

All this is done not ``in any definitive fashion... to resolve inherited problems of state, society and economy . . .''

Two, constitution-making hardly democratises inter-class political competition; it only addresses intra-elite political contestation and, not infrequently, rather unfairly and unsatisfactorily. Hence, the submission that ``in military constitutionalism, the state in effect elaborates its own relationship both with society and with itself.'' As ``a state-conditioned and dominated process'', the organising political authority carries the day, even though ``the initiative was taken by groups from outside the state with a primary interest in limiting state power or redefining its distribution.''[2]

There are at least two mutually exclusive `logics' of political restructuring and constitutionalism: formal or premeditated logic and informal or preemptive logic. The first relates to a genuine attempt, at a crisis point in the life of a nation, by leaders thrown up by the crisis to resolve them, *mutatis mutandis,* to the satisfaction of the mass-majority. The second works in the opposite direction by a deliberate undermining of the formal restructuring process in order that extra- or non-national interests may find full expression.

The formal logic is what everybody, including international observers, sees when they go to post-cold war African states to monitor sundry electoral consultations. They often return a verdict of clean bill of health, some even claim they are overwhelmed,[3] insofar as what they perceive is little more than the end-product of a process that is informed by both logics with more of informalism than formalism. On election day, however, both domestic and international observers see only the formally announced restructuring and recomposition programme at work. They are often ignorant of the fact that a large number of voters have had to be mobilised informally in order that formal objectives will be attained in full public glare and informal objectives also fulfilled at the political backyard.

Any student of Nigerian politics that has read the June 1994 inauguration address of the National Constitutional Conference by General Sani Abacha will be struck by the seeming candour and forthrightness of the speech. At a time the junta was in desperate search for legitimacy and acceptance at home and credibility internationally, the General's speech laboured to chart a new political course for the country. The emphasis of General Abacha was on a new national consensus anchored on an inclusive system where nobody and no group is marginalised or oppressed.

Thus, his major charge to the 380 delegates – 273 elected and ninety-four nominated – was to articulate an institutional arrangement capable of laying a solid foundation for:

> an inclusive system which will guarantee a stable society through its sensitive accommodation of all shades of political opinion harnessed by full participation of all the component units of our land... (and) restraints on government as will ensure that no man will be oppressed and no group will dominate or be marginalised.[4]

General Abacha also charged the conference delegates to fashion a ``conscious culture of national consensus conceived in the broadest sense''. For him, this is indispensable because ``the democratic nation we are building will be best sustained by *coordinative rather than subordinative relationships with proper sympathy for equal claims to political power, legitimacy and social justice*.[5]

Furthermore, perhaps conscious that the resolution of the political crisis does not pass through constitution-making, the General raised the question of honest, upright and conscientious leadership. He argued that what the country requires most is a leadership that serves, not oppresses, the people. Thus,

> the quality of leadership of this country must include courage, vision and a sense of history. A leader in a pluralist society such as ours has to be able to persuade (and) inspire trust and confidence and possess a capacity to attract men and women of talent into public office. Indeed, of necessity, *he should have the capacity to transcend all the various cleavages that hang around our country's neck like an albatross such as the propagation of ethnic, regional and religious extremism*.[6]

The Nigerian military ruler did not end his address without giving what appeared then as a firm commitment to keep faith with the submissions of the conference. First, he contended that, even though his junta's critics may not be convinced, ``it is neither in our personal interest nor that of the nation to perpetuate ourselves in power''. He added that ``nothing could be farther from our plans''.[7] Second, General Abacha assured the delegates not to entertain any fears whatsoever that their decisions and conclusions would be lightly set aside by him and his government. Hence, ``there need ... be no apprehension as to the nature of the freedom of the proceedings here (that is, at the conference)''.

Finally, the General spoke of the decision of the junta he leads – himself principally, by the play of logic – not to participate in the transition-to-civil rule programme to be unfolded after the conference. His words: ``We in the present government ... are committed to ensuring that there is *speedy and unimpeded transition to a civil democratic rule in which we shall not be participants. We are, in short, arranging to surrender power through a peaceful and orderly process*.[8]

The General's parting words to the delegates were equally assuring, namely, "You do your duty diligently and we shall not fail in ours". In view of what has transpired between 1994 and 1997, however, it is apparent that the Nigerian ruler only fulfilled all formal righteousness before the conference.

Elements of the Political Economy of Force

It has generally been argued that without a strong sense of nationhood or citizenship the Nigerian state is an easy prey to sectional and private interests (Forrest, 1995:3). The vulnerability is accentuated whenever state managers show no volition to open up the public space in order that extra-state classes/groups and actors could have self-expression.

Perhaps more than any regime before it, the Abacha junta has exacerbated the main elements of Nigerian politics, in particular ethnic, religious, regional and resource cleavages. By so doing, the cleavages have become so sharpened that, except the Abacha junta is compelled to stop exploiting the country's sundry divisions, war, however limited, and disintegration are not as totally far-fetched as many may think.

Current understanding of politics in deeply divided societies is that, far from being an albatross, ethnic pluralism may well be a blessing, not least in terms of healthy ethno-regional competition for overall national progress. As Clapham and Wiseman (1995:224) have argued, "it is autocracy rather than ethnic variety that has posed the most important threat to the maintenance of African states".

The Abacha junta inherited from its predecessors, in particular the Babangida regime, a compact legacy of force and coercion in which both the state and the civil society were in disequilibrium, unstable juxtaposition and mutual suspicion (M. Orkin, 1995:533). In inviting General Abacha to step in ostensibly to halt the seeming slide to anarchy under Ernest Shonekan, progressive members of the Social Democratic Party (SDP) and chieftains of the Campaign for Democracy (CD), expected him to rapidly cleanse the augean stables *a la* the Roman mythical warrior Cincinnatus and return to the barracks – after handing over to Bashorun M.K.O. Abiola.

Hopes that this would likely be the case were kept alive by the junta's self-imposed promise of brief tenure in Abacha's maiden speech on November 18, 1993. They were also fired by the composition of the junta's first cabinet in which some progressive politicians figured prominently even though the cabinet was really a hodge-podge of political incompatibles. We will return to this point later because the so-called invitation of Abacha by Abiola's entourage is a major plank in the junta's politics of force.

We need to understand the impending collapse of the Nigerian state under General Abacha in terms of the abandonment, so soon after his palace coup, as soon as the regime started to acquire some muscle of self-confidence, of its initial objective of closing political shop early. Thereafter, the junta became consumed with two mutual reinforcing objectives: establish its own political authority and re-establish northern political hegemony. This twin project necessarily entails the playing of exclusionary-inclusionary politics in an exceedingly manipulative manner. That is to say, inclusion in state patronage and preferment policies vis-a-vis pliant groups and individuals and exclusion in relation to those groups and individuals, who canvass for more innovative, public-regarding policies. Worse, a sectionalist and personalist drive to cling to power at any cost partly entails holding in abeyance some interests and crushing others so long as they are perceived as posing a formidable threat to core junta and northern interests. The aggregate of this phenomenon is that the junta continues to lose support, and, as J.D. Kandeh (1996:401) has argued, "When a regime loses public support, construction of effective institutions is difficult, if not impossible."

Yet in its early months, the junta's leading tandem, Generals Abacha and Diya, appeared, a la Buhari and Idiagbon, as a fairly balanced power equation. Both were mainly responsible for the appointment of the three service chiefs (Army, Air Force and Navy); the four General Officers Commanding (G.O.Cs) in the Army, which are very sensitive positions moreso in crisis times, and of several ministers. Further, in the early days of a seeming attempt to pacify pro-democracy and pro-June 12 elements and groups, Diya was extremely visible, multiplying contacts and somewhat reconciliatory statements nationwide. By the same token, it was reported that the two rulers either signed a pact or had a tacit agreement to consult with the service chiefs on issues of disagreement between them.

The northern hegemonists took unkindly to the workings of the tandem. Through representation to him and a widely-circulated editorial in the *Democrat,* a Kaduna-based daily, Abacha was urged not only to contain and curtail Diya's rising profile but also to assert his own political authority. According to a source, by July 1994 "Abacha (seemed) to have charted a course different from Diya's. Abacha has found another power group, leaving Diya in the lurch".[9]

The National Constitutional Conference provided the first litmus test for the hegemonists and the junta in their objective to regiment future politics in order to better control and manipulate it. The conference was a conceptual misnomer of sorts. What was on the nation's agenda since the Babangida years was a Sovereign National Conference (SNC) with full constituent powers to re-organise the country's politics and society. In its initial desperation for legitimacy, the junta had agreed to a SNC. It was on this platform that the first Justice Minister and Attorney-General, Dr Olu Onagoruwa, claimed he accepted to serve. As commencement date for the conference kept on shifting, the North and the junta went to work to limit its import and to hijack it.

None of the two really wanted the Constitutional Conference to hold. The North claimed that the conference was a threat to the country's existence, a euphemism for the continued good financial health of northern commercial and private interests who have, over the years become accustomed to regarding the Nigerian state as `a resource in itself', in the Morris Sfetzelian sense, and to live off it.[10] Usman Bugaje, a renowed Islamic scholar and pharmacist, alluded to this reality when he contended that ``those who clamoured for confab (sic) did so with one goal in mind: hatred of the North."[11]

It is not difficult to comprehend the political behaviour of the North when it comes to the issue of power rotation and a more or less dispassionate discourse on the form of Nigeria's federalism. For one, whatever the depth and intensity of communal, class and religious cleavages in the North, the hegemonists in the mafia and their allies often present the picture of a monolithic North. As Matthew H. Kukah (1993: 93-94) contends, ``all other forms of identities have ... been shown to collapse when northern interests are at stake, especially if there is a perceived challenge from Southerners". For the North, Nigeria is synonymous or coterminous with Northern Nigeria. Kukah (1993: 163,167) explains that when constrained by *force majeure* to share power, the Islamic North seeks by all means to guard power ``jealously and would continue to struggle for it". Thus, Chief Anthony Enahoro's scant remark that ``some think of national unity as a scenario in which they provide the star actors, while other parts of the country provide the bit actors and extras".[12]

On the part of the junta, its political behaviour on the National Question, before, during and after the Constitutional Conference resembles that of a typical `militariat'. According to Kandeh (1996:388ff), following Ali Mazrui, the chief characteristic of the militariat, that is the subaltern wing (lieutenant down to private) of the military is ``its access to, and operation of, the means of destruction in society". Drawing from the examples of the Gambia, the Sierra Leone and Liberia, Kandeh argues that:

> as a constitutive element of the repressive apparatuses of the state, the militariat more than any other subordinate group, is strategically positioned to play a central role in the deinstitutionalised politics of African states"

Thus, his submission that ``the militariat is an atavistic political force that is more likely to collapse the state than rescue it from institutional decay".

The conference was programmed by the junta to fail. It was flawed from the beginning; neither in terms of procedure nor in terms of content was it democratic. The concerns and anxieties of the opposition, both elite and non-elite, were at best, only marginally factored in, and, at worst, purely and simply ignored. For one, the Constitutional Conference Commission, the agency charged with the conference's organisation, consisted essentially of politicians, such as Dr Ibrahim Tahir, a scion of the `Mafia', who had openly opposed the idea of the conference. Alao Aka-Bashorun, former president of the Nigerian Bar Association, was prompted to query government's governance style:

> I don't believe in the way the government is handling this conference. You can't put the calibre of people you have in the constitutional commission there and say you are serious. Majority of the nineteen persons on the commission are opposed to the conference."[13]

For another, some nominations could hardly be justified except on grounds of immediate political expediency. In particular, the nomination of Umaru Dikko to represent Zaria caused a lot of disaffection between Abacha on the one hand and several senior military officers, including Diya, on the other. It would appear, given Dikko's antecedents in the Second Republic and his rabid anti-Abiola sentiments, that he was brought from self-exile in London to serve as the linchpin of the junta's anti-June 12 propaganda drive. Sanni Kontagora, publisher of the defunct rabidly pro-North *Hotline* magazine, not known for any anti-establishment opinion said the conference was not only a `farce', but also that Dikko's nomination was `morally wrong' [14].

Furthermore, the conference delegates were massively `settled', meaning that they were beneficiaries of far-ranging financial and material incentives. These included plots of land in choice areas of Abuja; completed residential buildings; mouth-watering financial inducements, etc. At critical points of decision-making, for example during the 1994 Christmas break after the conference had fixed an exit date for the junta for January 1, 1996, trunks of naira notes crisscrossed the federation for delegates. There were also group settlements. Delegates from the West were sometimes paid twice a month ostensibly to convert them to the junta's political world-view.

The junta also worked assiduously on northern delegates to prolong its own life by exploiting hegemonist sentiments of the North. Once it was clear that the South and the Middle Belt would settle for nothing else than a rotational presidency formula enshrined permanently in the constitution, the junta convinced the northern delegates to ensure that a Northerner (that is Abacha) held on to power ``for a little longer than a mere one year''.[15] In other words, Abacha's self-succession agenda, no more hidden by the middle of 1996, had earlier been voiced at the conference, perhaps before, and, significantly, was tied to the agenda of a continued domination of political power by the North.

The junta came out of the conference stronger and more assertive in dealing with the opposition. The conference having reversed itself on April 25, 1995 *a propos* the exit date of the junta, unwittingly gave the latter the leeway not only to undermine the corporate existence of Nigeria but also to undo the major decision, the *raison d'etre* as it were, of the conference. Foremost political economist, Claude Ake was right in his assessment that

> the ... conference leaves Nigeria more vulnerable than ever by closing yet another opportunity for peaceful change. In part, the minorities' problem will likely spread and intensify to threaten the political viability of Nigeria.[16]

Majorities' problem also intensified. In November 1995, the Ogoni Nine were hanged. In his famous October 1, 1995 broadcast in which he unfolded his transition programme, General Abacha abandoned any more pretences to a brief tenure. He declared *inter alia*, that "it is obvious that the duration of the timetable will be determined by the time required to complete each phase of the programme". Similarly, the junta ceased to 'dialogue' with NADECO, founded in 1994, and other pro-June 12 elements, even though Abacha met with its two foremost leaders, Michael Ajasin and Enahoro. It was not as if dialogue was conceptualised, *ab initio*, as a frank and constructive parley on how to bring Nigeria back on track. The establishment of transition agencies, especially the National Reconciliation Commission (NARECON) was, therefore, no more than a public relations gimmick vis-a-vis the international community.

I argue that since October 1, 1995, the junta has ceased to find solutions to the on-going political crisis. It would appear that for the regime there is no more crisis, since the opposition had been contained at the conference. It remained for the latter to be worsted politically and otherwise. With his regime increasingly mired in crisis by an arrogant refusal to open up the public space, General Abacha has had to reach for sundry sorcerers, diviners and seers to secure his power base. Increasingly, the General trusts no one except perhaps his chief security adviser, Ismaila Gwarzo; the head of his personal security staff, Major Hamza Mustapha and his spiritual consultants. He is also constituting his own home-grown 'Mafia' that could serve as a bulwark when every other fortress fails. The arrowhead is the Shehu of Bornu, Mustapha El-kanemi, whose ancestors were never conquered by the Sokoto Caliphate and who had always sought an autonomous politico-religious space outside the suffocating aegis of the caliphate.

What flagged off in January 1994, less than 100 days in office, as persecution of nationalities, classes and individuals who snubbed the junta's halting corporatist politics has, since the aftermath of the conference, snowballed into a full-blown dictatorship. The latter runs amock, etching on into the dark plain of fascism, seeking, *inter alia*, to rout civilo-military opponents (particularly Westerners) and to censor scholarship and chain thought and intellectual activities. Purely academic conferences are stopped usually in the South, rarely in the North, a pattern that has, increasingly, been unabashedly ethnicised,[17]

A major element in the political economy of force is to divide the South in order to better rule it. By working on and manipulating some personalities from the South-East, the historically healthy rivalry between the Igbo and the Yoruba elites and peoples have become highly politicised. As I have argued elsewhere (Amuwo, 1995), the Igbo political elites, save for isolated pockets, have not sufficiently appreciated the fact that the solution to their problem of marginalisation cannot but be a function of the resolution of the crisis of post-June 12 annulment. Rather, they tend to see the events of June 12 as a Yoruba problem – a ``tribal war" to quote the junta's loquacious information Minister, Walter Ofonagoro – as well as an opportunity to supplant their Yoruba[18] counterparts in national politics.

There are indications, however, that the opportunism of the Igbo political ``class" is being contested from within that nationality. For example, Joe Igbokwe criticises Uche Chukwumerije (Babangida's Information Secretary and anti-June 12 Chief propagandist), Ofonagoro and their likes for being ``bootlickers and paradigm of self-marginalisation". He continues:

> Blindfolded by ephemeral perquisities of office and intoxicated by the crumbs from the master's table, Igbo elite have become a willing lackey in the hands of their oppressors, singing hosanna, while their people are suffering in silence, feigning abundance in (the) midst of want.[19]

One Agwu Kalu Agwu, wondering whether some of the Igbo politicians who pose as leaders are really so, states what he considers to be the political wishes of the Igbo people:

> The Igbo population at large is determined to stay in one Nigeria, just, balanced and equitable... They want an open society with open competition and open programmes. They want their due share of the national dispensation. They do not like to be represented by bogey-men who only line their pockets and massage their own egos, rather than help fellow Nigerians, including Ndigbo.[20]

The SDP governor of Anambra State in the aborted Third Republic, Dr

Chukwuemeka Ezeife, reinforces the latter position by urging the Igbo to help redefine Nigeria's future – a future which, for him, rests on June 12.[21]

A second element in the political economy of force is a deliberate and pre-meditated policy of disparaging June 12 through sheer propaganda and, by extension, the Yoruba people and Abiola. On this score, Ofonagoro, S.G. Ikoku and Wada Nas, one of the junta's ministers for Special Duties, have behaved like veritable war-mongers and *agent-provocateurs*. Ofonagoro wrote a book on June 12 with the sole motive of establishing that (against the background of a rather bizarre court injection in the night of June 10, 1993 halting the election), there was never June 12. ``The Ofonagorian information machine'', writes Osifo-Whiskey,

> is the moral equivalent of a murder in the cathedral... official information is barefaced lies, blackmail, far-fetched conjectures, trumped-up charges and just any evil that may serve Aso Rock's designs and machinations.[22]

S.G. Ikoku, a former ideological theoretician in the Nkrumah School of Socialism and former disciple of Awolowo, metamorphosed in his later life into an effective tool in the hands of the northern military establishment. He led a group of so-called elder politicians who canvassed the French semi-presidential executive model to Babangida even as late as the eve of the June 12 presidential election. The essence was for Babangida to assume the *magistrature supreme* and then appoint a `safe' candidate from either the Yoruba or Igbo nationalities as prime minister. The idea has caught on. Ikoku transferred his services to Abacha. The latter reportedly offered Abiola the prime ministership which the president-elect promptly rejected.

Until his demise in April 1997, Ikoku was the Vice-Chairman of the Transition Implementation Committee (TIC), a position he exploited alongside the chairman, Justice Mamman Nasir, to serve as the arrowhead for Abacha's self-succession. A principal reason for this position was Ikoku's disdain for Abiola. During the Constitutional Conference, he remarked that Abiola and his mandate were ``a sick joke that should not be mentioned in a serious conference''.[23]

Wada Nas is the junta's linchpin against the umbrella opposition group, NADECO, and the Yoruba people. Shadowy and given to vituperations and outbursts that can hardly be substantiated, Nas has largely contributed to the permanence of the country's political impasse. In one of his several provocative interviews. Nas compared the political circumstances of Abiola in the 1990s with that of Awolowo, the acclaimed leader of the Yoruba in the 1960s:

> For God's sake, those people who are now asking for the release of Abiola, why didn't they ask for the release of Chief Obafemi Awolowo? Was he not arrested, interrogated, taken to court and jailed?[24]

Nowhere as in the use of literal, naked and crude force against NADECO, Yoruba leaders and Abiola has the agenda of the northern hegemonists found copious expression. NADECO has consistently been demonised in order to hit hard at its leadership – from the bomb blasts in Ilorin and the Ikeja military cantonment in April 1996 to the ones in quick succession that apparently targeted military personnel in December 1996 and January 1997. NADECO's home-based leaders have either been killed (e.g. Alfred Rewane), hounded, harangued and harassed by agents of the junta (e.g. Michael Ajasin, its Chairman, Faseun, Falae, Opadokun, Adebayo, etc). There are three main reasons for this development: One, the junta seeks to destroy credible and principled resistance to its power usurpation and misrule. Two, which is part of a larger agenda, to make possible presidential candidates in the organisation to contain their political ambition. Finally, force opposition to abandon the struggle to actualise the electoral verdict of June 12, 1993.

Members of NADECO abroad have also been treated to a menu of bestial political force. Nobel Laureate, Professor Wole Soyinka, has had his country-home despoiled and has been labelled a terrorist by General Abacha. General Alani Akinrinade's house in Lagos was bombed in May 1996. Rear-Admiral Omotehinwa may have been killed because of his closeness to Akinrinade. The Ogoni scenario has been duplicated in the West: in the same way the junta triggered off intra-communal crisis in order to get at Ken Saro-Wiwa and MOSOP, its agents – or perhaps some Hausa-Fulani hegemonists of fifth columnists working independently of the junta – may have used the gruesome assassination of Kudirat Abiola in June 1996 to further chain NADECO as well as implicate Abiola's family. NADECO is also blamed anytime any of its chieftains barely escapes the assassin's bullet (e.g. ex-Senator Abraham Adesanya, its deputy national chairman).

The assault on Abiola, his business empire and family has only a single objective, namely, to break the president-elect psychologically so that he could renounce his mandate. Soon after Abiola reportedly refused to accept a bribe of 300 million US dollars from the junta to let go of his mandate, the regime reacted by revoking the licence of Summit Oil, in which Abiola had massively invested, refusing to pay an ₦800 million naira debt owed ITT and other debts owed to Radio Communication Nigeria, an Abiola company, etc. Kudirat's business was also targeted for extinction perhaps on account of her being the anchor of Abiola's resilience. The junta might have asked three state governments owing her some millions of naira for contracts done to decline to pay her.[25]

The seeming total onslaught on NADECO and other opposition groups – including the Lagos-Ibadan media and pro-democracy groups – derives, in part, from the junta's understanding, in the light of the Babangidian experience, that only sustained pressure could force the junta to capitulate. Thus, the use of force by the junta is a rearguard and pre-emptive tactic. The political economy of force is also partly a function of a lingering controversy between the junta and NADECO chieftains.[26] The former and its supporters have persistently argued that Abiola and his entourage invited Abacha; that former CD Chairman, Dr Beko Ransome-Kuti, now in jail over the coup issue, had series of meetings with Abacha on how to get Shonekan removed; that Abiola was involved in the formation of Abacha's first cabinet; that Abiola met with Abacha on November 22, 1993 for ninety minutes, but June 12 did not feature in their discussion for Abiola only asked for assistance to recoup his electoral loss.

NADECO has also consistently countered that the junta's story is only one version of what transpired between the two groups: that there was some bargaining, a *quid pro quo* of sorts. True, Enahoro had, in his published agenda proposals to the junta, shown some optimism that the Abacha coup was a ``secondary coup''. For him, ``secondary coups, to cure the ill-effects of `primary coups' are not necessarily to be abhorred''. While calling on ``all true democrats ... to utilise this new opportunity with optimism'', he was careful enough to also ask them to utilise it ``with caution and robust vigilance''.[27] Yet, it is difficult to believe that the Kutis, Fawehinmis, Akinyemis etc could have been so naive enough to give Abacha a blanket cheque. We may never know exactly what transpired between the junta and the Abiola entourage. There is, however, a pointer in the direction of politics of deception: Colonel Nyiam affirms that Abacha and his military assistant, Colonel Yakubu Mu'azu, promised they would install Abiola.[28]

Within this context, the highly regimented and militarised transition programme fits into a predictable pattern. The two local government elections held so far have clearly exposed, through sheer military appointments inelegantly called 'elections',[29] the real agenda of the junta. They also reveal a grand design to subtly impose loyalists, political merchants and neophytes who would only be too willing once the price is right, at the grassroots, to do the bidding of the ruling junta at the most critical time.

The Future in Perspective

The problematic I have sought to elaborate upon in the foregoing is two-pronged. One, that a cabal of northern hegemonists, which is working for the perpetuation of political power in the North is using the Abacha junta to achieve its aim. Two, that, in a rather mutually reinforcing manner, General Abacha, a northern minority, rapidly appropriated by the

'Mafia', plays along insofar as his own private agenda to self-perpetuate in power is thereby ensured. What binds the northern Mafia with General Abacha is their common anti-June 12 sentiments and, by extension, their determination to stop the Yoruba nation from acquiring central political power.

It can be argued that had the cabal and the junta demonstrated any dexterity to rule well, both in the past and in the present, few would have minded the preservation of a self-appointed oligarchy. The issue, however, is that ethnic hegemonists, almost by definition, cannot rule well. They can only run a closed polity, when what a federal system requires is an open competition in which all groups and classes find both self-expression and self-fulfilment.[30]

Closed political systems can hardly survive for long, to the extent that they are assailed and contested both from within (intra-clique struggles for power) and without (inter-class and inter-group drives for hegemony). Carl Boggs (1993:182) has argued that:

> in a social order that dwells upon surface appearances and routinely depoliticises public discourse, radical insurgency is forced not only to articulate counter-hegemonic themes and possibilities but also to penetrate the dense world of media manipulation.

The capacity for 'radical insurgency' has always been present, even if latent, in the country's civil society. In the last ten years or so, this capacity has been given a filip, to a lesser or greater extent nationwide as the existential conditions become increasingly difficult. Olukoshi (1995:257) is therefore correct to have argued that:

> the 'Mafia' has certainly not always had its way on all issues of interest to it or its members as the Nigerian state has also had to contend with attempts by other interest groups to advance their own objectives.

In the countdown to the commencement of the Fourth Republic (October 1998?), the tandem northern hegemonists and General Abacha face formidable opposition on several fronts.[31] This is particularly because their agenda – that of perpetuating a northern oligarchy in power through a civilianised Abacha – has been made too open, too early in the day. This shows that the interests concerned have become more desperate and villanious, but the opposition is no less desperate and determined. If Babangida with all the goodwill and the benefit of the doubt he enjoyed until 1992-93 could fail, it is highly unlikely that an Abacha that has left his flanks too wide open will succeed.

In the impending duel between, on the one hand, the hegemonists and the junta and, on the other, the opposition forces, the future of Nigerian federal system will be determined in either of two ways: by the centrifugal push of ethnic particularism or by the centripetal pull of consensual, plural democracy. If the ethnic logic prevails, all the fine arguments about political restructuring and rotational presidency (cf Anthony A. Akinola, 1996: 58,61,71) will be put to nought. Indeed, the country will hardly ever get to experiment the much-vaunted blueprint on rotational presidency. If the pluralist or democratic logic triumphs, a sovereign National Conference will still be desirable in order that the terms and conditions of a new type of federal system are negotiated.

Notes

1. Randall Robinson, Executive Director of the Washington-based Trans Africa Forum has argued that the solution to the post-June 12, 1993 political crisis suffers in the face of a political mindset that "one section (of the country) must remain in power at all costs" in *Tell* (Lagos), July 10, 1995, pp. 12-16. Cf Odumegwu Ojukwu, ex-Biafran leader, used by the Babangida junta in the early days of the crisis to discredit the Abiola mandate and assault the sensibilities of the Yoruba and who would later find favour with the Abacha junta declared, perhaps in one of his most reflective moments, that "for those who enjoy the executive control of Nigeria, for those who enjoy almost exclusively the resources of this country, the term one Nigeria is like music to their ears. They love it, they want it to remain forever and if it becomes necessary to maintain one Nigeria by force, they would do so". See O. Ojukwu "That we may Survive", *African Concord* (Lagos), 7 March 1994 pp. 10-11.

2. On this important issue, Mahmood Mamdani (1995:249) has interrogated as follows: "What classes/groups have a capacity for constitutionalism? And, in turn, what are the contradictory conceptions of constitutionalism shaped by the contradictory interests of these classes/groups?".

3. During the zero-party municipal election in March 1996, in which the National Electoral Commission of Nigeria (NECON) claimed twenty-four million people voted, one Ron Innis, Chair of the US-based Congress for Racial Equality (CORE) said he was "overwhelmingly impressed". His words: "I have never seen this kind of outpouring of a desire of the people to vote and participate in the process towards democracy". See *Tell*,

April 1, 1996 p. 15). Innis and his three colleagues visited **only** Abuja, the Nigerian political capital and represented no known political interest. To all appearances the junta continues to battle with a serious credibility problem, thus the invitation to observers with dubious credentials. The same script would be played out during the party-based municipal elections in March 1997.

4. See Federal Government of Nigeria, *Report of the Constitutional Conference Containing the Draft Constitution* 1995, Volume II p.5.

5. *Report of the Constitutional Conference,* p.5. My emphasis.

6. *Report,* p. 9. Again, emphasis is mine.

7. The General was only reinforcing the 'brief tenure' notion of their power which they canvassed in the early months of their palace coup. While briefing senior military officers on November 23, 1993, Lt-General Oladipo Diya, the junta's formal Number 2, justified a brief tenure: "The mood of the nation and that of the international community is not for a military government". He added that "Nigeria is too great and important a country to the world to have a military regime". See *Newswatch* (Lagos), December 6, 1993, p.14.

8. My emphais.

9. See A. Oyinlola "Fire on the Mountain", *Tell,* July 25, 1994 p.23.

10. It is said that on hearing that Abiola had clinched the presidency in June 1993, the then Sultan of Sokoto, Ibrahim Dasuki, protested to Babangida that he would not be the one to undo Ahmadu Bello's legacy for the North. Babangida would later confide in some of his aides that "those Northerners who have lived on government for several decades cannot survive outside government. They will die"; see N. Igiebor "The Coup against June 12", *Tell,* June 26, 1995 p. 10-20;16.

11. *Tell,* 28 February 1994 p. 28.

12. See *Tell,* January 2, 1995 pp. 14-15. Osifo-Whiskey ("The Trouble with the North" *Tell,* August 15, 1994 p.3) elaborates on this: "Under the able scheming of the caliphal North, power alternates between its civilian and military minions in an unabashedly rabid power play that reduces the entire South to a glorified second-class people".

13. *Tell,* 28 February 1994 p. 29.

14. *Tell,* 5 September 1994, pp. 14-15.
15. *Tell,* January 23, 1995 pp. 14-15.
16. See Claude Ake, "A Plausible Transition" *Tell,* September 25, 1995 p. 34
17. Thus, whilst it was 'politically unsafe' to allow IFRA hold a Conference on "Political Restructuring and National Integration in Nigeria" in Ibadan (a NADECO stronghold?), it was okay to permit a group of mainly northern scholars to hold series of seminars on a more politically sensitive theme as "Extending the Nigerian Democratic Space" in Zaria.
18. Cf The *Tell* Editorial "The Way Forward" (November 27, 1995 p. 9)" Ours, with over 250 tongues is a failed federation. We run a federation where minorities, with all their wealth, are more of slaves than even second-class citizens. It is a federation in which a certain class sees itself as one with a divine right, sanctified by something higher than Papal infallibility, to rule forever".
19. J. Igbokwe, *Igbos: 25 years after Biafra* (Lagos: Advert Communications 1995) as reviewed in Y. Owolabi "Igbo, Igbokwe, Igbo-kwenu" *Tell,* December 4, 1995 p. 8
20. Agwu K. Agwu "Igbo Clowns or Igbo Leaders?' *The Post Express* (Lagos), March 17, 1997, p.8.
21. See *Tell,* July 17, 1995, p. 18.
22. Osifo-Whiskey, "Walter Ofona-Goebbels" *Tell,* May 27, 1996, p.5.
23. See Ikoku's interview, "Don't Rush the Military", in *Tell,* January 23, 1995
24. Interview with W. Nas "NADECO is dead", *Tell,* May 13, 1996 p. 21.
25. See Ade Olorunfemi "The Final Onslaught", *Tell,* July 1, 1996 pp. 8-13.
26. According to the Civil Liberties Organisation (CLO), by June 1996, no fewer than twenty-three pro-democracy activitists have gone on exile. At least twenty others are being held under the notorious Decree 2 of 1984 as amended in 1989.
27. See A. Enahoro "Agenda for Abacha", *African Concord,* January 10, 1994 pp. 36-37.
28. See Nyiam's interview, "Plans to Succeed Himself", *Tell,* September 18, 1995 p. 10.
29. In Ogun State, from where hails Abiola, the junta so much manipulated and regimented nominations and disqualifications

for the zero-party municipal election that `election' took place only in seven of the state's fifteen local government areas.

30. The northern hegemonists possess a feudal mentality which is antithetical to the ethic of development. A confidential source told me in August 1996 that according to a senior northern politician, Nigerians who blame their colleagues for ruling badly are ignorant of the fact that unlike in say, Yoruba and Igbo languages, there is no equivalent of "development" in Hausa language.

31. These include popular opposition, presidential ambition of top politicians; rampant poverty that is often a common denominator, intra-military fissures and June 12. Dissessions within the military have resulted in no less than eighty-seven June-12-induced purges since November 1993. Reuben Famuyibo, a close Yoruba ally of the junta (others include Dr Olunloyo, Olukoya, Ogundokun, Olumilua, Arisekola, Adedibu etc) is honest enough to admit that June 12 is a time-bomb. He says that "as we go about now, a lot of people keep asking us what about the June 12 election. *Only a fool would say there was no mandate* (emphasis mine)". See A. Akinkuotu, "The General's Hatchet Men", *Tell,* January 13, 1997 pp. 10-17, 17.

Bibliography

Adekanye, J.B. (1989) ``Politics in a Military Context'' in P.P. Ekeh *et al* (ed.) *Nigeria Since Independence: The First 25 Years, Vol. v Politics and Constitutions.* Ibadan: Heinemann Books pp. 186-205.

Akinola, A.A. (1996) *Rotational Presidency.* Ibadan: Spectrum Books.

Amuwo, K. (1995) *General Babangida, Civil Society and the Military in Nigeria: Anatomy of a Personal Rulership Project,* Travaux et Documents, No. 48, C.E.A.N., I.E.P., Universite de Bordeaux I, 41pp.

Berger, P.L. and T. Luckmann (1966) *The Social Construction of Reality, a Treatise in the Sociology of Knowledge.* N. York: Anchor Books, Doubleday.

Boggs, C. (1993) *Intellectuals and the Crisis of Modernity.* Albany: State University of New York Press.

Clapham, C. and J.A. Wiseman (1995) ``Conclusion: Assessing the Prospects for the Consolidation of Democracy in Africa ``in Wiseman (ed.) *Democracy and Political Change in Sub-Saharan Africa.* London and N. York: Routledge Publishers.

Durkheim, E. (1993) *Ethics and the Sociology of Morals.* Buffalo. N. York: Prometheus Books.

Ekeh, P.P. (1996) ``Political Minorities and Historically-Dominant Minorities in Nigerian History and Politics'' in O. Oyediran (ed.) *Governance and Development in Nigeria: Essays in Honour of Prof. B.J. Dudley.* Ibadan: Oyediran Consult International p. 33-63.

Fadahunsi, A.T. and T. Babawale (eds.) (1996) *Nigeria: Beyond Structural Adjustment: Towards a Popular Democratic Development Alternative.* Lagos: Frederich Ebert Foundation.

Fay Brian (1987) *Critical Social Science.* Ithaca, N. York: Cornell University Press.

Forrest, T. (1995) *Politics and Economic Development in Nigeria.* Boulder and Oxford: Westview Press.

Gramsci, A (1971) *Selections from the Prison Notebooks.* N. York: International Publishers.

Hutchful, E. (1991) ``Reconstructing Political Space: Militarism and Constitutionalism in Africa'' in Issa G. Shivji (ed.) *State and Constitutionalism: An African Debate in Democracy.* Harare: SAPES Books pp. 183-201.

Ige, B. (1994) *The Discovery of Nigeria.* Text of the University of Ibadan 1994 Alumni Lecture, December 2.

Ihonvbere, J.O. and O. Vaughan (1995) "Democracy and Civil Society: The Nigerian Transition Programme, 1985-1993" in Wiseman (ed.) *Democracy and Political Change...* pp.71-91.

―――― (1996) "Are Things Falling Apart? The Military and the Crisis of Democratisation in Nigeria". *Journal of Modern African Studies,* 34, 2, pp. 193-225.

Joseph, R.A. (1991) *Democracy and Prebendal Politics in Nigeria.* Ibadan: Spectrum Books.

Kandeh, J.D. (1996) "What does the 'Militariat' do when it rules? Military Regimes: The Gambia, Sierra Leone and Liberia". *Review of African Political Economy,* 69, p. 387-404.

Kukah, M.H. (1993) *Religion, Politics and Power in Northern Nigeria.* Ibadan: Spectrum Books.

Kunz, F.A. (1995) "Civil Society in Africa" *Journal of Modern African Studies,* 33, 1, pp. 181-187.

Mamdani, M. (1991) "Social Movements and Constitutionalism in the African Context" in Shivji (ed.) *State and Constitutionalism* pp. 237-250.

Olukoshi, A.O. (1995) "Bourgeois Social Movements and the Struggle for Democracy in Nigeria: An Inquiry into the 'Kaduna Mafia'" in M. Mamdani and E. Wamba-dia-Wamba (eds.) *African Studies in Social Movements and Democracy* Dakar: CODESRIA Books pp. 245-278.

Orkin, M. (1995) "Building Democracy in the New South Africa: Civil Society, Citizenship and Political Ideology" *Review of African Political Economy* 66, p. 525-537.

Rapley, J. (1994) "New Directions in the Political Economy of Development" *Review of African Political Economy,* 62, pp. 495-510.

Shaw, T.M. and S.J. MacLean (1996) "Civil Society and Political Economy in Contemporary Africa: What Projects for Sustainable Democracy?" *Journal of Contemporary African Studies,* 14, 2 pp. 247-264.

Government Publications

(a) Federal Republic of Nigeria (1995a) *Report of the Constitutional Conference Containing the Draft Constitution Volume I.*

(b) (1995b) *Report of the Constitutional Conference Containing the Resolutions and Recommendations of the Constitutional Conference,* Volume II.

SECTION TWO

Federal Character and Power Sharing

CHAPTER 6

J.A.A. Ayoade

The Federal Character Principle and the Search for National Integration

Nigeria, a politically arranged country, is the product of a British experiment in political cloning. It emerged piecemeal under different conditions. In fact, the British themselves only came to understand the nature and character of the territory after the acquisition. But the situation was even worse for the Nigerians. For some, it was, involuntary and traumatic. For yet others, it was at best, an affection for the unknown. But for all of them, it was a forced brotherhood and sisterhood which has been the subject of continual tinkering, panel beating and even attempted dissolution. In fact, an eminent Nigerian political actor described the product of the experiment as a mere geographical expression[1] while another equally prominent actor described the making of Nigeria as the "mistake of 1914.[2]" This problem is complicated by the size and complexity of the country called Nigeria. The political history of Nigeria has since been dominated by efforts at fashioning a system suited to the people's perception of the circumstances and needs of their new nation.[3]

Nigeria was made up of three parts administered by separate authorities. The colony of Lagos with its Yoruba hinterland was administered by the Colonial Office. By 1900, it became the Colony and Protectorate of Lagos. The Niger Coast Protectorate comprising the Bights of Benin and Biafra with their hinterlands was administered by the Foreign Office. In 1900, it became the Protectorate of Southern Nigeria and came under the Colonial Office. What later became known as Northern Nigeria was originally administered by The Royal Niger Company. In 1900 it became the Protectorate of Northern Nigeria and also came under the Colonial Office. Thus the whole territory now known as Nigeria came under one administration in 1900.[4]

Although there are three distinct units they appear to constitute two separate traditions. This duality had been anticipated by the Niger or Selborne Committee of 1898 which recommended that Nigeria should be divided into two provinces (i.e. Sudan and Maritime) each headed by a governor or an equivalent officer. The dual character of the country was consumated in 1906 by the fusion of the two southern administrations.

The dichotomy was clear cut. The South was seen as pagan and barbaric. It did not adopt either of the proselytising religions thus necessitating the mounting of a christian evangelical onslaught. Traditional southern administration had a taste of ungovernable liberalism. On the contrary, the Islamised North enjoyed at least a monotheist orderliness and respect for authority as canonised by the scriptures. The differences were a justification for the separate development of the Northern and Southern Provinces[5] and between 1900 and 1912 ``the administration of the North and South managed to develop strikingly different patterns – so different that they seemed more like products of the influence of different ruling powers than the offspring of the same secretary of state, brought up by the same ministry, the Colonial Office.[6]''

The British colonial officers took the dualism very seriously and tried to perpetuate it. They therefore instituted a policy of dual development in which contacts between the peoples of the two groups of provinces were kept to the absolute minimum.[7] The policy resulted in the separate quarterisation of the Southerners living in the North in Sabon Garis. They also initiated and perpetuated a policy of administrative dualism of direct and indirect rule. Thus, according to Afigbo, the colonial administration bequeathed to their Nigerian wards an enduring legacy of mutual suspicion and contempt.[8] The North derided the South as uncivilised pagan, undisciplined, rowdy and nakedly materialistic and the South in turn ridiculed the North as feudalistic, conservative, illiterate, pliant tools of the colonial masters.[9] This antagonistic duality was so deeply ingrained in the Nigerian system that Chief Awolowo saw the two parts as ``divergently and almost irreconcilably oriented.[10]'' This deleterious duality was worsened by the spatial imbalance between the North and the South. At best the North was equal to the land area of the South and that could have institutionalised a political stalemate but for the fact that the population of the North was put higher than that of the South. Consequently the Nigerian federation negated an important condition for a successful federation since the North was in a numerical position to be master of all joint deliberations. In such circumstances, all political dialogues must exhibit the characteristics of a monologue in essence. The conditions of an external political minority are unbearable to the same extent that the privileges of a permanent majority are non-negotiable. But the South as a political minority was even further incapacitated in 1939 when Governor Bourdillon in what he thought was a mere administrative exercise divided the South into the East and the West. The administrative partition of 1939 received constitutional backing in the Richards Constitution of 1946 and almost immediately gave vent to the differences between the East and the West. Thus the Bourdillon Act of 1939 gave greater political clout to an already strong North by initiating East-West conflict.

The strategy of conflict of the three parts determined the conditions of political victory. For the West with approximately a quarter of the population of Nigeria which includes a politically belligerent third in the Benin and Delta Provinces and an undependable liberal Yoruba core area it can only be victorious with assistance from the East and the North. Similarly the East with restive minorities in its southern and eastern extremities but a cohesive Igbo core area must win appreciable support in the North and the West to savour victory. Of all the three political contestants, it is only the North that can win victories by keeping to itself and warding off political trespassers. As it turned out, the East and the West were porous to mutual political infiltrations. Neither the East nor the West recorded any serious net political gain in the exercise because what the East gained in the Western political extremities it lost in the Eastern political periphery. The same was true of the West. Both the East and the West operated in the North through political intermediaries of the Northern Elements Progressive Union and the United Middle Belt Congress respectively. Their gains from the North were politically insignificant to neutralise the Bourdillon effect. Thus the North waxed stronger and perfected its strategy of coalition-building in contradistinction to the strategy of promoting belligerence in other regions. That strategy made coalition-building easier as it created less contradictions. For example a North plus East coalition only compromised the Northern Elements Progressive Union in the Kano-Emirate and nobody in the East. Similarly, a North plus West Coalition could only have compromised the United Middle Belt Congress and nobody in the West. On the contrary, an East plus West coalition would have compromised the members of the National Council of Nigerian Citizens in the West and members of the Action Group in the East. That contradiction could have resulted in the NCNC West and the AG East seeking refuge in the North. Such an eventuality would have greatly strengthened the North because the result would have been AG-AG(E)+NCNC-NCNC(W) +NEPU+UMBC<NPC+AG(E)+NCNC(W). Using the 1959 election results, this translates to (73-14)+(89-14)+8+25<134+14+21=167<169-legislative seats. This is because AG(E)>UMBC+NEPU. Therefore the original advantage of size of the North would have been further enhanced by the northern operational strategy. For the East/West Alliance to form the government it would have needed the support of the splinter minority parties which had a total of sixteen (16) legislative seats. In fact, this is the farthest that an East/West Alliance could go. The North/East Alliance would give NCNC-NEPU+NPC>AG which, using 1959 standards translates to 89-8+134>73=215>73. Similarly a North/West Alliance would mean NPC+AG-AG(North)>NCNC = 134+73-25>89=182>89. Therefore, because of the imbalance, the Bourdillon effect became a permanent constraint on the effective operation of the federal system.

The problem created by the territorial restructuring of 1939 was confirmed and compounded by the Nigerians themselves at the Ibadan Constitutional Conference in 1951. The Northern landmass was allocated fifty per cent of the total representation of the whole country because the North needed constitutional protection against the South. The effect of this constitutional guarantee is that the North can protect itself and equally determine the outcome of joint deliberations. This constitutional provision determined the locus of political power since then. For example, the Enahoro motion calling for self government in 1956 was stalled by this balance of political forces enshrined in the Nigerian Constitution. Sir Ahmadu Bello amended the motion to call for self government ``as soon as practicable''. The amendment was carried. This was what accounted for a later decision to grant internal self government for the Western and Eastern Regions in 1957, Northern Region in 1959 and independence for Nigeria in 1960. The construction of the Nigerian federation guaranteed a liberal veto for the Northern Region. In fact, rather than the position changing in favour of the South, it worsened. Although General Yakubu Gowon acknowledged the political immobilism imposed by this political configuration, his solution to the problem exacerbated the problem by ``restoring nominal federalism and northern dominance''[11]. He created Nigeria into twelve states – six in the North and six in the South. It was merely *plus ca change plus c'est la meme chose.* The northern octopus remained unruffled. The Northern States went on to establish the Interim Common Service Agency (ICSA) to manage joint assets and provide a forum for the continued harmonisation of policies through the governors' meetings. Although, it can be argued that the states of the Western Region also formed an association of Odu'a States and the states of the Eastern Region the Eastern States Interim Assets and Liabilities Agency (ESIALA), these groupings were not as homogenous as the ICSA. The ESIALA was made up of one Igbo State and two states made up of minorities who had objected to what they perceived as Igbo domination. But more importantly, the East and the West have been further polarised and thereby further incapacitated severally. The South at best was only equal to the North, therefore the polarisation of the East and West increased Northern political significance. The creation of states in the Eastern Region was part of the strategy to win the civil war, it was a deliberate act of ethnic differentiation which was not meant to bring about unity because unity was not the design purpose. The South Eastern and the Rivers States were created, according to Inya Eteng, ``to momentarily domesticate the vanquished Igbo''[12]. But, as the future was to prove, the twelve-state structure satisfied the conditions of **regional** parity on the surface. There was a North-South parity, an East-West parity, as well as a Yoruba-Igbo parity[13]. The Yoruba had only one state (i.e. the Western State) while the Igbo had East-Central state.

The Murtala/Obasanjo regime did not pay any attention to these three parities when it created nineteen states in 1976. The North-South balance was tilted in favour of the North in the ratio 10:9. Thus, the sixty-nine year old parity was also eliminated because the East had four states while the West had five. In the same manner Yoruba-Igbo parity was also cancelled as three states were created out of the Yoruba West while only two were created out of the East Central State. It was for this reason that Omoruyi argued in a strangely exaggerated manner that ``the nineteen State system constituted the greatest threat to a meaningful dialogue among Nigerians on the basis of equality of states, where states were supposed to be taken as the units of representation''[14]. Perhaps parity has assumed an unusual political salience because the various sections of the 1979 Constitution defined states as units of representation for the purpose of federal character. Therefore, the Igbo who have always been critical of the continued dominance of the economy and bureaucracy by the Yoruba felt further irked. Igbo leaders believed Igbo-Yoruba parity to be ``the greatest factor making for a sound federal political system''[15] as if only the two ethnic groups constitute the Nigerian federation. While the East-West competition continued, both sides paid no attention to North-South parity. And in order to neutralise the advantage of the West over the East, Dr. Chuba Okadigbo, an Igbo member of the Constituent Assembly proposed an amendment to a military clause of the Draft Constitution to read: *The composition of officer corps and other ranks shall reflect the federal character based on population of each state.*

If population then became the basis for the allocation of federal positions, the Yoruba advantage over the Igbo would disappear. But that even widened the gap between the North and the South and thus increased the disparity. It was clear therefore that the East and the West engaged in mutual destruction with the consequence of strengthening the North.

The population argument however failed. In 1989, General Babangida increased the number of states to twenty-one by creating one state in the North (Katsina) and one (Akwa Ibom) in the South. The North-South ratio then became 11:10 while East-West ratio became 5:5, although Yoruba-Igbo ratio stood at 3:2. The thirty-state structure created by Babangida in 1991 carefully increased the gap between the North and the South because the North had sixteen (16) states to fourteen (14) in the South. This gap was further increased by the fact that Abuja, the Federal Capital Territory, had virtually being classified as a Northern were even made in the Constituent Assembly in 1987 to declare it a state. Thus, to all intents and purposes, the North-South ratio had increased to 17:14. The balance between the East and the West was retained at 7:7 This was the situation until 1996 when General Sani Abacha created six additional states, i.e., three in the North, two in the East and one in the West. The North then had nineteen states plus Abuja; the East nine (9) states and the West eight (8) states. Thus, Northern political and distributive ascendancy has been assured. A relationship which stood at 50:50 in 1951 had by 1995 become 54:46. Similarly East-West relationship which started in 1951 as 50:50 has by 1995 become 53:47. Consequently, the North has gained at the expense of the South and the East at the expense of the West. Nigeria's solutions to the initial problem of regionalism failed to solve that nagging problem. It strengthened and exaggerated the disparity between the North and the South. Thus the North was given greater liberty to solely determine the political fate of all Nigerians. The East won a pyrrhic victory over the West but both of them remain political vassals of the North. Regionalism conveniently transformed into statism but the configuration of political forces did not change. If anything, the creation of states in the North has improved the northern argument for domination. Some members of the Political Bureau argued that those who criticise ``northern representation'' do not take into account the number of states in the North represented by the ``northern quota.''[16]

Federal Character

The problem of representational equity in Nigeria started with the problem of an unequal North-South duality. As if that was not problematic enough, the smaller southern component was split into two to create a deleterious southern duality and an equally debilitating national trinity. The attempt to redress North-South regional imbalance resulted in the creation of states but it resulted in weakening the South against the North. This then became the justification for other methods for the promotion of a sense of belonging in the country by eliminating or at least minimising domination resulting from imbalance in appointments.[17] Afigbo saw the solution as that of ethnic balancing such that there is a symmetry between the diversity of the nation and the representation of that diversity. He argued that ``the distinctive character of each federation, and by extension its stability, would appear to depend on the degree of harmony or congruence which exists between the structure and usages of the society on the one hand and the structure and usages of the constitution''.[18] Consequently the narrower the gap between both, the greater the stability and the wider, the greater the instability.

The purpose of the policy or principle of federal character is laudable. Unfortunately the debate preceding the constitutional provision was clumsy. The Constitution Drafting Committee was split into three on the issue. The first group argued that it would be dangerous and unrealistic not to ensure fair and equitable treatment of all the component states and ethnic groups in the country. However they believe that the creation of states and other provisions of the constitution are sufficient to ensure the protection of the rights of the various communities. Thus if the component states and all ethnic groups are accorded fair and equitable treatment then a combination of a few states cannot dominate the government to the exclusion of others. Therefore they concluded that the playing up of sectional representatives in the conduct of national affairs can only retard national unity. This school of thought submitted a draft clause of the Constitution as follows:

> The composition of the Federal Government and the conduct of its affairs shall be carried out in such manner as to ensure fair and equitable treatment for all the component states and ethnic groups in the country.[19]

The second school of thought agrees with the grounds of the above argument but felt that the views fall short of guarantees to secure and maintain stability in the country. It therefore felt that there must be a provision for equity in the composition of government or the appointment or election of persons to high offices in the state. Such participation must be in all tiers of government as well as governmental agencies like statutory corporations and companies. This group therefore suggested that the fundamental objectives should include the following:

i. The predominance in the federal government or any of its agencies of persons from some states, ethnic or other sectional groups to the exclusion of persons from other states, ethnic or other sectional groups, or the monopoly of the office of the president by persons from any state or ethnic group shall be avoided.

ii. The affairs of every government in the federation shall be conducted so as to ensure a fair and just treatment for all ethnic groups within the area of authority of such government.[20]

The third school of thought argued that the fundamental objectives must spell out clearly the ideals towards which every government should strive It however stated categorically that national unity is not a product of citizen's ethnic or linguistic affiliation. In fact, such primordial groupings must not be the primary definition of a citizen's quality as a human being. The Constitution should therefore render the area or ethnic origin of a person irrelevant in determining his suitability for an office. It therefore proposed a very simple clause for inclusion in the fundamental objectives as follows:

> The composition of every government in the federation and the conduct of its affairs shall be carried out in such manner as to recognise the need for national integration and the promotion of national unity.[21]

The members of the Constitution Drafting Committee succumbed to the argument to reflect the diversity of the polity in the governance of the country. The draft was approved as follows:

> The composition of the federal government or any of its agencies and the conduct of their affairs shall be carried out in such manner as to recognise the federal character of Nigeria and the need to promote national unity and to command national loyalty. Accordingly, the predominance in that government or in its agencies of persons from a few states or from a few ethnic or other sectional group shall be avoided.

> The composition of a government other than the Federal Government or any of the agencies of such government and the conduct of their affairs shall be carried out in such manner as to recognise the nature and character of the peoples within their area of authority and the need to promote a sense of belonging and loyalty among such peoples.

By 1986, the problems of this provision had to be addressed by the Political Bureau which was set up to examine the grounds for another constitution. It argued that "The constitutional definition of Nigerian citizenship should, as a matter of urgency, be studied with a view to removing the difficulties and anomalies arising from the interpretation of Section 277 of the 1979 Constitution."[22] A dangerous dichotomy has developed between Nigerian citizenship and nativity of a state similar to the situation in the colonial period when Nigerians living outside their states of origin were regarded as "native foreigners". This category of Nigerians did not enjoy full citizenship rights in those states to which they migrated. Thus the operationalisation of the federal character principle tended more to differentiate than to integrate. It was to prevent this untoward consequence that the Political Bureau recommended that laws should be promulgated to tie citizenship rights to either place of birth or residence such that any Nigerian who has lived in any part of the country for ten years can enjoy full residency rights, which must include all rights normally available to the traditional indigenes of the states.[23] This observation had been made as early as 1976 by Group Captain Dan Suleiman, then Governor of Plateau State. He had proposed for Plateau State that any Nigerian born in Plateau State or any Nigerian from any other state who has lived in Plateau State for twenty years should enjoy all the rights and privileges of a native of Plateau State. The "Suleiman Principle" as this progressive measure was called did not succeed because it was not adopted as a national policy. The application of the principle of federal character was a qualitative equal of the colonial policy of ethnic differentiation. In 1920, Sir Hugh Clifford, the colonial governor promised that he would seek to secure

> to each separate people the right to maintain its identity, its individuality and its nationality, its chosen form of government; and the peculiar political and social institutions which have been evolved for it by the wisdom and the accumulated experience of its forebears.[24]

The principle of federal character was the product of the contradiction between the ethno-moral debate and a politico-moral balance. The contradiction was reflected in the imprecision of its definition by its proponents. Quite appropriately Ahmed Talib argued that federal character is a subject which though vague in meaning is full of meaning especially with regard to the hopes and aspirations of Nigerians.[25] Afigbo was more trenchant in his assessment of this situation. He argued that the acceptance of the principle by most members of the Constitution Drafting Committee "lay partly in its novelty, partly in its cosmetic character, partly in its rhetorical appeal, but above all in its vagueness."[26] At best it was adopted only to pour oil on troubled ethnic waters. While the proponents showed revulsion of the fissiparous tendencies, the solution proferred in the name of federal character is a fecund source of ambiguity and a strategic retreat from the problem. Or how can one explain the contradictions in its definition by the Constitution Drafting Committee which defined the federal character of Nigeria as:

> the distinctive desire of the peoples of Nigeria to promote national unity, foster national loyalty and give every citizen of Nigeria a sense of belonging to the nation notwithstanding the diversities of ethnic origin, culture, language or religion which may exist and which it is their desire to nourish, harness to the enrichment of the Federal Republic of Nigeria.[27]

It is strange that the CDC only saw federal character as a *desire* to promote national unity. Therefore, federal character was only defined not substantively but by its objectives. But even within that definition is carefully embedded a contradiction which appears to be a freudian revelation of the CDC. It argued for instance that it is the desire of Nigerians to *nourish* and *harness* "the diversities of ethnic origin, culture, language or religion" for the enrichment of the Federal Republic of Nigeria. National integration was therefore not the intention of the proponents of federal character. If the methods of ethnic division, differentiation and particularism cannot achieve it, there is a contradiction between means and goals. The reason for this contradiction arises from the fact that it is a hegemonic device to strengthen the strong. It is a constitutional device for the disempowerment of the weak by the dominant northern elite. The ``self government in 1956'' motion by Anthony Enahoro had been opposed by the North for fear of southern domination in the bureaucracies. But by 1976, the North had discovered that political power is the final argument in all matters. Since it has achieved political ascendancy via the creation of states, the application of the federal character principle could then be used to whittle down southern dominance in the bureaucracy. In fact, civil servants from some states were retired particularly in the foreign service because their states were alleged to be overrepresented. Ibrahim Tahir saw federal character as a device for ventilating historical wrongs.[28] But historical wrongs were not only in the areas of federal public service, manpower, commercial and industrial development. The most critical historical wrong is political where the country has suffered from a divine right posture of the North. Federal character is therefore an instrument of eclectic redistribution of bureaucratic positions and industrial locations. Thus Ahmed Talib saw federal character as a method for the equalisation of persons, distribution of amenities and a formula for fair distribution.[29] This is to be expected from a concept which originated from the Cabinet Office headed by a Northerner who christened it as the ``Non-Exclusion Principle''. But robbing Peter to pay Paul cannot integrate Peter and Paul.

The regime of federal character in Nigeria negates various definitions of national or territorial integration. Even the definition by Ibrahim Tahir of national integration as the emergence of a situation in which every citizen is a perfect substitute for any other citizen for the purpose of selection and recruitment to perform socially determined roles subject only to qualification of residence and technical competence[30] is not appropriate. The caveat of residence neutralises the integrative component. The insertion of non-task considerations and a modish concern for ethnic representation offsets presumed merit and job skill related criteria. It is capable of resulting in a geometric diffusion of mediocrity. This definition even contradicts that of Coleman and Rosberg who define territorial integration as ``the progressive reduction of cultural and regional tensions and discontinuities in the process of creating a homogeneous territorial political community.''[31] While this definition emphasises the development of a homogeneous community federal character is based on the recognition of ethnic differences. Neither does the operationalisation of federal character agree with Ernest Haas definition of national integration as ``a process whereby political actors in distinct national settings are persuaded to shift their loyalties, expectations and political activities towards a new centre, whose institutions possess or demand jurisdiction over the pre-existing nation-state.[32] Federal character encourages the valorisation of the ethnic individuality rather than a dissolution of the ethnic personality.

Representative Bureaucracy

The need for a representative bureaucracy had been felt before independence. Actually, the most explosive issues, and certainly the most controversial ones, faced by Nigeria shortly before independence involved Nigerianisation, Expartriatisation and Northernisation.[33] The North had embarked on the Northernisation of the public service to keep away Southerners. If a qualified Northerner was available he was given priority in recruitment. If there was no Northerner available, an expatriate may be recruited. A Southerner was only recruited as a last resort and on contract terms only. In reality, the Northernisation Policy was directed more against southern Nigerians than against expatriates. The purpose was to make the Northern Public Service a representational cross-section of the northern society. In 1959, expatriates constitute 83.2 per cent of the senior posts in Public Service of Northern Nigeria (Table 1). And of the 315 Nigerians in that Service, Northerners were 207 while Southerners were 108. This meant that Northerners were only a paltry 11.2 per cent. This sharply contrasts with the figures for the East and the West. Easterners constituted 74.4 per cent of the Eastern Nigerian Civil Service and Westerners 76.2 per cent of the Western Nigerian Civil Service.

Table 1: Senior Posts in the Public Services of Nigeria

	Federal May 1,1959		Eastern April 1, 1959		Western April 30,1959		Northern Oct. 1, 1959	
	Number	%	Number	%	Number	%	Number	%
*Expatriates	1,739	48.5	259	25.6	387	23.8	1,577	83.2
Nigerians	1,844	51.5	753	74.4	1,239	76.2	0,315**	16.8

* Expatriates include a few officers from other African Countries
** Nigerians in the Northern Service include 207 Northerners and 108 Southerners.
Source: Ken Post, *The Nigerian Federal Election of 1959*. (London, OUP, 1964) p.23.

At the federal level, there was also a deliberate policy of Nigerianisation. The policy had started in the fifties. But since Northernisation and Nigerianisation were simultaneous, the North did not contribute much to Nigerianisation. Thus by 1959 the North which was the senior partner in the coalition federal government that received over 60 per cent of the parliamentary support from adherents of the Northern Peoples Congress had less than one per cent of the higher posts in the Federal Civil Service.[34] And even the posts vacated by the expatriates would be taken over by the Southerners thus further reducing northern percentage. Since there were no regional armies to preoccupy the North as the Northern Public Service the North pressed for the adoption of regional quotas for the recruitment of officers in the Nigeria Army. In the recruitment, the North had 50 per cent, the East 25 per cent and the West 25 per cent.[35] Gradually, the North started making strategic moves to gain political ascendancy. In 1951 it had secured for itself legislative parity between the North and the South. In 1960 it added military parity between the North and the South. By 1976 when political parity between both disappeared because the North had a majority of states over the South, it launched the constitutional principle of non-exclusion which the Constitution Drafting Committee christened the principle of federal character. The North abandoned parity for superiority and only sought to consolidate earlier gains establishing a bureaucracy in which it will have a majority. The North had sought to have a secure political base at the regional level before attempting to play with the boys at the federal level. It was a strategy of upward step-wise movement after consolidation at a particular level. The Nigerian civil war and its attendant Biafran propaganda necessitated and catalysed northern massive entry into the federal public service. The Igbo had argued that they constituted the backbone of the federal public service and that it would collapse with their exit. The lesson of this was not lost on the North and in order to prevent such future stalemate the North must have such presence in the federal public service as to neutralise such eventuality.

Apart from the lesson of the civil war, the North had come to accept the reality that the bureaucracy anywhere, is the blood, bone and sinews of political power[36]. The pivotal nature of bureaucracy lies in the fact that it is the policy-making, agenda-setting, preference-ordering and cue-giving apparatus for other sectors. Therefore, if the northern legislative and military victories must be meaningful, it must be guaranteed by victory in the bureaucracy. The bureaucracy fills in the deficiencies of the process of representation in the legislature.[37] It corrects the defect of the process of representation through the qualitative representation of such constituencies that fight shy of the political campaign rostrum. But perhaps more importantly, the convention of impartiality and neutrality can be achieved only where there is a political symmetry between the directing grades of the public service and the dominant political persuasion in government. If the directing grades of the public service are opposed to the programmatic concerns of the dominant political party, then there is a problem. Therefore the service must be able to respond to the prevailing political climate. This suggests a mechanism for the microreproduction of the community in the public service because group affiliations are taken as indexes of political beliefs. The loyalty of the public service in a plural society is seen as a function of its representativeness. Although this is a logical proposition, it is neither fool-proof nor the only way to guarantee loyalty. The Anglo-Saxon tradition of anonymity, objectivity and neutral competence appears to be a more viable recipe because it can cope with changes in the political and ideological environment. The bureaucracy must be flexibly apolitical in order to be congruent with all changing political persuasions. The principle of federal character does not address the abstract ideological issues but the near invariable concrete ethnic and regional differences. The effect will be that societal conflicts will be mirrored in bureaucratic disputes thus reducing its technocratic competence.

Another dilemma of bureaucracy in plural societies arises from the fact that the bureaucracy ``is historically the result of executive mitosis''[38]. As the executive expands, it tends to become amorphous, leaving more and more of its functions to the bureaucrats. In the Nigerian setting, this would mean a dominant northern executive leaving its functions to a southern dominated bureaucracy thus winning a political war and losing an all-important bureaucratic peace. The political executive needs a facilitator in the bureaucracy. But the Anglo-Saxon model did not appear to be a sufficient safeguard.

Representative bureaucracy has been seen elsewhere as having some advantages. The first advantage is that it creates support for government policies. ``No matter how brilliantly conceived, no matter how artfully contrived, government action usually also requires societal support''[39]. Such support is guaranteed by drawing a wide segment of society into the government ``to convey and merchandise a policy''[40]. While this may be true of political operatives, it does not appear true of the public servants who are more often than not indifferent to the general society particularly whenever their careers conflict with the demands of the society.

The second and related advantage that is often pleaded for such representation is the social penetration of such a bureaucracy. Members of the bureaucracy are seen as transmitters of government policies, and in the language of Nigeria, public servants are an index of federal government presence in their local communities. Thus to convert a bureaucracy from an army of occupation it must include people who are local and indigenous to the environment. In a more practical sense, therefore, government is brought closer to the people. But for it to serve the purpose of social penetration all sections of a nation must be taken into consideration. There must therefore be a just and national distribution of such personnel to avoid negative social penetration.

Finally, a representative bureaucracy also provides a mechanism for the government party to distribute patronage. This is particularly true when the American model is adopted such that the political officeholder (president or governor) can appoint the top echelons of his administration. That was the system in Nigeria from 1979 to 1997. The president and governors had a free hand to appoint directors-general. The power of appointment increased the social relevance of those offices and in a political party regime, would help in rooting the party of the president or governor in the local communities. This would ultimately increase the political appeal of the party. However, the distribution of clerical patronage requires care and tact. It may end up in creating nine enemies and one ingrate.[41] The operators must also be aware that the problem of social antagonism is never solved by excluding or marginalising a group. If anything, it only tends to exacerbate opposition and conflict. This observation on the Nigerian situation was aptly put by Momoh, who argued that in operating the principle of federal character, Nigeria must seek to level upwards rather than downwards.

> We do not have to make a poor man rich by making a rich man poor. The aim should be to make a poor man as rich as the wealthy in our midst. Our peculiar politics of envy that seeks deliberately to retard the progress of those who are making sacrifices to obtain their level of development in order that the less developed can catch up will impede rather than accelerate the process of national integration and cohesion[42].

The 1979 Constitution made special and specific provisions for federal character and national integration. These include;[43]

1. Relationship between government and the people – Section 14
2. Political and economic objectives of the federation – Sections 15 and 16
3. The rights of citizens to freedom of movement – Section 38
4. Freedom from discrimination – Section 39
5. Election of the president – Sections 125 and 126
6. Appointments to specific public offices – Sections 135, 157, 197 and 199
7. Formation, constitution and rules of political parties – Sections 202 and 203
8. Promotion of national unity, national loyalty and sense of national belonging – Section 277

Section 14(3) of the 1979 Nigerian Constitution stipulates that:

> The composition of the government of the federation or any of its agencies and the conduct of its affairs shall be carried out in such manner as to reflect the federal character of Nigeria and the need to promote National Unity, and also command national loyalty thereby ensuring that there shall be no predominance of persons from a few states or from a few ethnic or other sectional groups in that government or in any of its agencies.

It is hoped that this will "foster a feeling of belonging and of involvement among the various peoples' of the federation, to the end that loyalty to the nation shall override sectional loyalties". (Section 15(4)). In concrete terms, the president in appointing ministers must appoint at least one indigene of each state of the federation (Section 135(3)). Similarly, the appointments of the secretary to the government of the federation; head of the civil service of the federation; ambassadors or equivalent; permanent secretary or equivalent; or any personal staff of the president must take into account the federal character of Nigeria and the need to promote national unity (Section 157). Even the composition of the officer corps and other ranks of the Armed Forces shall reflect the federal character of Nigeria (Section 197(2)). The Constitution attempted an abortive architectural congruence between ethno-traditional and constitutional structures in a way to offset presumed merits and job skill related criteria. This is unfortunate because it highlights the internal incongruencies of the constitutional provisions. A Constitution full of incantations for the unity of the country emphasises the internal division of the country. As long as states which, by and large, are ethnic capsules remain the basis for appointments and the location of services, ethnicity cannot be erased from the minds of the people. In fact, ethnic particularisation becomes the surest strategy for capturing federal posts. Therefore, the application of the principle of federal character can only result in the fossilisation of ethnic differences.

The contradictions are also glaring in two major areas. The first is in the area of the freedom of movement while the second is that of freedom from discrimination. In an expansive interpretation of movement which includes career choice and upward mobility, the principle of federal character abridges career movement and stunts self-realisation in a discriminatory manner. For example, subjecting appointment and/or promotion to federal character discriminates against merit and is therefore unfair to certain sections of the country to the advantage of others. This is in contravention of Section 39(1) and (2) of the 1979 Constitution which states that

> 39-(1) A citizen of Nigeria of a particular community, ethnic group, place of origin, sex, religion or political opinion shall not, by reason only that he is such a person –
> (a) be subjected either expressly by, or in the practical application

of any law in force in Nigeria or any executive or administrative action of the government to disabilities or restrictions to which citizens of Nigeria of other communities, ethnic groups, place of origin, sex, religions, or political opinions are not made subject; or

(b) be accorded either expressly by, or in the practical application of any law in force in Nigeria or any executive or administrative action, any privilege or advantage that is not accorded to citizens of Nigeria of other communities, ethnic groups, place of origin, sex, religions, or political opinions. ·

39-(2) No citizen of Nigeria shall be subjected to any disability or deprivation merely by reason of the circumstances of his birth.

As long as the application discriminates against one group and favours another, no unity can result from such an exercise. The application is also falsifiable because distributive justice which it aims to achieve is of two types viz: arithmetical equality and proportional equality. Simple arithmetical equality has been applied where the equality of all states is assumed. But states are not equal in two main senses. They are not equal in population and they are not equal in the size of the pool of eligible candidates for appointment. There is no greater inequality than the equal treatment of unequals. Proportional equality would therefore be more just and less discriminatory than arithmetical equality.[44] But even more appropriately, the appointment must reflect the size of eligible candidates per state so that excellence is rewarded. Competent people who are disqualified on the grounds of state of origin and such other spurious criteria cannot be willing materials on which to erect the unity of the nation. They must feel wanted in order to volunteer themselves for national sacrifice.

But the interpretation of federal character which relies on state and ethnicity which are political synonyms in Nigeria is inadequate. It is oblivious of the multiple political realities which include social attitudes, class divisions, confessional divisions, temporal divisions and ideological persuasions, to name just a few. In a party-political regime, the president who makes all the appointments belong to only one political party. The appointments, more often than not, will therefore be limited to only the political party thus unrepresentative of the federal ideological character. Divisions in the nation are not only state and ethnic. In fact, it is advisable for the country to bridge ideological divisions which will be regionally diffuse and uniting. Such a posture will more likely than not detonate ethnic conflicts because trans-state alliances will easily emerge. This could be done by leaving appointments to federal positions to political parties controling each state. This process will make appointments representative of the national ideological spectrum and douse the feelings of punitive marginalisation. Secondly, it will remove hard and ill-feelings in states not controlled by majority party at the federal level because minority ideological entrepreneur would no longer be given a higher rating than the majority parties of those states. The present practice where the party controlling the federal government makes appointments in states that it does not control distorts the principle of representation. They often select such political reptiles to the chagrin of mainstream politicians in the state. Only objective selections can result in objective political conduct.

Closely related to the problem of ideological distortion is the fact that initially and universally equal opportunity provisions normally create enabling environments for minorities to be represented. Thus in Australia, it is meant to assist the Black Fellows and the Maoris just as in the United States it assists the Blacks, the Chicanos, the Indians etc. The operation of the federal character in Nigeria has given more powers to the politically superior groups thus creating a wider power disparity between the strong and the weak. The politically weak are subjected to double jeopardy, a situation that is patently antithetical to national integration. This situation is a natural consequence of the hegemonial ethnic political scheming that we have sketched out above. Secondly, it confirms the Austinian position that the Constitution cannot be enforced against the power that interprets it because Constitutions are essentially morality, not law. But in a politicised plural society like Nigeria morality is not a consensual value. If anything, in such environments morality is a strategic variable.

Even if the implementation of the principle satisfies the criterion of quantity the absence of a weighting formula makes it difficult to satisfy the criterion of quality. Power is not significant only in its quantity but in its quality. Thus the appointment of the same number of ministers or ambassadors from all the states as prescribed by the Constitution only guarantees nominal not substansive equality. The Ministry of Industries or the Petroleum Trust Fund wields excessively more powers than the National Planning Commission, the Ministry of Information or the Ministry of Youth and Sports. A proper implementation of the principle would require ranking or measurement criteria.

Conclusion

The principle of federal character is the archilles heel of Nigerian politics. It is the most recent epiphany in Nigerian troubled federal theology. It was aimed at redressing historical imbalance and integrate the country. Unfortunately, the attempt was to balance the ethnic groups in order to create a virile and united nation. It has turned out to be a mere substitute for substance. More recently the Constitutional Conference in 1994 recommended the establishment of a Federal Character Commission to superitend the implementation of the federal character provision of the Constitution. The gap between aspiration and reality showed quite clearly when protests greeted the membership of the commission which itself did not reflect the federal character. The Chairman was Alhaji Adamu Fika while the Secretary was Dr. Sabo Bako both from the North. The protest resulted in the replacement of Dr. Bako. But the damage had been done.

Diversity is both normal and necessary in a federation. Federal character became an issue because Nigeria has failed to operate true federalism. Over time, regional imbalance has been nurtured and exaggerated to a point that centralisation has become the order of the day. Unity has become synonymous with uniformity and a central octopus is the normal consequence. When states smart under such a central octopus they must clamour for representativeness and state individuality. "Representation of each region on the central decision-making body was seen as a way of guaranteeing to each region what it regarded as being its fair share of national resources."[45] Bureaucrats therefore play the role of informal brokers between the central government and their ethno-regions and engage in covert politics. The application of the principle of federal character can only perpetuate the primordial geography that it seeks to erase. The only solution to the problem of integration is adherence to true federalism and a reduction in the powers of the central government. A deconcentration of critical political power will result in a relaxed federal set-up and less-heated inter-ethnic relations.

Notes/References

1. Obafemi Awolowo, *Paths to Nigerian Freedom.* London: Faber and Faber, 1947, p.47.

2. Ahmadu Bello, *My Life.* London: Cambridge University Press, 1962. p.133

3. Ukwu I. Ukwu, ``General Introduction and Summary'' in Ukwu I. Ukwu (ed.) *Federal Character and National Integration in Nigeria.* Kuru: NIPSS, 1987, p.3.

4. A.E. Afigbo, ``Federal Character: Its Meaning and History'' in Ukwu I. Ukwu (ed.), *Ibid.,* p.24.

5. I.M. Okonjo, *British Administration in Nigeria 1900-1950.* Nok, 1974 p.335.

6. I.F. Nicolson, *The Administration of Nigeria.* Oxford.

7. I.M. Okonjo, *op. cit.,* p.335

8. A.E. Afigbo, *op. cit.,* p.24

9. *Ibid.,* p.26
10. O. Awolowo, *The Peoples Republic.* Oxford University Press, 1968, p.72.
11. Inyang A. Eteng, "Minority Rights Under Nigeria's Federal Structure," in Frederich Ebert Foundation, *Constitutions and Federalism.* Lagos: Frederich Ebert Foundation, 1997, p.129
12. *Ibid.,* p.129.
13. Omo Omoruyi, "State Creation and Ethnicity in a Federal (Plural, System: Nigeria's Search for Parity " in Dennis L. Thompson and Dov Ronen, *Ethnicity, Politics, and Development.* Boulder: Lynne Rienner Publishers, 1986, p.122.
14. *Ibid.,* p.125.
15. *Ibid.,* p.126.
16. Federal Republic of Nigeria, *Report of the Political Bureau.* Abuja: Directorate of Social Mobilisation, 1986, p. 202.
17. Federal Republic of Nigeria, *Report of the Constitutional Conference Containing the Resolutions and Recommendations, vol.11.* Abuja: National Assembly Press, 1995, p.145.
18. A.E. Afigbo, *op.cit.,* p. 23.
19. Federal Republic of Nigeria, *Report of the Constitution Drafting Committee containing the Draft Constitution, vol. 1.* Lagos: Federal Ministry of Information, 1976 p. ix.
20. *Ibid.,* p. ix cf. Oyeleye Oyediran, "Parties and Politics" in Ukwu I. Ukwu, *op. cit.,* p. 82
21. Federal Republic of Nigeria, *Report of the Constitution Drafting Committee ... op. cit.,* p. ix
22. Federal Republic of Nigeria, *Report of the Political Bureau, op. cit.,* p. 200.
23. *Ibid.,* p.200
24. J.S. Coleman, *Background to Nigerian Nationalism.* Berkeley: California University Press, 1958 p. 122
25. Ahmed Talib, "Keynote Address," in Ukwu I. Ukwu, *op. cit.,* p.17.
26. A.E. Afigbo, *op. cit.,* p.22.
27. Federal Republic of Nigeria, *Report of the Constitution Drafting Committee ... op. cit.,* p. x.

28. Ibrahim Tahir, "Political Party Organisation," in Ukwu I Ukwu, *op.cit.,* p. 75. cf. J. A.A. Ayoade, "Ethnic Management in the 1979 Nigerian Constitution." *Publius: The Journal of Federalism,* vol 16 No 2, 1986, p.77
29. Ahmed Talib, *op. cit.,* pp 17-18
30. Ibrahim Tahir, *op. cit.,* pp. 74
31. Quoted in Oyeleye Oyediran, *op. cit.,* p.81.
32. *Ibid...,* p. 81.
33. Robert O. Tilman and Taylor Cole, *The Nigerian Political Scene.* London: Cambridge University Press, 1962, p.108.
34. *Ibid.,* p. 109.
35. *Ibid.,* p. 109.
36. Samuel Krislov, *Representative Bureaucracy.* Englewood Cliffs, N.J: Prentice-Hall, Inc. 1974, p.40.
37. *Ibid.,* p.73
38. *Ibid.,* p.66
39. *Ibid.,* p. 4
40. *Ibid.,* p. 5
41. *Ibid.,* p. 5
42. R.A.I. Momoh, "State and Ethnic Interests", in Ukwu I. Ukwu, *op. cit.,* p. 57.
43. Ukwu I. Ukwu, *ibid.,* pp. 3-4
44. J.A.A. Ayoade, "Federalism in Nigeria: The Worship of an Unknown God", Paper Presented at a Special Seminar at the Institute of African Studies on February 10, 1982, p.20
45. J.A.A. Ayoade, "Ethnic Management", *op.cit.,* p.76.

CHAPTER 7

Adigun Agbaje

The Ideology of Power Sharing: An Analysis of Content, Context and Intent

One experience too many in its relatively short history as a country, Nigeria once again finds itself impaled on the horns of a three-headed dilemma. Since 1994, the concept of power sharing has been crafted in bits and pieces under the general direction of those who govern. That concept is meant to inform the constitution and practice of the Fourth Republic scheduled for 1998, even though a clean and final copy of that Constitution is yet to be crafted, and there is lingering doubt in certain quarters as to when and in what form the Fourth Republic will be inaugurated.

While these constitute immense problems for the student of Nigerian government and politics, the dilemma for Nigeria lies somewhere else. For one, it is not yet clear whether this concept can in fact lead to meaningful power sharing, although it is agreed that the country cannot continue with business as usual in regard of existing systems of asymmetrical relationships among its regions and groups of people and institutions.

At the same time, there is the nagging doubt over whether authentic frameworks for power sharing can be architectured under oligarchic regimes, themselves characterised by an absolute overcentralisation and overconcentration of power in its conception and deployment, or in the immediate post-oligarchic order, haunted by memories and lingering legacies of monistic intolerance and assertive abuse of power. This doubt persists, even as it is conceded that the diversities, sheer size, and unrepentant vibrancy of Nigerian life make permanent rule by oligarchs a most difficult, if not impossible, mission to accomplish.

Third, and finally, is that aspect of the dilemma that arises from the fact that the concept of power sharing as crafted since 1994 provides only temporary, short-term or fixed time solution to the problem of how to attain and maintain group (ethnic, regional, other) balancing in the polity, a problem that is more or less a permanent feature of virtually all political systems. Even if the problem was a temporary one, it would remain a moot point whether a temporary solution was preferable to a more permanent one, although this begs the point whether power sharing as a solution can assume permanent status.

What can the notion of power sharing produce and reproduce in situations of asymmetrical relationships in deeply divided societies, such as Nigeria, historically exposed more to oligarchic than democratic rule, if not the existing structure of power inequalities, or worse forms thereof, making the attainment of democracy beyond its nominalist pretensions more tenuous, if not impossible?

This is the central question that this chapter poses, and the line of argument it explores, in its analysis of the content, context and intent of the evolving notion of power sharing for the proposed Nigerian Fourth Republic. The pages that follow suggest that the evolving notion is likely to be unworkable, basically unnecessary, and potentially injurious to the polity. It is not likely to work because Nigeria exhibits at least three characteristics which traditionally have been identified in the comparative literature as toxic to power sharing arrangements. One is a network of deep social and territorial divisions, corresponding roughly with political loyalties, engaged in asymmetrical political relationships and with very little cross-cleavage allegiances. This structural network is underwritten by political memory distilled from historical experience informed more by the "politics of domination" than by the "politics of group equality",[1] as well as by contemporary political culture, including attitudes, that tend to concede, rather than contest, the existing power equation.

The second characteristic is the country's long experience with undemocratic rule. As is clear below, experience with democratic rule tends to be more facilitative of power sharing and related consociational arrangements.[2] Even in the proposed post-transition period, the potency of power sharing could be weakened by inexperience in the working of the democratic order, compounded by the legacy of undemocratic rule.

Taken together with these deep divisions and lack of experience with democracy, the third characteristic, involving the singling out of power sharing out of the other elements that constitute consociational democracy,[3] is likely to make the dream of a Fourth Republic erected on the politics of group equality and democracy unrealisable.

The notion is unnecessary, as is argued below, not only because aspects of its mandate are already being executed through the operation of a federal system of government and the related federal character principle but also because, in the long run, that mandate can be executed even more effectively by the untramelled and transparent implementation of the democratic idea retrieved and reconstructed via a sensitive application of the proportionality principle to make it more representative of all the peoples of Nigeria.

Finally, it is argued that the notion of power sharing as has been constructed since 1994 has the potential of doing more harm than good to the polity by further complicating the search for good governance, national integration, and democracy.

In essence, the rest of this chapter suggests that the evolving concept of power sharing can be understood only in the context in which it has evolved, and that its eventual consequence could in fact be at variance with its declared intent. It does appear that to make sense of the concept, it must be emphasised that it has been constructed under a largely illiberal and undemocratic manner, that the final product was decided by fiat by the unelected military government of General Sani Abacha, and that, logically, therefore, it would be wrong to expect the concept to be facilitative or supportive of democratic governance.

In that context, the notion of power sharing then becomes an ideology, an exercise in false consciousness meant to create a feeling of power dispersal in the face of continued power concentration, a feeling of symmetry even as the ``formation and perpetuation of asymmetrical relations between people, groups, institutions ... in which one partner in the relationship dominates or exploits the other''[4] partners in the relationship persists.

Not long ago, John Thompson[5] defined ideology as meaning in the service of power. In other words, power is exercised and exercisable in relations of asymmetry precisely because ideology mobilises everyday meaning in the service of such power by constructing, communicating and circulating symbols supportive of the production, sustenance and reproduction of relations of domination.

Against this background, the rest of this chapter examines in more detail the content, context and intent of what I call the ideology of power sharing as it evolved in Nigeria between 1994 and 1997.

The Content

The first steps toward codifying the ideology of power sharing were taken by the National Constitutional Conference inaugurated by General Sani Abacha on June 27, 1994, with

> the mandate to deliberate upon the structure of the Nigerian nation-state and to work out modalities for ensuring good governance; to devise for our people a system of government, guaranteeing equal opportunity, the right to aspire to any public office, irrespective of state of origin, ethnicity or creed, and thus engender a sense of belonging in all our citizens.[6]

Between July and August 1994, the conference sat in plenary session to establish the framework for its work, at the end of which it went into committee stage after setting up twenty-one committees including one on power sharing and another on the executive. These committees, along with most others, completed their work between August and September 1994 and submitted reports to the conference.

Noting that "the issue of equitable power sharing has been very contentious in Nigeria, especially since independence," the committee on power sharing adopted a concept of power, "not confined to political power alone," perceiving power sharing "as invariably touching on the question of equity, fairness and justice in the allocation of the fundamental indices of power which were identified as economic, military, bureaucratic, media and intellectual"[7]. The committee further declared that:

> in a country like Nigeria with its diverse peoples and their corresponding diverse political, cultural and economic endowments, true federalism must reflect a genuine attempt to regulate relationship among the groups, as well as a reflection of these identifiable divergencies within a framework of national unity .... (T)he particular complexion which a country's federal system takes reflects its diversities, historical experiences and the disposition of its peoples at a particular point in time, and ... each federating unit within a true federal system should have its powers and functions demarcated and guaranteed in such a way as to strike a compromise between local particularisms and national integration.... (W)e in Nigeria must evolve our own power sharing formula, take our own decisions and develop our own institutions anchored on our historical experiences, since the problem of power sharing had been responsible for much of the tensions, emotions, conflicts, stresses and strains in most countries.

Against this background, the committee made several recommendations, including those calling for rotation of the presidency, rotation of executive heads of government at the state and local government levels, zoning of other public posts, proportional representation at all levels of government, establishment of a federal character commission "to monitor and enforce federal character application and proportional representation in all aspects of our national life",[9] multiple vice-presidency to represent zones, power sharing among all levels of government with a view to reducing the functions of the federal government in favour of sub-national governments, equal opportunity for compulsory education up to secondary school level, trimming of the military, and empowering the press council to better control the use of information media.

In the conference report's own words, "no other single issue received a greater attention ... than the issue of rotational presidency."[10] The issue generated sharp division in the committee, with southern members largely opting for it, and northern delegates generally opposing it. The result was a deadlock, and the matter was referred to the conference for resolution. The conference was equally divided on the issue, and it was

The Ideology of Power Sharing.

not until a consensus committee was set up that the matter was resolved by the conference in October 1994.

In its own report, the committee on the executive reviewed and rejected several options, including what it called the presidential system (cabinet from legislature), presidential system (cabinet from outside the legislature), executive plus parliamentary (French) system, parliamentary (British) system, and "Afrocracy" (indigenous) system. It then recommended for adoption "the presidential system with a single Chief Executive."[11] The conference thereafter adopted the relevant provisions of the 1979 Constitution with certain modifications, including new provisions for three vice-presidents, one from the same zone as the president and the other two from the other zones, the conference having divided the country into two zones – North and South – for this purpose. It was also decided that any party with up to ten per cent of seats in the National Assembly should be entitled, if willing, to representation in the federal cabinet. Another decision was that majority of cabinet members should come from within the legislature.

In its deliberation, the conference came to the conclusion[12] that:

> Realising that the election of the Nation's Number One Citizen has been a major source of our political crises and upheaval, and determined to fashion out a constitution that will be acceptable to the majority of Nigerians, and mindful of the need to avoid concentration of power in the hands of a few, or a sectional group, and the need to allay the fears in certain quarters that the position of the number one citizen of Nigeria is reserved for a particular area of the country, or that particular sections of the country cannot aspire to occupy that coveted number one seat, the Conference, in its wisdom, and by consensus, agreed that the presidency shall rotate between the North and the South. In the same spirit, the Conference further decided that this principle of rotation shall go down the ladder and therefore the governorship of a state shall rotate amongst the three senatorial districts of the state, while the chairmanship of a local government shall rotate among the three sections into which each LGA shall be divided by the State Electoral Commission.

Subsequently the conference enshrined some of these decisions in Sections 133-229 comprising Chapter VI of the draft constitution that it submitted in June 1995 as Volume 1 of its two-volume report to the military government headed by General Abacha. Section 229(1-5) provided specifically that:

> The office of President shall rotate between the North and the South. The office of Governor shall rotate among the three

> Senatorial Districts in that state. The office of Chairman of Local Government Council shall rotate within the Local Government Area ... For the purpose of ... this section, the states, including the Federal Capital Territory, Abuja, carved out from the former Northern Region of Nigeria as at 1st October, 1960 shall be deemed to be the North and the states carved out from the former Eastern and Western Regions of Nigeria including the Federal Territory of Lagos as at 1st October, 1960 shall be deemed to be the South. No political party shall be registered under this constitution until it has reflected the provisions of this section in its constitution.

Section 15(3)(4) reechoed the provisions on federal character as contained in the 1979 and 1989 Constitutions, additional features including the establishment of the federal character commission (S.154(1) and Third schedule) and transforming federal character into a justiciable constitutional provision (S. 49(1)). Although there was much debate on the need to reduce the powers and reach of the federal government vis-a-vis other levels of government, the draft constitutional provisions did not depart much from previous practice, as expressed for instance in Parts I - III of the Second schedule containing legislative powers.

For purpose of comparison, it is important to describe the provisions on federal character, to the effect (S.15(3)(4), that:

> The composition of the government of the federation or any of its agencies and the conduct of its affairs shall be carried out in such manner as to reflect the federal character of Nigeria and the need to promote national unity, and also to command national loyalty thereby ensuring that there shall be no predominance of persons from a few states or from a few ethnic or other sectional groups in that government or in any of its agencies. The composition of the government of a state, a local government or any of the agencies of such governments, and the conduct of the affairs of the governments or such agencies shall be carried out in such manner as to recognise the diversity of the people within their areas of authority and the need to promote a sense of belonging and loyalty among all the people of the federation.

Shortly after receiving the reports of the conference, however, spokespersons of the Abacha government made it clear that the draft constitution arising therefrom would still be worked on by government,[13] which immediately set up a review committee as well as a constitutional analysis committee both comprising members of government, including senior military officers. In addition, several committees, comprising top civilian politicians and public officers, were set up to further explore aspects of the work already covered by the conference, including issues of creation of new states, devolution of power and national reconciliation. Those on devolution and reconciliation were still at work by 1997.

In essence, therefore, the full contours of the content of the ideology of power sharing were still being worked out by the end of 1997, but General Sani Abacha, in his Independence Day Broadcast to the country on October 1, 1995, has already announced changes in the notion as previously outlined by the Constitutional Conference. First, he indicated that the country would now be divided into ``six identifiable regional groupings'', namely the North-East, North-West, Middle Belt, South-West, South-East and Southern Minority, and not just North and South, for the purpose of ``rotating'' the presidency and effecting fully the notion of power sharing. Next, he jettisioned the conference's recommendation of an American-type presidency and three vice-presidents and endorsed a variant of the French system with a president, a vice, a prime-minister, and a deputy prime minister. He then expanded offices to be affected by rotation to include that of the president, vice-president, prime-minister, deputy prime minister, Senate president and Speaker of the House of Representatives. Finally, he limited the application of the power sharing arrangement spatially and temporally by insisting that it ``shall be entrenched in the constitution and shall be at the federal level and applicable for an experimental period of 30 (thirty) years''.[14]

This declaration, which is expected to be reflected in the constitution of the Fourth Republic when it is finally promulgated, was obviously an attempt to satisfy divergent southern and northern views as they crystallised in public and not-so-public debates within and outside the conference while it lasted. For instance, most southern delegates to the conference had pushed for rotation of power among the six groupings now endorsed in Abacha's speech while the compromise position of just two zones arrived at by the conference was closer to the position of northern delegates, who had moved from total rejection of the idea of `rotation' to reluctantly embrace it, subject to the zonal basis for rotating being limited to two.

On the other hand, limiting rotation to only thirty years and adopting a French-type executive system places the Abacha's speech closer to the northern position as reflected not only on the conference floor but also by such powerful groups of senior northern politicians and respected personalities as the Northern Elders Forum.

What emerges from this description of the content of the ideology of power sharing for Nigeria's fourth republic is that it is not too radical a departure from long-standing practice in the area of the politics of intra-elite accommodation, and in this regard it shares much in common with the federal character principle, first elevated to constitutional status in 1979 but reputedly predating Nigeria as a country in terms of practice, with historians tracing its appearance in the area now known as Nigeria to as far back as 1898.[15] The question that then arises is, to what extent is this ideology new in content, better in instrument, and more certain in intent, than its older variants of quota system and federal character?

An answer to this question can at the earliest be attempted only toward the end of this chapter, and even then the plea might be to await the unfolding of events yet in the future. For now, however, it must be emphasised that power sharing and its related notions of federalism, quota and federal character reflect at best two of the four props on which consociational practice, often portrayed as being conducive to democratic governance in divided societies, is erected. These two props reflected in the evolving ideology of power sharing are, first, the construction of a more or less grand coalition of the elite and, two, some use of the proportionality principle in the electoral distribution of public office. The other two that are largely unreflected for now and in the evolving prescription for the future relate to the use of what is called the mutual veto as well as the construction of and respect for spheres of segmental autonomy.[16]

The Context

To enrich our understanding and put in broader picture the evolving notion of power sharing, it is necessary to first put the Nigerian picture in comparative and historical context before examining the background immediately preceding and leading to its endorsement between 1994 and 1995.

The Nigerian tradition has been informed by insights from consociational theory and practice, the central thesis being that "under the unfavourable circumstances of segmentary cleavages, consociational democracy, though far from the abstract ideal, is the best kind of democracy that can realistically be expected."[17] The argument has been that simple majoritarian systems are grossly inadequate "for countries with sharp cultural divisions" partly because such societies cannot afford "winner takes all politics, and the consequent danger of creating a permanent minority."[18] For Arend Lijphart, a leading writer within this persuasion, "strict majority rule places a strain on the unity and peace of the system."[19]

In practice, however, the track record of consociationalism has been very mixed at best. Even in the four small European democracies where it is assumed to have attained some success, consociational practice is now perceived as having been "the outcome of prior events which cannot easily be replicated";[20] of having turned out principally as a transitional arrangement, already largely dismantled in three of such cases; while subsequent commentaries have suggested that two of these cases, including the oft-cited Switzerland, "never really satisfied the consociational model"[21]

As Joseph has pointed out, the record of consociational arrangements in non-western divided societies "is even more discouraging,"[22] with its record in stemming racial, ethnic and sectarian violence from the 1950s to the 1970s in such countries as Colombia, Malaysia, Cyprus, Uruguay, Lebanon and Nigeria being very unimpressive. Add to that the record of pre-Kerekou Dahomey (now Benin Republic) and what comes out is the point that power sharing could even facilitate military coups d'etat by fostering immobilism and attendant deadlock in governance.

On top of this, it has also been suggested by several writers that the consociational model might not be quite appropriate for African countries. It is argued, for instance, that such an approach is more applicable to class and religious cleavages rather than to ethnic cleavages,[23] a point worth noting, "since it is the ethnic dimension that is most prominent in many African countries, including Nigeria".[24]

In the specific Nigerian case, the statistics and geography of ethnic relations have ensured a structure described by Horowitz as the centralised variety, with a few groups (in this case the Hausa-Fulani to the North and the Igbo to the East and the Yoruba to the West in the South) "so large that their interactions are a constant theme of politics at the centre". Such a centralised structure tends to impede, rather than abet, interethnic cooperation, chipping away at whatever social infrastructure exists for the kind of cross-cleavage bridge-building required for consociational power sharing arrangements to produce meaningful results.

That mega-ethnic boundaries are also perceived in the practice and imageing of politics as coinciding with regional and religious divisions make the Nigerian terrain even more slippery for power sharing arrangements when compared with other societies with a more homogeneous population, those with a multiplicity of small ethnic groups or those whose ethnic populations are dispersed geographically, the latter ensuring that high public office acts as a "catalyst for coalition among interests that would normally be at loggerheads".[26] It was obviously the fear of the negative consequences of the further emboldening of divisive loyalties endemic in some of the features of power sharing that led the Political Bureau in the earlier botched transition under General Babangida to turn down arguments supportive of such endeavours, warning in 1986 that "a constitutional provision for rotation ... amounts to an acceptance of our inability to grow beyond ethnic or state loyalty".[27]

It is, therefore, a very interesting commentary on the road down which Nigeria has travelled since, and a tacit recognition of heightened ethnic and regional tension following the 1993 annulment by General Babangida, a

Northerner, of the first popular election to the most powerful office of the land to be won by a Southerner, that between 1994 and 1995 it was felt by those elected and selected into the Constitutional Conference under the oligarchy headed by General Abacha, another Northerner, that the best way to address ethnic and regional tension and manage the post-1993 crisis was to devise a system of power erected and feeding upon such divisive cleavages.

In addition, the hypothesis that the older Nigeria gets as a sovereign state, the more its terrain has become unsupportive of genuine experiments in power sharing seems to be getting more and more unassailable as history unfolds itself in at least three senses: in the sense of a tendency for increased overpoliticisation of life, overcentralisation of the federal arrangement, and in the increasing concentration of power in the hands of generals that govern and their oligarchs.

The first tendency is ably described by Larry Diamond, echoing the late Claude Ake and Richard Joseph, in a recent comment on what he identifies as the ``intense politicisation of social life:''[28]

> The state has been so central and pervasive in distributing what people want that every major group has wanted desperately to obtain access to or control over it.

As with every drive for hegemony in the context of resource competition, the more successful the hegemonic enterprise becomes, the narrower its recruitment base gets and the more exclusivist and monopolistic its hold on power.[29] When bandied around, the idea of power sharing then assumes the status of ideological cement for concretising the unity of the hegemon and deepening the fissures separating the various interests comprising the non-hegemonic. In any event, to talk about power sharing in the increasingly exclusivistic and monopolistic structure that is the Nigerian political process is to raise hopes about a more pluralistic future – hopes largely unsupported by structural realities and unfolding processes.

The second tendency is equally ably summarised by a Nigerian politician[30] from a minority ethnic group in the southern part of the country. Examining the travails of Nigerian federalism from the First Republic, when real power lay with the federating units and the centre was weak, to the present reality of a very strong centre and very weak federating units, turning Nigeria into what is now described as a unitary system in federal guise, he posed the question:

> Why did Ahmadu Bello, the late Sardauna of Sokoto, not come down from the North to Lagos? It was simply because the regions were strong and even more attractive than the centre. That time,

even a rotational presidency would be acceptable to Nigerians. Today, the head of state makes the law and executes it. It is like the centre is everything.

It could be validly argued that the absence of what Lijphart calls segmental autonomy in the contemporary federal experience in Nigeria is itself a legacy of many years of military authoritarian rule, and since power sharing is projected for post-military democratic rule, to that extent it would be illogical to talk about the impending failure of an arrangement expected to be put in place within a (democratic) political framework different from the (authoritarian) political arrangement that has made it largely unworkable in the past and at the moment.

This line of argument would be valid only in so far as there are indications that the post-military political arrangement would indeed be fully democratic, free from the legacy of years of military despotism. However, neither comparative democratic theory,[31] which underscores the uncertain and usually long drawn nature of democratisation and democratic consolidation, nor contemporary Nigerian realities, pointing to a deepening of oligarchic rule in the transition and immediate post-transition period, offers much hope of instant democratic consolidation.

Finally, the third tendency has involved the deepening since 1986 of the worse forms of repressive personal rule disdainful of plural democratic brakes on the use, non-use and abuse of power. Given that, in the best of times, consociational government including an arrangement for power sharing is ``largely a holding operation with an inherent tendency to maintain the socio-economic status'', to emphasise ``closed door negotiations'', encourage ``governmental immobilism, with the consequent growth of cynicism toward the political process'', and ultimately ``accentuates the oligarchical predilection of revisionist democratic theory''[32] and practice, it would be valid to expect in the post-transition Nigerian context the deepening of the oligarchic tendencies that have become the hallmark of contemporary Nigerian experience.

For this reason, therefore, it appears that only a sweeping and comprehensive move toward democracy and its attendant openings and dilemmas can begin to take Nigeria closer to the culture of patience, bargaining and restraint required for the emergence of a stable, integrated polity. By the time such a move is taken, however, there would hardly be any need for an ideology of power sharing or any other form of pacted democracy; given that power sharing is meant to facilitate the emergence of democracy in divided societies, but it has been found to also constitute a barrier to the full development of democratic forces, a move toward full democracy invariably portends the obsolescence of the instrumentality of power sharing.

What, then, can be deciphered about the future of power sharing and democracy in Nigeria?

Conclusion: From Intent to Prospects

Barely forty-eight hours after election day on June 12, 1993, it was clear that Nigeria was standing at the crossroads of history. For the first time in that country's history, election results were confounding optimists and pessimists alike, underscoring the fact that the electorate was moving away from unquestioning loyalty to ethnic, regional and religious considerations. By the time the Babangida government stopped further release of election results and then annulled the election, however, Nigeria and Nigerians were back along the well-trodden narrow path of ethnic chauvinism, regional jingoism and religious bigotry. As indicated earlier, the cross-regional, cross-ethnic and cross-religious pattern of voting as reflected in the 1993 presidential election is perhaps the best evidence not only of the irrelevance of official schemes for power sharing but of what democracy, untrammelled and largely uncensored, could do for national integration and nation-building. That the decision to annul the election, subsequently plunging the country into a crisis in which it was still enmeshed by 1997, was taken by an unelected oligarchy further makes the case for a democratic dispensation, rather than for an elaborate power-sharing formula that:

> seeks mechanically to balance the socio-economic attainments of the various ethnic groups while leaving intact the sources of these socio-economic insecurity of the individual, the regionalisation of the privileged classes and the inter-ethnic struggle among the various factions of these classes for the division of the national cake,[33]

as the lasting solution to the aches and pains of drives for unity in a multi-national state such as Nigeria.

On three obvious grounds, the ideology of power sharing for the Nigerian Fourth Republic as enunciated between 1994 and 1997 stands faulted. First, its promise does not square up with reality, in the sense that historical, structural and processual conditions toxic to its effective operation have remained in place. Second, like several other consociational arrangements, it aims principally at "elite integration" which, on its own, "may not lead to elite-mass integration"[34] and, not only for this reason but also because it is often supportive of oligarchic rule, it could ultimately subvert, rather than promote and deepen, democratic governance.

Third, it is perhaps only in its role as an ideology, mobilising meaning in the further service of asymmetrical, oligarchic power, that one can understand the emergence of power sharing in the lexicon of Nigeria's political landscape, since much of the ground that power sharing proposes to cover is already adequately covered by the related concepts of federalism and federal character. In fact, the demand for and cry over power sharing is enough evidence, first of the ineffectiveness of the current structure of federalism and federal character, and by extension the ``new'' and related alchemy of power sharing in addressing the problem of national integration. Second, this points to motives behind the ``new move'' other than the declared need for integration, equity and justice in the federal arrangement.

Whether such hidden motives exist is still a matter of conjecture, but it is interesting to note that, by 1997, the difficulties in implementing power sharing were already being used by officials of the Abacha administration as excuse for the delay in the promulgation of a constitution for the Fourth Republic. It is also instructive to reiterate that power sharing arrangements and attendant paralysis in the executive arm of government provided the background to the Kerekou coup in neighbouring Dahomey (now Benin Republic) in the early 1970s. Similarly, the 1996 coup in Niger Republic has been traced[35] largely to ``the dual president/prime minister constitution, modelled on the French Fifth Republic'' with the additional warning that ``even back in the 1960s, there were several countries where this caused problems''. To complete the cloud of suspicion is the fact that the French system as adapted for the Nigerian Fourth Republic actually concentrates more powers in the president than the American variant, although it also creates more impression of a dispersal and sharing of power among the president, his/her vice, the prime minister, and his/her deputy.

To the extent that power sharing perpetuates the Nigerian tradition in which ``government is conceived as sharing the fruits of power'', it is, to appropriate Ekeh's insightful description of federal character, a mere ``preservation of the Nigerian political character, not its reversal or indeed some new invention in Nigeria political history''.[36] This is a political history written largely by oligarchs and their fellow travellers.

A future that turns its back on this history and on the present should, therefore, involve the taking of urgent steps toward a democratic arrangement that involve a sensitive blending of majoritarian principles (for the election of executive heads of government at all levels of government) and principles of proportionality (for legislative elections and composition of cabinets) coupled with decisive steps to turn Nigeria into a truly federal state. For, it is only when power is de-concentrated and decentralised and made accountable that it can be shared. To argue for power sharing in any other context in divided societies is to bend meaning in the service of power, raising hopes that can only be dashed by reality, preparing the ground for the ruination of the next Republic.

Notes

1. On this, see Fred Onyeoziri, "Consociationalism and the Nigerian Political Practice" in P.P. Ekeh and E.E. Osaghae, eds., *Federal Character and Federalism in Nigeria*. Ibadan: Heinemann, 1989, p.435.
2. As the more successful Swiss experience has shown. Cf James L. Tyson, "Alternative Democracy: The American and British Model May Not Be the Best for all Emerging Nations", *The World & I*, December 1996, esp. p.327. Even then, however, the argument still holds that consociationalism is ultimately not facilitative of a full democratic order, which explains why Brian Barry, in his "Political Accommodation and Consociational Democracy: Review Article", *British Journal of Political Science*, 5,4(1975), p.501, informs that the Swiss have not really fully operated the consociational model.
3. For these elements, see below and Arend Lijphart, *Democracy in Plural Societies: A Comparative Exploration*. New Haven: Yale University Press, 1977, p.25.
4. Piet Human and Andre Zaaiman, *Managing Towards Self-Reliance: Effectiveness of Organisations in Africa*. Dakar: The Goree Institute, 1995, p.40
5. John B. Thompson, *Ideology and Modern Culture*. Cambridge, U.K: Polity Press, 1990.
6. Federal Republic of Nigeria, *Report of the Constitutional Conference Containing the Resolutions and Recommendations, Vol. II*. Abuja: National Assembly Press, 1995 p.3
7. *Ibid.*, p.143
8. *Ibid*., p. 143
9. *Ibid.*, pp. 144-145
10. *Ibid.*, p. 144
11. *Ibid.*, pp. 63-64
12. *Ibid.*, p.68
13. A. Agbaje, "The National Constitutional Conference," in O. Oyediran and A. Agbaje, eds., *Permanent Transition? Nigerian Politics and Governance, 1986-1996*. (forthcoming, 1998)
14. For comments, see A. Akinola, "The Concept of a Rotational Presidency in Nigeria," *The Round Table*, 337 (1996) pp. 13-24, esp. p.22

15. Cf. A.E. Afigbo, "Federal Character: Its Meaning and History", in Ekeh and Osaghae, eds; *Federal Character,* p.6
16. Lijphart, *Democracy in Plural Societies,* p. 25
17. *Ibid,* p. 48.
18. R.A. Joseph, *Democracy and Prebendal Politics in Nigeria: The Rise and Fall of the Second Republic.* Ibadan: Spectrum Books 1991, p.26,
19. Lijphart, *Democracy in Plural Societies,* p. 28
20. Joseph, *Democracy and Prebendal Politics,* p. 27.
21. Barry, "Political Accommodation," p. 501, and Joseph, *Democracy and Prebendal Politics,* p. 28.
22. Joseph, *Democracy and Prebendal Politics, p. 27*
23. Barry, "Political Accommodation", p. 503
24. *Ibid;* p. 28
25. D.L. Horowitz, *Ethnic Groups in Conflict.* Berkeley: University of California Press, 1985, p. 39
26. Akinola, "The Concept of a Rotational Presidency", p.21
27. Federal Republic of Nigeria, *Government's Views and Comments on the Findings and Recommendations of the Political Bureau.* Lagos: Federal Government Printer, 1987, p.23.
28. Larry Diamond, *Prospects for Democratic Development in Africa.* Stanford: Hoover Institution, 1997, p. 19.
29. A. Agbaje, *The Nigerian Press, Hegemony, and the Social Constitution of Legitimacy.* Lewiston, NY: Edwin Mellen, 1992, pp. v-x, i-18.
30. Senator Asemota, quoted in *Tell.* Lagos, March 14, 1994, p.16.
31. Cf. Diamond, *Prospects for Democratic Development.*
32. All in Joseph, *Democracy and Prebendal Politics,* p.28.
33. O. Nnoli, "Ethnic and Regional Balancing in Nigerian Federalism", in J.I. Elaigwu and R.A. Akindele, eds., *Foundations of Nigerian Federalism.* Abuja: National Council on Intergovernmental Relations, 1996, p.226.
34. A. Gboyega, "The 'Federal Character', or the Attempt to Create Representative Bureaucracies in Nigeria", *International Review of Administrative Sciences,* L, 1 (1984), pp. 22-23.

35. *West Africa*. London, February 5-11, 1996, p. 168.

36. P.P. Ekeh, "The Structure and Meaning of Federal Character" in Ekeh and Osaghae, eds, *Federal Character and Federalism*. p.36.

CHAPTER 8

Wale Are Olaitan

Rotational Presidency and State-Building in Nigeria

The Nigerian state is a state in dire need of organisational institutionalisation and coherence.[1] The history of the political process in Nigeria, characterised as it were by rhythmic dislocations and disruptions, significantly points to the absence of an institutional unifying appeal for the Nigerian state. Political instability in Nigeria would seem to have arisen out of a continuing contest on the underpinning mores and rules of the Nigerian state. The many Constitutional Conferences and Constituent Assemblies to fashion out workable constitutions for Nigeria represent varied attempts to grapple with this seemingly unending contest. These successive attempts signify the failure of past efforts to provide an abiding and workable platform for the institutional coherence and workings of the Nigerian state.[2]

The political uproar generated by the June 12, 1993 presidential election represents, perhaps in addition to the Nigerian Civil War of 1967 to 1970, the most frontal challenge to the existence of the Nigerian state, exposing the fragile underbelly of the state. The massive movement of Nigerians from their places of residence to their places of origin in the wake of this uproar, for instance, tellingly called attention to the absence of a national essence in the workings of the Nigerian state. This movement vividly portrayed the Nigerian state as lacking in unifying appeal as the citizens still felt more attached to their places of origin with the state unable to guarantee their existence and safety outside of such places of origin. It was, therefore, not surprising that the Abacha military government promised a Constitutional Conference of the representatives of all Nigerian segments and groups to (re)fashion a sustaining basis for the existence of the Nigerian state.[3]

The Constitutional Conference, under the aegis of the Abacha military government, has recommended extensive revision and reworking of the organisation and structure of the Nigerian state. These revisions include the creation of additional states, a change in the revenue allocation formula, the creation of geographical zones and the rotation of key executive and legislative offices among the zones of the federation. The overall aim of all these measures is to foster a positive sense of belonging in the diverse peoples and segments of the Nigerian state and ensure a more functional and workable existence for the state.

This chapter, against the background of the unending contest on the underpinning basis of the Nigerian state alluded to, and the imperative need to confront this situation and provide effective measure for its transcendence, assesses and evaluates the contribution of rotational presidency – as the symbolic term for the rotation of key executive and legislative offices among the political zones in Nigeria – towards the emergence of a Nigerian state that is institutionally coherent, workable and stable.

On the Imperative of State-building

The state, because of its being largely an *abstract entity* is concretised by the medley of institutions which operates in its name.[4] Indeed, as an organisational presence – something that can be related to concretely – the state is ``the overall network of institutional arrangements composed of the many diverse agencies which individually and collectively make public decisions".[5] This means that the concrete way to relate to the idea of the state is in terms of the institutions set up in its name to define it, and which make decisions as to the organisation and regulation of the public domain.

Yet, the state necessarily has to have more than an organisational presence. This is because it is not enough for the state to exist as a set of institutions for it to be able to make decisions on, and about, the public domain as these decisions ought to be binding on the people and ought to be predicated on acceptable rules and norms. In essence, the ability of the state, through its defining institutions, to make acceptable and binding decisions on the organisation of the public domain is not only related to the capacity of these institutions to translate decisions into action, but also depends, in a significant sense, on the acceptability of the rules and principles underpinning the activities and actions of the state's institutions. It is in this sense that the state, in addition to its organisational presence, has to exist as an organisational abstraction, an idea that is internalised and accepted by the people. This is why the state is also regarded as the

> set of broad organising principles which defines and constitutes the enduring and continuous pattern of rule and governance and which links and structures the many and diverse institutions of rule and governance into a coherent *whole* and *totality*.[6]

The need for the state to exist as an organisational abstraction internalised by the people becomes imperative when it is realised that the state's main function consists in ``homogenising and hegemonising...of a society conceived as inherently fragmented, atomised and centerless".[7] The society over which the state presides and superintends is essentially fragmented into `contrasting interests' that are perpetually in a contest over the public domain such that the actions of the state in that regard hold enormous importance and implications for these groups and interests.[8] It is, therefore, in order for the state to underpin its organisational presence with a normative acceptance by the people and this – the acceptance of the state as being technically necessary – has to be predicated, according to Gianfranco Poggi, not only on the end of state action – the good of the totality of the people – but also on an acceptable and workable process of proceeding towards such end.[9] It then means that a state has to devise appropriate mechanism and process for enlisting the support and interest of the contrasting groups in the society in its institutional framework for the institutions to perform effectively.

Incidentally, the reality that a state has to construct or devise appropriate institutional and normative framework for its existence means that the state can be seen as an artificial, engineered institutional complex and a deliberately created framework'.[10] This means that the state, in terms of its viable existence as an organisational abstraction and presence, is necessarily the result of conscious arrangement and design or what is called the `state-building process; the state necessarily has to be brought into existence by conscious arrangement and design to create appropriate institutions and framework for its existence. But this process, to be meaningful, has to be geared towards the emergence of acceptable framework for the existence of the state among the diverse groups and interests making up its society and ensuring normative acceptance of internalisation of the reality of the state. Effective state-building cannot but be the product of the interaction of the many interests and groups in the society; indeed, it is only through the unfettered interaction of these groups that acceptable compromises can be reached on the workings and running of the state and its institutions, making for the viable existence of the state.

However, there is a sense in which state-building can be seen as a continuous process that every state continuously and continually engages in as the dynamic essence of society demands changes and adaptation in the framework and principles of the state to meet changing circumstances. The functioning of state institutions at a particular time cannot meet the demands of the state and its society continuously because of changing demands and situations such that the state has to continuously adjust and devise appropriate mechanism and framework to meet such new demands. It, nonetheless, means that a distinction can be made between state-building efforts designed to bring into existence a (new) state where no state previously exists or where the state in existence has a fitful life without normative grounding and one designed to consolidate the existence of the state through changes to meet new circumstances given the different focus and latitude of the efforts demanded and required by the two processes. Without prejudice to this distinction, however, every state-building process has to be geared towards ensuring a viable existence for the state by reflecting the contrasting interests of its peoples in its institutions and principles in order to be meaningful.

The Case for Rotational Presidency in Nigeria

The coming into being of the Nigerian state as a colonial creation made it an imposed state obviously lacking in normative acceptance by the society.[11] This meant the need to transform the state from its imposed origin into a living, viable, normative state with a national, unifying appeal and institutional framework. Indeed, the history of the Nigerian state, since the beginning of the decolonisation process, has been that of a pre-occupation with this singular task of transforming the state. It can, therefore, be said that state-building efforts in Nigeria, instead of being for the consolidation of the existence of the state, have been essentially geared towards erecting the basis for the emergence of a true Nigerian state enjoying the widespread support of its diverse peoples and able to function effectively over its territory.

State-building efforts in Nigeria, particularly before independence, peaked with the nationwide debate preceding the Macpherson Constitution in 1951, a debate that was designed to elicit the true feelings of Nigerians on how the Nigerian state should operate and be administered.[12] This was subsequently followed by a series of Constitutional Conferences in the run-down to 1960 to usher in the 1960 Independence Constitution adopting a federal, Westminster system of government and a 3-region structure for Nigeria. This system unfortunately collapsed in 1966 due to enormous strains and dislocations prompting military intervention in the governance of Nigeria.[13] The political contests under the First Republic had shown a brazen lack of unanimity on the rules and the institutions animating the Nigerian state by the diverse groups and segments in the country.

This contestation was to continue even under military rule – military governments normally rely on force and order to elicit compliance instead of the ideal political norms of consultation, bargaining and compromise needed in meaningful state-building efforts – producing a thirty-month Civil War on the continued existence of the Nigerian state.[14] And other state-building efforts such as the change to a presidential system of government and the provisions on the emergence of national political parties for the Second Republic in 1979 did not produce appreciable results as the republic also collapsed under intense strain through another military intervention on December 31, 1983. Similarly, the political transition programme supervised by the Babangida military government in the mould of the introduction of a compulsory two-party system and creation of new states succeeded in taking the country to a virtual *cul-de-sac* with the annulment of the June 12, 1993 presidential election by the military government, an annulment that precipitated a dire political crisis out of which Nigeria is yet to emerge.[15]

It was against the background of the deep political crisis emanating from the June 12, 1993 presidential election debacle that the Abacha military government, on coming to power, promised a Constitutional Conference, with full constituent and plenary powers, to fashion out a new basis for the existence of the Nigerian state. For the crisis had brought up questions as to the perpetual marginalisation of some segments of the Nigerian polity in the political and power equation in Nigeria. Indeed, the annulment of the presidential election was perceived by not an insignificant number of the Nigerian people as a conscious attempt at denying a segment of the Nigerian polity the control of the Nigerian presidency.[16] The task before Nigerians, therefore, was how to devise a framework for the working of the Nigerian state that would give all segments of the polity a sense of belonging through real access to all important positions and offices of the state. There was the imperative need to ensure balancing in filling political offices especially the presidency as the arrowhead of the institutional representation of the state.

The effect of the complaints raised concretely by the June 12, 1993 presidential election debacle was such that had to be addressed through a formula by which significant segments of the Nigerian polity would be assured of access to important state offices if the Nigerian state was to be assured of continued existence. The reality was that significant segments of the Nigerian polity had come to associate their continued participation in the Nigerian enterprise and sense of belonging to assured and guaranteed access to important state offices particularly the presidency such that it became imperative to conceive of a framework of rotation by which all the segments of the polity would be guaranteed such access.[17] Indeed, state-building efforts, in addressing the particular issues raised by the June 12, 1993 presidential election imbroglio, had, of necessity, to initiate a process of rotational presidency since it was clear that only a guaranteed access to such state office could assuage the feelings of marginalisation responsible for the loud questioning of the existence of the Nigerian state. It is against the background of the virtual collapse of the existing framework for the institutional functioning of the Nigerian state under the pressure of the complaints of marginalisation, particularly with respect to the control of important state offices like the presidency, that the idea of rotational presidency becomes imperative and highly desirable in the Nigerian situation.

The Reality of Rotational Presidency in Nigeria

In spite of the desirability of the idea of rotational presidency in the Nigerian context to help infuse a sense of belonging in the state project in all segments of the Nigerian polity, it is regrettable that its adoption and reality bespeaks a monumental non-appreciation of the grave responsibilities accompanying state-building efforts. For the state-building process, properly conceived, has to accommodate the varying interests in a polity, to give them adequate expression, in order to reach acceptable national compromises and conclusions about the institution and workings of the state; it cannot, in a meaningful sense, be characterised by dictation, obfuscation, doubts and impreciseness as it is meant to assuage fears and complaints of segments of the polity pertaining to the control of state institutions.

Yet, the Abacha military government did not conceive of its Constitutional Conference as entirely a deliberative body composed of genuine elected representatives of all segments of the Nigerian polity as it conferred on itself the powers to appoint special representatives into the conference ostensibly to represent special interests. But, granted that there could be special interests like labour deserving of representation at the conference, such interests ought to have simply been identified and then allowed to democratically choose their representatives instead of the government using such opportunity to appoint ninety-six (96) members into the 369-member Constitutional Conference.[18] The end-result of the dictatorial appointment was to deny the conference of the legitimacy that should normally accrue to it as a deliberative body of genuine representatives of all interests and segments in Nigeria.

The legitimacy of the Constitutional Conference was further marred by the boycott of the election into the conference by the South-West section of the country. Though elections eventually held in the area, the insistence of significant political groups in the area to boycott the elections meant the symbolic non-representation of this section at the Constitutional Conference as the coast was then left for those who could exploit this boycott to advantage to contest and represent the area. In the end, questions continued to be raised about the representativeness of the Conference, a perception that was reinforced by the government's insistence on subjecting the conclusions and outcome of the Constitutional Conference to further debate in order to generate for them wider acceptance.[19]

With the legitimacy of the Constitutional Conference already impaired by the disputation on its representativeness arising from the direct nomination and appointment of many members by the military government and the boycott of its elections in some area, the minimum that could be done to make its conclusions partially credible was for such to be the decisions of perceived representatives of Nigerians on how the Nigerian state and its institutions should function. But the military government not only subjected the outcome of the Conference to further debate, it also conferred on itself the powers to tamper with the conclusions ostensibly in the higher national interest. It is within this context, for instance, that the military government announced the change in the nature of the rotational presidency, which the Constitutional Conference decided should rotate between the North and South of Nigeria as political blocs. Instead, the government prescribed the rotation of the presidency, vice-presidency, prime ministership, deputy prime ministership, senate presidency and the House of Representatives speakership among six newly-created (by the military government) geographical zones in Nigeria[20] This is outside of the persisting reluctance of the military government to make public other information about the workings of the rotational principle (such as which zones would take the first allotment of each of the offices) just as it is keeping a tight lid on the full Constitution that should simply have been promulgated on the basis of the outcome of the Constitutional Conference.[21]

It is, therefore, clear that the reality of rotational presidency in Nigeria is one springing out of the whims of the Abacha military government, instead of being the outcome of a conscious and deliberate desire of the Nigerian people, through their genuine representatives, to fashion a process for guaranteeing success to all important state offices for all segments of the polity against the background of loud complaints of marginalisation by some segments. Evidently, this is a reality that does not promote the ideal of state-building that Nigeria direly requires at present, suggesting that Nigeria, in spite of the present policy on rotational presidency, has to come to task with how to processually grapple with the continuing complaints of marginalisation by significant segments of its population.

Conclusion

The Nigerian state's search for institutional validation and re-validation, as has been argued, especially after the annulment of the June 12, 1993 presidential elections, requires that a process be devised for the guaranteeing of access of all segments of the Nigerian polity to important state offices. The virtual collapse of the state machinery in the context of the June 12, 1993 presidential election debacle arose out of a contention on the basis of distribution and control of important state offices as many segments complained of persistent marginalisation and a deliberate ploy to keep them out of such control. This means that deft moves were required to organise state-building efforts in the direction of working out acceptable basis of sharing and guaranteeing access to state offices in order to assure the Nigerian state of continued existence.

These imperative efforts in state-building, to be worthwhile and meaningful, need to accommodate the full expression of the demands and complaints of all segments in order to work out an acceptable compromise among the different segments; this is in contrast to the imposition of a formula as this would still be tantamount to a denial of the participation of these segments in the running and working of state institutions. In particular, it is important that genuine representatives of the different segments be allowed to work out an acceptable formula for the distribution and control of state offices in order to effectively cope with the debilitating demands.

It is observed that whereas the idea of rotational presidency satisfies, in theory, the quest for guaranteed access to state offices for all the segments of the Nigerian polity, its realisation in the Nigerian context through a Constitutional Conference with a flawed and questionable legitimacy, detracts from this satisfaction. A Constitutional Conference with questions as to its representativeness through the boycott of its elections and the appointment of a large number of its members by a military government cannot be set up as a deliberative body of the true and genuine representatives of the different segments of the Nigerian population with a mandate to reach acceptable conclusions on issues of state-building. Its deliberations and decisions would, therefore, not have the binding and crisis-relieving force of the compromises that would be reached through genuine state-building efforts.

Set against this background, the idea of rotational presidency in Nigeria, with the military government determining its context and operational mores, becomes another military imposition not promotive of genuine state-building. The imperative of rotational presidency in coping with the persisting complaints of marginalisation by significant segments of the Nigerian population suggests that a return to its true conception and realisation is desirable if Nigeria is to pursue the goals of true state-building. The military's hijacking of the idea of rotational presidency, in pointing at the problematic of state-building in the Nigerian context, does not preclude an eventual return to the path of true state-building especially when the military departs the governing scene. It then means that a true conception and realisation of rotational presidency, consistent with the aspirations of genuine and true state-building in Nigeria, is called for and required in the aftermath of the present military-sponsored, constitutional adventure.

Notes

1. Whereas every state necessarily reforms its institutions to meet changing needs and circumstances, the problem of the Nigerian state is that it is almost difficult to assign to it a period of institutional coherence and validity. Indeed, many scholars are wont to regard the Nigerian state as a state-in-formation, a state that is trying to grapple with the task of setting up appropriate institutions and mechanisms. See Sam Oyovbaire, "The Nigerian State as a Conceptual Variable", *Studies in Politics and Society,* Journal of the Nigerian Political Science Association, No. 2, Oct. 1984.

2. These efforts suggest a continuing failure to grapple successfully with the task of effective state-building and existence beyond the nominal existence of the Nigerian state. See *ibid.*

3. The maiden address of the military Head of State, General Sani Abacha, contained the promise on the Constitutional Conference. See Nigerian newspapers of November 18, 1993.

4. See Kunle Amuwo and Wale Are Olaitan, "The Military Presidency and the Poverty of State-Building in Nigeria: A Focus on the Babangida Era", *African Notes,* Vol. XIX, Nos. 1&2, 1994.

5. Shaheen Mozaffar, "A Research Strategy for Analysing the Colonial State in Africa", (Research paper for African Studies Center, Boston University, Boston, 1987)

6. *Ibid., p. 11*

7. Gianfranco Poggi, *The Development of the Modern State.* (London: Hutchinson and Company Limited, 1978)

8. *Ibid.,* p. 96

9. See *ibid.*

10. *Ibid.,* p. 95

11. The imposed nature and status of the colonial state is well recognised. See Crawford Young, "The African Colonial State and Its Political Legacy", Donald Rothchild and Naomi Chazan, (eds.), *The Precarious Balance: State and Society in Africa.* (Boulder: Westview Press, 1988)

12. The Macpherson Constitution was essentially the product of a nationwide debate. See Obafemi Awolowo, *Thoughts on Nigerian Constitution.* (London: Oxford University Press, 1970)

13. Billy Dudley, *Instability and Political Order: Politics and Crisis in Nigeria.* (Ibadan University Press, 1978)
14. Richard Joseph, *Democracy and Prebendal Politics in Nigeria: The Rise and Fall of the Second Republic.* (Cambridge: Cambridge University Press, 1987)
15. The Abacha military government's political transition programme and the continuing tension in the Nigerian polity are all outgrowth of the June 12, 1993 presidential election crisis.
16. The whole essence of the June 12, 1993 presidential election debacle is the perception of a deliberate ploy to deny a segment of the population access to and control of the Nigerian presidency after victory in a national election.
17. The reports of the deliberations of the Constitutional Conference in Nigeria suggest a widespread recognition and acceptance of the imperative of rotational presidency. Differences arose only on the nature of its implementation.
18. The military government simply announced the names of ninety-six delegates to the Conference without assigning to them the representation of any special interest.
19. The military government also insisted on subjecting the outcome of the Constitutional Conference's deliberations to further debate as a prelude to tampering with it.
20. The Constitutional Conference's decision on rotational presidency between the North and South zones was a product of splendid compromise by the members of the Conference. There was a long-drawn process of negotiation before the decision was reached. See *The Report of the Constitutional Conference Containing the Resolutions and Recommendations, Volume II.* (Federal Republic of Nigeria, 1995)
21. The Constitution for the Fourth Republic remains a matter of intellectual and political speculation as the military government continues to hold the country in suspense about its provisions.

CHAPTER 9

I. Bola Udegbe

The Constitutional Conference, Political Restructuring and Women's Access to Power

Overview

No doubt, women's organisations and groups in Nigeria have taken a leap from relative inactivity of the 60s and early 70s to higher levels in the 90s. This has been due in part to several programmes undertaken by several governmental and non-governmental agencies. However, this has not translated to significant access to political power in the past three republics and under military rule. The National Constitutional Conference of 1994-1995 presented an opportunity to restructure the Nigerian political system towards an enduring and equitable gender-balanced political arrangement. This chapter, therefore, examines from a gender perspective the extent to which the recommendations of the Constitutional Conference could bring about an equitable political arrangement.

Introduction

Nigeria has since independence been grappling with the problem of creating a fair, just and equitable political arrangement among its different peoples. After several unsuccessful attempts to entrench true democracy in the first, second and third republics (with attendant economic and social problems), frustration, deep dissatisfaction and alienation arising from perceived injustice in the political system have become the core elements of mass political culture in the country. The need for political restructuring and national integration of all peoples in Nigeria became even more pronounced with the threat to national unity created by the annulment of the June 12 presidential elections by the government of President Ibrahim Babangida.

Subsequently, and in response to calls from several quarters for a Sovereign National Conference, the government of General Sani Abacha set up a National Constitutional Conference (NCC) with the mandate

> (a) to pass resolutions and conclusions which shall form the framework for the governance to guarantee freedom and equality,

equity, justice and even-handed opportunities for social, political, educational and economic participation and enjoyment; establish a system of government reflecting the general consensus of Nigerians with due regard for our national expectations and aspirations as a united and indivisible Federal entity;...guarantee the promotion of social, economic and political cohesion of Nigeria;....acknowledge and encourage the harnessing of individual and collective initiatives aimed at the overall growth and development of the country; and (b) to propose a new constitution which shall be promulgated into law by the Provisional Ruling Council (pg. 51, Report of the Constitutional Conference).

The Conference perceived power as ``invariably touching on the question of equity, fairness and justice in the allocation of the fundamental indices of power which were identified as economic, military, bureaucratic, media and intellectual'. It also recognised that in Nigeria, with ``its diverse peoples and their corresponding diverse political, cultural and economic endowments, true federalism must reflect a genuine attempt to regulate relationship among the groups, as well as a reflection of these identifiable divergencies within a framework of national unity". The question that now arises is, how has this addressed the question of marginalisation of women in Nigerian politics?

Women and the Political Arrangement to Date

The past three decades have witnessed a global emphasis on women's issues. This has been marked by the decade for women (1975-1985) and international meetings on Women's issues such as those in Nairobi (1985) and Beijing (1995). These meetings centred on the strategies for women's advancement in various countries and have had significant effects on the political agenda and social life of several nations. In Nigeria, for example, the recent Beijing Conference has also increased to some extent the awareness for gender considerations in many issues. Phrases such as ``in the interest of Beijing" have become a common slogan *(The Guardian on Sunday,* April 27, 1997). Many development agencies have also encouraged research and placed greater emphasis on gender and development issues from interdisciplinary and multidisciplinary perspectives.

Similarly, women's development advocacy seems to have visibly gained ground in Nigeria. In response to women's global actions, the wives of the current and previous military presidents have initiated programmes and attempted some administrative restructuring to support activities which were intended to impact positively (directly or indirectly) on women's lives. These include the ``Better Life for Rural Women Programme" (BLP), the National Commission for Women, and the Family Support Programme (FSP). In addition, several nongovernmental agencies (NGOs), and women's associations and professional groups have initiated programmes, discourses and enlightenment programmes on issues such as ``women's advancement'' and ``women's empowerment'' and they have come to constitute pressure groups to the gender equality campaign.

These various groups differ in their feminist ideology, composition, areas of emphasis, strategies and their scope of operation. The organisations may meet only practical gender needs of the women by providing water, electricity, markets etc. Such organisations include those who are more service oriented with a focus on welfare. Some others may focus on issues of gender equity in all spheres of national life and engage in activities that have the potential to meet these strategic gender needs directly or indirectly through meeting practical gender needs (Moser, 1993). It must be emphasised that while it is important to meet short-term practical needs of women (a process that is usually time consuming and epileptic), it is only when significant proportion of women hold public offices and are given opportunities to initiate, mould and execute public policy and legislation, can they begin to effectively address the other problems faced by women.

On the whole, despite the level of activities and programmes carried out to advance the cause of women, it appears that much of the effect (as reflected in the collective psyche of the populace) is still insignificant. This is because women's direct access to political power in the last three decades has remained unimpressive. Figure 1 highlights and compares the characteristics of the pre-colonial and colonial eras with those of the First, Second and Third Republics.

Historical records show that even though pre-colonial Nigeria was patriarchal, women were not left out in the political arrangement (e.g., Awe, 1992; Nwanko, 1996). Generally, women's political power varied from one place to another; while in some societies women shared equal power with men, in others their roles were complimentary or subordinate (Olojede, 1990). From an analysis of precolonial power structure (Awe, 1992), three categories of women's involvement in the power structure are visible; they include palace women (e.g., Idia—King Esigie's mother), leaders of women (*Iyalode* Efunsetan of Ibadan), and rulers (e.g., Queen Amina of Zaria). Women who were successful had access to political power on merit and in several communities women emerged as leaders or rulers. Similarly, Awe (1992) has noted that:

> Most African oral traditions, surviving religious cults, and extant political institutions still attest to the significant position which women occupied in the social, economic, and political evolution of different African communities. Such evidence also shows that theirs was not merely a passive and supportive role, but was also dynamic and constructive. Indeed it has been suggested that an analysis of the leading figures of pre-twentieth century Africa will show that there were more women than men in the forefront of

social, political and economic life, than in contemporary Africa, and that during that period, the dominant position which the women held was both quantitative and qualitative(p.vii).

With colonial rule came a denial of equal access to power for women. Thus the era was characterised by women's disenfranchisement and massive erosion of their political power. In the First Republic (1960-1966) the running of government was largely monopolised by men. There were only three female legislators and no women in ministerial appointment. In addition, only women in southern Nigeria were enfranchised.

Participation in the Second Republic (1979-1983) remained significantly low. There were only one female of fifty-seven members of senate and three of 445 Federal House of Representatives. There were also only two female ministers. Although women from northern Nigeria got the franchise in the countdown to that republic, many were still *de facto* disenfranchised by electoral requirements and irregularities (Shettima, 1995). Not much can be said of the Third Republic because it was truncated at the level of presidential elections. However, the low participation of women was still evident; only 2.3 per cent of members of the thirty-odd state houses of assembly were females and there were only two female deputy governors. The female wings of political associations characteristic of the Second Republic were prohibited.

These highlights reflect women's low participation and under representation in the power structure of Nigeria since independence. It is evident that women's access to power in pre-colonial times was better than in post-colonial Nigeria. Consequently, the campaign for a gender - balanced power structure is neither foreign-inspired nor new to many African communities. Further details of the experience under military rule are outlined in other sections that follow.

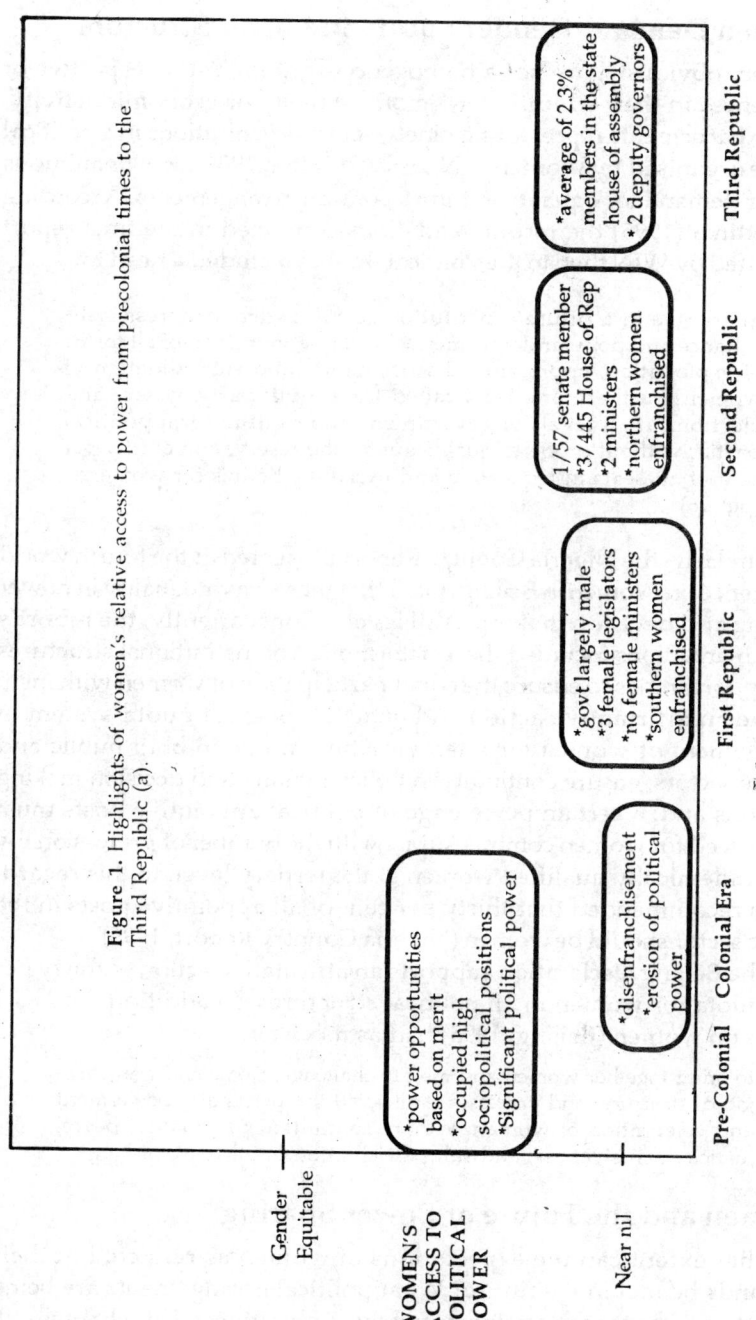

Figure 1. Highlights of women's relative access to power from precolonial times to the Third Republic (a).

a. The base of each rectangle indicates the level of relative access to power (on the ordinate)

Women Demand Gender Equity in Power Structure

Women, obviously, are not a homogenous group. Yet, irrespective of differences in their education, religion, ethnicity or economic activity, female participants representing ninety-seven organisations in a political debate organised by Women in Nigeria (WIN) in 1986 were unanimous in their demand for equality in future political arrangements. According to Shettima (1995) the recommendations contained in the final report submitted by WIN then to the Political Bureau included a need to:

> guarantee in a future constitution social justice, progress, self-reliance and popular democracy as well as elimination of all forms of exploitation, oppression, discrimination and subordination of women. Furthermore, WIN called for a multi-party system and elections at all levels of government; the right to form political parties without property qualifications; the reservation of fifty per cent of all seats in legislative and executive bodies for women;... (pg. 66)

Similarly, the Nigeria Country Report presented at the fourth world conference on Women in Beijing noted that there was inequality in power sharing and decision making at all levels. Consequently, the report's recommendations included the establishment of institutional structures and opportunities to ensure the equal participation of women with men; pursue an affirmative action and enact a policy of quota system in employment of women for a ten year time frame in both public and private sectors; ensure continuity in policy making and decision making positions and: a certain percentage of political appointive posts must be reserved for women commensurate with the number of professionally and academically qualified women at the tertiary level. In this regard, it was recommended that thirty per cent of all appointive posts in the public sector should be women (Nigeria Country Report, 1995).

The Beijing Declaration supports an affirmative action of thirty per cent quota for women in all political structures. In addition the NGO forum on women (Beijing, 1995) had as its vision

> to bring together women and men to challenge, create and transform global structures and processes at all levels through the empowerment and celebration of women. We are committed to equality, peace, justice, inclusiveness, and full participation of all (p.6).

Women and the Future of Power Sharing

To what extent can the expectations of women as reflected in their demands be met in the future? What political arrangements are being made to guarantee the attainment of these objectives? This chapter will examine these questions from the framework of the recommendations of the 1994-95 Constitutional Conference on power sharing.

The groundwork carried out by several women's organisations at the national and international levels and the increased awareness generated by the campaign for gender equality ought to have a positive impact on gender participation in the proposed Fourth Republic. However, an assessment of the report of the constitutional conference does not indicate that this hope will be realised. First, the emphasis on the principles of freedom, equality, equity and justice gives the impression of gender-neutral recommendations which prefer to subsume gender issue under geographical and ethnic considerations. In fact, the very composition of the conference produced was gender biased. Of the three hundred and sixty-nine (369) participants, three-hundred and sixty-one (361) were males while only eight (8) were females; thus reflecting only 2.2 per cent female participation. Although, seventy-four per cent of the members were elected while twenty-six per cent were nominated by the Provisional Ruling Council, deliberate effort should have been made to ensure significant participation of women as such considerations were employed to ensure representation from every part of the country. In the report of the Constitutional Conference, it was noted that the gender profile of the conference reflected "the under-representation of women in national affairs despite their numerical strength."

The National Constitutional Conference Commission (NCCC), the body that planned the conference was itself male dominated. Of the nineteen members of the NCCC inaugurated in January 1994 only one member was female. The composition of the commission, charged with the responsibility of working a final draft of the agenda for the conference from inputs from people would no doubt have had an impact on the items eventually drawn up. In addition to the National Council for Women Societies' observation of gender bias (*Daily Times*, February 2, 1994), the Civil Liberties Organisation observed that the body was composed of individuals "representing no known constituency other than themselves" (FEE, 1994). In this case, the group, ninety-five per cent male, was bound to pay less attention to issues of gender equity and more attention to issues reflecting traditional gender stereotypes.

Indeed, it is unfortunate that no appreciable progress can be observed in the representation of women in the preparations for the Third and Fourth Republics. Shettima (1995) also noted that of the 567 members of the Constituent Assembly (CA) formed in 1988 to discuss the draft constitution, only fourteen members were women. This reflects a 2.5% representation of women in the CA. Furthermore, nine women (7.8%) as against 106 (92.2%) men were nominees of the government.

The domination of the conference by a single group (male) has several implications. First, it reinforces patriarchy. Second, for women's organisations who have committed great amounts of resources to engendering a gender balanced Nigerian political system, it is retrogressive.

Third, it has a psychological effect of trivialising women's issues or ``inoculating'' people against women's issues in such a way that more effort would be required in future to achieve more positive results in consciousness raising; especially so among people who hold strong traditional stereotypical views about women and who already experience dissonance resulting from the new messages and calls for gender equity. Fourth, contrary to the theme of the NGO Forum on women, ``Look at the World Through Women's Eyes'', the conference was again, as in previous efforts at constitution making, looking at the Nigerian political structure through the eyes of men, and not even through those of ``men and women''. Consequently, it is not surprising that many of the recommendations on women at the national and international levels as highlighted above were absent in the report of the Constitutional Conference.

The insignificant contribution of women also raises questions of government commitment to the advancement of women. To what extent is the government willing to go in engendering the political system of the nation? Is the government only concerned with welfare packages for women or, as the shift from women (BLP) to women in the family context, (FSP) reflects, is there a concern for women only in the context of making them better mothers and homemakers? Is the government still controlling women's lives and restricting them mainly to the private sphere?

On power sharing, the conference noting that ``power sharing had been responsible for much of the tensions, emotions, conflicts, and stresses and strains in most countries'', warned that ``a properly structured and balanced federation implies that *all geopolitical areas and or major units* should have access to power in order to give all sections of the country a sense of belonging to the nation through well-worked out avenues for participation''. This implies that from the outset the committee did not consider gender in its formula for power sharing. The most important factor in power sharing was geopolitical and the strategy recommended to ensure representativeness was equally informed by geopolitical considerations.

Again, to take care of equitable geopolitical power sharing, the principle of Federal Character was reaffirmed. It was observed that the principle, which was needed to promote a sense of belonging in the country, would help eliminate or at least minimise domination resulting from imbalance in appointments.

Another element that was considered relevant in power sharing was the proportional representation of all parties who participated in each election. The conference, in seeking to discourage the policy of ``winner-takes-all'' in the practice of democracy in Nigeria recommended in Section 148 sub-section 6 of the 1995 Draft Constitution that to make for a government of national unity, all parties that participate in elections should be given positions proportional to the percentage of votes scored at the polls or the number of seats won at the general elections.

If one examines the above recommendations for power sharing for the Fourth Republic, it is evident that the trend of neglect of the gender question in political power structure still persists and the next republic does not hold much promise for women. It is unfortunate that despite international achievements and to some extent local milestones in increasing awareness of women's issues, such issues were not considered important enough to be factored into attempts at political restructuring. From a gender perspective, political restructuring must address the question of equity, fairness and justice in the fundamental indices of power not only from the context of ethnic and geographical but also from the perspective of gender. Since the CC represents another attempt to work out a formula which guarantees freedom, equality, equity, justice and even-handed opportunities in all areas of governance, its recommendations should not only have been stated in gender neutral terms, it ought also to have taken care of gender differences in access to power. Thus, a quota should have been agreed upon and stated in the form of recommendations rather than being left to the discretion of the Provisional Ruling Council or any government in power. Granted that reservation of seats or the Federal Character principle may be considered by some as contradictory to the principle of democracy; but since this principle has been adopted to address geopolitical differences, it would not be against constitutional norms to also apply it to gender differences.

Women's Issues – Seen Only in the Context of Social Welfare

As with the work of its committee on power sharing, women's issues were not factored into the recommendations of the conferences' other committees except that on social welfare, which examined its mandate under six headings:
1. Education, Science and Technology
2. Education, Social Welfare and Housing
3. Utilities e.g., water, roads, electricity, communication and transportation
4. Agriculture e.g., food production, livestock, veterinary and forestry
5. Social development
6. The environment e.g., pollution of rivers, lakes, the neighbourhood

Of these, women's issues were discussed only in the context of illiteracy, child marriage and teenage pregnancy, and women and development.

First, in terms of illiteracy, it was recommended that:

> Government should make adequate arrangement for the education of special groups like women and the girl child, the gifted as well as marginalised groups like the nomads. (pg. 168)

In addressing family and child welfare issues, the committee recommended among others that the government should:

> minimise the incidence of various forms of child abuse, child neglect and make provisions that will eliminate the incidence of child marriage and teenage pregnancy.

Thirdly, a subsection of social development addressed women and development. As the report noted, this is one of the aspects of policy programmes of the Federal Ministry of Social Development that the committee felt should be ``emphasised and steps taken to give... the Force of the law.'' The committee therefore recommended that the government should:

(i) Eliminate those aspects of our cultural beliefs and practices which are due to ignorance, superstition or misconception, and which tend to degrade and dehumanise women and militate against their full development.

(ii) Promote and protect the rights of widows, single parent, single women, and ensure that women who marry outside their ethnic origins have equal rights and benefits as indigenes of their husbands' state.

(iii) Ensure and guarantee security of employment for women and that both public and private business establishments employing a hundred or more female workers of child-bearing age, provide day-care centres for their children.

(iv) Establish a Ministry for the Women and Family Affairs. (pp.173-174)

No doubt, the provisions stated above reflect a continuation of the status quo, in which women's issues remain confined to welfare and family spheres. In other words, provisions in the social welfare recommendations are seen as being consistent with women's needs. For feminists, democratic family structure has positive implications for a democratic society. However, gender relations at the family level is conceived of in terms of equity in power structure. In addition, while on the one hand the government says it is out to eliminate cultural beliefs and practices which militate against the full development of women, on the other hand, the recommendations of the conference generally ignore strategies for ensuring gender equality or at the least significant representation in power sharing. If one compares the demands of the women with the issues emphasised and recommended by the CC, one would see that concrete gender issues which women consider to have serious impact on their lives have not been addressed.

Towards Gender Equity in Power Sharing: Enabling and Disabling Situations

A comparison of the two per cent representation of women in the CA and CC with the percentage of seats occupied by women in parliament in developing nations highlights the near-absent role of Nigerian women in their country's political power structure. The Human Development Report (1993) indicated that sixteen per cent and fourteen per cent of seats were occupied by females in the parliaments of Mozambique and Cameroon respectively. In Cuba and Guyana, the figures were thirty-four per cent and thirty-seven per cent respectively. Following the global call for gender equity in governance and the Beijing Declaration, there is also a trend towards gender equity in governance of some African countries such as Tunisia and Ghana by the adoption of quotas of almost 50/50. Yet, in Nigeria, the most recent attempt to review the constitution did not propose at least an interim measure to correct the imbalance. As was discussed earlier, the provisions and recommendations of the CC have the potential to perpetuate male domination in the Nigerian power structure in the immediate future. No doubt, some prevailing conditions and circumstances relating to the handling of women's issues in Nigeria may have contributed to the neglect of the gender factor in political arrangements. This section of the paper therefore examines problems and issues militating against the concrete entrenchment of women in power and also offers suggestions for improved women's participation. Table 1 summarises the current disabling situation and proposes enabling conditions for bringing about successful integration of women into the political power structure.

Mama (1995) used the term "femocracy" to describe the anti-democratic female power structure which claims to exist for the advancement of ordinary women but is unable to do so because it is dominated by a clique of women whose interest and power base derive from being the wives of powerful men rather than from any actions of their own. One fallout of this phenomenon is the imposition of a class based gender oppression which is characterised by the imposition of ideas and programmes on the ordinary women, and the assumption by a few of the role of spokesperson and "expert" on all issues concerning women. This is achieved through a top-down administrative structure made up of "First Ladies" in all the three tiers of government and run along the military line of control.

The roles and functions of the first ladies have created ambiguity and confusion in terms of the real representatives on women's issues in Nigeria.

Governmental structures such as the National Commission for Women put in place to handle women's issues are empty shells because of the interference from first ladies whose ambit of operation and activities eclipse functions of the personnel in the women's commission. Furthermore, recent experience buttresses the point that such first ladies' agenda tend to be synonymous with the agenda of the commission. For example, Mrs Maryam Babangida initiated the BLP and encased it in the National Commission for women (NCW) with the promulgation of Decree 30, which was later replaced with Decree 42 (1992). The objective of the NCW were to promote the full utilisation of women in the development of human resources, promote the welfare of women in general and carry out the aims and objectives of BLP..In addition to Women's Commissions at the state and local government levels there were other units such as Women in Development units in Technical Ministries, Women Education Unit, and Women in Agriculture Unit. All these units are not independent of the "offices of the first ladies" because most government activities on women are controlled by the first ladies. No doubt, women need to transform the very nature of politics and development in order to have the freedom to make choices and live full lives. Despite the efforts of many women's organisations and groups, there is insufficient mechanism at all levels to promote the advancement of women. Furthermore, women and advocates of women's advancement do not have adequate institutional backing and power base to operationalise their concerns.

The government-recognised umbrella body for women – the National Council of Women's Societies – suffers from undue interference by the government and thus largely plays the role of a supplicant. Consequently, in reality, with this politics of jurisdictional clashes, the governmental structures on women's issues lack autonomy and are not empowered to represent women's causes. A further implication of this is the subtle but strong institutionalisation of indirect rule of women through the offices of their husbands, thus leading to the reinforcement and legitimisation of the tendency for women to seek success and access to power mainly through men rather than through direct and democratic access based on personal merit.

Table 1. Towards integrating Women into Nigerian Political Power Structure: Enabling and Disabling Conditions.

Disabling	Enabling
1. Unstated percentage or quota for female representation in public office	1. Institutionalisation of a quota for female representation
2. Weak and undemocratic coalition of women's organisation.	2. A strong and recognised coalition of women's organisations responsible for monitoring and advocacy.
3. "Femocracy", advancement of individuals in different women's groups	3. Feminism and true concern for gender equality.
4. Shallow/superficial understanding of women/gender issues	4. Deep understanding of women/gender issues
5. Indirect access of women to power through their husbands	5. Direct access of women to power.
6. Problems and issues identified and solutions predetermined by a clique of the ruling elite	6. Coparticipation of mobilisers and beneficiaries in identifying problems and solutions
7. Jurisdictional clashes between government organs and first ladies	7. Clear and Separate lines of control between government activities and interests and activities of the first ladies
8. Lack of continuity in government programmes on women	8. Continuity in government's programmes on women
9. Women's activities characterised by desensitising propaganda	9. Women's activities/programmes characterised by serious empowering and enlightening programmes
10. "Funfairising" of women's issues by the media, thereby focusing on personalities and events.	10. Media fare that focuses on issues and therefore offers educative content.

Another factor that has contributed to the little attention being paid to women's issues is the fact that focus on women's agenda lacks continuity. The past two decades have witnessed situations whereby governmental responses (through the activities of first ladies and women's commission) are greatly influenced by the ideas of first ladies. For example during the Babangida regime the focus was on rural women while the Abacha regime focused on women principally in the context of family life. Also in 1993, the NCW drafted a policy document on women to address women's problems in all aspects of national life, but because of the change in government, the policy has been abandoned. If this trend continues, it will be difficult to predict the future of the campaign for gender equality from the angle of governmental intervention.

The few women who occupy high public office usually have access to power by virtue of their personal relationship with people who are in power, and do not necessarily see women as their primary constituency. For example, the profile of women who participated in the CA shows that even though they were highly educated they had limited backgrounds in the women's movement (Nwabuzor, 1992). In the BLP case, Udegbe (1995) noted that selection of BLP personnel was not based on competence, understanding of or sensitivity to women's issues, but rather on a combination of factors such as husband's status, social status and social relationships. As a result there has been widespread ignorance and lack of innovation in the running of BLP by personnel lacking clearly-defined gender perceptions.

The point has been made that the level of consciousness on women's issues amongst the populace has been on the increase leading to a high level of awareness of these women's issues (e.g., Ihimodu, 1996). While one may agree that debates and talk about women have increased and people are now aware of the fact that there is a global agenda for the advancement of women, there is still a lot of ignorance, misinformation and shallowness in understanding of women's issues. Many do not understand what the issues are or have only minimal or inadequate knowledge of the global agenda. For some, such agenda run contrary to traditional African norms and religious doctrines, are foreign and constitute a war against men. Such level of ignorance is not limited to males but is also common among females. It is, therefore, not surprising that this superficial awareness has encouraged the trivialising of women's issues by many. Udegbe (1995) has noted that:

> despite the fact that a serious focus on women's issues is very much needed in African countries, the prolonged exposure of the populace to women's programmes which only pay lip service to this important issue and which establish faulty institutional frameworks will only succeed in systematically desensitising them to women's needs (pg. 81).

Perhaps a major factor that has contributed to the trivialising of women's issues in Nigeria is the funfair, publicity and propaganda that is associated with programmes run by first ladies. The primary goal of group activism is often to promote change in power relations and not to advance individuals within or outside the organising group (Wittig, 1996). Significant change in people's attitude and respect for gender equality in power structure at the individual, interpersonal, collective and cultural levels can be facilitated by more sincere and serious efforts perceived as participatory by the populace.

Pratkanis and Turner (1996) have observed that true democratic social change can only be accomplished by encouraging deliberative persuasion (a process that encourages thought, reflection and critical analysis) and forestalling propaganda (a process that truncates thought through the use of simplistic symbols and images that play on prejudices and emotions). Indeed some NGOs are translating into local languages the Beijing Platform of action in order to provide adequate information to the populace about women's concerns. It is important not only to seek superficial awareness but increase people understanding of the issues raised by advocates of women's advancement. The media has an important role to play in this respect; the prevalent tendency of "funfairising" women's issues by focusing on personalities and events, contribute to the trivialising of women's issues. The media should therefore be reoriented and sensitised to focus on women and gender issues with the aim of educating and promoting thought, reflection and critical analysis.

Conclusion

Many critics of the campaign for gender equality argue that Nigerian constitutions since independence have guaranteed equal rights and privileges to all citizens irrespective of their gender. While this appears just on paper, it must be emphasised that women, especially in the political arena, are being asked to play with men on an uneven field. Unfortunately, the recommendations of the CC do not have the potential to address the problem of gender imbalance, indeed male domination, in the unfolding political arrangement. Not much has changed in terms of government's commitment to a gender-balanced political arrangement. Similar to the Third Republic government's reactions to the voices of women have been to either trivialise, neglect or displace (Shettima 1995). Compared to men, women by virtue of their low level of education, economic power, subordinate roles etc. are disadvantaged and thus operate in a situation where they are least likely to have access to political power. The implication is that to make the playing field even in such a way as to put them in a position to compete with men, there is a need for an interim affirmative action. This must be understood and provided for in the constitution. It is only then that a truly just and workable constitution that guarantees equal privileges to citizens, particularly in terms of power sharing, would have emerged.

In addition, NGOs and other relevant advocates of women's advancement should seek to truly mobilise and sustain women's commitment and actions by helping to build links at different levels in the country. Such sustainable links, with agenda, objectives and actions drawn by a broad coalition of women can constitute pressure groups in demanding for significant representation of women in power sharing. They will also be able to monitor women's progress in terms of access to power at the grassroots, community, governmental and NGO levels.

References

Awe, B. (1992) ``Women and politics in historical perspectives.'' In J.A.A., Ayoade, E.J. Nwabuzor, and A. Sambo (eds.) *Women and Politics in Nigeria.* Abuja: Centre for Democratic Studies.

Awe, B. (1994) *Nigerian Women in Historical Perspective.* Ibadan: Sankore/Bookcraft

Daily Times, February 2, 1994, pg.2

FEE (1994) The National Conference: Issues, Controversies and Assessment. A policy Research Report. Ibadan: Foundations for Economic Education (FEE) *Guardian on Sunday,* April 27, 1997.

Ihimodu, I.I. (1996) *The Impact of the Better Life Programme on the Economic Status of Women.* Ibadan: IFRA

Mama, A. (1995) ``Feminism or Femocracy? State Feminism and Democratisation in Nigeria.'' Africa Development, *XX (1),* 37-58

Moser, C.O.N. (1993) *Gender Planning and Development: Theory, Practice and Training.* New York: Routledge.

Nwabuzor, E.J. (1992) ``Profile of Women in Nigerian Politics during the Transition.'' In J.A.A. Ayoade, E.J. Nwabuzor and A. Sambo (eds.) *Women and Politics in Nigeria.* Abuja: Centre for Democratic Studies.

NGO forum on Women: Beijing '95. Look at the World Through Women's Eyes. Final Report. 30 August-8 September.

Nigeria Country Report. 4th World Conference on Women, Beijing, 1995

Nwanko, N. (1996) *Gender Equality in Nigerian Politics.* Lagos: Deutchetz.

Olojede, I.A. (1990). ``Women Power and Political System''. In L. Olurode (ed.) *Women and Social Change in Nigeria:* Lagos: Unity

Pratkanis, A.R. and Turner, M.E. (1996). ``Persuasion and Democracy: Strategies for increasing Deliberative Participation and Enacting Social Change''. *Journal of Social Issues, 52,* 187-206.

Shettima, K.A. (1995) Engendering Nigeria's Third Republic. *African Studies Review, 38,* 61-98.

Udegbe, I.B. (1995) ``Better Life for Rural Women Programme: An Agenda for positive Change?'' *Africa Development, XX, (3)* 69-84.

Wittig, M.A. (1996). ``An Introduction to Social Psychological Perspectives on Grassroots Organising''. *Journal of Social Issues, 52,* 3-14.

CHAPTER 10

Dauda Abubakar

The Federal Character Principle, Consociationalism and Democratic Stability in Nigeria

Introduction

For long, democratic stability, national integration and sustainable socio-economic development have eluded the Nigerian post-colonial state. Although the country attained formal political independence from British hegemony since October 1, 1960, Nigeria still remains one of the most underdeveloped post-colonial states in the Third World that is characterised by high external debt, inflation, poverty, malnutrition, institutional decay in health, education and general infrastructures, urban dislocation and violent crimes (Ihonvbere, 1996:5; Bangura, 1986; Forrest, 1993; Joseph, 1991 Iyayi, 1986; Olukoshi, 1990).

In spite of its enormous oil wealth and large population as well as agricultural potentials, Nigeria has not been able to establish the relevant socio-political and economic framework for transformation and development. Since independence, Nigerian politics has been essentially characterised by ethno-regional conflicts, secessionism, religious bigotry, coups and counter-coups, corruption and mismanagement (Joseph, 1991; Forrest, 1986; Falola and Ihonvbere, 1985; Ekekwe, 1986; Toyo, 1994).

Although efforts have been made by successive regimes – military and civilian – to resolve the basic problems of political stability and national integration through diverse structural reforms such as state and local government creation, introduction of the federal character principle in the 1979 Constitution and the use of "zoning system" as a mechanism for power sharing, the problematic of national question still looms large in Nigeria. In fact, the annulment of the June 12 1993 Presidential elections, the sacking of the Shonekan – led Interim National Government (ING), the return of the military on November 17 1993 and the subsequent reversal of the transition to civil rule programme are all pointers to the tortuous path of Nigeria's search for a stable democratic social order.

This chapter argues that the search for international and democratic stability must necessarily address fundamental questions such as: what constitutes the theoretical premise of federal character and its implications for political stability in Nigeria? Second, to what extent does resource allocation and distribution as advocated by federal character principle address the fundamental problem of national unity and integration? Third, does the behaviour of the political class in terms of access to state power and resources affect the stability of the country? Fourth, to what extent can the adoption of consociational principles enhance regime legitimacy and political stability in Nigeria?

In trying to answer the foregoing questions, the chapter is divided into three parts. The first section revisits the issue of federal character principle by examining the origins of that debate in the formative stages of the 1979 Constitution. It identifies the basic premise, content and implications of federal character principle as applied during the Second Republic (1979-83) under Shagari's regime. The second section of the chapter examines the concept of consociationalism, and argues that unless there is a basic attempt at accommodation and acceptance of one another by the political class and, indeed, Nigeria's diverse ethnic groups, democratic stability can hardly flourish in Nigeria. The third section is the conclusion of the chapter.

Federal Character Principle: Its Premise and Practice in Post-colonial Nigeria

Although the British colonialists dominated and exploited what came to be known as Nigeria through the agency of the colonial state under Lord Lugard, the Northern and Southern Protectorates were administered differently. While in the North, the British utilised the system of Indirect Rule and incorporated the Emirs into the colonial administrative structure, in the South, particularly among the Igbo, colonialism depended on its appointees – the warrant chiefs. As one analyst rightly put it, the policy of indirect rule which was premised on the principle of divide and rule,

> provided a strong argument for keeping the course of development in the Northern and Southern provinces rigorously apart, for reducing all contacts between the peoples of the two groups of provinces to the absolute minimum and for excluding the former group of provinces from the sphere of the Legislative Council (Afigbo, 1989)

This pattern of uneven development was exacerbated not only at the political level, but also in the educational sphere. While Christian missions were allowed to establish schools in the southern provinces, they were curtailed from doing so in the North under the pretext that the North was islámic in religious practice (Raufu, 1986:84; Kukah, 1993). The disparity in educational advancement between the North and the South unfortunately widened, and with it, the magnitude of prejudices. According to one scholar:

> ...the colonial administration passed on to their Nigerian wards the prejudices which had enabled them to think and act in the belief that this "informal federation" was a marriage of convenience between incompatibles. The North looked down on the South as uncivilised, pagan, indisciplined, rowdy and nakedly materialistic. The South returned this contempt with compliments, regarding the North as feudalistic, conservative, uneducated... and as the pliant tools of the imperial master (Afigbo, 1989:9).

The colonial policy of indirect rule not only exacerbated the North-South dichotomy but also introduced regionalism via the 1946 Richards Constitution (Post and Vickers, 1973; Mackintosh, 1966; Kirk-Greene, 1971; Dudley, 1982). Tom Forrest (1993:39) correctly argues that British colonial policy entrenched a tripartite regional system of government in which the three regions of North, East, and West were dominated by the major ethnic groups – Hausa-Fulani, Igbo and the Yoruba respectively. Underlying the competition between the ethno-regional groups

> ...was the struggle for economic advancement by individuals and communities and the fear of political and economic domination accentuated by the uneven development of disparate communities. These fears were strikingly evident in the bitter controversy over census and in the aggressive ethnicity that came to the surface. Despite the operation of a federal system of government that ensured considerable decentralisation of powers, there was too much at stake at the centre for a compromise to be struck.

The constant desire by the diverse ethnicities in Nigeria to either control the federal centre or ensure access to the "national cake" has constantly been at the centre of the national question and federal character debates (Raufu, 1986; Ekeh and Osaghae, 1989; NPSA, 1985). Under Gowon, Nigeria not only went through a bitter and destructive civil war, the federation was also restructured from four regions into twelve states. As the pressure for more states persisted, the Murtala-Obasanjo regime increased the number to nineteen states and introduced far-reaching reforms at the grassroots by giving autonomy to local governments. In its effort to return the country to civil rule, the Murtala-Obasanjo regime designed an elaborate transition programme and set up a Constitution Drafting Committee (CDC). It was at the 1975-76 CDC debates that the concept of federal character as a political lexicon emerged in Nigeria's search for a stable democratic order.

The tragic history of Nigeria's First Republic greatly influenced the perceptions and attitudes of the CDC sub-committee that examined the powers and functions of the Executive and Legislative arms of government in a multi-ethnic or plural society. In an effort to promote national unity and integration, the sub-committee proposed the adoption of what it termed Federal Character Principle which, according to the framers of the 1979 Constitution, is anchored on the:

> ....distinctive desire of the peoples of Nigeria to promote national unity, foster national loyalty and give every citizen of Nigeria sense of belonging to the nation notwithstanding the diversities of ethnic origin, culture, language or religion which may exist and which it is their desire to nourish, harness to the enrichment of the Federal Republic of Nigeria (Afigbo, 1989:4)

Simply put, therefore, federal character principle was aimed at creating a sense of belonging and participation by the diverse ethnic groups and political groupings in the governance of the post-colonial state. It was an outcome of the anxieties and fears of domination that characterises ethno-regional relation in Nigeria. Furthermore, federal character principle and its application in the governance of the Nigerian post-colonial state is symptomatic of the desire by the political class in the Second Republic to ensure access to and siphoning of national wealth through patron-client linkages (Joseph, 1991; Forrest, 1993:77).

Section 14(3) of the 1979 Constitution stipulates the fundamental premise of the federal character principle that:

> The composition of the federal government or any of its agencies and the conduct of their affairs shall be carried out in such a manner as to recognise the federal character of Nigeria and the need to promote national unity and to command national loyalty. Accordingly, the predominance in that government or its agencies of persons from a few states or from a few ethnic or other sectional groups shall be avoided

This provision with its emphasis on distribution of the "national cake" was not limited to the federal level and its parastatals; but it was also extended to cover states and local governments. Thus, patronage in governance was entrenched not only at the federal centre but also at the periphery i.e. the state and local government levels. Individuals that are elected or appointed into offices perceived their roles as primarily representing particular ethnic, regional or even religious interests. This process, according to Richard Joseph, leads to what he incisively describes as a prebendal system. Prebendalism, as he puts it, could be seen,

> not only as one in which the offices of state are allocated and then exploited as benefices by the officeholders, but also as one where such a practice is legitimated by a set of political norms according to which the appropriation of such offices is not just an act of

individual greed or ambition but concurrently the satisfaction of the short-term objectives of a subset of the general population (Joseph, 1991:67).

Federal character principle as practised during the tumultuous period of the Second Republic (1979-83) under Shagari's leadership, was essentially focused on enhancing the dominance of the National Party of Nigeria (NPN) through patronage. The constitutional provision of federal character and zoning system within the party provided the regime with a legal basis for appointing trusted prebends, clients and hangers-on in strategic offices who in turn manipulated their powers by allocation of contracts, import licences, access to bank loans, fertilizer etc. Thus through the control of state power at the federal centre, the NPN not only enhanced her leverage through patron-client alliances that cut across ethno-regional and religious cleavages, but also appropriated federal character principle to ensure its hegemony in the states by appointing Presidential Liasion Officers.

According to Tom Forrest (1993:76) the application of the federal character (as well as zoning) principle by the NPN not only led to poor appointments at ministerial levels and boards of federal parastatals, but also enhanced mediocrity rather than merit. Corruption and mismanagement of resources became the order of the day. As a weak party that drew its support from the so-called "Big Men" or patrons, indiscipline in both party and state governance became prevalent. Shagari could neither control the party nor provide a strong leadership and a sense of direction to national policies. As Tom Forrest (1993:89) perceptively argues, the organisational weakness of the NPN meant that:

> ...it was unable to effectively institutionalise patronage in ways that did not undermine the national economy. Its major concern was the distribution of state patronage on a national basis. This political preoccupation was built into the very structure of the party. Zoning at the level of party representation and the principle of federal character both served to distribute state patronage and secure a measure of national integration. Political dispute centred on the distribution of federal patronage and on federal-state relations where power shifted away from the centre to the states. These political concerns together with political weight of commercial interests intent on pursuing the accumulation of wealth through personal connection with those who held state power, helped to ensure that no clear issues or policies emerged from the process of political competition. Economic management, policy making and implementation were exposed to the political pressures of distributive demands, competition for rents, and party patronage.

The indiscipline of the political class manifested in intra and inter-party squabbles, corruption, economic mismanagement, rigged elections, political thuggery and violence provided the Nigerian military the opportunity to terminate the Second Republic in December 1983.

Nigeria's experience during the Second Republic, as shown above, exposes the limitations of federal character principle as a mechanism for enhancing national integration and participatory democracy in plural societies. One of the fundamental weaknesses of federal character as shown in the political practice of the Second Republic is that it tends to enthrone mediocrity in governance, at the expense of merit and professionalism. Also in the name of representation and national unity, federal character allows ethno-regional patrons and their clients to exploit and mismanage state resources without contributing to any meaningful development. Furthermore, by focusing on regional and ethnic representation, federal character exacerbates differentiation instead of enhancing mutual trust, accommodation and national unity. So long as national leaders perceive themselves as ethnic, regional or religious champions and ``warlords'' engaged in a struggle for the ``national cake'', socio-economic development and democratic stability will elude Nigeria. The 1983 squabbles within the NPN over the presidential ticket and the subsequent withdrawal of Chief M.K.O. Abiola shows how federal character and the manipulation of zoning in political practice could precipitate instability, ethnic chauvinism and bigotry. If the entrenchment of federal character principle in the 1979 Constitution did not enhance national integration, what model of democratic participation and accommodation could ameliorate instability in Nigeria? To what extent can the establishment of Federal Character Commission by the Abacha regime ensure participation, unity and political stability in the fourth republic? What lessons can Nigeria learn from consociational approach to political stability? In the next section, I shall examine the basic premises of consociational model of democratic governance with a view to identifying its applicability or otherwise to the Nigerian condition.

Consociationalism, Empowerment and Democratic Stability

In his major study on consociational democracy in plural societies, Arend Lijphart persuasively argues that the model of consociationalism can be defined in terms of four fundamental attributes: (i) government by a grand coalition of the political leaders of all significant segments of the society. Such grand coalition, Lijphart (1977:25) contends could take different forms, such as `a grand coalition cabinet in a parliamentary system, a grand council or committee with important advisory functions, or a grand coalition of a president and other top officeholders in a presidential system;" (ii) the mutual veto or ``concurrent majority ``rule, which serves as an additional protection, especially for vital minority interests; (iii) proportionality as the principal standard of political representation, civil service appointments, and allocation of resources and (iv) a degree of autonomy for each segment to run its own affairs.

In January 1966, Ironsi who took over power following the collapse of the First Republic attempted to restructure Nigeria's lop-sided federalism into a unitary system (Dudley, 1973; Kirk-Greene, 1971). However, this restructuring met with bloody resistance from the North because of the fear of domination. The pogrom that followed in most urban centres, particularly in the North, was directed against the Igbo because of the perception by the Hausa-Fulani that the January 15th 1966 coup was not only spearheaded by Igbo officers, but was also a calculated strategy to eliminate key political leaders from the North. Thus through cumulative ethno-regional fear of domination, prejudices as well as manipulation of socio-cultural cleavages by the political class in the First Republic, Nigeria drifted into anarchy and civil war. Inspite of the tragic lessons of the civil war, communal violence along ethnic and religious cleavages continues to pose serious threats to national integration and democratic stability in Nigeria (Elaigwu, 1993; Ihonvbere, 1996; Ibrahim, 1987; Bangura, 1986; Forrest, 1993; Falola and Ihonvbere, 1985; Ihonvbere, 1994; Nnoli, 1995; Diamond, 1982, 1984). Thus, the consociational model which explicitly defines specific modalities for power sharing has some relevance in resolving the national question problematic in Nigeria.

A major dimension of the national question which has plagued Nigeria since its amalgamation in 1914 has been the issue of marginalisation of minorities. The annulment of June 12 1993 elections as well as recent events in Ogoniland (Naanen, 1995) and the subsequent execution of Ken Saro-Wiwa along with eight other Movement for the Survival of Ogoni People, (MOSOP) leaders clearly suggest the necessity of adopting power-sharing mechanisms as spelt out in the consociationalist model to ensure national unity. A system of grand coalition at the national level with built-in mechanisms of mutual veto, proportional representation and segmental autonomy will go a long way in enhacing national unity and integration in Nigeria. As Bangura, (n.d) cogently asserts,

> ...power-sharing arrangements, in which all groups are represented in government, has the advantage of ensuring stability and of getting the parties that would otherwise be locked in conflict to understand each other's interests and develop a system of trust in governing the country. Such arrangements have the additional advantage of establishing a basic level of consensus in the management of the instruments of violence as all parties may be represented in the key institutions that deal with security.

Thus, in the Nigerian context, a grand coalition will draw representation not only from the various states of the federation, but also such interests as minorities, professional groups, students, workers and the peasantry.

The existence of mutual veto in the grand coalition not only enhances the empowerment of oppressed groups but also gives each segment a complete guarantee of political protection. As John C. Calhoun suggests, the principle of mutual veto or ``concurrent majority'' invests each segment in the grand coalition with ``the power of protecting itself, and places the rights and safety of each where only they can be securely placed, under its own guardianship. Without this there can be no systematic, peaceful, or effective resistance to the natural tendency of each to come into conflict with the others'' (Calhoun, 1953:28). According to Calhoun, since the veto is available to all as a potential weapon, it gives a feeling of security which makes the actual use improbable. In fact, by giving each segment the institutional power of self-protection, all strife and struggle between them for ascendancy is prevented, and thereby every feeling calculated to weaken the attachment to the whole is suppressed (Lijphart, 1977:37)

Another important element of the consociationalist model which is relevant in the resolution of Nigeria's national question is proportional representation. According to Lijphart, proportionality ``as a neutral and impartial standard of allocation, removes a large number of potentially divisive problems from the decision-making process and thus lightens the burdens of consociational government.'' Furthermore, it allows all groups not only to participate proportionally in the decision-making process, but also to influence policy outcome. Thus, in the Nigerian context, the proportional involvement of the diverse groups and interests in areas such as revenue allocation, and placement into strategic federal parastatals will not only enhance a sense of belonging, but it will increase trust, national unity and integration.

Unlike the federal character principle which emphasises the bridging of unequal development through sharing the ``national cake'', consociationalism through its basic principles of grand coalition, mutual veto, proportional representation and segmental autonomy not only enhances group participation – and therefore empowerment – but also provides guarantees against some forms of domination. According to Fred Onyeoziri:

> The much greater effectiveness of consociationalism derives from the fact that it seeks to restructure both the behaviour of the elite and the model of democracy which have hitherto provided the framework for Nigerian politics. The federal character principle, on the other hand, merely ``white-washes'' the surface while leaving the inner core of adversarial attitude and a conservative model of democracy largely untouched (Onyeoziri, 1989).

The adversarial attitude to politics and winner-takes-all or zero-sum syndrome in Nigerian politics have greatly contributed to instability of the post-colonial state. There is, therefore, the urgent need for considering models of governance that consciously takes into consideration the complex and plural nature of the Nigerian federation and prescribes power-sharing mechanisms that will ensure collective participation and empowerment of the generality of the populace (Leftwich: 1994; Ake, 1994). According to Ihonvbere, this must begin with:

> ... a struggle to remove the institutions, processes, and structures which have enabled... elites to dominate society without accountability. It is these institutions and structures which they privatised with the end of formal colonialism that have made it possible for the elite to exploit the people, to manipulate primordial loyalties, and to reproduce conditions of backwardness in [post-colonial Nigeria) (Ihonvbere, 1995)

More specifically, in the Nigerian context, the institutionalism of federal character principle, "zoning", arbitrary use of "quota system" in civil service appointments, admission into both federal and state institutions of higher learning, promotions within security apparatuses have all been turned into avenues for prebendalism, nepotism and the entrenchment of ethno-regional, religious and sectarian chauvinism which are destructive to the very survival of the country and its peoples. Thus, any agenda for political restructuring of Nigeria to resolve the diverse dimensions of the national question (Raufu, 1986) must proceed along the path of empowering the people, their organisations and communities. According to Mohammed Halfani (1993:33) "empowerment is the very essence of human development, not just a means to an end."

Within the last decade, Nigeria under military rule has experienced diverse restructuring at political and economic levels. At the political level, for example, the number of states in the federation was increased from nineteen in 1979 to twenty-one in 1987, and thirty in 1991. The Abacha regime increased the number of states to thirty-six and that of local governments to seven-hundred and seventy-two in 1996. A more far-reaching decision, however, centres on the adoption of rotational power sharing and zoning of offices as recommended by the Constitutional Conference. In the 1995 independence anniversary broadcast to the nation, Abacha declared that the Provisional Ruling Council had decided that:

> ...the proposal of *rotational power sharing* should be accepted. This option will apply to all levels of government. The PRC has also endorsed a modified presidential system (with) six identifiable geographical groups ... North-East, North-West, Middle Belt, South-West, East-Central, and Southern Minority. The national political offices, which will be filled by candidates on a rotational basis, are: the president, vice-president, prime-minister, deputy prime-minister, senate president and the speaker of the House of Representatives. This power-sharing arrangement, which shall be

entrenched in the constitution, shall be at the federal level and applicable for an experimental period of thirty years.

In addition to this, the Head of State announced the establishment of a Federal Character Commission charged with the responsibility of implementing, at different levels of government, the spirit and letter of federal character principle. It could be noted from the political restructuring that no effort was made to consciously involve the diverse groups and interests in the programme of the restructuring. By zoning offices along ethno-regional lines, the regime has not fundamentally incorporated workers, students, peasants and other oppressed minorities in the federation. Simply put, it has not empowered the people who are the agents and essence of development. Empowerment goes beyond ``zoning'' offices, restructuring the federation and clinging on to federal character. As Sandbrook (1993b:2) argues the process of empowerment ``involves transforming the economic, social, psychological, political and legal circumstances of the currently powerless;'' it involves ``the emergence of group identities (or community), the development of autonomous and coherent popular organisations and the defence of, and education about, the legal rights of the popular sectors.'' In the incisive words of Ihonvbere (1995:153) empowerment involves

> ...a form of socio-economic and political restructuring which removes the locus of power from the current custodians of state power, and enables the currently disadvantaged to meet their basic needs, fully participate in decision-making, and provide opportunities to challenge internal and external [oppression].

So far, our argument has basically been that although federal character principle has been conceived as a policy mechanism for addressing the contradictions of Nigeria's national question arising from British colonial policies of divide and rule, as well as uneven development; the political class which inherited power since independence manipulates state power, ethno-regional, religious and sectarian cleavages for its selfish ends. This is clearly illustrated by the political experiences of the Second Republic during which NPN as the dominant party at the federal level reduced the state and its institutions as avenues for patronage, rent-seeking, corruption and primitive accumulation. This political practice, in turn, undermined any possibility of enthroning popular democracy. I also suggested that in order to ensure democratic stability, political participation and empowerment, it is necessary to establish mechanisms of power sharing as exemplified by the consociationalist model.

Conclusion

Although efforts have been made by both civilian and military regimes to address the problematic of the national question in the Nigerian federation through policies of state and local government creation, federal character principle, ``zoning'', ``quota system'' and more recently ``rotational power sharing'' among six geo-political groups, the endemic problems of ethno-regional, religious and sectarian bigotry persist in Nigeria. These problems constitute serious threats to the survival of the Nigerian federation, retards the march to nationhood as well as the enthronement of a stable democratic socio-political order. Thus, any restructuring of the political space in the Nigerian post-colonial state should necessarily guarantee basic freedoms, the enthronement of a culture of public accountability, probity and responsibility as well as the empowerment of the generality of the populace within the framework of a national popular state (Ihonvbere, 1995:155). Such a state should draw its legitimacy from the people and anchor its operation on consensus-building mechanisms of power sharing rather than the dead-end zero-sum approaches that have characterised Nigerian politics since independence. The restructuring of the Nigerian state along consociationalist model of governance will enhance political stability which is necessary for economic transformation as we approach the twenty-first century.

Bibliography

Afigbo, A.E. ``Federal Character: Its Meaning and History'', in Ekeh, P.P. and Osaghae, E.E. (1989) (eds) *Federal Character and Federalism in Nigeria*. Ibadan: Heinemann Books Ltd., 1989

Ake, C. *Democratization of Disempowerment in Africa*. Lagos: CASS. 1994

Bangura, Y. ``Structural Adjustment and the Political Question''. *Review of African Political Economy*. No. 37, 1986 pp. 24-37.

――――― ``The Crisis of Underdevelopment and the Transition to Civil Rule: Conceptualizing the Question of Democracy in Nigeria''. *Africa Development*. Vol. 8, (1) 1988 pp.33-50.

――――― The Search for Identity: Ethnicity, Religion and Political Violence (UNRISD) mimeo, n.d.

Calhoun, J.C. *A Disquisition on Government*. New York: Liberal Arts Press, 1953.

Dudley, B.J. *Instability and Political Order: Politics and Crisis in Nigeria*. Ibadan: Ibadan University Press,1973.

Diamond, L. ``Cleavage, Conflict and Anxiety in Nigeria's Second Republic.'' *Journal of Modern African Studies*, 20, 4, 1982 pp.629-668.

Ekekwe, E. *Class and State in Nigeria*. Lagos: Longman, 1986.

Ekeh, P.P. and Osaghae, E.E. (eds) *Federal Character and Federalism in Nigeria*. Ibadan: Heinemann Books Nig. Ltd., 1989

Elaigwu, J.I. *The Shadow of Religion on Nigerian Federalism: 1960-93*. Abuja: NCIR, 1993.

Falola, T. and Ihonvbere, J.O. *The Rise and Fall of Nigeria's Second Republic*. London: Zed Books, 1985.

Forrest, T. *Politics and Economic Development in Nigeria*. Boulder, Colorado: Westview Press, 1993.

Halfani, M.S. "Constraints on Empowerment", in Richard Sandbrook and Mohammed Halfani, (eds)., *Empowering People: Building Community, Civil Associations and Legality in Africa*. Toronto: Centre for Urban and Community Studies, University of Toronto, 1993.

Ihonvbere, J.O. "The "irrelevant state," Ethnicity, and the Quest for nationhood in Africa". *Ethnic and Racial Studies*. Vol 17(1) 1994, pp.42-60.

───── "Beyond Governance: The State and Democratization in sub-Sahara Africa." *Journal of Asian and African Studies*, No. 50, 1995, pp. 141-158.

───── "Are things falling Apart? The Military and the Crisis of Democratization in Nigeria". *Journal of Modern African Studies*, 34(1) 1996, pp.3-33.

Joseph R.A. *Democracy and Prebendal Politics in Nigeria; The Rise and Fall of the Second Republic*. Ibadan: Spectrum Books, 1991.

Kirk Greene, A. *Crisis and Conflict in Nigeria: A Documentary Source Book* (2 Vol.) London: University Press, 1971.

Lijphart, A. *Democracy in Plural Societies: A Comparative Exploration*. New Haven: Yale University Press, 1977.

Mackintosh, J.P. (ed.) *Nigerian Government and Politics*. London: Allen and Unwin, 1966.

Nnoli, O. *Ethnicity and Democracy in Africa*. Oxford: Malthouse CASE Occasional Monograph series No.4, 1994.

───── *Ethnicity and Development in Nigeria*. London; Avery, 1995a.

───── "Ethnic Conflicts and Democratization in Africa". Paper for 8th General Assembly CODESRIA, Dakar, 1995b.

Nigerian Political Science Association (NPSA) "Military Rule and the National Question," Proceedings of 12th Annual Conference, 1985.

Olukoshi, A. (ed) *Nigerian External Debt Crisis: Its Management*. Lagos: Malthouse, 1990.

Onyeoziri, F.E. "Consociationalism and the Nigerian Practice"; in Ekeh, P and Osaghae, E.E. (eds.)

Post, K.W.J. and Vickers, M. *Structure and Conflict in Nigeria, 1960-66*. London: Heinemann, 1973.

Raufu, A.M. ``The National Question and Radical Politics in Nigeria'', *Review of African Political Economy* No. 37, 1986, pp. 81-96.

Sandbrook, R. ``Introduction'' to Richard Sandbrook and Mohammed Halfani, (eds). *Op. cit*, 1993b.

CHAPTER 11

C.C. Agbodike

Federal Character Principle and National Integration

Introduction

The problem of acrimonious existence among the diverse groups and interests in the federation of Nigeria leading to mutual distrust and inter-community conflicts has become perennial and endemic in the nation's body-politic and has militated against the political stability of the country since indepedence. The fear of domination of one ethnic group or section of the country by another and the national question of who gets what and how the 'national cake' should be shared constitute a major factor of this problem. This situation seriously hampers efforts at national integration as it applies to the building of a nation-state out of the disparate ethnic, geographic, social, economic and religious elements in the country.

The doctrine or principle of federal character was formulated and put into use by the government to address and hopefully mitigate this problem so as to ensure a peaceful, stable and integrated Nigeria.

In this chapter, efforts will be made, first to examine the historical antecedents to the problem of conflict and instability in Nigeria and the concern which the government has shown about the situation. This will be followed by a discussion of the concept and imperative of the federal character principle as a *sine qua non* for national integration in Nigeria. Next, we critically take a look at the problems and prospects of the federal character principle as a recipe for national integration. A few suggestions and recommendations on how to make the federal character principle a veritable instrument of national integration will then follow. Finally, we make concluding remarks.

Historical Antecedents to the Problem of Conflict and Instability in Nigeria

Nigeria is a nation state created as a result of British colonial enterprise in the territory and consists of a conglomeration of ethnic groups and fatherlands which are heterogenous in many respects. These include the diversity or pluralism of language, religion, socio-political and economic formations as well as administrative styles, social norms and personality types. There are also diversities among them resulting from factors of historical evolution, disproportionate population sizes, unequal economic resources and educational attainments. There are diversities, too, in social wants, needs and preferences as well as in talents and opportunities. These differences tend to generate mutual suspicion and misunderstanding which in turn give rise to conflicts. In fact, conflicts generated by these differences are such that at times, some writers and commentators expressed views showing that they are "highly sceptical about the continuing existence of Nigeria as a corporate entity." (Musa, 1985:112).

It is pertinent to trace briefly here the historical antecedents of these conflicts and how they sowed the seeds of mutual suspicion and disunity and consequently led to socio-economic disruptions and disarticulations which created situations of instability in the country.

The root cause of disunity, conflict and instability in Nigeria can be traced to certain colonial policies and practices in the country. For instance, the British colonial government evolved a piecemeal constitutional framework for the Northern and Southern segments of the country which were eventually amalgamated in 1914. Again, with the introduction of the Clifford Constitution in 1922 and the establishment of the Legislative council for Lagos (which generally legislated for Southern Nigeria to the exclusion of the North), Southerners were incrementally brought in to participate in the legislative affairs of their region ahead of their northern counterparts. This disparate constitutional and administrative arrangement, which went on until 1947 when the North and the South were brought together under a single legislative authority for the first time, was said to be fatal for nation-building and for the Nigerian nation state. According to one view, "the fact that a common constitutional framework for the whole country evolved piecemeal served to accentuate political diversities in an already diverse country" (*This Week*, 14 March 1988:10)

Again the Richards Constitution broke the country into three regions, the North, the East and the West. Each of these regions consisted of groups of majority and minority ethnic groups with the Hausa-Fulani being dominant in the North; the Yoruba in the West and the Igbo in the East, each of which was mutually distrustful of the other. With the emergence of the regions came sectional loyalties which, according to Osaghae (1989:443) "were built on the bogus theory of regionalism, that is, that one should be loyal to and protect the interest of one's region to the exclusion of others". Thus, the North was for the Northerners, the East for the Easterners and the West for the Westerners. Thus, the policy of regionalism, according to Ogunojemite (1987:226) created the federation after independence, this class "embarked on the use of political machinery to pursue their class interests ..." (Nnoli 1978:145). And more often than not, the struggles among factions of this class were transformed into struggles for state power. Nigerian history is replete with how the members of this class have unduly orchestrated the diversities in the nation and used them to spark off disruptive local and national cataclysms in the country. The events leading to the civil war and other controversies and clashes thereafter are reminiscent of such developments, which are inimical to the unity and stability of the country.

The successive governments of Nigeria were not unmindful of the explosive state of affairs in the country and so took steps to experiment on social and political engineering that would not only promote harmonious existence among the various ethnic groups and diverse interests but would also bring peace unity and stability to the country. For example, the NPC administration of Sir Abubakar Tafawa Balewa took steps to form a broad-based government through the establishment of alliances with other parties in 1959 and 1964. These alliances proved incapable of weathering the storms generated by regional and ethnic rivalries and so broke up no sooner than they were formed.

Again, the shortlived administration of Major-General Aguiyi Ironsi promulgated Decree 34 which abolished the federal structure of government and established a unitary system of administration. The aim was to do away with regionalism and its attendant ethnic and sectional loyalties which impeded efforts at national reconstruction and integration. Unfortunately, however, the move was not well received by many Nigerians, particularly from the North, who saw it as a ploy for Igbo ethnic dominance in the country. Similarly, the move to keep the regions slightly apart during the *Aburi Accord* in Ghana, at the heat of the Nigerian crisis in 1967, amounting to a confederation, was rejected as it could result in the end of Nigeria as a single country.

In 1967, following Colonel Ojukwu's threat of secession, and in order to restore the federal structure of government, General Gowon broke up the country into twelve states. The exercise was also aimed at redressing the structural imbalance in the federation and accomodating the demand of the minorities in the regions of self-realisation and self-assertion, and, "equalizing access to the means of development and political power" (Okpu 1989:358). The process of state creation was continued by the break up of the country into nineteen states in 1976, during General Murtala Mohammed regime, twenty-one states in 1987 and thirty states in 1991 respectively during General Ibrahim Babangida's administration; and thirty-six states in 1996 during the current General Ibrahim Sani Abacha regime.

disunity by reducing the country into a tri-national state.

Next, the Macpherson Constitution of 1951 introduced th[e] system of government which was finally adopted by the 1954 Constitut[ion]. 1954 federal constitution consolidated the regions, gave autonomy and effective power and made regional power attract[ive]. 1963, too, a fourth region, the Mid West Region, was carved out [of] then Western Region. But one significant feature of the Nigerian federation w[hich] impinged on the stability of the country was its unbalanced nature wh[ere] the northern region alone had more than half of the country's populati[on] and was larger than the other regions put together. This, in effe[ct] ensured vertical built-in control of the federation by that region. Surely thi[s] was a defective political framework for nation-building especially as the North which benefited from that arrangement held on to it and used it, even after the attainment of independence, to redress the claimed disadvantages of its people. The North, too, counting on its size and numerical strength argued for and won fifty per cent representation in the federal legislature and used its controlling position to wield power and appropriate the gains incidental thereof.

From the foregoing, it was not surprising that all the political parties formed to contest for power had ethnic/regional bases. Each was formed in response to the perceived threat of domination by the other. As a result, the NCNC led by Nnamdi Azikiwe, an Igbo, though it had nationalist orientation, nevertheless, had an Igbo ethnic perspective. The Action Group (AG) led by Obafemi Awolowo was formed to counter the perceived threat of Igbo domination. The Northern Peoples Congress (NPC) was founded, in response to the fear of southern domination, by the Hausa-Fulani aristocracy of the North. Thus, while these regional political leaders were united in the nationalist cause of securing independence, this sense of fear and the rivalry implicit in it, engendered severe political contradictions. The situation became very volatile after independence as the federal government exercised ascendant control over the regions as well as over the allocation of centrally-collected resources.

The relationship between majority and minority groups was also a veritable source of instability in Nigeria. The minority groups tried to assert their separateness and clamoured for a political structure which would free them from the domination of the major ethnic/cultural configurations. In support of these moves, Chief Awolowo and a few others preached the virtues of ethnic federalism based upon a large number of ethnic states. (Crawford Young 1993:302)

Again, as Ayam (1987:121) has contended, ``much of the instability of the Nigerian nation state is due to factional struggle and lack of unity within the Nigerian ruling class''. On acquiring political control of

The quota system was also introduced and practised from around 1958. The measure was intended to ensure equitable representation of the various groups in the country. According to Ekeh (1989:38) the system was meant "to give opportunities in education, appointment and employment... to disadvantaged groups and areas and to enable them to compete and catch up with the more advanced areas and sections of the nation". The quota system was also used for recruitment into the army, the police force and other defence and security services. Civil servants were also recruited and appointed on the basis of representative quota system.

The Concept and Imperative of the Federal Character Principle and the Quest for National Integration

The discussion above paints a gloomy scenario of the tensions, crises and problems that are endemic in the Nigerian body politic. The measures discussed above, too, sought to lay a solid foundation in terms of who gets what and to eliminate the tendencies and circumstances which give rise to mutual suspicion and unhealthy rivalries and which generate inter-group frictions and so exacerbate the disintegration rather than promote the unity of the country. But unfortunately, these measures failed to achieve the desired objective. For instance, the national question, which has found expression in such phenomena as the census, political party representation, revenue allocation, the failure of the unitarist administrative experiment of General Ironsi's government and the question of the survival of the federation after the bloody civil war (1967-70), continues to pose a serious threat to the country. The creation of new states institutionalised another political monster of statism in place of regionalism. What is more, there were serious grumblings, especially in the South, over the application of the quota system by the power brokers from the North.

Thus, to resolve these issues and to ensure structural balance of claims and gains by the various groups and interests in Nigeria, the federal character principle was conceived and its application became imperative as a directive principle of state policy. The term, federal character, was coined by the Constitution Drafting Committee (CDC) which drafted the 1979 Constitution of the Federal Republic of Nigeria. The term gained wide currency and usage after it was embodied in that constitution.

As defined by the CDC and enshrined in Section 14(3) of the 1979 Constitution:

> The composition of the government of the federation or any of its agencies and the conduct of its affairs shall be carried out in such manner as to reflect the federal character of Nigeria and the need

to promote national unity and to command national loyalty thereby ensuring that there shall be no predominance of persons from a few states or from a few ethnic or sectional groups, in that government or any of its agencies.

Section 14(4) of the said constitution also stipulates that:

the composition of the government of a state, a local government council or any of the agencies of such government or council and the conduct of the affairs of the government or council or such agencies shall be carried out in such manner as to recognise the diversity of the people within its area of authority and the need to promote a sense of belonging and loyalty among all the peoples of the federation.

These constitutional provisions were respectively repeated verbatim in Sections 15(3) and 15(4) of the 1989 Constitution of the Federal Republic of Nigeria.

In adopting the principle of federal character, the CDC recognised the heterogeneous nature of the Nigerian society. The CDC therefore decided to entrench the formula in the constitution to check these cleavages, ensure orderly progress of the country and "to promote national unity, foster national loyalty and give every citizen of Nigeria a sense of belonging to the nation".

The idea of federal character principle is not new. Its informal origins date back to the pre-independence days of nationalist agitation for participation in the administration of colonial Nigeria and especially after Nigeria became a formal federation in the fifties. Originally, during its informal application, the federal character principle was mainly concerned with legislative representation and equalisation of inter-regional opportunities in education and appointments at the federal level. But in its present formalised and institutionalised form, as embodied in the 1979 and 1989 Constitutions, virtually every sphere of federal, state and local government operation is involved and consequently politicised.

To ensure the smooth application and operation of the federal character principle, create a sense of belonging and hope in all Nigerians and strengthen the nation's unity and stability, the 1995 Draft Constitution went further to provide for a Federal Character Commission. This commission is empowered to work out an equitable formula for the distribution of all cadres of posts; to monitor, promote and enforce compliance with the principles of proportional sharing of posts at all levels of government; and to take measures to prosecute heads of any government ministry, body or agency who fail to comply with the formula.

Federal Character Principle for National Integration – Problems and Prospects

The *raison d'etre* of federal character principle, as noted above, is to ensure social harmony among all Nigerians and to promote the stability and national integration of the nation. National integration, is a process leading to political cohesion and sentiments of loyalty toward a central political authority and institutions by individuals belonging to different social groups or ... political units'. (Cf. Ogunojemite 1987:224) This meaning of integration is relevant to our present discussion. Thus, it becomes pertinent here to examine the problems and prospects implicit in the application of this formula in its bid to achieve the desired objective. In the first place, the successive state-creation exercises are seen as an expression and determinant of federal character and appear to have satisfied, to a large extent, statist claims to representation and at equalising access to the means of political power. However, these states are known to protect their interests very jealously, and to restrict the enjoyment of certain services and benefits provided by them and the federal authorities to their indigenes, by promulgating discriminatory laws, rules and regulations. Such a measure makes interstate mobility difficult. Yet the Constitution of the Federal Republic of Nigeria guarantees that `no Nigerian shall have cause to feel aggrieved or excluded on the grounds of his place of origin, sex, religion or ethnic grouping'. This situation, as Osaghae (1989:453) has rightly observed, is one of the emergent paradoxes of the federal character principle, whereby, instead of achieving unity through balancing, the country is further divided. To this end, Osaghae (1989:453) warns about the dangers inherent in consolidating statism in the guise of federal character principle which, according to him, threatens the appropriateness of the formula as well as the unity and stability of the federal system in Nigeria.

The principle of federal character emphasises the need for ethnic – balancing as a necessity in the evolution of Nigerian citizenship and for ensuring less acrimonious relationships among the various peoples of Nigeria. According to Saro-Wiwa (1985:7) the formula ``will make for a more equal federation to which more people will owe loyalty because they see themselves represented meaningfully therein''. To a quite reasonable extent, the formula has achieved this intention.

But unfortunately, the federal character principle, while stressing the imperative of ethnic-balancing, invariably enthrones ethnicity and de-emphasises the nation. In the process, too, it strengthens the parochial, particularist orientations and primordial ethnic attachments of Nigerians. These tendencies form the basis of disaffection among various groups in the nation. In addition, the formula has not adequately addressed the problems of the minorities especially in states made up of different and unequal ethnic groups.

The federal character principle has been manipulated by, and channelled to serve the overall interest of, the petty bourgeois ruling class. It is the members of this class who formulated and operate the principle. Even the debate on the principle, as carried in the Nigerian press, and noted by Agbaje (1989:117) "has been mainly an elite preoccupation...". Under the guise of the federal character principle, the members of the bourgeois class get themselves entrenched in power and exercise control over the machinery of state. Through the application of this principle, too, they strive to reconcile their class differences through the operation of acceptable formulae for the allocation, distribution and sharing of national resources and benefits among themselves. While they do this, they capitalise on, and fan the embers of, the ethnic differences among the various Nigerian peoples to win the support of the masses in their areas. And in the course of this elite game, members of this class climb to positions, amass wealth and enrich themselves.

But someone's meat is another's poison. As the members of the ruling class pillage and loot the nation on behalf of the groups and interests which they represent, they widen the gap between the rich and the poor in the society. The exploitation implicit in the propensity of the elite to amass wealth is exacerbated by the capitalist structure of the nation's economy which, according to Awa (1972:62), compels the people "to use essentially their own devices to get what they can from the proceeds of the economy". And what is worse, the interests of the masses are ignored as they do not get an equitable share of the resources, privileges and benefits of the state in the process. Thus, as Gboyega (1989:183) has rightly observed, the federal character principle is merely "an elite ploy which would not materially improve the lot of the downtrodden in whose name it is raised".

Under these circumstances, there is bound to be acrimony and socio-economic conflict between the haves (represented by the ruling elite class) and the have nots (represented by the masses). Unless the interests of the masses are taken care of in the application of the federal character principle, in such a way that they have access to the basic necessities of life, the formula is bound to have little relevance to the integration problems of Nigeria. It will at best provide an ambiguous and deceitful recipe for welding the federation together. Bourgeois solutions to instability in the country through the present structure of federal character can at best make the masses to "remain passive to elite-directed efforts at nation-building". In the opinion of Ogunojemite (1987:224), national integration can only occur "through the progressive bridging of the elite-mass gap on a vertical plane... and developing a participant political community."

The federal character principle satisfies the quest for representativeness and proportionality in allocating resources and in making appointments among various interest groups. However, in the application of the formula, as noted by Bodunrin (1989:307) ``choices are often made on the basis of criterion other than merit''. For example, the quota system as applied in education leads to lowering of standards against national interest. In the army it leads to the production of subgrade soldiers and officers. In the civil and public services of the federation, standards and professionalism are endangered and compromised. By eschewing meritocracy without recourse to standards, the quota system becomes morally reprehensible and an act of injustice. Viewed from this perspective, the quota factor in the federal character principle becomes not only counter-productive but divisive, and as such constitutes a cog in the wheel of the peaceful and orderly progress and development of Nigeria.

On the other hand, however, it has been argued that the quota system of the federal character principle is neither immoral nor unjust. Rather it should be seen as a variant of distributive justice. Ohonbamu (1968:130) and Kirk-Greene (1971:186) have argued that if the merit criterion is the only one used, most jobs would naturally go to the most enterprising and/or educationally advanced of the Nigerian tribes'. Thus, to ensure that the others do not feel deprived, the principle of federal character should be used to give them a sense of belonging. And as Lawson (1985:61) has conjectured ``the standards that enable this sense of belonging to be achieved are not necessarily the highest obtainable or available''.

In the civil and public services of the federation, it has been noted that as a result of the undue application of quota and lack of regard for merit in the application of federal character principle, standards and professionalism are also compromised and endangered. Moreover, the use of the formula is known to imbue civil and public servants in the country with a tendency to developing constituency consciousness and to remove the safeguards which protect them from the ravages of politics. Above all, it creates tension and frustration among some public servants, particularly in the South, whose career expectations are adversely affected by the need to reflect the federal character and who see the measure as a ploy to deprive them of jobs for the benefit of the Northerners. All these make the service an arena of sectional struggles and competition and make people to lose confidence in the impartiality of the government and the neutrality of the service as an instrument of state policy.

On the other hand, it has been argued by no less a personality than Alhaji Bargudu Shettima, a one time chairman of the Federal Public Service Commission, that the federal character principle can enhance the efficiency of the service. Gboyega (1989:182) believes this can be achieved through fair representation which would command public confidence and greater cooperation, mutual trust and mutual respect among the public servants themselves.

One of the major and most problematic features of the federal character principle, as presently operated, is the complexity of the interests and units as represented by the North-South, state, local government, ethnic and religious group affiliations. For example, the creation of more states and local governments and the establishment of federal educational institutions in every state to enhance greater representational opportunities leads to the multiplication of governmental and administrative units and facilities which become disturbingly expensive to the nation. This is often done against the evidence of the inability of the new states and local governments to discharge their statutory duties as a result of their unviability. As a result, the federal character principle, asserts Usman Yusufu Bala (1977:46-48) ``has deepened the problem it was devised to tackle''.

Recommendations and Suggestions

Despite the obvious shortcomings, and the controversies surrounding the notion and application of federal character, there seems to be a general acceptance of the principle as a normative expression of the equal rights of all Nigerians to participate in the political, administrative and economic affairs of the country. From the foregoing discussions, one significant fact has emerged, that is, that as long as Nigeria remains a federation, the need and the clamour to balance the diverse interests in the country will always be there. The federal character principle has been employed to take care of these diverse and sometimes conflicting interests. And by all indications, the formula has come to stay. What is therefore necessary is to seek ways and means to make it less rancorous and problematic, and to channel it in such a way as to ensure the overall unity and progress of the country. A few suggestions and recommendations are made below to help bring this about.

It has been noted that when states were first created in 1967, there were twelve of them, six in the North and six in the South. But today, the North-South balance is distorted in favour of the North. To assuage the mutual suspicion and ill-feelings generated by this situation, the original North-South balance should be restored and maintained.

However, the state-creation exercise should be carried out with caution. This is to ensure the viability of the states and their ability to discharge their statutory and other functions for the common good of all and orderly development of the country. Moreover, despite the present multiplicity of states and local governments, it is still not possible or feasible to give each ethnic group (some 250 of them) in Nigeria a state. The interest of the minorities in the present states and local governments who could not be given new states or local governments can be taken care of in other ways.

Efforts should be made through appropriate legislation to remove the `indigene syndrome' engendered by the federal character principle and the discriminatory policies, laws and regulations which legalise its operation. It is an aberration of nation building and national integration to see fellow Nigerians, some of whom were born and may have lived in a place all their lives, being thrown out of jobs and discriminated against because they are not indigenes of the area. To this end, we join Osaghae (1989:453) and Mark (1986) in asking the government to see that every citizen of Nigeria who settles in any part of the country is treated as an indigene of the place and endowed with residency rights as is the case, in the United States of America.

Again, the federal character principle should be applied with less stringency but with fairness among ethnic groups, states and local governments that are homogenous, to avoid creating cleavages and divisions where none may have, strictly speaking, existed. This will save such societies' from undue polarisation.

We share the view expressed by a former Head of State, General Olusegun Obasanjo, that the principle of merit should not be completely sacrificed on the altar of federal character (see Gboyega 1989:183). The appointment of persons to various positions should be made from the best available in any group or section in the country. Moreover, recruitment to posts which require specialist training such as those of medical practitioners, pilots, architects and engineers, should be essentially based on merit. (Adamolekun, 1985:185). To do otherwise would expose the citizenry to great peril. And to enthrone merit, efforts should be made to give equal access to education to all Nigerians, to bridge the educational disparities between the North and the South, and to give opportunities for further training and education to serving staff.

The present application of the federal character principle is all bourgeois-oriented and does very little to relieve the plight of the masses of this country. For example, the indigenisation policy which put capital in the hands of a few Nigerians did not benefit the masses. The latter need to be given equal opportunities for employment, equitable share in the distribution of the resources and benefits of the state in terms of education, access to goods and services provided by government and improved conditions of life. The political system should arrest the exploitation of the masses and redress their feeling of insecurity. It is by tackling these crucial welfare issues that the great majority of Nigerians can ``develop a sense of national identity... transcending parochial loyalties of... ethnicity, religion, language and region" (Rosberg 1971)

Conclusion

It is an acknowledged fact that the federal character principle has gone a long way to reduce various factors of mutual distrust and rivalries among the diverse groups and interests in Nigeria. But it is instructive to note that while some gain in the process, others lose and so the implementation hurts in certain quarters. There is therefore the need for all the groups, views and interests concerned to be consulted and taken into consideration in the course of its implementation. It is also important to ensure that those who implement the policy do not use it, as Bodunrin (1989:321) has cautioned, "as an instrument of stifling the progress and initiative of any groups nor as a punitive measure against any groups." This calls for the emergence of an enlightened leadership imbued with the requisite statesmanship to direct the affairs of the nation and ensure the continued survival of the peace, unity, stability and national integration of the country.

Ethnic differences and sectional interests should not be seen as an unmitigated evil. Rather, efforts should be made to transcend them, and to harness and incorporate their virtues in the march to stable and integrated nationhood. Nigerians should be made to stress more those things that unite than those things that separate them. They should see the Nigerian nation as the rope that ties up their common destiny. They should therefore endeavour to rekindle, as advised by Nwankwo (1986:75), the nationalist fervour which united all Nigerians from all corners of the country against colonial rule. In so doing, however, they should heed the warnings of Ogunojemite (1987:230) not to misconstrue the nationalism of the *nouveau riche* with the well-being of the masses. Above all, the federal character principle should not only concern itself with the inter-ethnic distribution of national resources, privileges and benefits, but should also ensure that modalities are worked out by which its beneficiaries can make reciprocal contributions to the overall common good, progress, stability and national integration of the country.

References

Adamolekun, Ladipo. (1986) *Politics and Administration in Nigeria*, Ibadan: Spetrum Books Ltd.

Adebisi, Busari. O. (1989) `Federal Character and Social Class' in P.P. Ekeh and E.E. Osaghae (eds) *Federal Character and Federalism in Nigeria*. Ibadan: Heinemann Educational Books (Nig), Ltd.

Agbaje, Adigun. A.B. (1989) `Mass Media and the Shaping of Federal Character: A Content Analysis of Four Decades of Nigerian Newspapers 1950-1984' in P.P. Ekeh and E.E. Osaghae (eds) *Federalism Character and Federalism in Nigeria*.

Awa, E.O. (1972) `Foundations For Political Reconstruction in Nigeria' in *Ikenga – A Journal of African Studies*. University of Nigeria Press.

Ayam, John. A. (1987) `Intra-Class Struggle and the State – Towards Resolving the Problem of Instability in Nigeria' in Stephen O. Olugbemi (ed) *Alternative Political Futures for Nigeria*. Lagos: Political Science Association.

Bala, Usman Yusufu (1977) `National Cohesion, National Planning and the Construction' in Suleiman Kumo and Abubakar Aliyu (eds.) *Issues in Nigerian Draft Constitution*. Zaria: Baraka Press Ltd.

Bodunrin, Peter (1989) `Federal Character and Social Justice' in P.P. Ekeh and E.E. Osaghae (eds.) *Federal Character and Federalism in Nigeria*.

Ekeh, Peter. P. (1989) `The Structure and Meaning of Federal Character in the Nigerian Political System' in P.P. Ekeh and E.E. Osaghae (eds.) *Federal Character and Federalism in Nigeria*.

Gboyega, Alex. (1989) `The Public Service and Federal Character' in P.P. Ekeh and E.E. Osaghae (eds.) *Federal Character and Federalism in Nigeria*.

Kirk - Greene, A.H.M. (1971) *Crisis and Conflict in Nigeria*, Vol. I. London: Oxford University Press.

Lawson, C.O. (1985) `Experiences at the Federal Level' in Ladipo Adamolekun (ed) *Nigerian Public Administration 1960-80: Perspectives and Prospects*. Ibadan: Heinemann Educational Books (Nig.) Ltd.

Mark, David. (1986) *New Nigerian*. February 14

Musa, S.A. (1985) `Developments at the Federal Level' in Ladipo Adamolekun (ed) *Nigerian Public Administration 1960-80: Perspectives and Prospects*.

Newswatch, September 11, 1995.

Nnoli, O. (1978) *Ethnic Politics in Nigeria*. Enugu: Fourth Dimension Publishers.

Nwankwo, Arthur. A. (1986) *Thoughts on Nigeria*. Enugu: Fourth Dimension Publishing Company Ltd.

Ogunojemite, L.O. (1987) `Federal Character as an Integrative Mechanism: The Nigerian Experience at Nation Building' in Stephen. O. Olugbemi (ed) *Alternative Political Futures For Nigeria*. Lagos: Political Science Association.

Ohonbamu, O. (1968) *The Psychology of the Nigerian Revolution*. 1 Infracombe, Devon: A.H. Stockwell.

Okpu, Ugbana (1989) `Ethnic Minorities and Federal Character' in P.P. Ekeh and E.E. Osaghae (eds) *Federal Character and Federalism in Nigeria*.

Osaghae, Eghosa E. (1989) `Federal Character: Past, Present and Future' in P.P. Ekeh and E.E. Osaghae (eds) *Federal Character and Federalism in Nigeria*.

Report of the C.D.C. Containing the Draft Constitution (1976). Lagos: Federal Ministry of Information, Vol. I.

Rosberg, Carl. G. (1971) `National Identity in African States' in *The African Review*. Vol. I, No. 1., March, 1971.

Saro-Wiwa, Ken (1985) *The Guardian*, January 22, Also in Gboyega `The Public Service and Federal Character' in P.P. Ekeh and E.E. Osaghae (eds) *Federal Character and Federalism in Nigeria*.

The 1989 Constitution – *The Constitution of the Federal Republic of Nigeria*, Extra-Ordinary Gazette, No. 29, Lagos, 3rd May, 1989, Vol. 76, Printed and Published by the Federal Government Press.

The Guardian, January 22, 1985.

The 1979 Presidential Constitution.

This Week, Vol. 8, No. 1, March 14, 1988.

Young, Crawford. (1993) *The Politics of Cultural Pluralism*. Ibadan: Heinemann Educational Books (Nig), Plc.

CHAPTER 12

Chris O. Uroh

On the Ethics of Ethnic Balancing in Nigeria: Federal Character Reconsidered

Introduction

How do we ensure fair play in a plural society characterised, as it were, by *diversities* and *inequalities* of various magnitudes and dimensions? This is one question that has continued to confront, or better still, torment policy makers in Nigeria right from the colonial days to the present time. Every regime has fashioned out what it considers the appropriate response to this rather enduring problem: The colonial overlords got around the problem by consolidating the distance between the various ethnic groups in the country. That way equals were treated equally and the converse went for the unequals. With that the basis for comparison and therefore, the ground for rivalry was reduced, if not totally eliminated. But things, changed after independence in 1960. For with political independence and the imperative of common governance and government, especially with the indigenisation of the civil service, educational institutions and job placements, among others, the *dual mandate* became rather defective as a principle of administration of the new Nigeria.

After independence in 1960, it dawned on Nigeria and Nigerians that Arthur Richard (1979) was in everything right when he noted that:

> It is only the accident of British suzerainty which has made Nigeria one country. (That) it is still far from being one country or one nation, socially or even economically. (That) socially and politically there are deep differences between the major tribal groups. They do not speak the same language and they have highly divergent customs and ways of life and they represent different stages of culture.

The handwriting was on the wall early enough in post-colonial Nigeria. The bubble however burst open in 1967, and for thirty months, language and accident of birth defined one's position on the rather blurred line of symmetry demarcating the ``enemies'' camp from that of the ``loyalists''. The war ended, and in spirit at least, without ``victors'' and ``vanquished''. But rather than suppress the question, of the best socio-political structure for Nigeria, it further played it up. And so, with the memory of the *war of unity* haunting them, Nigerian policy makers, saddled with the responsibility of fashioning a new political formula for Nigeria, opined and so recommended that:

> There had in the past been inter-ethnic rivalry to secure the domination of government by one ethnic group or combination of ethnic groups to the exclusion of others. It is essential to have some provisions to ensure that the predominance of persons from a few states or from a few ethnic or other sectional groups is avoided in the composition of government or the appointment or election of persons to high offices in the state (CDC, 1977: ix).

In line with this recommendation, section 14 (3) (a) secured a space in the 1979 Constitution of the Federal Republic of Nigeria and, accordingly, the Statute book declares:

> The composition of the government of the federation or any of its agencies and the conduct of its affairs should be carried out in such manner as to reflect the *federal character* of Nigeria and the need to promote national unity and also to command national loyalty thereby ensuring that there shall be no predominance of persons from a few states or from a few ethnic or other sectional groups in that government or in any of its agencies.

Basically, what the principle of federal character has come to mean, in what Adiele Afigbo (1986) rightly describes as ``unsophisticated everyday usage'', is ``Nigeria's multi-ethnic character''. And in that case, to reflect federal character means simply to ensure ``that Nigerian affairs are not dominated by persons'' from a few states or ethnic groups. (*Ibid.*). In practice, the notion of federal character has manifested, among other things, in the application of quota system in job placements and recruitments into military services, in the granting of special considerations for *educationally disadvantaged states* in admission into institutions of higher learning, and in the requirement for *national spread* in appointment into public offices and so on.

This chapter examines the principle of federal character first, as a scheme that was supposed to ensure fair play or justice among the various groups that have, as a result of colonial conquest, been *chaotically crowded* (Ake, 1993) within the Nigerian state. The question here is, to what extent can a principle based on preferential treatment or reverse discrimination, as federal character has turned out to be, fall in line with the idea of fair play or justice? Second, as a corrolary to the above, can the federal character principle achieve its goals of promoting national unity and national loyalty, or above all, ``give every citizen of Nigeria a sense of belonging to the nation...''? (CDC, 1977: X).

Social Justice and Reverse Discrimination

The notion of justice, like most social science concepts, has remained a contested one among scholars. Therefore, at various times and under different historical, cultural and ideological influences, justice has been variously interpreted, (see for instance, Plato., 1973; Rawls 1973; Carr, 1981; Campbell, 1988; etc). Nevertheless, it is a settled matter that justice is a distributive term. By this, it is meant that justice has to do with the ``allotment of something''; to persons (Frankena, 1976; 433). And these things could be ``duties, goods, offices, opportunities, penalties, punishments, privileges, roles, status, and so on'' (*Ibid.*). The point should be made here, however, that justice ``has to do, not so much with the quantity of good or evil'' that is being distributed, but more ``with the *manner* in which it is distributed'' (*Ibid.* 432). To put the matter differently, ``the subject matter of justice (is) the manner in which benefits and burdens are distributed among men'' (Miller, 1979; 19). And a just distribution has been described as that in which ``each individual has exactly those benefits and burdens which are due to him'' (*Ibid.*). This I believe is also what Bodunrin (1989:31) has in mind when he states that a society would be considered just ``if everybody is treated fairly in respect of the distribution of the society's goods''.

But the question of what treatment should qualify as fair treatment, and by implication, what a just distribution is, is not a settled one. This is where the question of *conception* of what justice means becomes knotty and sometimes naughty. However following John Rawls' (1973:5) position, we can say, if only tentatively that, even people who hold different views or conceptions of what justice is, can ``still agree that institutions are just when no arbitrary distinctions are made between persons'' in the assignment of ``basic rights and duties and when the rules determine a proper balance between competing claims to the advantage of social life''.

One way of interpreting Rawls' view here is that, justice entails the avoidance as much as possible, of discrimination in the distribution of social benefits or costs. To achieve this goal, Rawls suggests that every society should be organised so that:

(1) Each person should have equal rights to the most extensive basic liberty compatible with a similar liberty for others.

(2) Social inequalities are to be arranged so that they are (a) reasonably expected to be to everyone's advantages, and (b) attached to positions and offices open to all (*Ibid*:60).

It is important to note here that Rawls recognises the plausibility of unequal distribution of costs and benefits of the society leading to the attainment of justice. In other words, he foresees a situation whereby ``an unequal distribution of any or all of (liberty, opportunity, income and wealth, and the bases of self-respect) ``is to everyone's advantage" (*Ibid*: 83). This can happen when ``an unequal distribution" is to ``the advantage of the least favoured groups in the society (*Ibid*.).

The implication of this is that an unequal distribution is not necessarily unjust. It is the principle inherent in this type of position which protagonists of *reverse discrimination* or *affirmative action*, have used to justify their claims. Here, the argument is that some social and/or historical circumstances could be the basis for giving *preferential* treatment to some groups without compromising justice.

Let us examine closely what the idea of preferential treatment entails, and more importantly, the justifications given for it. First, preferential treatment means giving to somebody what she might not have, under a *prevailing* circumstance, obtained on her own (Yinger, 1964). It equally means, though not necessarily, a denial of somebody else's right. As earlier noted, preferential treatment is usually justified on the ground of historical antecedents and the inequalities these had created. As Judith Thompson (1973) puts it, ``if we have wronged A, we must make amends, justice requires it and failure to make amends is not merely callousness, but injustice".

Preferential treatment therefore is more a *reparation* so to say, paid for a *past wrong*. Lyndon B. Johnson (1971:166) in affirming this view notes as follows:

> You do not take a person who, for years has been hobbled by chains... and then say you are free to compete with all the others and still just believe that you have been completely fair.

One major argument that has therefore been used to justify affirmative action or reverse discrimination in a place like the United States is the fact that certain state policies in the past were biased against certain groups and that it is not just enough to stop such policies but that conscious efforts should be made to correct some of the disequilibrums created by the past policies.

For instance, it was the case that with slavery in America, racism became almost institutionalised. Blacks and other minority groups suffered as a result. Education is one area where such discrimination was manifest: There were laws such as the 1740 South Carolina Statute that made it an offence for slaves to be educated. Says the law:

> And whereas the having of slaves taught to write, or suffering them to be employed in writing, may be attending with great inconvenience; be it enacted that all and every person and persons whatsoever, who shall hereafter teach, or cause any slave or slaves

to be taught to write, or shall use or employ any slave as a scribe in any manner of writing whatsoever, hereafter taught to write, every such person or persons shall, for every offence, forfeit the sum of one hundred pounds current money (See Gates Jr. 1985:9).

In this light therefore, the whole idea of affirmative action is first, a recognition of the fact of this kind of discrimination in the past (Mogekwu, 1992: 215; Uroh 1996a). Second, it is equally applied as a *compensation* for the past misdeed. Putting the matter in another way, "reverse discrimination", especially as it is being pursued through the principle of affirmative action in the U.S is based on the need to achieve the following objectives, among others:

(a) To ensure that past discrimination against blacks and women does not continue

(b) To offer officially and explicity a symbolic denunciation of past racism and/or sexism in America;

(c) To provide role models for victimised blacks and women;

(d) To compensate victims of discrimination by *preferring* them over beneficiaries of injustice (i.e. those who had gained from the *status quo* (Mogekwu, 1992)

Whichever way one views the matter, therefore, the idea of affirmative action is based on a sense of collective *guilt* and the *moral* obligation to pay compensation to the group which had been wronged in the past. What is thus implied is that preferential treatment for a group, especially when this leads to the denial of some other groups' rights, can only be justifiable in instances where the *preferred* group can really be shown to have suffered some wrongs or denials in the past through a policy or policies that were beneficial to the group that now "suffers". Conversely, if group A cannot be proved to have been the cause (or beneficiary) of B's present predicament, or better still, where B's present denial did not in any way benefit A, the basis for preferential treatment in favour of B would hardly be sustained on any principle of social justice. In fact, to do that would amount to injustice against A.

Having thus concluded, I shall in the next section examine the principle and practice of the federal character policy in Nigeria to see the extent to which the policy could be justified.

Federal Character and Social Justice

The major argument of protagonists of the federal character principle is that it would help to right the wrongs of the past. The question that arises at this juncture is, what are these past wrongs that the practice of federal character is expected to put straight? Let me start by noting the most visible and in fact most widely discussed, namely, the educational disparities between the North and South. It is a common fact of history that at independence, the South, by which is meant the former Eastern and Western Regions, was ahead of the North in terms of western education. This is how Ahmadu Bello, former Premier of Northern Nigeria, put it in his autobiography, *My Life:*

> We were very conscious indeed that the Northern Region was far behind the others educationally. We know that individually the educated Northerners could hold their own against the educated Southerners, but simply had not got the numbers they had; nor had we people with university degrees necessary as a qualification ... for some of the higher posts. (Bello, 1962, 110).

Bello is simply stating the obvious here; but the question then arises, can we blame the South for the educational disparities in the country? Let us for the meantime forget the disputed question of whether or not the northern leadership, especially the emirs, blocked the chance of western education up North. The process of colonisation or better, the contact with western civilisation just created a situation where the southern parts of the country had to be on the lead in terms of western education and in fact, westernisation in general. As Obaro Ikime (1979:7) rightly notes:

> Abeokuta received missionaries in 1846, Benin did not till 1897, a whole half century later. The *Day Sprint* brought cargo of missionaries to Onitsha in 1857. The more hinterland parts of Igboland did not receive missionaries till after 1914. (What's more) The first grammar school in Lagos was founded in 1859. There are parts of this country where there were no grammar schools till a whole century later.

The North was one of such places without schools. In fact, the first educational institution in the north, the Sokoto Elementary School was founded only in 1914 while Kaduna College, the first secondary school in any part of northern Nigeria was established in 1948, the same year the University College, Ibadan was founded.

The question now is; to what extent can the South be held responsible for the educational backwardness of the North? There appears to be none. Let us recast the question and say; how has the South benefitted, in the *past* as a result of a state policy which kept the North in the background educationwise? If there is none, then on what basis are we applying a discriminatory principle in admitting Nigerian citizens into public institutions of higher learning? These questions arise because the practice of federal character as it relates to intakes into higher institutions appears to work only to hold down a part of the country considered to be educationally advanced states, so that those fellow compatriots who are from the reverse side could catch up with them. This is so since candidates from the so-called educationally advanced states are supposed to score higher than their counterparts from the disadvantaged states. In this sense, federal character means lowering of standards in favour of some preferred groups, and against others who cannot be said to have wronged the preferred groups in the past.

Furthermore, and in fact this is the crux of the matter, the present reality in Nigeria is such that, those from the educationally advanced states do not hold any *advantageous* position when it comes to politics, economics and other spheres of state power. This point needs elaboration. When one looks at the American society or any other society for that matter, where the principle of affirmative action or "reverse discrimination" is in place, the tendency is that the preferred groups are usually marginalised in the scheme of things. In fact, it is this marginalisation which qualifies them for preferential treatment in the first place. In America, for instance, Blacks, the Hispanics and women, belong to the marginalised groups. This is why the affirmative action principle is in their favour.

Interestingly, the reverse is the case in Nigeria. People who are discriminated against either in admission into public schools or employment into government establishments, are the same group of people who do not have access to political or economic powers of the country. They are therefore discriminated against in more than just one way. What is more, the application of the principle of federal character has not been total. For instance, while it is supposed to be used in the recruitment into the armed forces, it is not always, followed when appointments are being made, irrespective of whether such appointments are political or military. A case in point was the appointment made in 1987/88 under the regime of Ibrahim Babangida. It favoured a part of the country. Babangida's reply was that the appointments were purely military postings. This has been interpreted to mean that "such postings did not need to be guided by the principle of quota system" (Mogekwu, 1992:214). The impression this creates is that "the principle of federal character was applied only when it brought some group at *par* with others and not necessarily to objectively create a balance". (*Ibid.*).

When one weighs the principle and practice of federal character in Nigeria on the scale of social justice and fair play one finds it weighing so low. The reason is simple; not only are those discriminated against not holding any enviable position, despite what is considered to be their attainment, educationwise, the *preferred* group;

> cannot be described as victims of past discriminatory governmental or social policies; they have not been exploited by any group. Here, there is no guilty group which is morally bound to make reparation for past misdeeds (Bodunrin, 1989:304).

Lastly, it is appropriate to ask whether or not the federal character principle can ensure unity among Nigerians and loyalty to the Nigerian state. The answer here is obvious. It cannot. The principle is *unjustifiably* discriminatory. This runs counter even to some other provisions of the 1979 Constitution. For instance, section 15(2) provides that: "Discrimination on the ground of place of origin, sex, religion, status, ethnic or linguistic association or ties shall be prohibited". Federal character principle in fact emphasises one's place of origin and discriminates against one on that ground. The result has been that sometime more qualified personnel are denied employment or promotion mainly on the ground that the available position is not for their state or places of origin. Thus the principle of federal character or quota system, contravenes the provision of section 17 (3) (a) of the 1979 Constitution which requires that; "All citizens without discrimination on any ground whatsoever have adequate opportunity to secure suitable employment".

In this circumstance, rather than foster national unity, the practice of federal character has only heightened mutual suspicion and acrimonies among Nigerians (Uroh 1988, Olukoshi and Agbu, 1996). For, if anything, federal character has made Nigerians to look inward, to see themselves foremost as members of their primordial group before anything else. Thus, at every available opportunity they demand for their own separate state. The reasoning here being simply that, one's state is where she he really belongs (Ekeh, 1989).

Conclusion

In this rather short conclusion, I want to state simply that, one of the reasons why the principles of federal character, quota system, educationally (dis)advantaged states and so on have appeared inevitable in the present dispensation in Nigeria is because there is so much power —political, economic, bureacratic — that is concentrated at the centre. For this, every group wants to control the power at the centre just the same way the hegemony of the central government is visible everywhere. To solve the problem of unhealthy rivalry, Nigeria should operate a truly federal system in which, in the words of Obafemi Awolowo (1966:47) every section or even ethnic group is "autonomous in regard to its internal affairs". The country should, in other words, liberate itself from what Claude Welch (1995:635) rightly describes as a "misleading federation".

References

Afigbo, A.E. (1986), *Federal Character: Its Meaning and History*. Owerri: RADA Publishing Company.

Ake, C. (1993) "Is Africa Democratising?" *The Guardian* Annual Lecture, Lagos.

Awolowo, O. (1966). *Path to Nigerian Freedom*. London.

Bello. A. (1962). *My Life*. Cambridge: Cambridge University Press.

Bodunrin, P. (1989). "Federal Character and Social Justice" in P.P. Ekeh and E.E. Osaghae (eds) *Federal Character and Federalism in Nigeria*. Ibadan: Heneimann. pp. 303-324.

Campbell, T. (1988) *Justice*. London: Macmillan Education Ltd.

Carr, C.L. (1981) "The Concept of Formal Justice" in *Philosophical Studies*, Vol. 39.

CDC, (1977) *Report of the Constitutional Drafting Committee* Vol. 1, Lagos.

Ekeh, P.P. (1989) "The Structure and Meaning of Federal Character in the Nigerian Political System" in his edited *Federal Character and Federalism in Nigeria op. cit.*

Frankena, W.K. (1976) "The concept of social justice" in Samuel Gorowitz *et al* (eds) *Moral Problems in Medicine*. New Jersey: Prentice-Hall Inc.

Gates Jr, H.L. (1985) "Writing, Race and the Difference It Makes" *Critical Inquiry 12*.

Ikime, O. (1979) *Through Changing Scenes: Nigerian History Yesterday, Today and Tomorrow*. Inaugural Lecture, University of Ibadan, 26, October.

Johnson, L.B. (1971). *The Vintage Point*. New York: Holt Reinhart and Winston.

Miller, D. (1979) *Social Justice*. Oxford: Oxford University Press.

Mogekwu, M. (1972). "Federal Character and the Question of Equal Opportunities in Nigeria: Lessons from America's "Affirmative Action". *Nigerian Journal of American Studies*.

Olukoshi, A.O. and Agbu, O. (1996). "The Deepening Crisis of Nigerian Federalism and the Future of the Nation-State" in Olukoshi A.O. and Laakso, L. (eds) *Challenges to the Nation – State in Africa*. Uppsala: Nordiska Afrikainstitutet, pp 74 - 101.

Plato, (1973) *The Republic*. Oxford: Oxford University Press.

Rawls, J. (1973) *A Theory of Justice.* Cambridge Mass: Harvard University Press.

Richard, A. (1979). Cited in Osuntokun's "The Background of Nigerian Federalism" in Akinyemi, A.B. *et al* (eds) *Reading in Federalism.* Lagos: Nigerian Institute of International Affairs.

Thompson, J. (1973) "Preferential Hiring". *Philosophy and Public Affairs.* Vol. 2, No 4.

Uroh, C. (1988a) "The Dilemma of Federal Character". *Nigerian Tribune* (November 4).

─────── (1996) "The struggle for self-determination and the crisis of governance in Nigeria: A Theoretical Statement". Paper presented at the CODESRIA Governance Institute, Dakar Senegal, August.

Welch, C.E. (1995) "The Ogoni and Self-determination: Increasing Violence in Nigeria." *Journal of Modern African Studies*, Vol. 33, No. 4, pp.635-649.

CHAPTER 13

David A. Utume

Federal Character as an Equity Principle

Introduction

Equity has been an enduring principle, perhaps a value, in the determination of political action by individuals and groups. Scholars have not so much heralded its impact in this regard as they have *power*. We have thus often by-passed *equity* to arrive at *power* as the central concern of political action and of political study. However, we must recognise that the person who desires power and strives after it is engaged in a struggle to circumvent such events as might visit privation upon himself and/or his group. In other words, he tries to ensure that he is in a position to ensure equity to himself, and perhaps to others. At most, by being in power, he hopes to escape from such injustices as might be inadvertently or otherwise visited upon his person by those in power. It is for this, we believe, that political arrangements may stand or fall on the basis of equity.

Indirectly or otherwise, equity has recently assumed more prominence in national discussions, although it has featured in such discussions since the establishment of the political union called Nigeria. In his keynote address at an International Conference on Federalism in Nigeria, Shridath Ramphal directed the conference to one of the questions that touch on this essential principle in the context of a planned transition from military to civil democratic rule, ``whether taking account of the declared objective of the Federal Military Government to create a just and lasting democratic society. . . in a more equitable Nigerian Republic'', this noble aim could be furthered by federalism and, if so, by what particular federal arrangement''.[1]

Since 1979, the equity principle has always been reflected in the ``fundamental objectives and directive principles of State Policy''.[2] This concern does not merely reflect the need to be fashionable, since equity has been at the heart of many revolutions, including the American, French and Chinese revolutions, as well as wars of liberation which have made sense only when rationalised as a necessary step towards social and economic justice for the oppressed. And, generally, forms of rule, the more democratic and the more autocratic inclusive, have heightened the stakes of equity, such that no political community can claim to have found the final solution to the problem of ensuring equity amongst its peoples. Nigeria is one such community. Since 1979, the federal character principle has become entrenched in her constitution.

This chapter examines federal character as an equity principle essential for national integration. The intention here is to clarify issues and further interpret this principle with the aim of showing how it can foster the goals of national integration for Nigeria in the context of the demands of pluralist democracy and the consequences of military rule, the politics of appointment and the economics of public office.

The Demands of Pluralism

In political studies, pluralism has come to assume different meanings to different analysts. For example, Sartori refers to cultural, societal and political pluralism[3] in his effort to show which of these better suits party formation and stable party politics. Such early pluralists focused more on the organic elements of group and inter-group dynamics, although other writers like Young hold the view that human beings' cognitive endowments are capable of creating and recreating identities by which groups can be defined. It is the very subjective nature of group identities which renders pluralism significant in politics.[4] What remains constant and central to pluralism is its penchant for colouring relationships within given communities. Political contests are seen along lines of group interests, and individuals in government are perceived as representatives of their groups. Pluralist forms of governance demand, therefore, that, as individuals in their group, member participate both in policy determination and in the distribution of values and/or benefits in a given community. This suggests that the political arrangements must be such that group interests are fully taken care of for them to qualify as democratic. It is no wonder Lijphart has cause to describe his political model as ``consociational democracy''[5] which recommends four cardinal principles for accommodating group interests in plural societies: that government has to comprise a grand coalition where all main segments of society are represented; that the decision-making process must be based on the mutual veto principle; that it must not only recognise but also respect segmental autonomy.

Federal arrangements have come handy to contain these demands of pluralism. These usually ensure that local values are preserved despite commitment to the larger union. With many such unions, it is claimed, federalism has grown from below,[6] rendering the central government dependent on the federating units. But in such ex-colonial states as India and Nigeria, the modern state and its federal structure were plural societies from above, by imperial fiat. The stability of the system became suspect. For, whereas the federating units, jealous of their local autonomy, feared they might be compromised by any growth of federal power, the demands of unity in the modern state arose from fears of disintegration emanating from the challenges of localism. The ultimate loser was the individual citizen who could neither be served by benefits derived from the larger union nor by guarantees of local autonomy. On the whole, however, we can say that federalism has endured, despite break-downs here and there. But the challenges of the modern state have rendered federal might suspect vis-a-vis local autonomy in both old and new states. It is for this reason that reviews of federal arrangements are frequently advocated to ensure that advantages do not tilt unduly in favour of particular segments such as to endanger the entire scheme. The need is more urgent for the new societies of the world experimenting with this type of arrangement.

Nigeria is a relatively young federation which, over the last generation, has been feeling its way through with different types of arrangements in the hope to achieve a stable and progressive polity. It is one of the very few new states that have survived a civil war. Moreover, there seems to be an unwritten covenant among Nigerians for the continued unity of the country. Of course, there are explanations for the constituent groups' commitment to the continued survival of the country; but that is beyond the scope of this chapter. What remains is for Nigeria to devise ways of achieving stability so as to bring about development and advance the well-being of its people. This stability, it is argued below, can only be achieved under an equitable arrangement for everybody and every group in the society. The proper implementation of federal character as an equity principle can enhance individual and group commitment to the country.

The Politics of Appointments

It was Richard Joseph who once argued that ``even in the absence of multi-party system, offices of state in Africa are often captured by individuals and their support groups and exploited to favour their interests within the marketplace of civil society as well as in the appropriation of the resources of the state itself.''[7] This principle he referred to as prebendal politics, a definitive feature of Nigerian politics. To him, such use of prebends is corrupt and thus politically unhealthy. While one may not associate with the perjorative use of the terms ``captured'', ``exploited'' and ``appropriation'' as used above, it approximates to the Nigerian view of public office in which it is expected that there can be legitimate prebends accruing from public office.

Nigeria has come a long way in establishing the notion that public office attracts special privileges that are of significance not just to the individual officer alone, but also to the group he or she purportedly represents. It is for this reason the history of Nigeria is full of protests and agitations, as well as policies, over access to and appropriation of public office. This is what is here termed the politics of appointment. Conventionally, public appointments have always been categorised into political and career appointments. It may not make much difference trying to distinguish between the two for purposes of discussion in this chapter for, in the final analysis, they have the same political (and even economic) significance for Nigerians. A brief review of the records is attempted below.

Among the earliest demands made on the colonial administration by the Africans were demands that would ensure African appointment into both political and career offices. In 1920, the National Congress of British West Africa (NCBWA) sent a delegation to the Secretary of State for the colonies to demand among other things, that each territory (of British West Africa) should have a legislative council half of which membership should be elected Africans; and that racial discrimination (usually against Africans) in the Civil Service be abolished,[8] such as to enable Africans take career appointments in the public service. It is significant to note that Nigerians were represented on the NCBWA delegation. It is also worth noting that, right from such early times, the belief that public appointments should be representative was a prominent one.

This was why early nationalists felt deprived when they could not secure public offices, political or otherwise, in the colonial service. Because Nigerian nationalists set greater store on political office, most agitations following upon those of the NCBWA concerned the magnitude of African involvement in government at the political level. Thus from the Clifford Constitution of 1922, following upon the 1920 demands of the NCBWA, gradual progress was made in African political participation up to 1960 when Nigerians assumed full political control of their affairs. And despite the progress made with appointment of Nigerians into the civil service, deliberate effort was needed to ensure that Nigerians took over from the British civil servants in the country – the Nigerianisation policy of 1956. Though regionalisation of the services in 1954 contradicted this policy in some instances (i.e. by slowing down Nigerianisation of the Northern service so as to make regionalisation succeed), this policy was to remain the ultimate objective for the entire country. And twenty years later Nigerianisation was being pursued in the industrial and commercial sectors of Nigerian life,[9] not just in ownership of business but also in their management. It shows that Nigerians place high stakes on appointments, both in public and private sectors of her national life.

But since the 1970s, the pendulum has swung to the other side. The change in the country's federal structure, in her economic fortunes and educational advancement of all regions and states (which are now smaller and economically weaker with limited career opportunities), has increased the stakes in the federal service. These factors have conspired to weaken the centrifugal forces. Thus, the section that does not have access to the federal service now feels greatly cheated. And from the 1970s, talk of `quota system' became common, the advocacy of which was a euphemistic protest against undue preponderant representations of some sections of the Nigerian community in the federal service. The other older dimension of the argument was the fear of political domination of some section (i.e. the North) of national appointments. Interestingly, Nigerians were now raising eyebrows not about European domination but sectional domination. To this latter one was found an answer in the jettisoning of the Westminster system adopted in the First Republic. The 1979 Constitution was presidential and went further to recognise federal character in the appointment of ministers and other officers of government.[10] The 1992 (reviewed) version of the Constitution went further to require the federal character principle in all public services of the country for which Federal Character Commission is provided.[11]

These policies, in positive response to public demands, are by themselves proof of the validity and rationality of the demands. As indicated by the Constitution, to the extent that its implementation achieves `a sense of belonging' among those affected, to such extent does it advance the cause of national integration.

The Economics of Public Office

Employment and unemployment are problems of economics the world over, though they may hold different meanings to the parties involved, sometimes, i.e. between the employer (usually government) and the employed (the individual worker). For here, we are only concerned with what surrounds the office held by the individual worker in the public service, and how that may also affect his immediate sub-national community. We refer to the tangible and intangible prebends that accrue to an office, not only to the benefit of the individual, but also of the community from which he comes, but especially the `extended family', the kindred, the clan or village, etc.

We may start looking at this from the policy level which roughly represents the intangible aspect. Individuals in public offices determine, in large measure, what becomes the economic fate of a people. In other words, they are in a position to exercise great power over the affairs of others. The significance of this is that it easily translates into politics. For as asserted by Alexander Hamilton, "in the general course of human nature... a power over a man's subsistence amounts to a power over his will'"[12] it is not surprising that those who are unrepresented in any public sphere feel deprived. However fair and well considered, policies become impositions as they are `alien' to those not represented at its formulation. On the positive side of it, a community whose son occupies an important public office feels secure and satisfied, especially given that even if no direct benefits are immediately forthcoming, they feel confident that they will not be cheated when the opportunity offers itself. And experience has shown that officeholders are influential in attracting development projects to their communities of origin. Many a time they endeavour to make their communities thrive after meeting the minimum conditions to qualify for these projects. Where they fail to achieve that as individuals, they have even used the lobby technique through their community development associations, often showing their prominent members who and who matter in the decision-making process. It is also true that very important projects have not been considered at all, or have been given low priority because the people in charge cannot fully appreciate their importance to the immediate community. Recently, a prominent Nigerian had cause to lament the abandonment of roads and other projects embarked upon during his tenure in government, which he considered, like his community, very important. But, alas, his successor was not in a position to appreciate how it feels to live a rural life.[13] Given the above, the cliche `If you have nobody in the capital, you have no say in the capital' holds so true. And besides, projects, scholarships and employment opportunities have gone to certain areas because they are well represented in the offices that matter. Call it nepotism, but it cancels itself out if other areas are equally or fairly represented. Regional disparities, in terms of development, can thus be attributed to this factor of lopsided representation. It is partly used to explain the difference in federal industrial presence between the land East of the Niger and that West of it. The civil war and `bad politics among the Easterners' deprived them of the opportunity to be at the strategic places when decisions were being taken. This is held as the common view in the `East'.[14] Similarly, if you ask a man from the middle-belt area of Nigeria, he will advance comparable reasons to explain the paucity of federal industries in the area.

At another level, public office held by an individual is of tremendous economic benefit to his community, at times. Some of these benefits can still be unquantifiable, though we intend to deal here with the tangible prebendal trappings of office. In the extended family system, an officeholder is seen as an economic benefactor for many of his kinsmen.

Many a time it proves to be so. Apart from financial assistance which he is always called upon to give, he fulfills other obligations such as offering hospitality to many members of his community who come to town for different businesses, such as schooling, attending interviews or searching for employment, looking for contracts, or trading. Besides accommodation, this same officer sometimes has to help out, by making necessary connections to make it easier or possible for his relations to achieve their goals. A successful public officer may be a source of inspiration to his community whom young men and women are made to look up to as well as to emulate. Many have won chieftaincy titles for such contributions.

It is for such benefits that public office is seen in many quarters as special privilege which should not be limited but instead be fairly, if not equally, spread. This expectation is achievable only through such a policy principle as federal character.

A Critique

We have stated much in favour of the federal character principle. It is only fair that we also attempt to answer to what negative views or arguments may be held against it. The strongest opponents of federal character are those apostles of meritocracy; who think only merit is good enough in determining who gets a public appointment. The fear is that upholding the federal character principle will compromise on the requisite competence for holding such appointments.[15] This is a genuine fear if the holders of such views are sincere about public good. But classrooms do not make geniuses. The merit problem becomes a technical one which poorly fits in with politics. If it dealt only with matters of technical competence such as flying of planes, operation of computers etc. and stopped at that, there might be good sense in the arguments of meritocracy. But it is not about the categories of the competent and the incompetent, but about the categories of the competent and the more or less competent. Were it possible to say that the candidate A is a better achiever than candidate B, and that candidate B is better than candidate C and so on, there would be no problem. But for most examinations, there are only two categories, the F (failure) category and the rest of them who then arrange themselves from E up to A. This means that it is not only A that is useful. It follows logically that there is a minimum standard of competence determined by examinations, and the rest is politics – the one for the classroom and the other for the place of employment. Besides, merit by itself is not foolproof, considering the human elements that go into the determination of merit.

The foregoing has cleared the air over the issue of merit to make our position clear. But we must be honest to accept that something shall certainly give way in the face of accepting the federal character principle. For example, there is genuine fear that officers, secured by the provision, may begin to act like political representatives without paying due attention to their duties. Secondly, given that federal character is the twin brother of proportionality, it is feared we may start on a very shaky note if special care is not taken. However, we may stop to ask; How much shall we lose by embracing federal character and thereby risking the aforementioned? One is tempted to say the loss will be negligible compared with possible gains.

We return to the fundamental question, i.e. that a people only need to dedicate themselves, or `commit themselves', as suggested by Ramphal, to make federal formulae work.[16] Thus even though we accept that every arrangement may only approximate the federal ideal, a people must cultivate the necessary political will to see them work. For Nigeria, federal character may thus be better both in spirit and in practice than alternative arrangements, in the circumstances i.e. in a plural society with a high degree of identity creating awareness among diverse cultures such as Nigeria represents.

Conclusion

We have tried to argue that in a `deeply' segmented society[17] such as Nigeria's, equity is one of the strongest ways of establishing confidence among the groups. For it is by it that they can feel the sense of belonging and so commit themselves to the continued existence of the union. Thus federal character as an equity principle is an integrative principle if arrangements are made to respect it in a political set up. A brief survey of Nigeria's experience suggests that the equity principle, through public office appointments, is realisable. It is so appreciated by Nigerians. Thus, despite some of its obvious shortcomings there are benefits it offers if Nigeria adopts and applies it to the operation of its federation, such as it now purports to do by the constitutional acceptance of the principle.

There is a little more we may add here to the necessary conditions which may ensure its success in the country, beside the political will of Nigerians to make it succeed. First, is the honesty and impartiality of those charged with implementing it or supervising its implementation. This suggests that only men of proven integrity should be charged with ensuring its operation. Only such persons are capable of standing firm and yet preventing a slide into an impasse with the arguments whether or not it has been respected. And because federal character is a closely related principle to proportionality, there must be technical resources to ensure its realisation. It shows that reliable data must always be available. Necessary data will have to be assembled and constantly updated, which must be dependable. In addition, the guidelines to its implementation must also be unambiguous. This is to avoid a situation where mischievous elements take advantage of ambiguities to perpetrate their inequities. In the absence of such prerequisites, what obtained between Benue State and Igala people at the creation of Kogi State in 1991 can easily obtain.[18] It is suspected that the Igala community simply exploited the loopholes in the employment policy to fill the junior cadre of the Benue Service with its men and women. Of course you may only blame the policy or the inefficiency of its supervision. Again, a local complaint is germane to the argument. In the present Benue State, the Tiv people comprise about three-quarter of the population. But in each year's admission into the Nigerian Defence Academy (NDA), not up to 1/3 of the total successful candidates come from the Tiv. The continuity and consistency of the pattern now worries many Tiv young people. For this phenomenon cannot be blamed on their inability to cope in the selection process, as such incompetence should have been reflected in other spheres of Benue life. The suspicion is that there is an abuse of `state character' and proportionality in the selection of NDA candidates for Benue State.

Another serious challenge in the successful implementation of the federal character principle is the requirement of manpower planning and development. For it is only by careful manpower planning that the services should expect what to take in and what to shed off at different times, all other things being equal.

All in all, the federal character principle should be a potent tool with which to pursue and perhaps achieve national integration for Nigeria.

Notes

1. Akinyemi, A.B. *et al* (eds), *Readings on Federalism*. (Lagos: Nigerian Institute of International Affairs, NIIA, 1979), p. xvii.

2. Federal Republic of Nigeria, *The Constitution*, 1979.

3. Sartori, Giovani, *Parties and Party Systems: A framework for Analysis Vol. 1.* (Cambridge: Cambridge University Press, 1976)

4. Young Crawford. *The Politics of Cultural Pluralism*. (Wisconsin: University of Wisconsin Press, 1979).

5. Lijphart, Arend, *Democracy in Plural Societies: A Comparative Exploration*. (New Haven: Yale University Press, 1977).

6. Bapst, Eric, for example, has argued that it is the autonomy of the Swiss Communes that makes unique the national federal

arrangement of Switzerland, *The Autonomy of the Commune; The Swiss Experience,* a National Council for Intergovernmental Relations (NCIR) Lecture Series No. 2, 1993.

7. Richard, Joseph A., *Democracy and Prebendal Politics in Nigeria: The Rise and Fall of the Second Republic.* (Ibadan: Spectrum Books Limited, 1991) p. 186.

8. See for example Crowder, Michael *The Story of Nigeria.* (London: Faber and Faber Limited, 1978) p.208, for the demands of the NCBWA.

9. See the 1972 Nigerian Enterprises Promotion Decree and the 1977 Indigenisation Policy.

10. Section 144(3) and Section 15(3) of the Constitution of the Federal Republic of Nigeria, 1992.

11. Third Schedule of the Nigerian Constitution, 1992.

12. Quoted in Kling, Merle, "Towards a Theory of Power and Political Instability in Latin America" in Bendix, Reinhard, *et al* (eds) *State and Society; A Reader.* (Berkley: University of California Press, 1968), p.493.

13. Chief B.A.I. Gemade in a speech at a reception on 28th December, 1996 for his honorary doctorate award from the University of Calabar. The speech is yet unpublished.

14. This writer studied at the University of Nigeria, Nsukka, 1980-1982 and had the opportunity to often listen to such discussions. Some such claims could make interesting subjects for further investigation.

15. The valedictory speech of the graduating students at the 15th Convocation of the University of Calabar on 21st December, 1996, made reference to this.

16. See note 4 above.

17. Lijphart, A., *op.cit.* He prefers to describe societies with cultural pluralism as those 'deeply segmented', though we are not told how deep is 'deeply'.

18. When Igala land was excised from Benue State to make up the present Kogi State, it was discovered, to the embarrassment of the remaining Benue Community, that Igala people, accounting for hardly a quarter of the total population of the then Benue State had about half the population of the state's public service, mostly in the junior cadre.

SECTION THREE

Political Restructuring and the Economics of Federalism

CHAPTER 14

Gini F. Mbanefoh and Festus O. Egwaikhide

Revenue Allocation in Nigeria: Derivation Principle Revisited

I Introduction

A large body of literature exists on Nigeria's fiscal federalism, particularly with reference to revenue allocation. Despite the profound and lengthy discussions that have taken place on the subject for about four decades, consensus has not been reached concerning the optimal formula to adopt. Thus, the issue of revenue allocation has been a recurring theme in Nigeria's fiscal federalism.

There is the problem of how to allocate revenue to the different tiers of government in relation to the constitutionally assigned functions. The discordance between fiscal capacity of the various levels of government and their expenditure responsibilities, the non-correspondence problem, is a striking feature of the Nigerian federal finance. There is also the problem of how revenues should be shared among the states and local councils. Since the late 1940s, several criteria have been used to allocate revenues among the regions/states. The principles adopted to date include derivation, fiscal autonomy, national interest, equality of states, population, balanced development, social development and absorptive capacity. Each of these principles has attracted a number of criticisms from fiscal federalists, economists, social scientists, among others. The debate about what principles to use and the weight has been intense, giving rise to different theoretical and political positions.

The principle of derivation has unequivocally attracted the most significant attacks and protestations, however. Indeed, it was the dominant criterion up to the mid-1970s. Following the Aboyade Technical Committee on Revenue Allocation in 1977 and the submission of the minority report of the Okigbo Revenue Allocation Commission in 1981 (that this principle should not feature again in the revenue allocation scheme)[1], the use of the derivation principle has paled into insignificance. Empirical enquiries have shown that derivation principle significantly influenced the revenues allocated to the regions/states (see Teriba, 1966, Phillips, 1971, 1975; and Omorogiuwa, 1980). Derivation that was initially suggested because it is an innocuous principle has been proved to be ruinous by some fiscal federalists. One major plank of their argument is the patchy data on the items on which the derivation principle was applied. Arising from this is the conclusion that derivation principle unjustifiably raised the revenue to some regions/states at the expense of others. This made the principle incompatible with the objective of balanced development stressed in the various National Development Plans and policy statements.

This chapter examines the arguments in favour of derivation principle in horizontal revenue allocation in Nigeria. It is acknowledged that the proposed weight of 13 per cent attached to the derivation principle at the 1995 Constitutional Conference is a welcome development. This figure should be substantially increased since oil production that contributes to the bulk of the nation's revenue generates negative externalities with intergenerational adverse consequences.

The rest of the chapter is organised into five sections. Section II presents the developments in revenue allocation formula in recent years. Examined in Section III is the distributional pattern of revenue among states. The profile of derivation revenue and the need to reconsider the application of derivation principle in the horizontal revenue sharing arrangement are the main focus of section IV. Recent developments in Nigeria's fiscal federalism are compiled in Section V. Section VI concludes.

II Changes in the Revenue Allocation System

This discussion focuses on the 1980s and after, as many authors have comprehensively analysed the developments in the previous years (see for example, Phillips, 1971; 1975; Mbanefoh, 1980, 1993; Emenuga, 1993). The two major criteria, which dominated the horizontal revenue sharing formula, were equality of states and population. In response to the call by individuals and pressure groups for a review of the revenue sharing formula, the Aboyade Technical Committee on Revenue Allocation was set up in 1977. Almost all the recommendations of this committee were considered too technical relative to the stage of Nigeria's development and were consequently disregarded by government.

Soon after the swearing-in of the Shagari-led civilian administration on October 1, 1979, the Presidential Commission on Revenue Allocation headed by Pius Okigbo (also called the Okigbo Commission) was constituted. Although, the Okigbo Commission's recommendations were invalidated by the Supreme Court of Nigeria, the 1981 revenue Act that was passed by Parliament was based on the recommendations of the Okigbo Commission. By this Act, the federal government was to receive 55 per cent of the Federation Account; state governments, 30.5 per cent local government, 10 per cent; and 4.5 per cent for special funds.

Further modifications were made in 1984 by Decree 36 and in 1992 on approval of the recommendations of the National Revenue Mobilisation, Allocation and Fiscal Commission (NRMAFC) by the Armed Forces Ruling Council (AFRC). Since 1992, the share of the federal government has remained at 48.5 per cent, state and local government are allocated 24 per cent and twenty per cent, respectively; and the remaining 7.5 per cent belongs to special funds. Out of the 7.5 per cent, three per cent is set aside for the development of oil producing areas, while 1.0 per cent is shared among mineral-producing states on the basis of derivation.

For the sharing of revenue among state governments, four principles were considered. These were: population with a weight of 40 per cent minimum responsibility of government (also called equality of states), 40 per cent; social development factor, 15 per cent; and internal revenue effort, 5 per cent. The same principles with the corresponding weights were also used to allocate revenue to local governments from the Federation Account. The weights have been adjusted since then: equality of states 40 per cent; population reduced to 30 per cent; internal revenue effort, 10 per cent; social development factor, 10 per cent; and the balance of 10 per cent is assigned to land mass and terrain, a static principle quietly introduced by the NRMAFC. Thus, these principles influenced the distributional pattern of statutory revenues of state and local governments since the 1980s.

III Profile of Revenue Allocation in Recent Years

In general, the magnitude of revenue allocated to states leapt significantly during the period of 1980 to 1995. Specifically, the amount allocated to states increased from about ₦2.4 billion in 1980 through ₦10.9 billion to ₦38.4 billion in 1989 and 1995 respectively. The general rise in revenue allocation to this tier of government largely reflected developments in the federally-collected revenue, and was also a function of the percentage given to it by the revenue sharing formula. Following the promulgation of Decree No. 36 of 1984, for example, the percentage share of state governments in the Federation Account was raised from 30.5 per cent to 32.5 per cent.

Reliable statistics on non-statutory allocation (or conditional grants) to state governments at the discretion of the federal government are not readily available. It will be recalled that these grants were tied to vital sectors of the economy (e.g., health, education, water resources and industry). Indeed, it is argued that non-statutory allocation substantially raised revenues accruing to state governments in the 1970s (Phillips, 1975; Omoroguiwa, 1980). The disappearance of these conditional grants in the 1980s may have been due to amendments in the revenue allocation system that placed all revenues collected (with minor exceptions) by the federal government to the Federation Account for vertical sharing among the three layers of government.

The distributional pattern of statutory revenue allocation to states for the period between 1980 and 1995 is shown in Tables 1a and 1b. It is clear that there were no significant variations in the relative shares of states from year to year in the 1980s; though, differences exist across states. On average, Kano State received the highest allocation of 7.2% during 1980/89 period, a figure that is marginally above the share of Bendel and Rivers States that each received 7.14%. The population of Kano State possibly explains its high share in the Federation Account relative to other states. A closer look at Table 1b reveals that the shares of Kano, Katsina and Rivers were generally higher than any other state in the 1990s; but could not compare favourably with the figures for the 1980s.

Test statistic indicates the relatively evenly distribution of interstate statutory revenue allocation from the Federation Account during the reference period. The computed index, which is basically the standard deviation divided by the mean, deviated significantly from absolute equality (i.e., zero) on an annual basis in the first half of 1970s, with the minimum being 0.41 in 1972/73 (see Phillips, 1975:12). The highest this index recorded in the 1980s was 0.41 (see Table 2) and it tended to decline thereafter.

A comment on the overall trend is basic. The fact that no particular state's share in the Federation Account was outstanding is a clear demonstration of the improvements over the allocations in the 1970s when Mid-Western (later Bendel) State and Rivers States dominated. Technically, this trend reflects fairer inter-state shares deriving possibly from the principles and weights used. In this respect, the less emphasis on derivation principle may have played a significant role. But, the results of the computation should be seen as only being statistically fair since they deviate significantly from reality.

Table 1a: Percentage Distribution of Revenue Allocation to States in Nigeria, 1980-1989

State	1980	1981	1982	1983	1984	1985	1986	1987	1988	1989
Akwa-Ibom								1.6	4.1	4.1
Anambra	5.1	5.1	5.5	5.5	5.5	5.1	5.6	5.5	5.4	5.4
Bauchi	4.1	4.2	4.3	4.3	4.3	4.1	4.4	4.3	4.2	4.2
Bendel	10.0	8.9	7.0	6.9	6.9	5.9	6.4	6.5	6.3	6.4
Benue	4.2	4.2	4.5	4.5	4.5	4.1	4.5	4.4	4.3	4.3
Borno	4.6	4.6	4.9	4.9	4.9	4.6	5.0	4.9	4.8	4.8
Cross River	5.2	5.1	5.3	5.3	5.3	4.9	5.4	4.3	2.9	2.8
Gongola	4.3	4.3	4.5	4.5	4.5	4.2	4.6	4.5	4.4	4.4
Imo	6.4	6.3	6.1	6.1	6.1	5.5	6.0	6.0	5.9	5.9
Kaduna	5.4	5.5	5.9	5.9	5.9	5.5	6.0	5.0	3.4	3.4
Kano	6.7	6.8	7.4	7.4	7.4	6.8	7.5	7.4	7.3	7.3
Katsina								1.6	4.2	4.1
Kwara	3.6	3.6	3.6	3.6	3.6	3.4	3.7	3.6	3.5	3.5
Lagos	3.4	3.4	4.0	4.0	4.0	3.7	4.0	4.0	3.9	3.9
Niger	3.2	3.2	3.1	3.1	3.1	2.9	3.2	3.1	3.0	3.0
Ogun	3.5	3.5	3.5	3.5	3.5	3.2	3.5	3.4	3.3	3.3
Ondo	4.4	4.4	4.7	4.7	4.7	4.4	4.8	4.7	4.6	4.6
Oyo	6.3	6.4	6.7	6.8	6.8	6.8	6.9	6.8	6.7	6.7
Plateau	3.9	3.9	3.9	3.9	3.9	5.0	3.9	3.9	3.8	3.8
Rivers	10.0	10.5	6.8	6.8	6.7	5.6	6.1	6.2	6.0	6.2
Sokoto	5.8	5.8	6.3	6.3	6.3	5.9	6.4	6.3	6.2	6.2
FCT			1.9	1.9	1.9	1.7	1.9	1.0	1.5	1.7
Total	100.0	100.0	100.0	100.0	100.0	100.0	100.0	100.0	98.5	100.0

Source: Federal Ministry of Finance

Table 1b: Statutory Revenue Allocation to States in Nigeria, 1992-95 (%)

State	1992	1993	1994	1995
Abia	2.34	2.65	2.74	2.88
Adamawa	3.44	3.46	3.03	3.10
Akwa Ibom	4.15	3.26	3.11	3.95
Anambra	2.73	2.587	2.54	2.66
Bauchi	4.23	3.98	3.55	3.68
Benue	2.59	3.92	2.96	2.66
Borno	2.25	2.93	2.95	3.63
Cross River	2.4	2.56	2.74	3.25
Delta	2.80	3.29	3.36	3.51
Edo	1.99	2.69	2.52	3.54
Enugu	2.43	2.53	2.89	3.62
Imo	3.84	3.34	3.21	3.13
Jigawa	4.0	2.84	2.87	2.96
Kaduna	3.12	3.61	3.98	2.44
Kano	3.34	5.26	5.54	4.13
Katsina	5.52	4.26	4.32	4.03
Kebbi	2.29	2.56	3.28	2.72
Kogi	2.42	2.71	2.29	2.40
Kwara	2.18	2.35	2.56	2.15
Lagos	5.25	3.34	3.21	3.35
Niger	1.94	2.56	2.85	2.97
Ogun	2.26	2.83	3.02	2.58
Ondo	2.71	2.22	3.55	2.88
Osun	4.04	3.23	3.22	3.36
Oyo	4.58	3.08	2.96	3.36
Plateau	2.95	3.67	3.47	3.50
Rivers	5.34	4.77	3.48	4.72
Sokoto	5.02	4.78	3.60	3.92
Taraba	1.87	2.41	3.46	2.56
Yobe	2.74	2.40	2.73	2.77
FCT, Abuja	3.14	3.64	3.96	3.58
Total	**100.00**	**100.00**	**100.00**	**100.00**

Source: Central Bank of Nigeria, *Annual Report and Statement of Accounts*, various issues, Lagos

Revenue Allocation in Nigeria. 219

For clarity of exposition, it is essential to examine the role of state creation on revenue allocation. Since this issue has been discussed for the earlier years by Omorogiuwa (1980), interpretations are limited to the more recent years. A close inspection of Table 1a shows that the relative shares of Cross River and Kaduna States that used to oscillate around 5.0-5.5 per cent and 5.4-6.0 per cent, respectively, declined after 1987. The creation of Akwa-Ibom State (from the old Cross River State) and Katsina State (out of the former Kaduna State) accounts for the observed outcome. In 1991, additional nine states were created, bringing the total number to thirty. Thus, two States – Delta and Edo –were created from the former Bendel State; Osun State was carved out from the erstwhile Oyo State; Kebbi State was excised from the old Sokoto State, etc. This development altered the pattern of revenue allocation to states. Between 1980 and 1986, the share of Kaduna State from the total revenue allocated to all the states averaged 5.7 per cent annually. Katsina State was created from Kaduna State, a development which raised their combined share to 7.8 per cent in the four years, 1992-95. The lowest share recorded by Bendel State in the 1980s was 5.9 per cent and that was in 1985. With the bifurcation of the state into Delta and Edo States, the combined percentage allocation averaged 5.9 per cent, a far cry from the figures of the 1980s. It is doubtful if the joint percentage allocation to Osun and Oyo States ever improved even marginally over the period when they were in a single state. Juxtaposed against this is the increasing statutory allocations to Sokoto and Kebbi States when compared to the single state before 1991. In October 1996, six additional states were created, Sokoto State was further divided into Sokoto and Zamfara States. By this, the former Sokoto State has been divided into three states.

Perhaps, the effect of state creation on revenue allocation is easily understood when the data are organised into the four former regions. It is evident in Table 1 in the Appendix that the share of the Northern region (that is, all the Northern States) has tended to increase from 48.4 per cent of 1982-84 period, to 49 per cent during 1987/89 and averaged about 51.7 per cent for 1992/95 period. It is almost incredible that the allocation to the Western States that fluctuated between 17.5 per cent and 19 per cent fell to an average of 15.4 per cent between 1993 and 1995. Since 1982, the allotment to the Eastern States only varied in 1993-94 when it registered about 21.4 per cent, while Mid-Western States (Edo and Delta

States) declined in 1992/94.

Table 2: Coefficient of Variation for Inter-state and Inter-local Government Shares in Statutory Revenue Allocation 1980/1995

Year	State	Local Council
1980	0.375	0.301
1981	0.410	0.210
1982	0.262	0.242
1983	0.254	0.242
1984	0.256	0.242
1985	0.228	0.242
1986	0.240	0.234
1987	0.335	0.325
1988	0.278	0.269
1989	0.281	–
1992	0.331	–
1993	0.235	0.284
1994	0.192	0.307
1995	0.180	0.368

Note: Coefficient of variation of inter-local government on state basis for 1980-81 are based on estimates.

Sources: Data used to compute this index were obtained from:
(i) Federal Ministry of Finance; and (ii) Central Bank of Nigeria, *Annual Report and Statement of Account*, various years

Two plausible factors account for the observed pattern of revenue allocation. These are the use of land mass and terrain, and equality of states to which 40 per cent and 10 per cent weights are attached respectively. On the basis of the principle of equality of states, the region that is balkanised into more states received more from the Federation Account. Land mass may have favoured northern states more than the states in the other regions. From the relatively high weights attached to the principles of equality of states and land mass, it can be argued that they are being used as instruments of resource redistribution, from regions where revenue are generated to poor regions. This is not a transparent way of redistributing financial resources in a federal setting. These principles have formed part of the latent factors for the creation of more states and local councils in recent years.

Local governments also use the same principles that are applied to states with corresponding weights. This suggests that states with more local councils got more from the Federation Accounts using the principle of equality.

IV Trends in Derivation Revenue and Derivation Principle

Derivation principle has been de-emphasised. In place of derivation, 2 per cent of the total revenue collected was allocated to mineral producing states and it was shared in proportion to the value of minerals extracted. There was 1.5 per cent set aside as federal fund that was directly administered to oil producing states. It is obvious that not all the states benefitted from the application of derivation principle since the early 1980s. States that received revenue in the 1980s from derivation were: Akwa-Ibom, Bauchi, Bendel, Cross River, Imo, Kaduna, Kano, Katsina, Ondo, Plateau, and Rivers. However, the revenue from this source by each of these states – Bauchi, Kaduna, Ondo, and Plateau – was less than ₦1 million annually in the years 1982/88 (Kaduna State, however, received about ₦4 million in 1987). Thus, the revenue realised by these states on the basis of the applied derivation principle as a proportion of statutory allocation was negligible.

Contained in Table 3 are statistics on revenue allocation, based on derivation, to Akwa-Ibom, Bendel, Cross River, Imo and Rivers States for the period between 1982 and 1989. Akwa-Ibom State, which was created in 1987, obtained less than 1.5 per cent of its statutory allocation from the Federation Account in 1987/89. For Imo, the relative share of derivation in statutory allocation averaged 6.6 per cent during the period. However, both Bendel and Rivers States, the major oil-producing states derived, sizeable revenue from derivation principle. It follows that without the use of this principle, the statutory revenue to these states would have been relatively low. In this sense, the inference is drawn that derivation served as an instrument of fiscal equalisation; implying that Bendel and Rivers States, each received a paltry sum based on the principle of derivation.

Table 3: Derivation Revenue as a Percentage of Statutory Revenue Allocation for Selected States in the 1980s

Year	Akwa-Ibom State	Bendel State	Cross-River State	Imo State	Rivers State
1982		25.4	0.1	6.8	3.2
1983		34.2	1.6	9.5	45.8
1984		n.a	n.a	n.a	n.a
1985		25.0	1.5	6.7	33.5
1986		27.5	1.1	6.5	78.8
1987	0.7	12.5	6.8	5.5	25.0
1988	1.1	16.7	11.6	5.6	30.5
1989	1.3	25.4	–	5.9	61.4

Notes: n.a. denotes 'not available'. The revenue received on the basis of derivation as percentage of total allocated revenue received by each of the following states – Bauchi, Kaduna, Kano, Ondo, and Plateau – is less than 0.5 per cent yearly. This is why they are excluded from this table. The other states did not receive revenues based on derivation since they do not produce any minerals. Allocation to local councils are not included.

Source: Computed from data obtained from the Federal Ministry of Finance.

Derivation principle may have been replaced by land mass and terrain, a principle whose introduction was not thrown to public debate or whose acceptance has not officially been tested. Like the principle of equality of states, the use of land mass serves as a device to divert financial resources to some parts of the country. The conclusion is easily appreciated that a large part of expenditures in non-oil producing states are incurred at the expense of oil-producing areas. This is a huge subsidy, suggesting that the horizontal revenue allocation principles be reviewed and redesigned to favour the use of derivation principle. It is only in this way that the minority group that contributes the substantial part of the total revenue can derive adequate benefit and have a sense of belonging to the Nigerian federating units.

Historically, the principle of derivation as a criterion for horizontal revenue allocation in Nigeria was first recommended by the Phillipson Fiscal Commission of 1942[2]. Thereafter, it featured prominently in all the other fiscal commissions set up by the government. Following the Aboyade Technical Committee on Revenue Allocation Report in 1977, the principle of derivation was de-emphasised; and its use became worrisomely negligible. Indeed, the Volume IV of the Okigbo Report of the Presidential Commission on Revenue Allocation (1980) argued indefatigably that this principle should not be used again in the revenue allocation scheme.

According to the principle of derivation, each region should receive revenue from the central government in proportion to its contribution to the centrally collected revenue. In the views of Phillipson, the recommendation of this principle was informed by the need to promote fiscal discipline in the region. On the basis of derivation, therefore, it was envisaged that each region must necessarily relate its expenditures to available revenue. This principle was also proposed in anticipation that the regions should have some degree of fiscal autonomy with time[3]. On these scores, the use of derivation as a principle for revenue allocation among the regions is desirable and in particular, it should be favoured on equity considerations.

The principle of derivation was used to share revenue collected from import and excise taxes on tobacco; import duties on motor fuel, salt, and spirit; export duties, and mining rents and royalties in accordance with regional consumption of the products on which tax revenues were obtained. This principle was attacked: that, it negates equity principle due to several factors. Central to the criticisms was the lack of accurate statistics on the regional distribution of imported items (other than tobacco and motor fuel) on which duties were imposed. Indeed, it was reported that figures for regional consumption of the affected items were based on broad assumptions and approximation. Moreso, the country at its stage of development then, did not possess the capacity to effectively handle the calculations required from time to time. Thus, to share revenue generated from customs duties to the regions on the basis of the amount of imported goods consumed represented a blatant violation of the principles of equity and fairness.

The point has also been made that the application of derivation promoted regional hostility and disunity because it supported uneven development. It was expressed that derivation principle tended to favour wealthy regions at the expense of the poor ones; and so, it is not only anti-redistributional, it negates the macro objective of rapid growth and development (see Teriba, 1966; and Phillips, 1971). Thus, it was common for a region not favoured by it at one period to oppose its use. Despite the criticisms levelled against derivation, it was used to its fullest degree up to the mid-1960s.

With the emergence of oil, the antagonists of the use of derivation increased with rapidity. The core of their arguments was that derivation excessively favours the oil-producing states[4]. Relying on the coefficient of variation as an index of inequality, for example, statistical estimates by Phillips (1975) reveal that there was increased inequality in interstate revenue between 1970/71 and 1974/75 fiscal years (it increased from 0.48 in 1970/71 to 0.74 in 1974/75), a result attributed to the use of derivation. This trend may have been invidious in two senses. The first was the unbalanced development that the use of this principle could foster. Second, which is political, was that derivation could lead to a radical shift in revenue from majority groups, which are very influential and powerful, to minority groups that are politically powerless. Accordingly, the persistence of this trend may lead to a shift in political power which should not be.

Despite the structurally weak statistical base of the principle of derivation, it represented the sole determinant of revenue allocation to the regions. This possibly demonstrates the strong direct correspondence between regional control of the political process and the use of derivation in Nigeria's fiscal federalism (Federal Republic of Nigeria, 1987:169-70). On this score, that the use of derivation as a major principle for revenue sharing would have persisted, had the dominant groups are the oil producing areas, is doubtless.

There is little doubt that the use of derivation was unjustifiably de-emphasised. The arguments for its resurgence with a substantial weight attached are easily appreciated. If there were no statistical problems associated with the regional consumption of imported goods (other than tobacco and motor fuel), derivation would have been used till today. But, mineral production does not suffer similar statistical weakness that would warrant the non-application of this principle. Even during this period there were no arguments against the use of derivation to allocate revenue obtained from mining rents and royalties.

Second is the proposition that the continued use of derivation will accelerate uneven progress. This claim possibly finds explanation in the hypothesis of geographic dualism. That, favouring a particular region through derivation would precipitate cumulative expansion in the region at the expense of other regions. But, by the very nature of fiscal decentralisation, disproportionate growth and development is inevitable. This is directly related to the important issue of unequal fiscal capacity of fiscal federalism. Reference can hardly be made to a developing country with a decentralised fiscal system that has achieved balanced development. In this respect, this argument is not only untenable, it can hardly be sustained. Interregional differences in terms of development indicators are only expected to diverge significantly if the `backwash' effects of the rapid growth in one region overshadow the `trickling down' effects[5]. It is generally acknowledged that the polarisation effects of interregional differences would not persist indefinitely due to increasing costs and external diseconomies that may emerge. Even so, regional planners generally recognise that regional disequilibrium situation tends to move towards equilibrium through movements of factors across space. Based on the equilibrium model of development and the conclusion of the disequilibrium theory, the fear of the antagonists of derivation principle that it would engender spatial inequalities is, perhaps, unfounded. Policy advisers would normally favour this line of reasoning that should increased regional inequalities arise following the application of derivation, policies should be implemented to strengthen the `spread' effects of the expanding region. In any case, the problem of unequal fiscal capacity is usually resolved through grants.

There is a third argument in favour of derivation principle and it uses the case of oil production as an illustration. There are negative geographic spillovers associated with crude oil production. The intensity and dimensions of pollution in oil-producing areas have increased over time. Some indications of this are the increased persistent clashes between oil-producing companies and oil communities in recent years. Pollution has led to soil degradation with adverse consequences on food production. Water contamination has tended to increase water-borne diseases and has impaired aquatic life. In general, pollution has been detrimental to human health and wildlife in oil-producing areas. Oil pollution has both short and long-run effects on man and the environment, and so, they affect one generation to another. Even the distributional effects of oil pollution are not evenly distributed, with women and children having to suffer most from the negative externalities of oil production. A direct import of this is that the indirect costs of oil production are borne more by the communities. By implication, the current revenue arrangements do not guarantee net benefits to the affected communities. Crop and imported goods on which derivation had been applied to the fullest did not generate the negative externalities mineral production such as oil has on the immediate environment. Attaching a substantial weight to derivation principle will provide adequate funds to implement development projects that will enhance the living standards of the people directly affected. This is particularly necessary when it is realised that poor health caused by pollution can, in fact, affect future generations. The fact that crude oil is a wasting asset even makes it the more imperative to consider derivation principle in allocating revenue from its production.

To these three reasons can be added a fourth. One argument explored to liquidate derivation principle is that it breeds regional conflicts and hostility; and as a result, it is a factor of disunity. The corollary is that the elimination of derivation will promote and reinforce unity and, therefore, induce the development process. Although, the importance of derivation has tapered off for more than a decade, interregional antagonism, discontent and tension have deepened rather than abated. There was a consensus agreement at the 1995 Constitutional Conference that derivation should not only be one of the principles for sharing revenue, it should attract a minimum weight of 13 per cent. Since members of this conference were representatives of the people, their recommendations on derivation must be seen as politically acceptable and ethically desirable. This is a strong indication that the use of derivation principle, with a reasonable weight attached, is not an element of factionalism.

V Recent Developments

Following the economic crisis of the early 1980s that led to the implementation of economic reform programme, the federal government established special accounts. The accounts are: Stabilisation Fund; Dedicated Accounts; and Petroleum Trust Fund (PTF)[6]. The funds paid into these accounts are federally collected revenue that ought to be paid into the

Federation Account for vertical sharing among the three levels of government. The PTF, for instance, was set up by the federal government to manage the revenue generated from the substantial upward review of prices of petroleum products in October 1994. Specifically, the PTF funds are to be used to improve the deteriorated social services and economic infrastructure.

That the PTF is predicated on the principle of earmarking can hardly be denied. But, earmarking reduces budgetary flexibility since the budget cannot easily be adapted to the changing preferences of the various groups, particularly under a decentralised fiscal system. It is argued that the arbitrary procedure of earmarking does not allow revenue to be allocated among competing uses. Thus, the principle of earmarked taxes does not permit efficient allocation of government revenue[7]. Weaker states and local councils who are unable to persuade the PTF management about the seriousness of the problems of their social services and economic infrastructure are not likely to receive attention. States and local councils that got relatively higher revenue allocation from the Federation Account may, in fact, also benefit more from the expenditure programme of the PTF. By the very nature of the PTF that is operated as a benevolent fund, the federal government undeniably sees itself as a benefactor. This argument only highlights the fact that state and local governments do not have any say regarding how the funds in this and other accounts should be used.

The concentration process in Nigeria's fiscal federalism reported by Mbanefoh (1986), a phenomenon in which states and local councils share very little in the growth of total government outlay is possibly exacerbated with the establishments of special accounts by the federal government. Even the striking imbalance between the assigned constitutional functions and taxes to carry out such functions – the non-correspondence problem – has been provoked by the existence of the special accounts. In a democratic setting, the use of special accounts that does not take into consideration the principle of fairness and equity will certainly be challenged and opposed by the lower levels of government. Where special accounts are used to foster the development of a few selected states/local councils, inter-state hostility and rivalry will inevitably intensify.

The point should be made that Nigeria can hardly qualify for fiscal decentralisation presently. Perhaps, it is more appropriate to say that Nigeria operates administrative decentralisation, as most of the buoyant taxes are collected by the federal government and the revenue allocated to lower levels of government through the Federation Account for them to carry out their expenditure responsibilities[8]. In carrying out their expenditure functions, the federal government imposes regulations and controls on states and local governments. Indeed, a one-size-fits-all technique, which is more relevant to a centralised fiscal system, has always been adopted under the military. In consequence, there is little or no room for experimentation and innovative creation on the part of the federating units. All this does not permit a viable and enduring fiscal decentralisation; and it negates democratic principles that fiscal decentralisation should promote.

VI Concluding Remarks

This chapter has examined the distributional pattern of revenues among states in Nigeria during the 1980s and argues in favour of derivation principle. Historical evidence indicates that there was no striking disparity in the statutory revenue allocation among the states of the federation, a significant departure from what obtained prior to the 1980s. This was attributed to the weights attached to the principles used in the horizontal revenue sharing arrangements. Despite this trend, it was noted that the pattern exhibited may not have reflected the needs of the various states.

It was argued that the principle of derivation was unjustifiably de-emphasised because of the shift in revenue generation from the majority groups that are politically powerful to the minority areas that are politically powerless. Because the principle of derivation meets equity consideration, its use with a substantial weight should be considered in order to enhance the benefits derivable from oil production by mineral producing areas. The justification for the increase in the weight attached to derivation is anchored on the negative externalities which oil production, in particular, generates. The destruction of the ecosystem of the oil-producing areas demands huge budgetary allocations to such areas to meet their developmental needs. The relegation of derivation has undoubtedly sustained the dogmatic use of the principle of equality of states that now serves as an effective apparatus for redistributing financial resources from one region to another.

The establishment of special account (with the PTF as an example) attracted some interpretative comment. It was expressed that the use of special accounts does not guarantee fairness and equity often stressed in multilevel finance. Thus, it is only proper for such accounts to be repudiated.

Notes

1. See, for example, the articles by Phillips (1971,1975) and his minority report to the Presidential Revenue Commission headed by Okigbo in 1980.

2. It has been acknowledged by Phillipson that revenue estimates from certain sources – licenses, fees, direct taxes, rent of government for the year 1919 were shared among the Central Government, the Northern Region, and the Southern Protectorate and the Colony on the basis of derivation. On this, see Phillipson (1948:7)

3. *Ibid*, p.20, The views of the other fiscal commissions on derivation can be found in Hicks and Phillipson (1951), Chicks (1954), and Raisman and Tress (1958)

4. In particular, Phillips (1975) argued that the application of derivation principle excessively favoured Mid-Western (later became Bendel) and Rivers States, the major oil-producing states.

5. See Myrdal (1957) who developed the hypothesis of cumulative causation to explain regional dualism.

6. See Central Bank of Nigeria (1995) *Annual Report and Statement of Account*, pp. 62-63.

7. For a discussion on earmarking, see Buchanan (1963), and McMahon and Sprenkle (1970).

8. On the distinction between fiscal and administrative decentralisation, see Tanzi (1995).

References

Chick, A.L. (1954) *Report of Fiscal Commmmission.* Lagos: Government Printer

Emenuga, C. (1993) ``Nigeria: The search for an Acceptable Revenue Allocation Formula'', *Proceedings of the 1993 Annual Conference of Nigerian Economic Society*, pp. 79-105

Buchanan, J.M. (1963) ``The Economics of Earmarked Taxes'', *Journal of Political Economy*, Vol. 71, pp. 457-69

Federal Republic of Nigeria (1980) *Report of the Presidential Commission on Revenue Allocation* Vol. IV. Lagos: Federal Government Press, Apapa

Federal Republic of Nigeria (1987) *Report of the Political Bureau.* Lagos: Government Printer

Federal Republic of Nigeria (1989) *National Revenue Mobilization, Allocation and Fiscal Commission.* Main Report

Hicks, J.R. and S. Phillipson (1951) *Report of the Commission on Revenue Allocation.* Lagos: Government Printer

Mbanefoh, Gini F. (1986) ``Military Presence and the Future of Nigerian Fiscal Federalism'', *Faculty Lecture Series* (Faculty of the Social Sciences, University of Ibadan, Nigeria), No.1.

──────── (1993) ``Unsettled Issues in Nigeria's Fiscal Federalism and the National Question''. Proceedings of the 1993 Annual Conference of the Nigerian Economic Society, pp. 61-77.

McMahon, W.W. and C.M. Sprenkle (1970) ``A Theory of Earmarking'', *National Tax Journal*, vol. 23, pp 255-262

Myrdal, G. (1957) *Economic Theory and Underdeveloped Regions* London: Duckworth.

Omorogiuwa, P.A. (1980) *Nigeria: The Effect of State Creation on Revenue Allocation and Economic Development.* Published for the Association of Graduates of American Universities: Nigerian Chapter

Phillips, A.O. (1971) ``Nigeria's Federal Financial Experience''. *The Journal of Modern African Studies,* vol. 9, No. 3, pp. 389-408

──────── (1975) ``Revenue Allocation in Nigeria 1970-80''. *The Nigerian Journal of Economic and Social Studies.* vol. 17, No.1 pp. 1-28

Phillipson, S. (1948) *Administrative and Financial Procedure under the New Constitution: Financial Relations Between the Government of Nigeria and the Native* Administration. Lagos: Government Printer.

Raisman, J. and R.C. Trees (1958) *Preliminary Report of the Fiscal Commission.* Lagos: Government Printer

Tanzi, V. (1995) "Fiscal Federalism and Decentralisation: A Review of Some Efficiency and Macroeconomic Aspects". *Annual World Bank Conference on Development Economics.*

Teriba, O. (1966) "Nigeria Revenue Allocation Experience". *The Nigerian Journal of Economic and Social Studies.* vol. 8, No. 3, pp. 361-382

Appendix

Table 1: Statutory Revenue Allocation to the Four Former Regions

Region	1977	1978	1979	1980	1981	1982	1983	1984
East	24.25	25.7	24.7	26.7	27	23.7	23.7	23.6
North	47.03	47.4	48.1	45.8	46.1	48.4	48.4	48.4
West	17.6	18.1	18.4	17.6	17.7	18.9	19	19
Mid-West	11.12	8.87	8.83	10	8.9	7	6.9	6.9

Region	1985	1986	1987	1988	1989	1992	1993	1994	1995
East	21.1	23.1	23.6	24.3	24.4	23.2	21.7	20.7	24.2
North	46.5	49.2	49	49.1	49	49.9	54	53.4	49.6
West	17.6	19.2	18.9	18.5	18.5	18.8	14.7	16	15.5
Mid-West	5.9	6.4	6.5	6.3	6.4	4.79	5.58	5.88	7.05

Note: These data do not include those of local councils

Sources: Figures for the period between 1977 and 1979 were obtained from Omorogiuwa (1980). Data for the other years were computed from Central Bank of Nigeria, *Annual Report and Statements of Accounts;* and statistics collected from Federal Ministry of Finance.

CHAPTER 15

Olutayo C. Adesina

Revenue Allocation Commissions and the Contradictions in Nigeria's Federalism

> *When eminent economists confess that their own techniques and intellectual tools, applied to an area in which they claim absolute supremacy, have led to conclusions which violate ordinary commonsense, what more is there to say about their contribution to the national search for a revenue allocation formula?*
>
> Aliyu, A.Y. (1977).[1]

Introduction

The dialectic of revenue allocation has more ominous reverberations for Nigeria's federalism[2] than hitherto acknowledged, especially by the post-independence Revenue Allocation Commissions.[3] The instabilities which ensued from this phenomenon and the inadequate attention paid to it, have diminished and precluded the exultant promise of a dynamic and integrated polity. From independence in 1960, till 1981, Nigeria's revenue allocation system was neither efficient nor equitable. Indeed, it manifested a wide spectrum of vulnerability. Ethnicity, language, region and religion interactively form Nigeria's matrix of cultural pluralism.[4] In the face of such complexities therefore, several revenue allocation principles had to be adopted, faulted and discarded. The central thrust of this chapter is that, revenue allocation formulae are warped because they have not been "open covenants openly arrived at". Rather, they reflect the views of commissions, individuals, or groups within the commissions, which have shown proclivity for embracing theories, beliefs, ideals and approaches which have not only proved unrealistic, but have thereby contributed to the dislocations within the Nigerian state.

The point being stressed here is that a historical analysis of the revenue allocation commissions is vitally important in unravelling the paradoxes of our time, and to understand our contemporary predicament. Decisions of individuals, men and women, determine what policies states pursue. This is why an understanding of the human actors and the reports of the commissions between 1960 and 1981 are very crucial to the proper appreciation of the whole concept of Nigeria's revenue allocation strategies, as well as the strength and weaknesses it manifested in the present epoch.

The Burden of the Nigerian State

A major disability under which Nigerian federalism laboured was how to equitably share revenue between constituent parts of the federation.[5] Prior to independence, and shortly after independence, the political elites from each of the three regions, viz: North, East and West, exhibited the fear of domination of one over the other and distrust for one another.[6] Each of the regions wanted to control the government from the centre. Consequently, federalism planted the most potent seed of instability into the evolution of Nigeria as a nation. At first, in the early years of independence, the constitution seemed in spite of its limitations, able to contain the various strains to which it was subjected. Yet within less than seven years of independence, civilian rule was to be discredited and military rule which replaced it was unable to hold the nation together. Nigeria was then plunged into a thirty-month civil war.[7] At the root of the crises that engulfed the nation was the question of the equitable distribution of resources and *ipso facto,* power. For at independence, Nigerians were presented with a state disposing enormous powers and privileges.

The balance of power in the country became further complicated by the discovery of oil in the East and from a region seeking a centralised constitution under which natural resources could be jointly shared, the East became potentially the richest region and its leaders were less willing to tolerate a subordinate political position.[8] The sickening atmosphere of distrust between the regions was further exacerbated by the ethnic politics which characterised the Nigerian political milieu.[9]

Until Nigeria's independence, the most contentious aspect of the nation's federalism, revenue allocation, remained the responsibility of the colonial masters. Then, politicians accepted compromise as the price of access to state office, and thus to the revenues of state.[10] The colonial state set up the Phillipson Commission in 1946 to formulate the administrative and financial system to be adopted under the Richards Constitution.[11] The 1951 Macpherson Constitution led to the inauguration of the Hicks-Phillipson Commission, while the Chick Commission was appointed in 1953 in anticipation of the Lyttleton Constitution of 1954.[12] It was the 1954 Constitution which made Nigeria a federation of three regional governments and a central government, each with specific powers and responsibilities.[13] In 1958, the Raisman Commission was appointed in anticipation of Nigeria's independence.[14]

After independence, another commission, also headed by a foreign expert, was again inaugurated to find solutions to the endemic problem of revenue allocation. This was the Binn's Commission of 1964. However, within one year of the Binn's report, the First Republic was aborted by a military putsch.[15] It is appropriate at this juncture to highlight the fact that all these commissions at various times caused to be adopted or foisted on the country revenue principles such as derivation, even progress, need, national interest, independent revenue, fiscal autonomy, equality of status of states, geographical peculiarities, population, minimum responsibility of government, financial comparability and balanced development.[16] Scathing criticisms and disagreements attended all these principles. Their problems were summarised by the Aboyade Technical Committee thus:

> Population has been characterised by illogicality, inconsistency and inequity; derivation had done much to ``poison intergovernmental relations and hamper a sense of national unity''; need had ``little if any operational relevance''; even development was ``analytically ambiguous... (and was) not technically feasible to measure in any meaningful way''; equality of status of states was a ``consolation prize to states not favoured by the population and derivation principles''; geographical peculiarities defied any ``concise definition... (and had) little or no merit''; national interest was ``capable of many interpretations (and) circumstances''.[17]

Shortly after the fiasco that attended the failure of the democratic experiment of the First Republic and in view of the inadequacies of the previous Revenue Allocation principles, the military regime of Yakubu Gowon decided that Nigerians themselves should handle the recurrent problems of federal finance. This led in 1968 to the inauguration of the first `home-made' Revenue Allocation Commission.

The Politics of Revenue Allocation

The nature and conditions of the financial relations in any federal system is crucial to the continued existence of such a system.[18] Fiscal matters transcend the purview of economics. They have in most cases, especially in plural societies, assumed political, religious and social dimensions. Allotments of money, according to James O'Connor in *The Fiscal Crisis of the State,*[19] reflect... social and economic conflicts between classes and groups''. Others have similarly recognised fiscal and budgetary matters as a kind of code for the political economy of the society. It is in recognition of the foregoing that members of Revenue Allocation Commissions should not act independent of the realities on the ground. A historical evaluation of the outcomes of the commissions set up on revenue allocation have revealed results found lacking in integrative ethos of justice. This had been at the root of the immanent flaw in the logic of revenue allocation since the period of the Nigerian civil war.

The Nigerian nation, a polyglot composition of over 250 different ethnic groups, was convulsed at independence by the presence of competitive regional and ethnic blocs of population and this rendered the issue of revenue allocation one of uncommon intensity.[20] Between 1960 and 1968 the distributional basis of revenue was found anaemic and this necessitated the setting up of a commission to look into the issue. Subsequent grievances also led to the inauguration of two others between 1968 and 1981.

Revenue Allocation Commissions and Nigerian Federalism, 1968-1981

A key element of the Revenue Allocation Commissions set up by various Nigerian governments between 1968 and 1981 was the need for necessary and immediate adjustments that would make the revenue allocation principle, one that is fair and just. The creation of new states in 1967 and the issue of equitable distribution of the nation's resources led to the inauguration by the Federal Military Government of the Interim Revenue Allocation Review Committee (IRARC) headed by Chief I.O. Dina, Permanent Secretary in the Western State, in July 1968. The Committee was to, "look into and suggest any change in the existing system of revenue allocation as a whole as well as new revenue sources."[21] In 1977, the Aboyade Technical Committee on Revenue Allocation was inaugurated by the Obasanjo regime as part of the plan to return the nation to democratic rule. In 1979, the Shehu Shagari administration picked Pius Okigbo to head what was named the Presidential Commission on Revenue Allocation.[22] Like its predecessors, the Okigbo commission was mandated to examine the existing formula for revenue allocation between the federal, state and local governments, having regard for the need to ensure that each tier of government in the federation had adequate revenue to enable it to discharge its functions as laid down in the constitution of the Federal Republic.[23]

The setting up of three commissions on revenue allocation within a short period of twelve years is a manifestation of the instability that characterised the Nigerian polity. Between 1968 and 1980, income from petroleum constituted over eighty per cent of federal revenue. The importance of the federal centre therefore increased proportionately. As a consequence of this major shift in revenue generation, a desperate struggle to win control of state power ensued since this control meant for all practical purposes being all-powerful and owning everything. The issue of revenue allocation therefore became not a matter of pure economics but a political factor. It is in this light that the recommendations of the commissions shall be evaluated.

The Dina Commission had among its members Professor Ojetunji

Aboyade of the Department of Economics, University of Ibadan and A.E. Ekukinam, Director of Research at the Central Bank of Nigeria. The 1977 Technical Committee was headed by Ojetunji Aboyade and included Professor R.O. Teriba an Ibadan-based economist as member. The committee also commissioned experts to submit memoranda and these included Professor Dotun Phillips and Dr. Adebayo Adedeji. The Okigbo panel comprised Dotun Phillips, Dr. G.B. Leton and Alhaji Ahmed Talib.[25] The implications of each commission's reports for revenue allocation and Nigeria's federalism shall be based on its recommendations and the views of some of its key members.

There is no doubt that the commissions, especially the latter two, contributed by their acts of commission or omission to the aggravation of the inequities inherent in the revenue allocation system. Paradoxically, the Dina report whose recommendations were neither accepted by the government, nor published officially has been regarded as not only one of the best documentations on the country's fiscal system, but also one which was too far ahead of its times.[26] Its recommendations and proposals would be placed side by side with the other two to reveal their inadequacies.

The two latter commissions no doubt exhibited a rigid adherence to a formula based on principles that enforced their goals of efficiency, rather than the realistic allocation that emphasises considerations of equity in a highly combative plural society. In fact, the Dina report was considered controversial not because of its explicit economic proposals but because of its political assumptions and related issues which were pivotal to the realisation of a realistic revenue allocation principle, but which powerful forces, unfortunately, considered outside the committee's terms of reference. The committee fell foul of the power-brokers when it declared:

> We believe that fiscal arrangements in this country should reflect the new spirit of unity to which the nation is dedicated. No more evidence of this is necessary than the present war to preserve this unity at the cost of human lives, material resources and the radical change in this country's structure. It is in the spirit of this new-found unity that we have viewed all the sources of revenue of this country as the common funds of the country to be used for executing the kinds of programmes which can maintain this unity.[27]

In order not to be accused of exceeding their briefs, the latter two commissions gave a wide berth to the issues of politics and concentrated absolutely on the economics of the revenue allocation. As a result of this they ran into serious problems with the Nigerian polity. The Aboyade Technical Report recommended that the Federation Account, should be distributed on the following basis: Federal - fifty-seven per cent, state –

thirty per cent and local governments – ten per cent. It also recommended that three per cent be put in a special account to be operated by the federal government.[28] It is essential here to point out some of the views enunciated by individuals or groups within the commission. As far as Phillips was concerned, it would do a lot of good if solutions to the revenue allocation crisis be found ``without significantly changing the basic revenue allocation philosophy and without generating intense dislocation in the country's polity''.[29] Another expert involved in the Committee, Adebayo Adedeji had advocated as early as 1969 that emphasis be placed on the goal of efficiency rather than equity.[30] It is necessary at this stage to fault the positions of the two key members of this group because a number of facts about revenue sharing in Nigeria give an indication of the need for reforms. Firstly, the wide disparities in the revenue that eventually went to each regional or state government depending upon the principles of allocation adopted or emphasised, tended to favour the states of northern Nigeria. Secondly, local governments were not given fair treatment in the revenue-allocation systems. Administratively, the local councils were weak, and financially they were poor, even after they were granted ten per cent of the share of the federation account by the Aboyade Technical Committee.[31] In fact, Phillips claimed in 1980 that local councils should not be treated as separate entities. As far as he was concerned: ``there should be no revenue transfer directly or indirectly from the federal government to the local government.''[32]

No wonder therefore that the committee found it difficult to suggest radical departures from the existing system. Rather it took refuge in the subtle subterfuge of econometrics. The Technical Committee translated the principles they had recommended into statistical and mathematical calculations that would require a huge volume of accurate statistical details to back them up. As a result of the pungent criticisms that attended the committee's report,[33] and because of its obvious over-dependence on statistics, it was considered too unrealistic to last for more than a few years.

In 1979, Pius Okigbo who had helped to discredit the Aboyade report was chosen to head the Presidential Commission on Revenue Allocation. This initiative was bedevilled by contradictions. Perhaps this was what was responsible for its submitting one majority report and two minority reports in 1980.[34]

The Commission's recommendations ran contrary to the firm conviction among a large percentage of Nigerians that the federal government was acquiring too much powers disproportionate to the principles and philosophy of federalism. The aspects of the commission's reports which drew the ire of people were the proportion of federally collected revenue that was assigned to the federal government; the inclusion of the Federal Capital Territory in the vertical sharing scheme; federal government's control of the special fund; and the proportion of the special fund earmarked for mineral-producing areas; and on the relative share of the federal government from the federation account, *vis-a-vis* the other layers of government. One of the basic reasons for the high rate of turnover witnessed in the revenue allocation principle has to do with the relative share of each layer of government in the federation account. The total effect of the overbearing lopsidedness in the sharing formula was the strengthening of the position of the federal government *vis-a-vis* the regions or states and local governments. Eventually the other layers became heavilly dependent on the federal government through patronage, thus making nonsense of their independence, fiscal and otherwise, as envisaged by the federal principle and the constitution.

It was therefore not surprising when the formula recommended by the Okigbo Commission,[36] and which the federal government adopted as the Revenue Allocation Act of 1981 was declared null and void by the Supreme Court as a result of a suit challenging its validity in 1981.

Conclusion

The Dina Committee, which presaged the other commissions, had its recommendations rejected on the basis for which the other two stumbled, the political assumptions of revenue allocation in a plural federal state. Ironically, while the Aboyade and Okigbo Commissions which tried to ``conform" ran into serious problems, most of the Dina committee's supposedly controversial recommendations were implemented with suitable amendments where necessary.[37] From the foregoing, it seems clear that many members of the commissions or the commissions themselves simply took Nigerian federalism for granted, thereby negating the process whereby the federal qualities of the Nigerian society are articulated and protected. Thus, the federal government, because of the acts of commission or omission of the Revenue Allocation Commissions became so powerful that it was capable of holding any individual or group of states and local governments to ransom. Thus, both the prevailing socio-economic and political processes and the lessons of the Dina report, make it difficult to permit other conclusion than the following: until the main constitutional questions are settled, there can be no firm basis for a workable Revenue Allocation System. No revenue allocation formula indepedent of the fears and aspirations of the component parts, and which try to operate within the false parameter that groups within the nation are apt to accept common objectives for the nation, is likely to succeed.

Postscript

PREAMBLE

The revenue allocation formula in Nigeria is a phenomenon that appears to be in permanent disorder. The ad-hoc and inconsistent Revenue Allocation principles adopted by various Nigerian governments partly explains the frequent creation or the need for new revenue allocation commissions. The other explanation has to do with the fact that the Nigerian society, has emerged out of the bringing together of over-250 ethnic groups which now co-exist in various degrees of inter-dependence.[38] In such a situation, any genuine attempt to eradicate numerous micro-loyalties and thus re-orientate the multi-ethnic society into manifesting a national identity and outlook would require a sound and just revenue allocation formula that would, to a large extent, satisfy the expectations of the diverse interests within the polity.

In 1981, after the Supreme Court had voided the Okigbo-inspired Revenue Allocation formula, a new Revenue Act was passed by the National Assembly. It went into operation in January 1982. The Act which lasted until December 1989 and which thereby remained the longest-lasting revenue formula to date, distributed federally collected revenues as follows: Federal government (53%), state governments (35%) and local governments (10%).[39] The revenue act survived for so long, not because it was equitable or just, but because the military government in power after December 1983 ignored criticisms and agitations against it.[40] There were obvious inconsistencies in the revenue act. For example while some states received more than their statutory allocations, others received less. Except for 1983, Lagos received more than its statutory allocation during the entire period. In 1986-89, Anambra state got far more than its statutory allocation while the middle belt state of Plateau received less than its share of the federation account.[40] There is no doubt that economic, political and social pressures resulted in cases of excess allocation. The entire scenario thus made a mockery of the revenue allocation system and the federal structure within which it subsisted.

The inability to stick to the allocation guidelines and the persistent cry for equitable distribution of revenue inevitably led to the inauguration of another revenue allocation commission by the Babangida administration.

THE BABANGIDA REGIME, 1985-93

By this regime's peculiar circumstances, the revenue allocation principle it inherited, and the formats adopted or recommended for it clearly represented a classical case of a travesty of the principles of federalism. It also represented a negation of the ideals of the Structural Adjustment Programme (SAP) which the regime introduced in 1986.[42] One of the cardinal principles of SAP is social justice which proclaimed the equity and distributional objectives of government intervention in the economy.[43] This objective therefore called for a whole panoply of changes in the insalubrious political, social, economic and fiscal principles prevalent within the polity. It would be recalled that prior to this, Nigeria's calculations were not based on the totality of the collectivity.[44] It was this that rendered the issue of revenue allocation one of uncommon intensity.

Thus, in order to address the equity issue, the Babangida administration in line with the principles of SAP and federalism, inaugurated in 1988, the National Revenue Mobilisation, Allocation and Fiscal Commission under the chairmanship of General T.Y. Danjuma (Rtd.). In December 1989, the government modified and then accepted the recommendations of the commission.[45] The revenue allocation regime that came out of this effort utilised what has been regarded as a cumbersome, static and arbitrary yardstick to wit:[46]

Equality of states	40	per cent
Population	30	per cent
Land Mass	10	per cent
Social Development	10	per cent
Internal Revenue Generation effort	10	per cent
Total =	100	per cent

The government added a new dimension to revenue allocation when it gave 2 per cent of the revenue from mineral exploitation in direct proportion to the value of minerals extracted from each state, and another 1.5 per cent allocated to the fund to be administered by the federal government for the development of the mineral-producing areas of the country. Although this formula was supposed to be an improvement on the previous formulae, a studious perusal of the formula revealed that it not only retained some of the anachronisms of the earlier ones, but also introduced obnoxious aspects of its own. First of all, the act of picking a soldier to head a revenue allocation commission at a period when the nation was trying to grapple with the negative effects of a commandist structure was in bad taste. Also, whatever claims the formula may make on equitability, reasonableness and acceptability was circumscribed by its adherence to among others, the low percentage weight it assigned to derivation, and the disproportionate weight given to population and population-related factors in relation to "Equality of states. The introduction of land mass as an index of revenue allocation was also regarded as retrogressive and unfair.[47]

The new revenue allocation also encouraged a fiscal centralisation which allowed the federal military government to perpetuate an inescapable sense of dependence among the states. In fact, the disposal of funds over statutory allocation by the F.M.G. empowered it to facilitate an inequitable distribution of official patronage, and at the whim of the president. This was clearly revealed in 1992 when the Minister of Finance, Alhaji Abubakar Alhaji, while reacting to Governor Segun Osoba of Ogun State's call for F.M.G. assistance to all states declared:

> I am glad to announce to you that President Babangida has directed me to release some amount of money to all states of the federation on Monday. Criteria to be used will depend on the needs of each state as the needs of the states are not the same.[48]

Even the so-called innovations in the formula, the derivation fund and the fund for the ecological repair of the areas affected by mineral production, raised more delicate and sensitive issues, especially as each local authority had to make a good case for allocation.[49] On the other hand, oil-producing local governments also felt that the goals of the derivation fund would remain unrealised if state governments continued to administer the fund.[50]

There is no doubt that the pattern of fiscal structure and relationships under this regime followed the awkward approach adopted by previous regimes and under such a climate, the principles of federalism became its most potent victim.

THE FISCAL REGIME, 1994-97

The Sanni Abacha administration which came into power on 17 November 1993, promised an end to many of the problems confronting the nation. It thereafter inaugurated a constitutional conference to find solutions to the country's endemic problems of power sharing and transfer.[51] To demonstrate its seriousness in its programme of equity and fair play, the government set up among others the Transitional Committee on Devolution of powers, and the National Revenue Mobilisation and Fiscal Commission.[52] Most of the recommendations of these bodies may however not be implemented until the promulgation of the draft constitution in 1998. As an interim measure, the government adopted an ad-hoc revenue allocation formula which is more or less a continuation of the previous regime. The adoption of this formula was, however, accompanied by strident calls by different tiers of government[53] and even the Central Bank of Nigeria,[54] for a review of the indices that determine allocation of revenue in the country.

As a result of continued agitations, the F.M.G. gave its approval to the National Revenue Mobilisation and Fiscal Commission, to carry out the review in view of the creation of six new states and 183 local councils in October 1996.[55]

The paradox of the whole situation was that the attempt to find solutions to the intractable problem of revenue allocation went hand in hand with the subversion of the same process. The most basic problem manifested under the Abacha administration so far was succintly put by the Akwa Ibom State administrator, Navy Captain Joseph Adeusi. In his speech to members of the Committee on the Devolution of powers, he affirmed that:

> ... the current practice of military federalism had tended to raise fears of an overcentralised federal structure which denied states the autonomy to decide their constitutional responsibilities to the people as a result of close supervision and control.[56]

Further testimonies reveal that the federal government (FG) has been guilty of the rapacious accumulation of power and the nation's wealth to the detriment of the federating units which had been further balkanised from nineteen in 1976 to twenty-one in 1989, thirty in 1991 and thirty-six in 1996. The octopoidal tendencies of the FG have been intensified with the promulgation of decrees strengthening its position in relation to the other tiers of government. The massive increase in revenue accruing to the F.G. and the unilateral decreeing as to how it would be shared between it and the states eroded the financial autonomy of states and enabled the F.G. to venture into areas exclusive to, or shared concurrently with the states.[57] The Value Added Tax (VAT), the Autonomous Foreign Exchange Market (AFEM) and the Petroleum Trust Fund (PTF) were public policy thrusts which underlined the F.G.'s takeover of a larger chunk of the nation's resources without respect for the revenue allocation formula. The VAT as a proxy for sales tax, should accrue largely to the states which initially were to receive eighty per cent, with twenty per cent accruing to the F.G. as cost of administration and collection. But the F.G. inverted this to be eighty per cent for itself and twenty per cent for the states.[58] It took a clamour by the states for the formula to be reviewed to 33-35-30 for the Federal, State and local governments.[59] The AFEM gains on the other hand were regarded as the joint property of the three tiers of government. This sector yielded a profit of ₦78 billion in 1995 and ₦128 billion in 1996. But without consultation and in disregard of the wishes of the other tiers of government, the F.G. unilaterally invested the profits allegedly "in the productive sector of the economy".[60] Such infractions by the F.G. no doubt, are well replicated in other spheres of national life.

Thus, by the time six new states and 183 local governments were created in October 1996, the depredations of the F.G. had all but wiped out the other tiers of government as tools for catalysing development. The onus now rests on the proposed 1998 Constitution to restore the balance of power and functions between the three tiers of government and thereby enthrone a genuine and equitable federal polity.

Notes and References

1. Aliyu, A.T. "The New Revenue Allocation Formula: A Critique," in *The Nigerian Journal of Public Affairs* (Zaria), vii, May-October 1977, pp. 134-5.

2. For details on Nigeria's Federalism see, Akinyemi, B., Cole D., and Ofonagoro, W. (eds.) *Reading on Federalism*. Lagos: NIIA, 1979; Awa. E.O. *Issues in Federalism* Benin: Ethiope Publishing Corporation, 1976; and, Oyovbaire, S.E., *Federalism in Nigeria*. London: Macmillan Press, 1985.

3. This study is basically concerned with the Revenue Allocation Commissions. For discussions on Nigeria's Fiscal Performance and the nature and character of fiscal relationships between the different tiers of government see, Ekpo, A.H. "Fiscal Federalism: Nigeria's Post-Independence Experience, 1960-90" *World Development* vol. 22, No. 8, Special Issue, August 1994, pp. 1129-1146.

4. Young Crawford, *The Politics of Cultural Pluralism*. Ibadan: Heinemann Educational Books (Nigeria) 1993. P. 276. See also Onosode, G. *Three Decades of Development Crises in Nigeria*. Lagos: Malthouse Press 1993, pp. 34-39.

5. Phillips, Adedoti ., Nigeria's Federal Financial Experience". *The Journal of Modern African Studies* ix, 3 October 1971, p. 389.

6. Nwabueze, B.O. *A Constitutional History of Nigeria*. Ikeja and Essex: Longman Group Ltd. 1982, pp. 147-148.

7. Crowder, Michael, *The Story of Nigeria*. London: Faber and Faber, Publishers, 1978, p. 259.

8. Ade-Ajayi, J.F. "Recent History of Nigeria" in *Africa: South of the Sahara*. 12th Edition, London: Europa Publications 1982-83, p. 774.

9. For details see, Nnoli, Okwudiba, *Ethnic Politics in Nigeria.* Enugu: Fourth Dimension Publishers, 1978.

10. Williams, Gavin, *State and Society in Nigeria.* Idanre: Afrografika Publishers, 1980, p. 74.

11. Mbanefoh, F. Gini ``Public Finance'' in Kayode, M.O. and Usman, Y.B. *Nigeria Since Independence. The First Twenty-Five Years,* vol. II: The Economy. Ibadan: Heinemann Educational Books (Nigeria) p. 191.

12. Sklar, L. Richard, *Nigerian Political Parties: Power in an Emergent Nation.* Princeton: Princeton University Press, 1963), p.24: See also, Chick Louis, *Report of Fiscal Commissioner on Financial Effects of Proposed New Constitutional Arrangements.* Lagos, 1953.

13. Dudley, Billy ``Federalism and the Balance of Political Power in Nigeria.'' *Journal of Commonwealth Political Studies,* vol iv, No. 1, March 1966, p.16

14. Mbanefoh, F. Gini, *op. cit.* p. 192.

15. *Ibid.,* p. 195.

16. Okigbo, P.N.C. *Nigerian Public Finance.* Evanston, Illinois: North western University Press, 1965, chapter 2; see also, Mbanefoh. F. Gini. p. 194.

17. Federal Republic of Nigeria, *Report of the Technical Committee on Revenue Allocation Under the Military.* Lagos, 1979, pp. 23-8.

18. Badmus, Adejare G. ``Contradictions in Nigerian Federalism'' (Unpublished M.A. Thesis, Department of History, University of Ibadan. 1997), p. 39.

19. For details see, O' Connor James, *The Fiscal Crisis of the State.* New York: St. Martin's Press, 1973, p. 276.

20. Joseph, A. Richard, *Democracy and Prebendal Politics in Nigeria.* Ibadan: Spectrum Books Limited, 1991 p. 4.,

21. Ayida, A.A. *The Nigerian Revolution, 1966-1976.* Ibadan: Ibadan University Press, 1973, pp. 7-8.

22. Adebayo, A.G. ``The ``Ibadan School'' and the Handling of Federal Finance in Nigeria''. *The Journal of Modern African Studies,* 28, 2 (1990), pp. 245-264.

23. Mbanefoh, F. Gini, *Op. cit* 202.

24. Joseph, A. Richard *op.cit.* pp. 73-75; see also Ake, Claude Presidential Address to the Annual Conference of the Nigerian

Political Science Association, 1981, Printed in *West Africa*, 25 May 1981, pp. 1162-3.

25. Adebayo, A.G. *op. cit.* pp. 1-2.
26. Ayida, A. *op. cit.* pp. 8.
27. Federal Republic of Nigeria, *Report of the Interim Revenue Allocation Review Committee*, para 77. See also Ayida, A. *ibid,* p.8.
28. Adebayo, A.G. *op. cit.* p. 256
29. Phillips, Adedotun, ``Reforming Nigeria's Revenue Allocation System'', in *The Nigerian Journal of Public Affairs (Zaria)*, vi, 1, May 1976, p. 80.
30. Adebayo, A.G. p. 254. See also, Adedeji, Adebayo, *Nigerian Federal Finance: Its Development, Problems and Prospects.* London, 1969.
31. *Ibid.* p. 255.
32. Phillips, Adedotun, ``Three Decades of Inter-Governmental Financial Relationship in the Federation of Nigeria'' in *Quarterly Journal of Administration.* XIV, 2, 1980, p. 175.
33. See Nigeria, Federal Ministry of Information, *Proceedings of the Constituent Assembly,* Official Report No. 96, May 29, 1978 Lagos, 1978, for the speech made by Pius Okigbo to discredit the committee's recommendations. See also, Aliyu, A.Y. *op. cit.* pp. 134-4, and Adebayo, A.G. *op. cit.* p. 258
34. Okigbo, Pius *et al, Report of the Presidential Commission on Revenue Allocation.* Lagos, 1980, vols. I and II.
35. For details see Mbanefoh, G.F. *op. cit.* p. 203; and also, Mbanefoh, G.F. ``Purchasing votes and the Politics of Vertical Revenue sharing Debate among Civilian Governments of the Second Republic'', mimeo, University of Ibadan, 1985.
36. Federal Republic of Nigeria, *Report of the Presidential Commission on Revenue Allocation,* Vol. 1, Main report and minority views''. Lagos: Office of the President, 1980.
37. Ayida, A.A. *op. cit.* pp. 8-9.
38. Sanda, A.O. *Lectures on the Sociology of Development.* Ibadan and Lagos: Fact Finders International; 1992, p. 59.
39. Ekpo, A.H. *op. cit.* p. 1133.
40. *Ibid. p. 1134.*
41. *Ibid.* pp. 1135-1136.

42. Federal Republic of Nigeria, ``Structural Adjustment Programme for Nigeria June 1986 - July 1988'' Lagos: Government Printer, 1986.
43. Mbanefoh, G.F. ``The Public Sector and the Structural Adjustment Programme'' in Phillips. A. and Ndekwu, E.C. (eds) *Structural Adjustment in a Developing Economy.* Ibadan: NISER, 1987, p. 105.
44. Ikime, O. ``Facing up to our Realities''. *The Post Express.* Lagos, April 16, 1997, p. 9.
45. Federal Republic of Nigeria, ``The Approved Revenue Allocation Formulae, National Revenue Commission''. Ikoyi, Lagos: Government Printer, 1990.
46. Nwankwo, U. *Economic Agenda for Nigeria.* Lagos: Centrist Productions Ltd., 1992. p. 276-77.
47. *Ibid.* p. 278
48. *Daily Sketch,* Ibadan 14 March, 1992, p.1.
49. Ayida, A. ``The Wealth of the Nation'' *Daily Times,* Lagos, June 22, 1992, p. 36.
50. *The Guardian,* Lagos 31 August 1992, p.2.
51. *Newswatch,* Lagos 12 May 1997, p.6
52. *West Africa,* 22-28 January 1996, p. 104; *Vanguard,* Lagos, 20 March, 1996, p.3.
53. See, *Third Eye,* Ibadan 16 September, 1996, p. 1; *The Guardian,* Lagos, 9 October, 1996 and *This Day,* Lagos, 19 March, 1997.
54. *Daily Sketch,* Ibadan, 24 June, 1996, p.1
55. *The Guardian,* 9 October, 1996, p. A.I.
56. *Post Express,* Lagos, 20 September, 1996, p. 24.
57. See Alex Ekwueme's lecture on ``The Changing Faces of Nigerian Federalism: which way forward'' *The Guardian,* Lagos, 2, May 1997, p.1.
58. *Nigerian Tribune,* Ibadan, 2 May 1997, p.2
59. *The Guardian,* Lagos, 2 May 1997, p.1
60. *Ibid.*

CHAPTER 16

G.D. Olowononi

Revenue Allocation and Economics of Federalism

Introduction

Revenue allocation has a very great potential for conflicts, especially between rich and poor regions or states, in Nigeria. In fact, it was ethnic conflict which largely explains the origin of centralisation of fiscal powers in Nigeria today. With central control over a wide range of policies the federal government has been able to effect a redistribution of income from the richer to the poorer states. The highly unitary tendencies are however being questioned since Nigeria has adopted a federal rather than a unitary system of government.

This chapter examines the methods and techniques of inter-governmental resources transfer which could be used to foster national integration in Nigeria. Revenue allocation is broadly defined to include allocation of tax powers and the revenue sharing arrangements not only among the three levels of government but among the state governments as well.

Revenue allocation under a federal system of government creates complex problems. The complexity stems from the distinctive nature of federalism as a form of government in which the legislative, executive and judicial functions or powers of the state are shared among three levels of government.

The success of a federal system depends on an acceptable distribution of resources and functions among the three levels of government so that efficiency in the use of scarce resources is encouraged while reducing inequality in the treatment of individuals among different states. Given the heavy dependence of these governments on the federation account, it is neccessary to examine the principles which govern its allocations among the state governments.

Conceptual Framework

The discussion of contemporary federalism seems to have started with Wheare (1943) who defined federal government as a constitutional arrangement which divides law-making powers and functions of the state between two levels of government which are co-ordinate in status. He believed that each level of government should have adequate resources to perform its function without appealing to the other level of government for financial assistance. He emphatically argued that:

> If state authorities, for example, find that the services allotted them are too expensive for them to perform, and if they call upon the federal authority for grants and subsidies to assist them, they are no longer coordinate with the federal government but subordinate to it. Financial subordination makes an end of federalism in fact, no matter how carefully the legal forms may be preserved. It follows therefore that both state and federal authorities in a federation must be given the power in the constitution each to have access to and to control, its own sufficient financial resources. Each must have a power to tax and to borrow for the financing of its own services by itself.

The rights of both the federal government and the constituent state governments in a federal structure are enshrined in the constitution. Modern federal countries have three levels of government each distinguished by the scope of the geographical areas over which their respective jurisdictions extend. The jurisdiction of the federal (Central) government covers the entire country in some subject-matters. Regional (State) government's jurisdictions cover sub-sections of the country. Local governments exercise responsibility over non over-lapping areas within a state. Federalism is a standard concept of government units based on area to cater for racial, religious, linguistic and other differences. Ideally a system of multi-level government should be structured from the point of view of ensuring an efficient supply of public services.

Federalism and Development

It is now widely argued by economists that the principles and practice of public finance which concentrates functions, and power in the hands of the federal government will accelerate economic development. This is because they are convinced that classical federalism creates less - than - optimum allocation of resources. Besides, classical federalism prevents economies of scale in government and increases cost of administration. Furthermore, the conventional macro-economics favours centralisation and integration of fiscal powers which enables the economy to combat depression and inflation. It was in this regard that Hanson and Perloff (1965) argued that autonomous taxing, borrowing and spending activities of the state and local governments collectively have typically run counter to an economically sound fiscal policy of the central government and have therefore intensified the violence of economic fluctuation. They were of the view that unless the states' fiscal systems "are planned in relation to the federal stabilisation programmes, they are likely to nullify in large measure the national counter-cyclical activities".

Not everybody believes that the centralisation of fiscal powers is what is required to accelerate the rate of economic development. Scot (1965) for example, argued that a short-run misallocation of scarce resources is not dysfunctional for a federal political system in the long-run. Bauer (1961) argued, in the same vein, that:

> Policies which seem paradoxical or even self-defeating in terms of promotion of economic development in the sense of raising living standards may come to be readily explicable by reference to alternative aims which take precedence over the promotion of economic development and which may require measures incompatible with it.

The three levels of government, in most federations, are finding the pressure of expenditure on revenue resources great. This increasing pressure is a serious handicap in devising fiscal arrangements in accordance with the classical federal principle, that is to say, to match taxable resources with individual responsibilities of these three levels of government.

Fortunately, the borrowing powers of the state and local governments are no longer restricted. Such powers have been used widely to acquire the required resources for the purposes of government services. In some federations, the taxing and borrowing powers of government are not used solely to acquire resources for development but to regulate the economy. This means that the preservation of the federal structure is not only what is important in devising fiscal policy. The current practice in some federations is that the federal government does not only have the sole responsibility for levying and collecting the most lucrative taxes but also for deciding, in the light of changing circumstances, how the federally collected revenue should be shared out between itself and the other two levels of government. Such an arrangement is not only very economical but permits the efficient use of tax as a regulator of the economy. It also enables the federal government to facilitate the process of even development throughout the country through the revenue allocation system and its own spending.

For various reasons to be explained later some people are objecting to this arrangement in Nigeria saying that it makes the states to sacrifice a great deal of their autonomy because a large percentage of their revenues is dependent on the federation account whose size is freely controlled by the federal government.

We now turn to revenue allocation among the state and local governments. The main principles which are generally used are compensation, derivation and fiscal needs. All of these have been used in Nigeria. Compensation has been used to ease out the financial difficulties arising from the federal take-over of erstwhile state governments' tax powers. Compensation has however enjoyed only a limited vogue in Nigeria. Australia also attempted to apply the principle on a large scale but did not succeed.

Derivation is closely related to compensation. The derivation principle, as it has been used in Nigeria, is a method of sharing revenue among the various units making up the federation in the proportion of certain taxes assumed to have been paid by the citizen (Olaolu, 1979:115). Revenues allocated on the basis of derivation penalises the relatively backward or poor states. Besides, the principle is not easy to apply as the burden of taxes collected within a state is not necesarily borne by the residents of that state alone. This fact has been stressed by Hicks (1961:73). Revenue allocation among the regional governments in Nigeria was largely based on derivation from 1954 to 1975, but it was found unworkable as it threatened national integration.

Consequently, both the Aboyade Committee (1977) and Okigbo Commission (1980) de-emphasised the principle in the revenue allocation formula. The experience in India also demonstrates unsatisfactory nature of the derivation principle. Consequently most federations are emphasising the principle of needs for sharing the distributable pool account. The principle of needs can be grouped in two ways – national interest and state need. Revenue may be allocated among the state governments not to level up development disparities but to undertake projects considered to be of high value to the whole country. Revenue allocated on this basis may even widen the disparities in the levels of development among the states. Revenue allocated on the basis of state needs are consciously designed to achieve a high degree of equalisation among the states in the provision of public services. Horizontal fiscal equalisation becomes necessary because of the differing tax capacities and the uniform tax rates in the country. The economic rationale for equalisation is that it checks the outflow of skilled labour from the poor states. Graham (1964) has also supported the principle. According to him.

> It appears that the argument that fiscal transfers induce, accentuate or perpetuate misallocation of resources is too tenuous theoretically and too remote economically to be taken seriously as a proposition, it transfers accord with the principle of fiscal equity.

Genesis and Magnitude of Fiscal Dependence in Nigeria

Regional governments were almost fiscally self-independent from 1954 to 1966. This fact can be seen when we consider independent revenues as percentages of current revenue. The regional governments were fiscally very powerful viz-a-vis the federal government. In fact, the federal government played second fiddle to the regional governments.

The trend has, however, been revised since 1967 with the creation of twelve states which were increased to nineteen in 1976, twenty-one in 1987, thirty in 1991 and thirty-six in 1996. As more states were created, the tax base of each diminished. Besides, the rapidly growing sources of federal revenue such as petroleum profit tax, mining rents and royalties, company incomes tax, customs and excise duties contributed significantly to reverse the trend. Various constraints which impeded the raising of more internal revenues within the states also contributed significantly to reverse the trend. For example, the federal government either took over or controlled important taxes previously controlled by the regional governments. The marketing boards were taken over and their export duties accruing to states abolished. The states' Produce Sales Tax was also abolished. Personal income tax, the largest tax of the states has come under federal government's control since 1975. The rates have not only been made uniform but have been continuously reduced since 1986 to cushion the effects of the structural adjustment programme. Besides, the tax allowances have been generously increased thus reducing the revenue accruing to the state governments.

In 1994, the federal government abolished the sales tax and introduced Valued-Added Tax in its place. The tax is made uniform throughout the country and is collected by federal government. These serious incursions into the state rights have made the states fiscally dependent on the federally collected revenue. The seriousness of the internal revenue situation is underscored by the fact that between 1991 and 1995 only Lagos State was able to raise above fifty per cent of its current revenue internally (See Table 1).

Table 1: Internal Revenue as Percentage of States' Current Revenue

State	1991	1991	1993	1994	1995
Abia	4.85	12.75	22.27	14.42	14.57
Adamawa	14.52	6.64	6.39	6.64	7.16
Akwa-Ibom	5.79	6.90	10.31	18.11	13.97
Anambra	21.33	11.31	19.60	22.88	20.00
Bauchi	6.18	5.85	6.27	11.55	11.40
Benue	4.53	4.13	4.90	8.79	11.35
Borno	11.37	23.04	6.78	12.15	14.79
Delta	12.61	12.09	33.75	27.74	43.44
Kaduna	7.94	28.92	24.00	19.57	38.23
Kano	13.10	14.23	8.70	11.33	21.22
Kwara	11.11	16.33	6.79	10.46	11.10
Lagos	41.19	48.70	66.24	61.32	69.21
Ondo	10.76	9.82	21.50	14.44	18.25
Oyo	13.67	28.29	18.02	27.83	26.03
Rivers	15.84	29.66	43.12	50.74	32.67
Sokoto	11.29	6.88	7.78	9.80	10.62

Source: Computed from Central Bank of Nigeria, *Annual Report and Statement of Accounts for the Year Ended 31st December, 1995*.

Internally generated revenues constituted only 12.84 per cent of all the states' total current revenue in 1991, 17.76 per cent in 1993 and 24.19 per cent in 1995, (CBN Report, 1995). The internally generated revenues were low in relation to the state expenditures imposed by the statutory responsibilities. In other words, their revenues were not growing rapidly enough to keep pace with the growth of expenditures. The list of statutory responsibilities of the states can be found in the concurrent and exclusive lists of the 1979 Federal Constitution of Nigeria. Among them are economic, social and community services. These services include specifically education, roads, health-care, water supply, agricultural development, regional planning and so on. The Federal Constitution provides various sources of revenue to be used to provide these services. They may be broadly grouped as internal and external sources of revenue. The internal sources include personal income tax, entertainment tax, capital grains tax, stamp duties, estate duties and motor vehicle licence and registration fees. There are other taxes depending on the level of development of each state and the ingenuity of each state administration. The external sources include statutory revenue, grants, value-added tax and transfers from Stabilisation Fund Account.

The bulk of revenues accruing to the states are from the external sources. Table 2 shows that the states have had financial crises since 1991. The overall budget deficits rose from ₦2,251.5 million in 1991 to ₦3,500.3 million in 1993 and ₦5,504.7 million in 1995. The precarious financial crises have forced the states to neglect their important functions of providing essential public services.

Table 2: Financial Positions of State Governments including the Federal Capital Territory (₦ Million)

Sources	1991	1992	1993	1994	1995
Current Revenue	24,772.2	32,673.6	42,333.0	49,246.0	63,686.1
Current Expenditure	15,872.3	20,780.3	29,992.3	35,178.6	45,356.9
Current Surplus (+) and Deficit	8,889.9	11,893.3	12,340.7	14,067.4	18,329.2
Capital Expenditure	11,151.4	16,280.3	15,841.0	16,942.1	23,893.9
Total Expenditure	27,023.7	37,060.6	45,833.3	52,120.7	69.250.8
Overall Surplus (+) Deficit	-2,251.5	-4,387.0	-3,500.3	-2,874.7	-5,564.7

Source: Central Bank of Nigeria, *Annual Report and Statement of Accounts for the Year Ended 31st December, 1995.*

Like the state governments, the local governments had financial crises which resulted from their structurally weak revenue base. For example, they generated internally 5.24 per cent, 6.24 per cent and 7.93 per cent of their total current revenues in 1993, 1994 and 1995 respectively. This means they were heavily dependent on external financial resources.

Table 3: Federation Account as Percentage of Federally Collected Revenue

Year	Total Federally Collected Revenue (₦ Million)	Federation Account	Federation Account as % of Federally Collected Revenue (₦ Million)
1991	100,991.6	54,000.0	53.47
1992	190,453.2	77,800.0	40.85
1993	192,769.4	106,799.4	55.40
1994	201,910.8	110,641.0	54.80
1995	459,987.3	161,998.5	35.22

Source: Central Bank of Nigeria, *Annual Report and Statement of Account for the Year Ended, 1995.*

The functions of local governments include the provision and maintenance of primary schools, refuse disposal, markets, health centres, fire services, roads, and so forth. They derive revenue to provide these services from internal and external sources. The internal sources are expected to be property tax, licences for bicycle, trucks (other than mechanically operated trucks), Canoes, wheel barrows and carts, rates and levies on radio, television, fees and fines, earnings from commercial undertakings and so forth. The external sources include the Federation Account, Value-Added-Tax and grants from the state governments.

The statutory functions of the federal government include defence and internal security, social and economic services, general administration and so forth. Under the 1979 Constitution, the federal government has the exclusive power to levy and collect customs and excise duties, company income tax, petroleum profits tax including mining rents and royalties. In 1994, the federal government introduced the Value-Added-Tax and has been collecting its proceeds. Federal revenues, other than those from the oil, have been relatively buoyant since 1991. The liberalisation of imports accompanied by the depreciation of the naira exchange rate for example, has caused significant increases in the receipts of import duties. Revenues from the Value-added-tax have also shown impressive growth. The 1979 Constitution states that:

> the Federation shall maintain a special account to be called the Federation Account into which shall be paid all revenues collected by the Government of the Federation, except the proceeds from the personal income tax of the personnel of the Armed Forces of

the Federation, the Nigeria Police Force, the Ministry or Department of government charged with the responsibility for External Affairs and the residents of the Federal Capital Territory.

Money paid into the Federation Account is currently shared among the federal, state and local governments in the ratio of 45.5:24:10. The balance of 7.5 per cent is allocated to special funds to cater for ecological problems such as soil erosion, desertification, flood control, oil pollution and the principles of derivation.

Given the structure of the Nigerian economy, the state and local governments have had to be heavily dependent on the federally collected revenues. The transfers of funds from the federally collected revenue have however diminished the size of the Federation Account. The federal government has recently created Stabilisation Fund, Dedicated Accounts, Petroleum Trust Fund, all of which in effect reduce the amount of revenue available directly to the state and local governments from the Federation Account.

There is also no doubt that revenues allocated statutorily to the state governments have not fostered any sense of financial responsibility on the part of state and local governments as they have increasingly become inefficient in the use of the meagre funds they get. These governments, are tempted to spend on questionable projects. Besides, the revenue allocation formula has not sufficiently given incentives to these governments to exploit fully their own sources of revenue. In fact, they have found it more rewarding to concentrate their energies on attempting to obtain larger transfers from the federally collected revenue rather than attempting to generate more revenues internally. This is a problem created by federalism which must be urgently solved.

As a result of these problems, the expenditures to which the state and local governments are committed now far exceed their revenues. While state and local governments revenue showed little growth potential, their expenditures showed high growth potential. Thus, not only was there a large excess of their expenditure over revenue, but the extent of imbalance was progressively rising.

The problem is currently being solved by the enormous federal government's powers of control over state budgets. Estimates of revenue and expenditures are submitted to the federal government for approval. With the incoming of civilian government, the states will no longer be obliged to submit their annual estimates to the federal government for approval. The new constitution is designed to enhance the state autonomy and initiative which means that they could decide whether or not to expand a particular service without reference to the federal government.

The formula for sharing revenue among the states between 1980 and 1990 was as follows:

Minimum responsibilities of government: .... 40 per cent
Population:... 40 per cent
Social development factor:...15 per cent
Internal revenue effort:..5 per cent

In 1990, the formula was modified as follows:
Minimum responsibility of government.................40 per cent
Population..40 per cent
Social development factor...10 per cent
Internal revenue generation effort..........................10 per cent
Land mass and/or terrain..10 per cent

Local governments have been using the same principles and weights for sharing revenue among themselves. Some states have, however, started, in recent years, to agitate that the principle of derivation should be re-emphasised as it was between 1954 and 1975. Yielding to their demand will create a potential threat to national integration. During the fifties and sixties, the application of the derivation principle engendered inter-regional imbalance and friction. (See Adedeji, 1969).

Remedies

(1) It is suggested that the principle of fiscal needs should be given a dominant weight in the future revenue allocation system. Our suggestion is not new as it had earlier been proferred by the Dina Committee (1969), Aboyade Committee (1979) and Okigbo Commission (1980). One of the biggest problems facing the country today is the imbalance in economic development. Consequently, the revenue allocation system must be used to address the problem.

(2) The power of the federal government to vary the proportion of the federally collected revenue which goes to the federation account must be checked. This power has made nonsense of the revenue allocation formula among federal, state and local governments.

(3) The federal government has changed the tax structures at the federal and state levels in recent years. General sales tax has been abolished at the state level while Value-Added Tax has been introduced in its place at the federal level. Under the 1979 Constitution only the state governments are authorised to levy and collect sales tax. Value-Added Tax should therefore be administered by the state governments. The collection system could be privatised in order to enhance efficiency and greater revenue yield.

(4) An important tax which is yet to be efficiently utilised is the property tax. An important function for the tax beside revenue generation is that of optimal utilisation of property, some of which are currently either under-utilised or not utilised at all. Property taxation is currently under the jurisdiction of local governments and very few local governments collect the tax even where the legal basis exists. Property tax could generate about ₦30 billion yearly. Property Values are rising everyday and the incomes attributable to property are also rising fast. The manner in which the property tax base ought to be tapped has been a mirage in the air for most local governments in Nigeria. The federal government should take over the administration of the tax for the next five to ten years, after which it should be reverted to local governments.

(5) Furthermore, the state governments should be allowed to collect and retain the proceeds from the toll gate. It is a reliable source of revenue.

(6) The personal income tax is low partly because the extent of wage employment is limited and partly because the system of tax withholding from wages and self-employed professionals is faulty.

I do not know of any federation in which the federal government lacks the power to control incomes and profit taxes. If these taxes differ from one state to the other, the variations in the tax structure could hinder free mobility of labour and employees will be reluctant to move to those states where the tax rates are relatively high. The decision of the federal government to continue with a uniform income tax structure throughout the country is a welcome measure.

The preservation of the states' autonomy requires that every state government be allowed to set its own tax structure. Such a measure will however result in a duplication of taxes which will constitute a heavy burden on productive effort.

(7) Generally speaking, for reasons earlier adumbrated and which are already very familiar, revenue should be allocated among the state governments as follows:

Length of federal road	25 per cent
Population size	35 per cent
Tax effort	15 per cent
Equality of state	25 per cent
Total	100 per cent

The suggested revenue allocation formula is designed more to raise the level of the backward states than to push forward the level of the relatively advanced states. It is based on equity considerations.

(8) If the existing functional responsibilities of the three levels of government are to continue, the federation account should be shared in the ratio by which the Value Added is currently shared. This is to say that the sharing

formula will be as follows:

Federal government..35 per cent
State governments..40 per cent
Local governments..25 per cent

In addition, the federal government should set aside 7.5 per cent out of the states share as Special Fund to be applied as follows:

Special Problems of the Mineral Producing Areas....2.5 per cent
Flood and desert control (etc)..2.5 per cent
Revenue Equalisation Fund...2.5 per cent

It follows therefore that the degree of fiscal autonomy for the states must be viewed in the wider context of inter-state relations and of national integration. If the states are to be at peace with one another, maximum efforts must be made to remove those forces that divide them and hinder economic growth. Inter-state commerce should be promoted while free flow of goods and persons across the state boundaries must not be restricted by fiscal measures.

Summary and Conclusions

This chapter has shown that the structure of revenue allocation has had a great impact on the nature of Nigerian federalism. Although it was federalism which created the need for revenue allocation, the system of revenue allocation has radically altered the structure of federalism itself. Virtually all the state governments are so heavily dependent on the federation account that the federal structure has almost been transformed to a unitary system. The new structure has denied the component units direct access to lucrative taxes. It has therefore necessitated balancing transfers to fill the gaps created by revenue and responsibilities at the lower levels of government. Equalisation transfers have also been effected because of the variations in the revenue raising capacities of the state governments. This is aimed at preventing poorer states from imposing heavier tax burden on their residents.

The chapter argues that it is efficient to transfer a part of the financial resources generated in one part of the country to another especially from the surplus areas to the deficit areas to promote optimum resources use and balanced development in the country.

The receipt of a very high percentage of state governments' revenue in the form of statutory allocation shows a weakness in the use of locally controlled taxes. However, statutory revenues are not federal government's revenues. They are revenues collected by the federal government on behalf of the state and local governments primarily for efficiency objectives and must be fairly shared among the three levels of government.

The federal government should no longer unilaterally vary the proportion of the federally collected revenue paid into the federation account or the revenue allocation formula. Finally, this chapter believes that undue emphasis on the application of derivation principle will again distort the pattern of development in the country. Such a discriminatory principle is likely to be vehemently opposed by the majority of the state governments and this may create problems for national integration.

Notes and References

Aboyade Technical Committee on Revenue Allocation (1977)

Adebayo, Adedeji (1969). *The Nigerian Federal Finance: Its Development, Problems and Prospects.* London: Huutchinson

Anusionwu, Chukwuma (1987). ``Fiscal Dependence and Need for Diversification of State Government Revenue Sources in Nigeria'', paper presented at the 1983 Annual Conference of the Nigerian Economic Society, Jos.

Banner, P.T. (1961). *Indian Economic Policy and Development.* London.

Buchanan, J.M. (1959). ``Federalism and Fiscal Equity'', in R.A. Musgrave and C. Shoups (eds) *Readings in the Economics of Taxation.* Homewood: Richard D. Irwin.

Carnel, F.G. (1961) ``Political Implications of Federalism in New States'' in U.K. Hicks (ed). *Federalism and Economic Growth in Underdeveloped Countries.*

Dare, L.O. (1980), ``Intergovernmental Relations in Federalism''. *Ife Social Science Review,* Vol. 2, No.1.

Graham, John F. (1964), ``Fiscal Adjustment in a Federal Country'' in R. Robertson (ed). *Intergovernmental Fiscal Relationships.* Toronto: Canadian Tax Foundation.

Hanson, A.H. and S. Perloff (1963) ``State and Local Finance in the National Economy'', in R.A. Musgrave (ed). *Essays in Fiscal Federalism.* Washington.

Hicks, S.R. (1961). ``The Nature and Basis of Economic Growth'' in U.K. Hicks *et al* (eds). *Federalism and Economic Growth in Underdeveloped Countries.* London: Allen and Unwin.

Odama, J.S. (1986). ``The New Revenue Allocation Formula. A Mere Residual or New Fiscal Policy Tool?'', in *Nigerian Journal of Policy and Strategic Studies.* Kuru, NIPSS.

Okigbo Commission (1980) *Report of the Presidential Commission on Revenue Allocation,* Vol. 1, Federal Government Press, Apapa.

Olaloku, F.A. (1979), Nigeria Federal Finances: Issues and Choices in A.B. Akinyemi *et al* (eds) *Readings on Federalism.* Lagos: Nigerian Institute of International Affairs.

Olowononi, G.D. (1991) ``*Fiscal Centralisation in Nigeria*''. An Unpublished Ph.D Thesis submitted to Post-Graduate School, Ahmadu Bello University, Zaria.

Ozayimwese, I.Z. and S.O. Iyare (1990), ``Economic Management Issues in Nigerian Federalism'', *Nigerian Journal of Policy and Strategy,* Vol. 5, No. 1 & 2.

Rupley, Lawrence (1978) ``Personal Income-based Taxation in the Northern States of Nigeria and the Effect of Uniform Income Taxation'' *Bulletin for International Fiscal Documentation* Vol. 32, Aug/Sept.

Topham, Naveille (1983) ``Local Government Economies'' in R. Millward *et al* (eds), *Public Sector Economy.* London: Longman.

Wheare, K.C. (1944) *Federal Government* (4th ed).

CHAPTER 17

Cyril I. Obi

The Impact of Oil on Nigeria's Revenue Allocation System: Problems and Prospects for National Reconstruction.

Introduction

Since its inception, and especially after the oil-boom of the 1970's, the Revenue Allocation System remains one of the critical destabilising factors in Nigeria's federal experiment.[1] This chapter examines the ways in which oil fuels the destabilising tendencies of the politics of revenue allocation, as well as the deepening of the economic crisis in which the Nigerian federation is immersed.

The choice of oil is tied to its status as the fiscal basis of the Nigerian state, accounting for over eighty per cent of all federal revenues and 90 per cent of all foreign exchange earnings. Beyond this, it feeds into struggles over control, access and distribution by various factions of the ruling class. With revenue allocation largely implying the allocation of oil revenues, oil is central to the politics of inter-governmental relations in Nigeria, the economic crisis, and the transcendence of the destabilising tendencies within the system.

Another aim of this chapter is the exploration of how at this critical point in the evolution of Nigeria's federalism, alternative possibilities for economic reconstruction within a democratic federal framework could be opened up.

In going about the analysis of how oil fits into the scenario of a troubled federal experiment through the dynamics of revenue allocation, and proferring solutions directed at moving away from divisive and destabilising struggles over the sharing/allocation of oil revenues, this chapter is divided into four broad parts. The first part, the introduction, sets out the parameters of the discourse. It is followed by the section that deals with the background and conceptual issues relating to the political economy of Nigeria's fiscal federalism. The third part, which is the analytical fulcrum of the study, examines the dynamics of the revenue allocation system in Nigeria vis-á-vis the allocative functions of the oil rentier state. While the fourth and conclusive part, sums up the arguments and prospects within the rubric of the challenge of national reconstruction in the Fourth Republic.

The Political Economy of Nigeria's Fiscal Federalism: Some Conceptual and Background Issues

The political economy of fiscal federalism, confronts the power relations that underlie the `authoritative allocation of resources' among the various tiers of the Nigerian federation. By the same logic, it deals with the outcomes of the allocative process and the conditions under which it breeds crisis. Rather than be limited by the straight jacket of specialised approaches, which provides a narrow view based on how ``the principles of horizontal equity and efficient allocation of resources are fulfilled in the context of fiscal federalism,''[2] a holistic approach goes beyond the treatment of revenue allocation as the distribution of resources to defined tiers, responsibilities and functions, and addresses the power relations in which the struggle between factions of the ruling class are rooted: territorially, regionally, locally or atimes ethnically or numerically. Such factional struggles for access or control over national resources are meant to consolidate the gains of those in power or advance the ambitions of those who seek entry into the `circle of power'. In other words, the issue of revenue allocation, strikes at the very basis of the existence of the Nigerian federation and the rules of entry and exit from the ruling class. Furthermore, it shows that the evolution of a `non' crisis generating approach to revenue allocation is germane to the stability and development of the Nigerian society.

Thus, a conceptual treatment that limits itself to the `economics' of fiscal federalism, or divorces it from its political context would not serve as appropriate tool for analysis. By inserting a historical perspective into our holistic framework, we are able to connect the political economy of the revenue allocation system to the current crisis besetting the federation, and proffer concrete suggestions for national reconstruction.

In discussing the revenue allocation system, it is apposite to understand revenue allocation as an expression of a balance of social and political forces within the state. For ultimately, the power of allocation resides in the state, and can be threatened when the struggle for power and access to resources `get out of hand'. Thus, the contending forces over power and access to oil, the locus of state power, extraction and accumulation of resources, constitute the major conceptual issues that must be objectively confronted in seeking to grasp the full ramifications of the impact of oil on Nigeria's revenue allocation system.

Some Background Issues

The background to the oil-revenue allocation nexus lies in the economic structure of the colonial state, the history of revenue allocation, and the emergence of oil after the civil war as the fiscal basis of the Nigerian federation.

The Colonial State

Nigeria was the creation of the (British) colonial state. Through its coercive apparatus, the colonial state defined Nigeria territorially, and forcefully integrated the various political forms and pre-capitalist modes at different stages of development into the global economic system. While it pursued different administrative styles towards Northern and Southern Nigeria (which were initially separate until the amalgamation of 1914), the economy was structured towards satisfying the demand of British and global capital for raw materials, primary exports, and local markets for imported finished products. Essentially, the Nigerian colonial state served the interests of global accumulation at the periphery through the local extraction and transfer of resources to the metropolis. As such it exacerbated local differences and spawned uneven development through vertical channels of extraction, accumulation and transfer. Uneven levels of penetration, regional disparities in the emergence of the local elite in areas of concentration of accumulation and commerce (to the detriment of those excluded), created cleavages, distrust and rivalry. This was worsened by the centralised nature of colonial patrimonialism which gave elite factions of the numerically dominant ethnic groups a headstart in the sharing of spoils within the colonial state.

The adoption of federalism and the creation of regions then provided a framework within which the dominant regional elite sought access to regional power as a basis for their exclusive control over the regional cash crop economic base, and for defending it from extra-regional competitors. It was this that gave Nigerian federalism a divisive and regionalised character. With ethnicity as a ready tool for elite mobilisation for access to power and resources, and regionalism as a framework for class formation and politics alongside the structural inequities embedded in the colonial state, the stage was already set for a troubled federalising process in Nigeria. A critical flashpoint of tension, conflict and struggle was the issue of revenue allocation, and the fiscal relations between the tiers of government.

Revenue Allocation: A Historical Background

The inception of the revenue allocation system in Nigeria has been put at

1946[3] when the Richards Constitution came into effect. As Adebayo puts it, ``although the constitution was not strictly federal, the creation of the regional level of government immediately raised the question of allocating revenue among the central government, the new regional centres and the old Native Administration.''[4] This gave the process a political character quite early and tied it to the class formation (highly regionalised) project of the nationalist elite which was then involved in the competition to inherit political power from colonial Britain. In this way, revenue allocation became central to Nigerian federalism, and the struggle for power and resources. As it turned out, the Phillipson Commission's recommendation in 1946 of derivation as the allocation principle through which `a region would benefit from its non-declared revenue according to the proportion of its contribution to the central revenue',[5] set the pace for the struggles that were to follow. The principle of derivation was unacceptable because it was believed that it unduly favoured some regions at the expense of another. Thus, ``by 1948, the elite from the Northern Region had begun to question the derivation principle, and made revenue allocation a major issue at the general conference on the review of the Richards Constitution in Ibadan in 1950.''[6]. In addition to other pressures relating to the accuracy of the data on which derivation was calculated, the principle was jettisoned as the sole basis of allocation and replaced with need (population) and national interest by the Hicks-Phillipson Commission. Yet, the struggle to correct fiscal imbalances between the regions was far from over, as the regional elites struggled to corner larger chunks of resources. By the time the federal constitution of 1954 came into existence, the derivation principle had come back into reckoning as recommended by the Chick Commission of 1953. Yet, in 1957 the principles of derivation which indeed had favoured the elite of the western region (thanks to the cocoa boom of the 1950's) became once more the chief allocative principle. That same year, the Raisman and Tress Commission sought to remove the fiscal imbalances between the Western and other regions by narrowing the application of derivation, and setting up the Distributable Pool Account (DPA) for other taxes which were not declared regional or federal[7]. This was made up ``of 30 per cent of mining royalties and rents and 30 per cent of general import revenue to be allocated to the regional governments in the following proportion: North 40 per cent, West 24 per cent, East 31 per cent and Southern Camerouns 5 per cent''[8]. The Raisman and Tress recommendations formed the core of Nigeria's revenue allocation system up till the late 1960's. Its significance lay in its creation of the DPA as a counter-balance to derivation thus defining to a large extent, the poles of conflict around which the struggles over revenue were to take place after independence.

Although the Dina Commission of 1968 attempted to review the Raisman and Tress report and did recommend federal control of the larger part of revenues within the context of a new twelve state structure, its proposals failed to see the light of day thus creating a vacuum in which the federal military government effectively centralised the allocative process. Thus through decrees 15 of 1967, 13 of 1970, 9 of 1971 and 6 of 1975[9] the balance of control and access to revenue tilted towards fiscal centralisation at the federal level. This process of transformation was effected through the progressive reduction of the principle of derivation and the strengthening of the principles of the DPA. It is however important to note that fiscal centralisation was partly informed by the lesson of the civil war: to reduce the power of the regions and prevent them from being strong enough to challenge the centre, ensuring that a `neutral' centre could mediate relations and provide equal access to resources to all the tiers in the pursuit of balanced development. Most fundamentally, perhaps was the transfer by the ruling junta of the military culture of the single command to issues of governance. Its main consequence was the centralisation of power at the federal level, and the dependence of the other tiers of government on federal benevolence.

The federal government as the very vortex of power thus became the ultimate prize in politics, and all attention shifted to the contest for access to power and the capacity to authoritatively allocate resources at the centre[10]. Worse still, the nature of oil wealth spawned a political culture in which emphasis was on how to share the providential wealth, rather than how to engage in the production of renewable and viable alternatives. As such, other sources of revenue were neglected in the rush for oil resources at the centre, thus giving the federal government a lot of leverage, which unfortunately was channelled into unproductive pursuits. Although oil fed into the rapid expansion of the public economy and the import-dependent private sector, the economy did not undergo any real structural development. A lot of energy was dissipated on the destabilising struggles for federal power, while the economy remained dependent on a single commodity whose fortunes were externally determined. Under oil, fiscal federalism in Nigeria and the revenue allocation system has gone through several convulsions which culminated in the tightening of the grip of federal power over the entire process, with the concomitant increase in the struggle for access to, and control over, federal power.

What the preceding shows, is that the politicisation of revenue sharing and its immersion in the contests over access to state (and later oil) power are at the root of the unresolved question of inter-governmental fiscal relations in Nigeria.

Oil and the Allocative Rentier State: The Dialectics of Revenue Allocation in Nigeria

The main thesis here is that while oil has overdeveloped the allocative capacities of the federal state in Nigeria, it is possible to discern a corresponding `underdevelopment' of its productive base. While the basis of class reproduction and national unity remains the fragile oil economy, itself totally dependent on volatile global oil markets and foreign, vertically integrated oil multinationals, the locus of struggle is concentrated at the levels of the collection and distribution of oil surplus. As such, the politics of allocation is heavily dominated by the rentier nature of oil revenues. It also implies, that the `capacity to allocate', is divorced from control over production, but inheres in location within, or access to state power. Furthermore, it explains the structural distortions spawned by oil in the Nigerian economy and how this feeds into crises.

From the preceding, it is clear that the oil-state nexus is at the heart of the dialectics of revenue allocation in Nigeria. What follows is to locate the contradictions spawned by oil within the processes of fiscal federalism. The major contradictions are: federal government versus the other tiers, federal government versus the states, federal government versus the oil-producing states, oil-producing states versus the non-oil producing states, federal government versus the oil minorities and oil minorities versus the oil multinationals. As such, these oil-related battle lines are both locational and situational, being influenced by their position in oil-based accumulation, the distribution of spoils, extent of control of territorial space, and the position within a historically determined structure of domination, resistance and access. It is important to caution here that the intention is not to define or theorise the Nigerian state. It is merely to show the connection between providential state-controlled oil revenue and its distributive/allocative politics. This is predicated on the notion of rent which refers to ``the sharing of a produce or natural stock of wealth without contributing to it.''[11]

As Beblawi explains further:

> The emergence of the oil states in the 1970's and their promotion to the forefront óf world trade and finance resuscitated the concept of rentier economies. A windfall wealth of unprecedent magnitude in such short time revived the idea of unearned income, hence the epithet of the rentier economy.[12]

Nigeria was a beneficiary of an oil boom of the 1970's and early 1980's. From an insignificant contribution to the nation's coffers in the early 1960's, earnings from oil shot up from a few hundred million naira to ₦4.733 billion in 1975, ₦10 billion in 1979 and an unprecedented ₦15 billion naira in 1980.[13] The state in spite of being awash with petrodollars remained outside the actual production of oil which remained firmly in the hands of foreign oil multinationals led by Shell. As such the state was reduced to a collector of `oil rents or toll booty.'[14]

Once captured by `the few', state power in a rentier oil context is transformed into an authoritarian core sustained by a series of patron-client networks terminating at the feet of a grand patron, and involving the repression of contending/opposition groups.[15] The power over allocation is therefore highly prized and closely guarded, being fundamental to the reproduction of class rule. For the same reason, it remains vulnerable to destabilisation due to pressures by rival factions within the ruling class for access and control. It is perhaps out of the desire to mediate those pressures and the fact of military dictatorship that led progressively to the strengthening of central/federal control over the allocative process in a zero sum context marked by the narrowing of access which undermined intergovernmental fiscal relations to the advantage of federal power. This led to the intensification of struggles for access to federal power, amidst growing protests against federal neglect, marginalisation and unfairness. The roots of such protests lay in the changes effected in the revenue allocation system after the advent of the oil boom. Since most of the oil was contributed by the minority ethnic states of midwestern and south eastern Nigeria, the abandonment of derivation was interpreted as a treacherous ploy of denying those states of the full benefit of their contributions to the federal purse. In reality, it was more of an intra-class struggle over which faction of the regionalist bourgeoisie (now broken up along state lines) would maximise the benefits from oil rents. Such struggles were bitter and deepened in intensity as the effects of the economic crises bit deeper and oil rents shrank further.[16]

There was no alternative to oil rents as the crisis in the oil sector destabilised the federal system. The latter became the object of increased struggles by `the constituent political units and nationalities in Nigeria for greater access to the revenues accruing to the federal state from oil exports and the challenges to the existing structure of the nation-state.[17] These pressures also fed into a crisis of legitimacy and governance amidst growing calls for a revision of the revenue allocation formula, and the renegotiation of the very basis of the Nigerian federation.[18] In this way, the allocative state in the rentier context is having its monopoly over the revenue allocation system contested by political units and nationalities within Nigeria on the grounds of unfairness, inequity and alienation. The very fact of power over distribution bereft of power over production defines the dialectics of revenue allocation and its links to the deepening of the crisis of Nigeria's federalism.

The Federal Government Versus the other Tiers

This contradiction lay in the shift of fiscal power from the regions (and states) from derivation, to the federal government which from the 1970s assumed *defacto* control of the bulk of national revenues (oil). Being tied to the class project of the regional elite and their continued participation in the processes of domestic accumulation, the shift in the 'power of allocation' to the centre in a context in which production was largely divorced from distribution bred vicious intra-class competition for access to, and control over resources. The process of the transfer of fiscal power was shaped by several factors: military rule, splitting of the four regions into twelve states in 1967, the progressive abandonment of derivation as the sole allocative principle and the convergence of oil on the main revenue earner. With the shift in power, the arena of contest moved to the federal level.

By decree 13 of 1970, the share of allocation based on derivation was reduced to 50 per cent, while the 50 per cent of the DPA each went to population and equality of states. This was against the background of Decree 51 of 1969 and 38 of 1971 which gave the federal government, complete ownership and control of all petroleum produced in Nigeria, while decree 9 of 1971, gave the federal government control over the collection of all offshore oil receipts.[19] By 1975, derivation was further reduced by 5 per cent, while only 20 per cent of onshore oil receipts went to states of origin, 80 per cent went to the DPA from where it was distributed on the basis of population and equality of states. By 1977 when the DPA was replaced with a single federation account distributed on the basis of a ratio of 60:30:10, there was no doubt that the federal tier had fully reversed the allocation formula to its own advantage. Ever since, it has progressively come under pressure from the states which have increased from twelve to nineteen, twenty-one, thirty and now thirty-six, which seek to maximise their share of oil rents. In 1985 the formula had a ratio of 53:35:10, and in 1997, the ratio of allocation of the Federation Account is 48.5:24:7.5[20] still reflecting federal hegemony.

What the preceding shows is that with the advent of oil the other tiers have 'lost' the power over national resources to the federal government. The underdevelopment of other revenue sources in spite of shrinking oil revenue (arising from the economic crisis of the 1980s) have further served to increase the pressure by the other tiers for more funds from the federal government, or as in the case of oil-producing states, for the control of their natural resources. The process of allocation has become more politicised, feeding into imbalances in Nigeria's intergovernmental fiscal relations. The contradictions arising from the growing economic crisis and the distribution of oil revenues have fed into the intensification of intra-ruling class struggles for access to, and control of the critical oil resource. As a result, federal hegemony in the multicultural and multi-national context of Nigeria is increasingly being questioned.

The Federal State Versus the Oil Minorities

This contradiction is one of the most critical within Nigeria's troubled federal experiment. Its roots lie in the aftermath of the Nigerian civil war when the hopes of the oil minorities that they would gain full rights over the oil mined in their territory were dashed by the shift from the allocative principle of derivation to those of equality and population of states which benefitted the big ethnic-nationality groups which had historically marginalised the minorities.[21] Federal fiscal centralisation under military rule further alienated and shut off the oil minorities from any direct access to oil, the new wealth of Nigeria[22]. Ever since, the oil minorities have mounted pressures for the return to derivation as a major allocative principle that would ensure justice, equity and fairness.

Of recent, the struggle of oil minorities against the federal state has intensified.[23]

The deepening of the economic crisis after the introduction of SAP in 1986 largely radicalised the struggles of the oil minorities. The demands of the newly formed oil minorities social movements included, the restructuring of the federation in a manner that gives more autonomy to the other tiers, self-determination to the minorities within the federation and the return to the allocative principles of derivation, while providing for compensation for oil pollution of the environment. Prominent among such groups were the Movement for the Survival of the Ogoni People (MOSOP), the Ethnic Minority Organisation of Africa (EMIROAF) and the Ijaw Ethnic Minority Rights Protection Organisation and the Southern Minorities Movement.[24] So heightened were the pressures that in some parts of the Niger Delta they led to local resistance to continued oil exploitation. As such struggles intensified, the oil minorities increasingly questioned the capacity of the state to protect their welfare and meet their needs in the face of shrinking oil revenues and an allocative system that is stacked against them.[25] It was partly in response to the demands of the oil minorities, and to mediate the contradictions spawned by oil that the Babangida junta raised the statutory allocation to mineral-producing areas to 3 per cent, and set up the Oil Mineral Producing Areas Development Council

(OMPADEC) to administer the fund. But the gesture failed to stem the tension. The intensity of the demands for fiscal redress and the fundamental restructuring of the federation portend a crisis of state legitimacy and the fostering of the unresolved volatile national question.

Oil Producing Versus Non-oil Producing States

The contradiction between oil producing versus non-oil producing states is embedded in intra-class squabbles over oil rents. The battlefield of this struggle has been the revenue allocation system. Since most of the oil is found in the coastal areas of midwestern and south eastern Nigeria and the adjoining offshore areas, the process of states creation and the growing profile of oil have made the issue of the modality of distribution a sore point in inter-state relations. Thus, while the oil producing states insist on derivation, the non-oil producing states insist on the principles of the equality of states and the size of population. Furthermore, the non-oil producing states accuse their oil-producing counterparts of greed, arguing that they do not have a sole right to the oil within their territory since they did not put it there, nor contribute anything to it[26]. Undeterred, the oil- producing states have remained as resolute as ever on the grounds of equity, justice, fairplay and the need to protect their environment from the deletrious impact of oil pollution. They also complain that they are marginalised by the other (numerically dominant) groups of the federation who (even though they contribute little or nothing to federal revenues) continue to feed fat on the oil rents and plum federal jobs.[27] Through media campaigns, political fora, court cases and well-articulated views of pressure groups within civil society, the oil-producing states have pushed their case. During the Babangida regime's transition programme, they formed themselves into the Association of Mineral Oil States (AMOS),[28] to fight for a derivation-based redress in Nigeria's fiscal federalism. Yet, concessions in the form of OMPADEC and the small increase in the statutory allocation to mineral producing areas have neither appeased the oil minorities nor allayed the fears of the non-oil states, thus worsening the tension in inter-state relations.

The collapse of the external oil sector and the sharp decline in living standards partly caused by the implementation of SAP further worsened inter-state relations. The contests over the shrinking oil revenues amidst the growing authoritarianism of the state meant that peaceful calls for redress remained unanswered, while intra-ruling class struggles over oil deepened[30]. Although the lid has been kept on as a result of military rule, it remains clear that the non-resolution of the contradiction between oil-producing and non-oil producing states remains a latent threat to the federally dominated nation-state in Nigeria.

Oil Minorities Versus the Oil Multinationals

While oil is a source of profit to the oil multinationals, the oil-rich environment is fundamental to the survival and reproduction of the oil minorities and the local host communities. Due to the fragile ecology of the Niger Delta, oil production has the impact of upsetting the delicate balance between land, water and life.[31]

Apart from the threat to the ecosystem (which is well documented).[32] most of these communities lack basic infrastructure, while their local economies are ruined by pollution. The contradiction arising from oil production and pollution fuels demands for adequate compensation, basic infrastructure, community development projects, employment of indigenes, payment of reparations for past exploitation and degradation of the oil-producing environment. The refusal of the companies to respond to these demands have provoked tension and a rash of protests in the oil minority areas of the Niger Delta.[33] In 1994, Shell, Elf and Agip, three of Nigeria's major oil producers lost millions of barrels of oil due to forced stoppages by protesting villagers in Delta and Rivers States.[34] In the case of Ogoniland, MOSOP had forced Shell to stop operations since May 1993, leading to a daily loss of ₦9.9 million.[35]

The foregoing clearly shows the clash between the profit motives of the oil multinationals and the rights of the oil minorities. There is no doubt that the clash of interests between the profit motives of the oil multinationals and the rights of oil minorities remains a sore point, and has further fuelled the feeling of the oil minorities that they are being marginalised and unjustly punished on account of their small size. Such feelings directly question their status in Nigeria's federalism, and the ability of the state to protect their interests vis-a-vis the exploitative oil multinationals. It is this loss of faith, that poses some danger to the Nigerian state as presently constituted.

Prospects for National Reconstruction

From the foregoing, a strong link exists between oil and the crisis facing Nigerian federalism. The economic interface of this linkage has also been shown to be equally grim, with the immersion of Nigeria in a deep-seated debt and economic crisis in the past decade; a crisis partly fuelled by "the struggle among dominant groups in Nigeria as they seek to expand their niches, each trying to out-do the other in the belief that it would be, or it is being subjugated and marginalised or schemed out by others."[36] The result of this state of affairs is recurring instability, the endangering of the nation-state project as presently constituted, and the viability of economic reforms in the context of a highly centralised form of federalism which has evolved over time in Nigeria. As it is, the issue of sharing revenues has become a bitterly contested point in the on-going intra-class and inter-tier struggles, even though the allocative system has not been able to give life to a productive base or any real development. The highly politicised nature of the revenue allocation system has not been resolved by the post-civil war commissions such as those of Aboyade, Phillips and Okigbo, nor the legal tussles between the states and the federal government during the Second Republic. Indeed, its current destabilising nature is recognised by the Committee on Revenue Allocation of the 1995 constitutional conference which among other things recommended a "less crisis-laden approach to the question of revenue allocation."[37]

To cite the report further:

> .... allocation should be strictly based on equity and justice and should serve as inducement to the federating units to achieve self-generating growth. A good revenue allocation formula induces the federating units to try to excel in economic growth and revenue generation, and since it is based on equity and justice, it breeds peace.[38]

Although the committee did not go to the extent of defining the parameters of `justice' and equity, nor deal with how this can be brought about within the context of a monocultural and crisis-ridden economy, it goes far enough in terms of identifying some basic short-comings of the present formula.

Thus, certain fundamental steps need to be taken to transcend the present crisis-ridden conjuncture. The first step is the full democratisation of the centre of political and economic power, to provide equality of access to power to all groups. The concentration of power over oil has to be systematically broken down, with emphasis on the devolution of power and accountability. This would provide the basis for fairness to all groups and federating units. There should also be a thoroughgoing process of democratisation within existing political and economic spaces. Of immediate importance is the imperative of democratic governance in place of the current authoritarianism and centralisation. Also current demands for local autonomy need to be addressed as an essential building block for a democratic and equitable federation.

In relation to the oil nexus, there is no doubt that the structural roots of the contradictions generated by its production and distribution can only be resolved through the `deconstruction' of the rentier political economy. Also, the demand of the oil minorities for restitution and access cannot be ignored. As is known, the costs of denial have been heavy locally and even globally, and tug at the very life-chords of the Nigerian state.

Beyond the diversification of the monocultural, dependent Nigerian economy and the proliferation of new taxes (including Value Added Tax) at all tiers of government in the drive towards expanding the fiscal base of the federation, is the need to democratise the state, and move towards people-centered economic paradigms. At the heart of the transcendence of the `travails of Nigerian federalism,'[40] lies the challenge of transforming distributive inequity and state authoritarianism.

Endnotes

1. A.G. Adebayo, `Revenue Allocation: A Historical Analysis of the Nigerian Experience', in, Richard Olaniyan (ed) *Federalism in a Changing World*. Lagos: The Presidency, 1988.

2. F.A. Olaloku, `Nigeria's Federal Finance: Issues and Choices, in A.B. Akinyemi, P.D. Cole, Walter Ofonagoro (eds) *Readings on Federalism*. Lagos: Nigerian Institute of International Affairs, 1979, p. iii.

    Also see T. Danjuma, `Revenue Sharing and the Political Economy of Nigerian Federalism, in Isawa Eliagwu *et al* (eds), *Federalism and Nation-building in Nigeria*. Abuja: NCIR, 1994, pp.87-115.

3. A.G. Adebayo, *Embattled Federalism: History of Revenue Allocation in Nigeria 1946-60*. New York: Peter Lang, 1993.

4. Adebayo, (1988), *op.cit.* p.172.

5. *Ibid*

6. *Ibid*

7. *Ibid*, p. 174.

8. *Ibid*

9. *Ibid*, p.175.

10. Kayode Soremekun and Cyril I. Obi, `Oil and the National Question', in F. Onah (ed), *The National Question and Economic Development in Nigeria: Selected Papers of the 1993 Annual Conference of the Nigerian Economic Society*. Ibadan: NES, 1993, p.223-224.

11. Hazem Beblawi and Giacomo Luciani, `Introduction', in Hazem Beblawi and Giacomo Luciani (eds) *The Rentier State*. London: Croom helm, 1987.

12. Hazem Beblawi, `The Rentier State in the Arab World', *Ibid*.

13. Adebayo O. Olukoshi, 'The Role of the International Monetary Fund and the World Bank in the Management of Nigeria's Foreign Debt', in Adebayo Olukoshi (ed) *Nigeria's External Debt Crisis: Its Management*. Lagos: NIIA and Malthouse, 1990 p.84

14. Cyril I. Obi, 'Oil Minority Rights Versus the Nigerian State: Environmental Conflict, Its Implications and Transcendence,' Paper presented at CODESRIA'S 8th General Assembly and Conference, Dakar, Senegal, June 26 to July 2, 1995.

15. Ibid

16. Adebayo O. Olukoshi and Osita Agbu, 'The deepening Crisis of Nigerian Federalism and the Future of the Nigerian State', in, Adebayo Olukoshi and Lisa Laakso (eds) *Challenges to the Nation-State in Africa*. Uppsala: Nordiska Afrikainstitutet (in cooperation with the Institute of Development Studies, University of Helsinki), 1996. p. 80.

17. Ibid, p.81.

18. Ibid, Also Soremekun and Obi, *op. cit.*

19. Cited by G. Etikerentse, 'Some Aspects of the Law Relating to the Oil Industry,' Paper presented at the National Oil Seminar September 21-25, 1975 and published in the presentations and proceedings of the Fourth Annual Oil Seminar, GOCON, Lagos, 1995.

20. Adebayo, *op. cit.* Also see *The Guardian*, January 18, 1997 p.1.

21. Rotimi Suberu, *Ethnic Minority Conflicts and Governance in Nigeria*. Ibadan: Spectrum and IFRA, 1996.

22. Obi, 1995, *op. cit.*

23. Cyril I. Obi and Kayode Soremekun, 'Oil, the National Question and Crises in Nigeria: A Critical Review of Current Developments', in R.T. Akinyele and J. Owoeye (eds), *The National Question in Nigeria*. (Forthcoming).

24. Obi, 1995, *op. cit*

25. Ibid

26. Adebayo, 1993, *op. cit*

27. 'What all Southern Minorities Must Know,' Adopted Position Paper of the Southern Minorities Forum, Eket, 24th March, 1994.

28. Ibid
29. Obi and Soremekun, 1995 op. cit.
30. Cyril I. Obi, *Structural Adjustment, Oil and Popular Struggles: The Deepening Crisis of State Legitimacy in Nigeria.* Dakar: CODESRIA Monograph Series, (Forthcoming).
31. Obi, 1995, op. cit.
32. Dappa-Biriye, Briggs, Idoniboye-Obu and Fubara, `The Endangered Environment of the Niger Delta; Constraints and Strategies: An NGO Memorandum of the Rivers' Chiefs and Peoples, for the World Conference of Indigenous Peoples on the Environment and Development and the United Nations', conference on the Environment, Rio De Janeiro, Brazil, 1992.

 Also see, A. Rowell, *Shell Shocked: The environmental and Social Costs of Living with Shell in Nigeria.* Amsterdam: Greenpeace, 1994.
33. Obi (Forthcoming) op. cit
34. Tayo Lukula, `Oil Firms Count Losses, Proffer Solutions to Community Agitation', *The Guardian,* January 25, 1994.
35. Ifeanyi, Izeze, `Nigeria Loses ₦2.732 billion to Ogoni Crisis', *Daily Sunray,* February 3, 1994. p.1.
36. Attahiru Jega, `The Political Economy of Nigerian Federalism', in J. Isawa Elaigwu and R.A. Akindele (eds) *Foundations of Nigerian Federalism 1960-1995.* Abuja: National Council of Intergovernmental Relations, 1996. p. 87.
37. Federal Republic of Nigeria, *Report of the Constitutional Conference Containing Resolutions and Recommendations,* Vol. II, Abuja, 1995.
38. Ibid.
39. Cyril I. Obi, *Oil, Environmental Conflict and National Security in Nigeria: Ramifications of the Ecology-Security Nexus for Sub-Regional Peace.* Urbana-Champaign, ACDIS Occasional Paper (Forthcoming).
40. Rotimi Suberu, `The Travails of Federalism in Nigeria', *Journal of Democracy,* Vol. 4, No. 4, October 1993.

CHAPTER 18

Rotimi T. Suberu

States' Creation and the Political Economy of Nigerian Federalism*

A striking, yet sobering, feature of Nigerian politics has been the severe instability in the internal territorial configuration of the country's federal system. Since her independence from Britain in 1960, the federation's internal composition has been altered six times. The Mid-West region was excised from the Western region in 1963, thereby modifying the colonial tripodal regional structure into a four-region system. In 1967, in what became the first in a series of military-mediated territorial reconfigurations, General Gowon overturned the four regions and replaced them with twelve states. In 1976, the Murtala Mohammed-Olusegun Obasanjo junta transformed the twelve-state structure into a nineteen-state system. During General Ibrahim Babangida's eight-year tenure (1985-1993), the states increased from nineteen to twenty-one in 1987, and from twenty-one to thirty in 1991. In 1996, General Sani Abacha established an additional six new states, thereby instituting the federation's current thirty-six state-structure. However, far from receding or diminishing, the agitations for territorial changes have tended to increase and intensify with each round of reorganisations.

This chapter discusses the unrelenting pressures for new states in Nigeria in terms of the convoluted structure of the federation's political economy. The chapter is divided into four sections. The first sketches the broad elements and conditions of the political economy of Nigerian federalism. The second chronicles the manner in which the distributive pressures inherent in Nigeria's political economy have shaped the historical legacy of state-creation in the country. The third section focuses more specifically on the political economy of the latest (1996) reorganisations. The fourth and final section reiterates the essay's main implications and arguments.

The Political Economy of Nigerian Federalism

The nature of Nigeria's politics, in general, and the character of the federal system, in particular, have been shaped by two critical features of the country's political economy, namely, economic statism and ethnic

---

* The preparation of this paper was facilitated by a 'policy appraisal' research grant from the Development Policy Centre, Ibadan.

pluralism¹. As Otwin Marenin succinctly puts it, `Nigerian society is characterised by an overpowering statism which inextricably intertwines political and economic power. The line demarcating politics and economics has been erased as state power equals wealth and wealth is the pathway to power'². The economic centrality of the Nigerian state derives significantly from the underdevelopment of the country's economy, the limited elaboration of capitalist agricultural and industrial accumulation, the attendant popularity and attractiveness of the ideology and practice of centralised, state-led development planning and, especially since the seventies, the expansion of public finances by petroleum export revenues. By giving the Nigerian state a preeminent role in the use of resources and in the dispensation of patronage, these factors also elevate distributive considerations, rather than ideological or programmatic contestation, into the primary impulse for political competition.

Nigeria is also, of course, one of the most ethnically diverse countries in the world, with over 250 ethno-linguistic groups, some of which are bigger than many independent states of contemporary Africa. Given this profound ethnic heterogeneity, and the relative underdevelopment of socio-economic processes and identities, it is inevitable that the public competition for the resources of the state would take place predominantly among `ethnically-defined constituencies'.³ In essence, ethnicity, and the associated `primordial' paradigms of communalism, religion and regionalism, have emerged as the primary organising principles for conceptualising, articulating, protecting or promoting collective distributive interests in Nigeria⁴.

The Nigerian federal system plays a preeminent role in this distributive process. Succinctly, owing to its explicit legitimation and accommodation of sectional-territorial constituencies, the federal system provides the structural and institutional framework for the organisation and mediation of the ethnic competition for public resources in Nigeria. Thus, Peter Lewis refers to the `central role of federalism as the formula for governing Nigeria's fractious political economy'⁵. Indeed, according to Tom Forrest, the `strength of distributive pressures that have made up much of the substance of political debate and controversy and affected the allocation of resources (in Nigeria) is not explicable without reference to the evolution of the federal system and the structure of political competition'⁶. In essence, the development of a `distributive approach' to federalism in Nigeria represents the political corollary and institutional response to the country's economic statism and ethnic pluralism.⁷

In order to relate the foregoing discussion to the issue of new states, it is necessary to highlight some key, closely intertwined features of distributive federalism in Nigeria. In the first place, because national oil revenues constitute the pivot of the Nigerian economy, the financial resources of the federation are concentrated overwhelmingly in the central government. Specifically, the revenues generated from the taxation of petroleum profits, companies' profits, customs and excise, and a number of other lucrative revenue sources, are collected by the federal government and paid into the Federation Account. Although this Account is expected to serve all the three tiers of government, it is often unilaterally, arbitrarily and illegally operated, approriated and manipulated by the central authorities. Thus, although its current statutory share of the Federation Account is only 48.5 per cent, the federal government actually spends up to 70 per cent or more of the federally-collected revenues[8]. This discrepancy arises from the absence of sufficient intergovernmental accountability and transparency in the management of the Federation Account, the federal government's manipulation of the dollar to naira exchange rate in making export revenue transfers to the subnational governments and, most importantly, the various, largely extra-constitutional, deductions which the federal government makes from the Federation Account before it is shared between the three orders of government. Such deductions are meant to cater for such centrally-controlled items as the Stabilisation Fund, Dedicated Accounts, Petroleum Trust Fund, external debt service and other so-called national priority projects. These anomalies have been largely sustained, if not generated in the first place, by the reality of authoritarian military rule, and the concomitant inability of state and local administrations to enforce their constitutional rights as primary stakeholders in the Federation Account.

In the second place, the states and localities lack viable sources of revenue of their own. For instance, the key state-based revenue sources – personal income tax, vehicle licensing fees, land charges and sales tax – are inherently limited as sources of public revenues, are often weakly or inefficiently exploited by state administrations, or are sometimes regulated, restricted or even brazenly appropriated by the centre. For example, the federal government has imposed uniform national rates for income tax since the seventies. It also currently appropriates a huge chunk of the potentially lucrative sales tax, which has been administered as a federal Value Added Tax (VAT) since 1994. In essence, as noted by a recent report of the Central Bank of Nigeria:

> As presently constituted, only few states and local governments can provide up to 30 per cent of their planned expenditures from their internal revenue generation efforts. The statutory allocation from the Federation Account between 1990 and 1994 constituted, on the average, over 70 per cent of the current revenues of the state governments, while internally generated revenues accounted for only 17.8 per cent and the balance was by special (discretionary) grants from the federal government. The finances of the local governments reflect a similar overdependence on statutory allocations from the federal and state governments.[9]

The financial hegemony of the centre and the fiscal incapacity of the states and localities create a dual effect; they reinforce the structural vulnerability of the states and localities, while simultaneously intensifying the pressures among their populations and administrations for federal economic patronage. A third feature of Nigeria's distributive federalism is, therefore, the tendency for the states and localities to function as no more than conduits for the dissemination of federal resources to subnational populations, and for the representation of the distributive claims of these communities at the centre. Hence, some authors have characterised Nigeria's subnational governments as `agents or outlets of centrally coordinated development' or, better still, as `luxury consumer item(s)' which `clearly enhanced the prospects for the inflow of federal government revenues'[10]

Fourthly, the aforementioned role of Nigeria's subnational units as outlets for federal patronage has been reinforced and legitimised by the practice of dividing federal resources and opportunities on an equal basis among the states and among the localities. The horizontal (inter-state, inter-local) revenue sharing formula, and the `federal character' principle are perhaps the most important and systematic examples of this distributive rule.

For instance, since the seventies, between 50 and 40 per cent of the states' shares of the Federation Account, and up to 80 per cent of discretionary federal allocations to the states, have been shared equally among these units. The pervasive influence of the norm of inter-unit equality is also reflected in the practice of providing equal federal financial aid to new states. Thus, when Babangida created nine new states and 140 new localities in August-September 1991, he announced federal take-off grants of ₦30 million for each new state, and five million naira for each locality. What is more, the Babangida government approved expenditures of about ₦150 million for each state for the provision of key infrastructural facilities – office complex, secretariat, township roads – in their respective headquarters.[11]

Similarly, the constitutional principle that the composition and conduct of federal agencies should reflect the country's `federal character' has been widely interpreted to mean the equal distribution of federal appointments, amenities, and opportunities among the states. Indeed, according to an elaborate sharing formula developed by the newly established Federal Character Commission (FCC), the states `are to be equally represented in all federal ministries, departments, agencies, national institutions as well as public enterprises and organisations'. This rule is also to apply in `the siting of economic projects, and in the distribution of health and educational facilities and development infrastructures like roads, electricity and telecommunication equipment'.

Furthermore, according to the FCC, the principle of inter-unit equality in the distribution of patronage is to apply between council areas within states, and between wards within local government areas.[12]

The inevitable and predictable impact of these distributive practices is to reduce the creation of new territorial units of government into an avenue for economic aggrandisement by local elites and their communities. But, contrary to the positions of noted scholars like Okwudiba Nnoli and Eme Ekekwe, who have portrayed the agitations for new states as purely bourgeois in character, statehood aspirations embody both elitist and populist – communalist impulses.[13] Privileged local elites are the primary beneficiaries of the proliferation of political offices, bureaucratic appointments, public works' contracts and other individual goods or perquisites attendant on the creation of new subnational administrations. Mass-based communal constituencies, on the other hand, stand to benefit from such communal benefits of reorganisations as the provision or expansion (especially in the headquarters of the new states or localities) of public and private economic activities as well as basic infrastructures like roads, pipe-borne water supply, electricity, schools, telecommunications and clinics. As it is the case with most socio-political processes, however, there can be little doubt that the benefits to the elites from the state-creation project far exceed the more nebulous and vicarious advantages to mass-based communal groups.

While distributive pressures lie at the roots of the clamour for new subnational units in Nigeria, the actual processes and outcomes of territorial reorganisations usually reflect the interests, perceptions, calculations and manipulations of national governing elites. These considerations, as the next section should illustrate, are embedded in diverse political goals, including the augmentation of central hegemony, the cooptation or mortification of restive local elites and constituencies, the maintenance of some equity among the major regions and geo-political segments of the federation, the promotion of the federation's stability and, perhaps most importantly, the creation or expansion of regime support or legitimacy.

The Politics and Economics of States' Creation, 1954-1991

The original impetus for state agitation and creation in Nigeria derived from ethnic minority opposition to the British-instituted three-region Federal structure, which secured autonomy and hegemony for the Hausa-Fulani, Yoruba and Igbo majority nationalities in the Northern, Western and Eastern regions respectively. As recognised by Larry Diamond, this ethnic minority ferment had important distributive dimensions:

> ethnic minority fears and grievances centred around obtaining a fair share of the rewards and resources of an expanding economy

and state; contracts, loans, scholarships, processing plants, water supplies, street lights, schools, hydro-electric projects. Minority demands for separate states were based on the belief, actively promoted by their leaders, that minorities were being cheated in the distribution of these resources by the majority-dominated regional governments....[14]

However, apart from assuaging ethnic minority grievances, the creation of states was also expected to correct the politico-structural imbalance arising from the disproportionate size of the North, which accounted for over half of the federation's population and three-quarters of the national territory.

Yet, save for the rather isolated creation of the Mid-West in 1963, no significant restructuring of the federation could be implemented throughout the over ten-year period starting from the formalisation of Nigeria's federal status in 1954, up to the military overthrow of the First Republic in January 1966. Political factors account for this rather cold response to the state-issue.

For instance, largely in deference to the opposition of the conservative and pro-British northern political class to the fragmentation of its redoubtable regional base, the British colonial authorities had resisted all proposals to restructure the federation in the immediate pre-independence period (1954-1960). Indeed, a British-appointed commission of inquiry into minority fears (the 1957 Willink Commission) not only dismissed minority grievances as exaggerated, but also ingeniously sought to demonstrate that the creation of new states was both undesirable and unnecessary.[15]

The southern nationalist political class acquiesced in the retention of the three-region structure, and ultimately in its own political marginalisation, when it allowed itself to be blackmailed by a British position that any meaningful consideration of the issue of new states would require a postponement of the proposed 1960 date for the independence of Nigeria. In essence, the statehood aspirations of minorities in the immediate pre-independence period were `sacrificed before the Nigerian altars of ethnic chauvinism,... political sovereignty ... and political expediency', as claimed by Billy Dudley.[16]

Predictably, the excision of the non-Yoruba, partly Igbo, Mid-West population from the Western region in 1963 did not arise from a genuine concern by the nation's leaders for the predicament of the minorities. Rather, the reorganisation was part of a vindictive campaign by the ruling federal coalition parties – the Northern Peoples Congress (NPC) and the Eastern-based National Council of Nigerian Citizens (NCNC) – to destroy the Western regional base of the main federal opposition party, the Action Group (AG).

In essence, while resolutely resisting the statehood aspirations of minorities in their respective home regions, both the NPC and NCNC reaped enormous political and/or ethnic benefits from their decision to capitalise on an intra-party crisis in the AG to declare a state of emergency in the West, and then dismember the region.

The establishment of a twelve-state framework in 1967 derived from the political ascendancy of new, military-based ethno-political coalitions and the urgent need to undercut the imminent secession of the oil-rich Eastern Region from the Federation. The military counter-coup of July 1966, in particular, effectively transferred the reins of national power from ethnic majority politicians or their cohorts in the military to a minority-dominated military-bureaucratic governing coalition. The key ethnic minority elements in this coalition included the military head of state himself, General Yakubu Gowon, and such prominent civil-servants as Allison Ayida, Eme Ebong, Philip Asiodu and Abdulaziz Attah. These elements naturally favoured the restructuring of the ethnically inequitable and politically unsustainable regional system. However, it was the imminent secession of the Igbo-dominated Eastern Region, and Gowon's desire to undermine support for the secession among the Eastern minorities, that precipitated the 1967 reorganisations.

Consequently, the Eastern Region was fragmented into three new states, two of which comprised oil-rich minority–populated areas, leaving the Igbo landlocked and economically isolated in the third state. A similar attempt to contain centrifugal pressures in the federation informed the excision of the colony-province of Lagos from the Western region, which thus became landlocked, and less attractive or viable as a prospective independent Yoruba Republic. The Mid-West region was left intact, while the North, like the South, was fragmented into six states.[17]

In essence, the 1967 reform not only ended the structural imbalance engendered by the disproportionate size of the North, it also created a federal structure in which the interests of minority ethnic groups, and indeed the nation at large, could no longer be abused by any one ethnic majority group. All of this was, of course, consistent with the military's emerging commitment to manipulating the state-structure to augmen the hegemony of the centre and tame the divisive tendencies inherent in Nigeria's cultural diversity.

While ethnopolitical imperatives were a paramount factor in the 1967 reorganisations, distributive issues dominated the 1976 state-creation exercise. The latter exercise was implemented in the wake of both a phenomenal expansion in federal petroleum export revenues and revenue allocation arrangements that enthroned inter-state equality as the preeminent standard of financial devolution. As noted by the Justice Ayo Irikefeled Commission that was appointed to advise on the 1976 reorganisations: '... the basic motivation in the demand for more states is rapid economic development. All other reasons adduced by state agitators are to a large extent mere rationalisation to achieve the basic purpose of development'[18].

The main features of the 1976 reorganisations can be briefly summarised as follows. First, owing to the explicit association of state-creation with the devolution of central revenues, there was an official commitment to making the states as equal in population as possible. This was in order to ensure some per capita equity in the access of territorial communities to federal revenues. Consequently, many statehood requests were rejected on no other grounds than that their relatively limited population did not justify any reorganisations. The palpable casualties of this policy were the numerically disadvantaged ethnic minorities; the obvious beneficiaries were the three large ethnic majority groups. In essence, while as many as six of the twelve states created in 1967 were minority-controlled units, only about seven of the nineteen states in 1976 could be regarded as ethnic minority states[19]. Moreover, the nineteen-state structure consisted of ten and nine states in the North and South respectively, thereby overturning the preexisting equality between the admittedly more populous North and the apparently smaller South in the distribution of states. To date, the theme of ethnic and regional inequality in the distribution of states has remained an important source of contention in the Nigerian federation.

A second and related feature of the 1976 reorganisations was the explicit transformation of the rationale for state-creation from its original role as a sop for minority fears into a scheme for the dissemination of central revenues (derived mainly from southern ethnic minority communities) to predominantly ethnic majority populations. Henceforth, state-creation would cease to be a vehicle for extending political and economic self-governance to distinct ethnic communities; rather, it became an administrative strategy for the devolution of federal largesse to an omnibus and amorphous array of territorial communities and coalitions.

Third, partly in order to reduce the obviously insatiable distributive pressures for new states, and mollify the numerous unsuccessful candidates for statehood, the 1976 reorganisations were accompanied by a nationwide reform and revitalisation of the local government system. This reform, which constituted the federation into 301 Local Government Areas (LGAS), sought to transform these governments into an effective third tier of Nigerian federalism, and a genuine instrument for decentralisation, development and democracy at the grassroots.

Fourth, and finally, the 1976 reorganisations were explicitly linked to a programme of transition from military to civilian rule. Thus, the creation of new states was officially presented as a divisive and disruptive issue, which a 'corrective' military regime should resolve before handing over power to civilian rulers. Unlike the Gowon government, which procrastinated on the issues of democratisation and state-creation, the Murtala-Obasanjo government saw the prompt resolution of the state issue, and the disengagement of the military from politics, as essential to its image and legitimacy as a corrective government. However, while the Murtala-Obasanjo government correctly perceived the state-issue as potentially equally capable of disrupting and delaying the process of demilitarisation, and had resisted further agitations for changes to the nineteen-state structure on this ground, its successor military regimes have been quite eager to use the issue as a ploy to legitimise and/or prolong military rule.

Nevertheless, the issue of new states did resurface as 'perhaps the most prominent and volatile issue' in the Second Republic (1979-83)[20]. As it is well known, however, the attempts to create new states during this period were stymied by constitutional complexity, partisan acrimony, economic uncertainty, and unfettered sectional recrimination and suspicion.

In an attempt to resolve this festering issue, and as part of his political transition programme, General Ibrahim Babangida created two new states in 1987, namely, Katsina in the North, and Akwa Ibom in the South. Two years later, in 1989, General Babangida increased the number of localities in the federation from 301 to 449, excluding the mayoralty of Abuja.

In an important sense, the 1987, state-creation exercise sought simply to complete the unfinished business of the 1976 exercise. This is because the creation of Akwa Ibom had been explicity recommended by the Irikefe Commission, while the Zaria-Katsina imbroglio in Kaduna State, and the attendant agitations for the separation of the two communities, had become extremely strident even before the military's disengagement in 1979.

An additional achievement of the 1987 reorganisations was to make the number of states in the federation exactly divisible by three. This was widely considered to be necessary in order to avoid a rerun in the proposed Third Republic of the unfortunate constitutional-cum-electoral controversy in 1979 over what constituted two-thirds of the states in the federation.[21]

While the 1987 reorganisations genuinely appeared to be in the 'national interest', as claimed by Babangida, the 1991 reforms underscored both the continuing popular pressures for new states and Babangida's desire to exploit these demands to promote his personal rulership project[22]. The demands emanated largely from the Igbo and intelligentsia and political leadership.

These Igbo elements claimed, quite forcefully and persuasively, that they had been economically shortchanged and politically marginalised by the various reorganisations of the federal structure since 1967. Babangida responded to this particular grievance by creating two new Igbo states – Abia and (New) Anambra – and locating the capital of a third state, Delta, in the Igbo city of Asaba. The six remaining states that were created in 1991 gave satisfaction to distributive pressures emanating from Hausa-Fulani and Yoruba sub-groups (Jigawa, Kebbi and Osun) or responded to the need to extend political and economic decentralisation to geographically large, administratively unwieldy and/or culturally incompatible areas (Kogi, Taraba and Yobe). However, the location of five of the nine states in the North compounded the problem of inter-regional inequality in the distribution of states; the new thirty state structure consisted of sixteen states in the North against only fourteen in the South. The minorities were similarly shortchanged; they had only twelve of the thirty states.

The 1991 reorganisations trivialised and degraded the process of territorial reform in Nigeria. The creation of the nine new states, and the accompanying reorganisations of the localities, were done in a precipitate and prejudiced manner. Consequently, the reorganisations provoked an unprecedented orgy of protests, demonstrations and arson involving tens of fatalities.[23]

What is more, Babangida's decision to establish nine additional state administrations, and 140 new local governments, severely undermined the Structural Adjustment Programme (SAP) that he had announced in 1986 in response to the profound national economic crisis engendered by the steep decline in the country's petroleum export revenues since the early eighties. As claimed by Peter Lewis, the reorganisations underscored the government's `descent into unbriddled corruption and patronage politics' which `reversed many of the previous gains of SAP and left the country in its worst economic plight in a decade'[24]

Most importantly, however, the 1991 reorganisations reflected Babangida's increasingly wilful manipulation of his own democratic transition project. Among the more immediate consequences of the reorganisations were the disorganisation and destabilisation of state-level branches of the two official parties, the National Republican Convention (NRC) and the Social Democratic Party (SDP); the disruption or postponement of key items on the transition agenda, including the National Population Census and gubernatorial elections; and an intensification of the orchestrated campaigns for Babangida to continue in power beyond his promised 1992-93 handover date. Babangida's continued perversion of the transition programme eventually culminated in the 1993 presidential election crisis, which led to the dictator's forced abdication of power to an Interim National Government (ING) in August 1993, and the full reintroduction of military rule under General Abacha during the following November.

The 1996 Reorganisations

From the outset the Abacha government laboured under severe economic and political pressures. These pressures engendered contradictory perspectives and attitudes towards the issue of state-creation. The negative implications of any further state-creation exercises for the country's troubled economy were eloquently stated in a speech in January 1996 by the nation's former civilian president and a prominent supporter of the Abacha government, Alhaji Shehu Shagari;

> ... it is hard to see what contribution the creation of yet more states will make to our recovery and progress ... Civil Servants will earn rapid promotion and businessmen and women a fresh wave of contracts for more prestigious buildings and projects. That will be it ... No new resources are likely to be generated either from taxes, production or services. Dependent on federal hand-outs and ill-equipped to perform their functions, the new states will simply be a drain on already limited resources ... That is not development. It is absurdity.[25]

General Abacha himself appeared to set great store by this kind of analysis or prognosis when he argued that consideration of the issue of new states could 'only be done against the background of their economic and other wider implications', and that only economically viable states could be created by his administration.[26] Since virtually all the Nigerian states were in financial disarray, many observers interpreted Abacha's position to mean that no major restructuring of the federal state-system was imminent.

Nevertheless, given the contentious circumstances surrounding his assumption of power, his widely rumoured civilian-presidential ambition, and his government's consequent need to secure some basis of support and legitimacy, Abacha could not ignore the deluge of distributive and political pressures emanating from the Nigerian society.

Consequently, as a way out of the crisis engendered by Babangida's aborted transition, General Abacha inaugurated a National Constitutional Conference (NCC) in January 1994 to provide a framework for a fourth Nigerian republic. Among the topics that featured prominently in the deliberations of the conference was the issue of state-creation. Two separate committees, headed by Dr. Peter Odili and Mr. Paul Unongo respectively, were set up to investigate and advise on the matter. Yet, because both committees failed to produce an acceptable resolution of the issue, the Conference ultimately resolved to entrust absolute responsibility for state-creation to the Abacha government.[27]

On 13 December 1995, General Abacha inaugurated a committee on the creation of states and local governments. Headed by Chief Arthur Mbanefo, the committee was asked to investigate all demands for territorial reorganisations, and make appropriate recommendations to the government. The committe received a total of seventy-two requests for new states (twenty-seven requests more than the number received by the constitutional conference – see Table 1) 2,369 demands for local governments, and 286 proposals for boundary adjustments.[28] Although the committee made specific recommendations for the creation of some states and local governments, such proposals were never publicised, and the government itself did not publish any White Paper on the committee's report.

Nevertheless, on the occasion of the country's thirty-sixth anniversary on 1 October 1996, General Abacha announced the creation of six new states as follows:

> Bayelsa, with headquarters at Yenagoa, was created out of Rivers State. Ebonyi, with headquarters at Abakaliki, was excised from Abia and Enugu States. Ekiti, with capital at Ado-Ekiti, emerged from Ondo State.
> Gombe, with headquarters at Gombe, was excised from Bauchi State.
> Nasarawa, with capital at Lafia, was created out of Plateau State.
> Zamfara, with headquarters at Gusau, emerged from Sokoto State.[29]

Table 1: The 45 Requests for New States Received by the National Constitutional Conference, 1994.

Present State	Proposed States	Proposed Capital
Abia	(1) Aba	Aba
Adamawa/Taraba	(2) Sardauna	Mubi
Akwa Ibom	(3) Itai	Ikot Ekpene
	(4) Atlantic	Oron
Anambra	(5) Ezu	Awka
Bauchi	(6) Gombe	Gombe
	(7) Katagum	Azare
Benue	(8) Apa	Otukpo
	(9) Katsina-Ala	Zaki-Ibiam
Cross-River	(10) Ogoja	Ikom/Ogoja
Delta	(11) Anioma	Asaba
	(12) Toru-Ebe	Patani
Edo	(13) Afemesa	Auchi
Enugu/Abia	(14) Ebonyi	Abakaliki
Imo	(15) Njaba	Okigwe
Jigawa	(16) Hadejia	Hadejia
	(17) Lautai	N/A
	(18) Bayajida	Daura, Kazaure or Gumel
Kaduna	(19) Gurara	Zonkwa or Kanfanchan
Kano	(20) Tiga	N/A
	(21) Gari	N/A
	(22) Tigari	Gwarzo
Katsina	(23) Karadua	N/A
Kogi	(24) Okura	Anyigba
	(25) Okun	Kabba
Kwara	(26) Oya	Kabba
	(27) Yoruba/Ekiti	Ilorin
Niger/Kebbi	(28) Kainji	Kontagora
	(29) Ndaduma (Nupe)	Bida
Ogun	(30) Ijebu-Remo	Odogbolu or Ijebu-Ode
Ondo	(31) Ekiti	Ado-Ekiti
Osun	(32) Oduduwa	Ile-Ife or Ilesha
Oyo	(33) New Oyo	Ogbomosho
	(34) Oke-Ogun	Shaki, Iseyin, or Igboho
	(35) Ibadan	Ibadan
Plateau	(36) Nasarawa	Akwanga
Rivers	(37) Bayelsa/Niger Delta	Yenagoa, Brass or Sagbama
	(38) Orashi	Ahoada
	(39) Ogoni/Rivers East	Bori
	(40) Port Harcourt	P/Harcourt
	(41) New Rivers	South P/Harcourt
	(42) Oloibiri	Ogbia or Nembe
Sokoto	(43) Zamfara	Gusau
	(44) New Sokoto/Sakkwato	N/A
Taraba	(45) Mambila	N/A

Source: Adapted from Federal Republic of Nigeria, *Report of The Constitutional Conference Vol.2* (Abuja: National Assembly Press, 1995) Appendix 1.

Note: N/A = Not Available.

In addition to these six new states, Abacha approved a 30 per cent increase in the number of localities in the country. Ultimately, 183 new local government areas (LGAS) were established thereby bringing the number of localities in the country from the 593 inherited from the Babangida era to 776.

Abacha justified these reorganisations on four interrelated grounds. First, he argued that, although the exercise could be economically and administratively disruptive, the establishment of new units of state and local government was not new to the country. Rather, according to Abacha, the exercise had become a familiar and inevitable feature of the country's post-independence government and politics. Second, Abacha claimed that his government could not ignore the popular demands for states and localities, especially as some of the demands appeared to be `genuine and capable of improving the administrative machinery of government.'[30] Thirdly, Abacha alluded to the broad support for new states at the NCC, as well as the conference's decision to transfer responsibility for the creation of the states to his government. Fourth and finally, Abacha said that it was necessary for his government to address all genuine demands for new states and localities in order to minimise the volume of unresolved issues that could `impede the stability of a democratically elected government'.[31]

The foregoing arguments offer rationalisations for the creation of new states, but do not really account for the choice and distribution of the six created states. According to Abacha, the creation of the six states was guided by the need to `ensure a fair spread and balancing within the geopolitical zones of the country, applying such criteria as population and land mass, among others.'[32] Accordingly, one state was created from each of the six recognised geopolitical zones of the country, namely, the North-West (which produced Zamfara), the North-East (Gombe), the lower North or Middle Belt (Nasarawa), the South-West (Ekiti), the South-East (Ebonyi) and the South-South (Bayelsa). These zones, which Abacha had previously named as the basis for power-sharing in the proposed Fourth Republic, reflect longstanding, if informal, axes of political jockeying, bargaining and bonding among the Nigerian political class.

Perhaps, the most significant feature of the 1996 reorganisations was the federal government's decision not to give any special take-off grants to the newly created states and local governments. This decision, according to official pronouncements, reflected government's intention to avoid extra-budgetary expenses or budgetary deficits (a familiar symptom of financial indisicipline under Babangida), correct the popular perception that new states and localities were instant avenues to federal largesse, and encourage the indigenes and protagonists of the new states and localities to assume a significant part of the responsibility for the development of such new units.[33]

Yet, the new states, like their precursors, face enormous economic constraints. Bayelsa, Ebonyi, Ekiti and Nasarawa States, in particular, have had to contend with severe infrastructural problems in their respective capital cities. In the absence of special grants from the federal government, financial and/or material succour for the new states has come from the Federation Account, the Federal Ministry of Works, some neighbouring or parent state governments, development appeal funds and rich indigenes. Many prosperous indigenes, in particular, have offered their properties to new state administrations for use for official purposes. But, according to the *Vanguard*, `those who offered accommodation to the new administrations are not doing it for the love of the new states but purely for selfish reasons. Some do-gooders are hoping that the new administrations would put their dilapidated properties in good order for them to claim back later.'[34]

Indeed, the states appear destined to relive the economic pathologies of the older states, including dwindling budgets; decreasing federal government allocations; derisively low internally generated revenues; excessively high wage bills or recurrent expenditures (which account for some 60 per cent of most state budgets); the disproportionate (mis)allocation of scarce resources to unproductive capital projects (radio and television stations, office and residential accommodation); wanton neglect of social services and regenerative capital projects; and massive corruption and waste through inflated contracts, abandoned projects, the sale of government properties (land, plants and automobiles) to cronies or fronts of government functionaries at ridiculous prices, arbitrary deductions from state-chanelled federal allocations to the localities, and outright theft of public monies.

The economic implications of the 1996 reorganisations are compounded by political factors. While giving satisfaction to some communities, the reorganisations have left many statehood aspirations unsatisfied and, in some cases, ignited previously latent grievances and tensions. In Nasarawa and Ebonyi, for instance, the sectional competition to be named as the headquarters of the new states has marred relations between the dominant blocs of Lafia and Akwanga, and Abakaliki and Afikpo, respectively. Ekiti State, on the other hand, is embroiled in fierce disputes over assets-sharing with Ondo. Meanwhile, the major unsuccessful candidates for statehood – Oke-Ogun, New Delta, Katagum, Itai, Ijebu-Remo, Hadejia – are bemoaning their misfortunes, while anxiously awaiting another future round of territorial reorganisations.

The geopolitical distribution of the states has also generated some strictures. Critics contend that the thirty-six states should have been distributed equally among the six geopolitical zones. However, there are only five states in the south-eastern zone, against seven in the North-West, and six in each of the remaining four zones. The inter-regional distribution of the thirty-six states has also been criticised: there are nineteen states, plus the federal capital territory, in the North, while the South has seventeen states.

More significantly, the 1996 reorganisations may have compounded the marginalisation of the minorities. Only two (Bayelsa and Nasarawa) of the six new states can be regarded as minority-populated states. This gives the minorities a total of fourteen states, against twenty-two for the `big three'.

The most disturbing political result of the 1996 reorganisations, however, was the spate of violent protests over the reorganisations of the localities. The reorganisations, it should be noted, were initially announced in October 1996.

They were, however, implemented only during the following December, and further `amended' on the eve of nationwide local government elections in March 1997! As was the case with Babangida's infamous and equally tumultuous reorganisations of 1991, the protests over the local reorganisations of 1996 were largely the result of the government's capricious handling of this emotive matter. The protests assumed particularly dangerous dimensions in three states: Delta, where the Ijaws and Itsekiris engaged in bloody and destructive conflicts over the relocation of the headquarters of the Warri South-West LGA from Ogbe-Ijoh to Ogidigben; Ondo, where comparable communal violence greeted the government's relocation of the headquarters of the Akoko South-West LGA from Oba Akoko to Ishua Akoko; and Osun, where the relocation of the capital of the Ife East LGA from Enuwa to Modakeke revived age-old tensions between the Ife and Modakeke. Bayelsa, Ekiti, Kwara, Kaduna, Niger and Plateau were some of the other states affected by communal tensions over the 1996 local reorganisations. These conflicts broadly underscore the inherent limitations of direct federal involvement in the politics of local reorganisations.

Conclusion

The unrelenting pressures for territorial changes in Nigeria reflect the insatiable pressures by territorial communities for easy access to central (rentier) revenues. The attendant proliferation of subnational units in Nigeria has added a pathological and cyclical dimension to what has been characterised as the `deepening crisis of Nigerian federalism'.[35] The more perverse consequences of the practice of territorial fragmentation in Nigeria have been shown to include: the promotion of the `cake-sharing syndrome; the augmentation of the centre's political and economic hegemony via the erosion of the size and resource base of subnational governments; the proliferation of unproductive, corrupt, wasteful and unviable political and administrative units; the intensification of ethnic, regional and communal tensions over the beneficiaries and modalities of territorial restructuring; the stimulation of `neo-ethnicity', or new forms of parochial, divisive and exclusionary identities; and the legitimisation of autocratic, military rule[36]. Indeed, far from demonstrating `its interest in an administratively simple, small number of states', as claimed by William Graf, the military has become the preeminent culprit in the saga of state-proliferation in Nigeria.[37]

Perhaps the only real argument for new states and localities lies in their presumed capacity to spread federal resources and developmental undertakings more evenly among territorial communities in the federation. However, given the declining productivity and viability of the national economy, even this redistributive role is becoming a mirage. Other than the rehabilitation or expansion of some infrastructures in the new administrative headquarters, the creation of new subnational units no longer carries the prospect of any real, mass-based benefits beyond the enrichment or advancement of bourgeois elites. Hence, the popular demands for new territorial units in Nigeria have degenerated into increasingly vicious inter-communal struggles for the headquarters of such units.

Quite obviously, the only real solution to the perennial crisis of territorial reform in Nigeria lies in the reinvention of the political economy of Nigerian federalism: It lies, in other words, in the creation of institutional and fiscal incentives that can promote the efficient mobilisation and utilisation of resources, and thus the expansion of the national cake, by all governments and segments, while discouraging the current preoccupation with sharing a shrinking national cake. General Abacha's modest effort to introduce the notion of financial viability to the process of state-creation in Nigeria, and the emergence of various other stimulating proposals for reforming the Nigerian federal system, appear to carry some promise for federal renewal in Nigeria.[38] However, the debilitating dynamics of the rentier oil-economy, and the predatory orientations of dominant national political elites, do not give much immediate ground for optimism about Nigeria's federal future.

Endnotes

1. See Larry Diamond, `Nigeria: Pluralism, Statism and the Struggle for Democracy', in Larry Diamond, Juan Linz, and Seymour Martin Lipset (eds.), *Democracy in Developing Countries: Africa.* Boulder, Colo: Lynne Rienner, 1988, pp. 33-92.

2. Otwin Marenin, `The Nigerian State as Process and Manager: A Conceptualization', *Comparative Politics,* 20, 2(1988), p.21.

3. Gavin Williams, *State and Society in Nigeria.* Idanre: Afrografika, 1980, p.69.

4: Henry Bienen, `The Politics of Income Distribution: Institutions, Class, and Ethnicity , in Henry Bienen and V.P Diejomah (eds). *The Political Economy of Income Distribution in Nigeria.* New York: Holmes and Meier, 1981, p.162.

5. Peter M. Lewis, `Economic Statism, Private Capital, and the Dilemmas of Accumulation in Nigeria', *World Development* 22, 3(1994), p.442.

6. Tom Forrest, *Politics and Economic Development in Nigeria.* Boulder, Co: Westview Press, 1995, p.2.

7. See Daniel Bach, `The Mamman Dike Challenge: Ethnicity, Nationality and Federalism in Nigeria' (Paper Presented to the Conference on Democratic Transition and Structural Adjustment in Nigeria, Stanford, U.S.A. August 1990), p.15.

8. See Weneso Orogun, `States Open Sheath Against Revenue Allocation', *The Guardian,* Lagos, 24 July 1996, p.18.

9. Cited in *Sunday Punch,* Lagos, 18 August 1996, p.23.

10. See Eghosa E. Osaghae, `The Status of State Governments in Nigeria's Federalism' *Publius: The Journal of Federalism,* 22, 3(1992), p. 183; and John N. Paden, `National System Development and Conflict Resolution in Nigeria', in J.V. Montville (ed.) *Conflict and Peacemaking in Multiethnic Societies.* Lexington; Lexington Books, 1990, p.415.

11. See Rotimi T. Suberu, `Recent Demands For New States in Nigeria', *The Nigerian Journal of Federalism,* Vol. 1,2 (1994), p.70

12. See *The Guardian,* Lagos, 18 October 1996, pp. 1-2.

13. Okwudiba Nnoli, *Ethnic Politics in Nigeria.* Enugu: Fourth Dimension Publishers, 1978; and Eme Ekekwe, *Class and State in Nigeria.* London: Longman, 1986.

14. Larry Diamond, `Class, Ethnicity and the Democratic State: Nigeria, 1950-1966'. *Comparative Studies in Society and History* 25(1983), p. 475.

15. See *Nigeria: Report of the Commission Appointed to Enquire into the Fears of Minorities and the Means of Allaying Them.* London: Her Majesty's Stationery Office, 1958.

16. Billy Dudley, *An Introduction to Nigerian Government and Politics.* London: Macmillan Press, 1982, p.58

17. See J. Isawa Elaigwu, *Gowon: The Biography of a Soldier-Statesman.* Ibadan: West Book Publishers, 1986.

18. Federal Republic of Nigeria, *Federal Military Government Views On the Report of the Panel On Creation of States.* Lagos: Federal Ministry of Information, 1976, p.10.

19. Eghosa E. Osaghae, `Do Ethnic Minorities Still Exist in Nigeria?', *Journal of Commonwealth and Comparative Politics* 24, 2(1986), pp. 158, 160.

20. William Graf, *The Nigerian State.* London: James Currey, 1988, p.141.

21. See Dudley, *Nigerian Government and Politics,* pp. 169-178.

22. See *The Guardian,* 24 September 1987; Kunle Amuwo, ``General Babangida, Civil Society and the Military in Nigeria: Anatomy of a Personal Rulership Project', *Travaux Et Documents,* No. 48, 1995.

23. See Rotimi T. Suberu, `1991 State and Local Government Reorganisations in Nigeria', *Travaux. Et. Documents,* No. 41, 1994.

24. Peter Lewis, `End-Game in Nigeria? The Politics of a Failed Democratic Transition', *African Affairs* 93, 372 (1994), p. 338.

25. Shehu Shagari, `The Time For Muddling Through Is Over', (Acceptance Speech on The Award of Honorary Doctorate Degree, Usman Dan Fodio University Sokoto, 13 January 1996).

26. See `Address by General Abacha On the Inauguration of the National Constitutional Conference on 27th June 1994', in Federal Republic of Nigeria, *Report of The National Constitutional Conference Vol. 2.* Abuja: National Assembly Press, 1995, p.8.

27. See *Newswatch,* Lagos, 19 December 1994, pp. 17-19.

28. Daily Times, Lagos, 2 October 1996, p. 21.
29. Ibid.
30. Ibid.
31. Ibid.
32. Ibid.
33. See, for instance, the statement by Alhaji Abu Gidado, the Minister of State for Finance, in Vanguard (Lagos), 3 October 1991, p.1.
34. `Headache For New States', editorial in the Vanguard 11 November 1996, p. 6.
35. Adebayo O. Olukoshi and Osita Agbu, `The Deepening Crisis of Nigerian Federalism and the Future of the Nation-State', in Adebayo O. Olukoshi and Lisa Laakso (eds.) *Challenges to the Nation-State in Africa.* Uppsala: Nordiska Afrikainstitutet, 1996, 74-101.
36. On neo-ethnicity, See Onigu Otite, *Ethnic Pluralism and Ethnicity in Nigeria.* Ibadan: Shaneson 1990, pp. 124-141.
37. Graf, *The Nigerian State,* p. 146.
38. See Rotimi T. Suberu, `Travails of Federalism in Nigeria', *Journal of Democracy.* 4, 4(October 1993), pp. 49-53; and Larry Diamond, `Issues In The Constitutional Design of a Third Nigerian Republic', *African Affairs,* 86, 343 (1987), pp. 209-26.

SECTION FOUR
The Executive in Comparative Perspective

CHAPTER 19

J.D. Ojo

The Executive Under the Nigerian Constitutions, 1960-1995.

Nigeria became an independent country on October 1, 1960 under a parliamentary system of government of the Westminster type of democracy. There was a governor-general who was the head of state representing the Queen and a prime minister who was the effective head of government. There were also regional governors in charge of regional governments and regional premiers who were the effective leaders of state governments. By this arrangement, the governor-general and the governors were meant to be ceremonial heads of state without executive powers. Just like the British monarch, they had three powers, the power to be consulted, to advise and to warn, but the persons who wielded real power at the centre and the regions were the prime minister and the regional premiers.

This arrangement worked perfectly for only a while. In no time, strains and stresses developed. Indeed, it is very difficult for a head of state in Africa to occupy the position of a titular head. Even if he reluctantly accepted such a position, there was bound to be personality clash between the effective head of government and the constitutional head of state because such a concept is still alien to the African who has been used to seeing his leaders (traditional rulers and local union leaders) wield enormous power"[1]

In 1961, Dr. Nnamdi Azikiwe, the first indigenous head of state, made a passionate plea that Nigeria should become a republic with the governor-general as president with executive powers[2]. He felt disenchanted with the weak position of the governor-general and he believed that it was wrong giving all the powers to the prime minister.

The plea by Dr. Azikiwe for an executive presidential system was considered at an all party-conference in July 1963. At that conference, it was agreed that Nigeria should become a republic in October 1963 with the governor-general as constitutional president. Dr. Azikiwe was not pleased with this arrangement which did not vest executive powers in the president. The pre-eminent role of the head of government was clearly demonstrated during the federal election of December 1964 when the head of state advised that the election be postponed from December 30,

1964 to a later more convenient date. Alhaji Abubakar Tafawa Balewa, the prime minister and head of government at the centre refused and he ordered that the election should go on as scheduled. The threat by the United Progressive Grand Alliance UPGA that if the elections were held on December 30, 1964, the party would boycott the election did not deter the prime minister. Despite total boycott in the East and partial boycott in the West and the Midwest, the election went ahead. During the election, there were electoral malpractices and the election was massively rigged. Despite the fact that the Nigerian National Alliance, NNA won the election through rigging, the President, Dr. Azikiwe was still bound to call on Alhaji Tafawa Balewa to form his cabinet since he won majority support in parliament.

Another problem Nigeria had was that under the parliamentary system of government, whoever had majority support in parliament had to form the cabinet. Under this practice, it was possible for a leader to confine himself to his region and if he could win majority support in parliament without campaigning for votes in the other regions of Nigeria, he was alright. This meant that Nigeria could have a prime minister whose knowledge of many parts of Nigeria was dim.

This was why Ojo[3] suggested that:

> to make democracy meaningful, we now need a leader that would be acceptable to all the people. For this purpose, it is being strongly suggested that a party or person must have overwhelming support in at least two thirds of the states in the country before being entitled to form a political party. That would stop the mushroom-like proliferation of parties. It would also enable the leader of a viable party, who owes his office not merely to a narrow sector of the Nigerian public, to speak with greater authority and to take far-reaching decisions on behalf of the country without fear or favour.

With the census controversy in 1962 and 1963, the Treason trial of 1963, and rigging of both the federal election of December 1964 and the Western regional election of October 1965, the army had to seize power on Saturday, January 15, 1966,[4] when the civilian government could not arrest the worsening political turmoil.

Between January 15, 1966 and October 1, 1979, the army was in power in Nigeria. No serious effort to get a new Constitution for Nigeria was made until Brigadier Murtala Mohammed (as he then was) assumed office as Head of State on July 29, 1975. In his 15th anniversary Independence broadcast on October 1, 1975, he assured the nation that he would soon set in motion the machinery for a new Constitution for the country. In his address to the Constitution Drafting Committee, Brigadier Mohammed told the members (i) that he wanted them to examine the possibility of introducing an executive presidential system with the president and vice-president popularly elected. (ii) That the choice of the members of the cabinet should reflect the federal character of the country; (iii) that he wanted to establish an independent judiciary[5].

At the end of the debates, the members recommended to the Constituent Assembly a presidential executive system of government. During the Constituent Assembly proceedings, members like Dr. Kumo[6] suggested that the presidential system be set aside and the parliamentary system continued. Similarly, Chief Adebo was of the view that Nigeria failed under the Westminster model for reasons unconnected with the defects of the system[7]. But there were members like Dr. Mbadiwe[8] and Wodi[9] who were fully in support of the presidential system. At the end of the debate, the Constituent Assembly settled for a presidential system of the American type.

Under the presidential system of government, there is separation of powers. Wade and Phillip argue that separation of powers may mean three different things:

(a) that the same persons should not form part of more than one of the three organs of government e.g. that ministers should not sit in parliament;

(b) that one organ of government should not control or interfere with the exercise of its functions by another organ e.g. that the judiciary should be independent of the executive or that ministers should not be responsible to parliament;

(c) that one organ of government should not exercise the functions of another e.g. that ministers should not have legislative powers[10].

This is in conformity with the doctrine of separation of powers propounded by Montesquieu in his *De L'Esprit des lois*, 1748, that:

> When the Legislative and Executive powers are united in the same person or in the same body of magistrates, there can be no liberty. Again, there is no liberty if the judicial power is not separated from the legislative and executive powers. Were it joined with the legislative power, the life and liberty of the subject would be exposed to arbitrary control – for the judge would be the legislator. Were it joined with the executive power, the judge might behave with violence and oppression. There would be an end of everything were the same man or the same body to exercise these three powers.

This doctrine really influenced American people when they were drafting the American Constitution. Madison, one of the architects of the Constitution, commented as follows, in his appreciation of the doctrine, that:

> the accumulation of all powers, legislative, executive and judiciary, in the same hands whether of one, a few or many, and whether hereditary, self-appointed or elective, may justly be pronounced the very definition of tyranny[11].

But the impractical nature of a full separation of power has been pointed out by Woodrow Wilson, when discussing the American Constitution;

> The trouble with the theory is that government is not a machine, but a living thing... No living thing can have its organs offset against each other as checks and live ... Government is not a body of blind forces, it is a body of men, with highly differential functions, no doubt in our modern day of specialisation, but with a common purpose. Their co-operation is indispensable, their warfare total[12].

Under s.4(1) of the 1979 Constitution, legislative power is vested in the National Assembly while s.4(6) of the Constitution vests legislative powers of a state of the federation in the House of Assembly of the state. Again s.5(1)(a) vests executive powers of the Federation in the President while s.5(2)(a) vests executive powers of the state in the State Governor. Similarly s.6(1) vests judicial powers of the Federation in the courts established for the Federation while s.6(2) vests judicial powers of a state in the courts established for a state[13].

Under the presidential constitution of Nigeria, there is a countrywide selection of the President and a statewide selection of the Governor[14]. This is unlike the parliamentary system of government where the leader that has majority support in parliament has to be called upon to form the government, even if he is not known outside his own constituency. This is why it is possible under a presidential system for a leader who has popular support among the people to win an election as president or governor whereas his party does not command majority support in parliament. In Kaduna State in the Second Republic, Alhaji Balarabe Musa won the gubernatorial election in Kaduna State while his party the People's Redemption Party only won few parliamentary seats in the Kaduna State House of Assembly. Similarly, in the 1991 gubernatorial election in Lagos State, Sir Otedola won the election while his party, the National Republican Party, won only a few parliamentary seats in the state.

Under a parliamentary system of government, the executive arm of government forms part of the legislative arm and its fortunes are tied to the fortunes of the legislature. This does not happen in a presidential system where members are elected to serve by the electorate for a specific duration of time. The condition for the removal of the president, vice-president, governors and their deputies are well provided for in sections 132, and 170, of the 1979 Nigerian Constitution, and section 144 and 188 Nigerian Draft Constitution, 1995[15].

Under the 1995 Nigerian Draft Constitution, the term of the office of the president, vice-president, governors and the deputies were increased from four to five years[16]. The members of the Constitutional Conference felt that five years was long enough for a president or governor to make his impact felt by the people and that four years was too short to demonstrate his effectiveness[17]. This is questionable as a popular president or governor can be re-elected for another term. The additional year is unnecessary.

One of the innovations in the 1995 Report of the Constitutional Conference is the declaration that:

> determined to fashion out a constitution that will be acceptable to the majority of Nigerians, and mindful of the need to avoid concentration of power in the hands of a few, or a sectional group, and the need to allay the fears in certain quarters that the position of the number one citizen of Nigeria is reserved for a particular area of the country or that particular area or that particular sections of the country cannot aspire to occupy that coveted number one seat, the Conference in its wisdom, and by consensus, agreed that the presidency shall rotate between the North and the South[18].

However commendable and far-sighted this provision may be, it is most likely to be rejected since the North still finds it extremely difficult to surrender political power voluntarily. The general belief in the North is that the northern leaders have a divine right to rule. Only a revolt or a threatened secession by any of the major ethnic groups can force a change in policy. In this respect, one cannot but refer to the June 1993 election in Nigeria. Following the promulgation of the Federal Government (Basic Constitutional and Transitional Provision) Decree, the National Assembly was constituted and the presidential election of June 12, 1993 was held. However, when it became apparent that Alhaji M.K.O. Abiola, a Southerner would win by defeating, at the polls Alhaji Tofa, a Northerner, the government of General Babangida annulled the election.

Ojo was also very critical of the action when he said in another context that:

> Why should the North assume that it must produce a ruler for Nigeria at all cost? That is preposterous and unacceptable in a democratic polity. Democracy cannot thrive in a society where certain segments of the society are regarded as underdogs[19].

It is hoped that commonsense would prevail so that an acceptable solution is found to this nagging problem which has eluded all solutions yet. The North has to accept the fact that it cannot indefinitely impose itself on the country. No federation of unequals can last for long.

The problem created under the 1979 Nigerian Constitution was the interpretation of section 34A (1) (c) (i) and (ii). The section provided that

A candidate for an election to the office of president shall be deemed to have been duly elected to such office where there being more than two candidates (i) he has the highest number of votes cast at the election and (ii) he has not less than one quarter of the votes cast at the election in each of at least two-thirds of all the states in the Federation

When the presidential election was held on August 11, 1979, five candidates contested the election. After the results had been compiled, it became obvious that Alhaji Shehu Shagari had the highest number of votes but he only scored one quarter of the votes cast in twelve states.

The bone of contention was the correct interpretation of "in each of at least two-thirds of all the states in the Federation". The Tribunal which tried the case held this to mean $12^{2}/_{3}$[20]. But the counsel for Chief Awolowo held that $2/3$ of nineteen states in the federation could not be less than thirteen states. The case went to the Supreme Court on Appeal. By a majority of five to two, the appeal was dismissed[21]. Justice Kayode Eso, JSC, in his dissenting judgement, held that the thirteenth state, like the first twelve states, should have been measured by physical territory and not by votes[22]. The Supreme Court held *inter alia* that $2/3$ of nineteen states was $12^{2}/_{3}$.

To correct the controversial decision in the case above, s.133 of the 1989 Nigerian Constitution rejected the Supreme Court's interpretation in *Awolowo* V. *Shagari* by providing that:

> where the computation of two-thirds of all the states of the federation or one third of the votes cast in a state, as the case may be, results in a fraction, the figure obtained shall be rounded up to the next higher whole number[23]

As Ijalaiye said:

> In essence, these constitutional provisions have once and for all put to eternal rest the menacing controversies which the decision of *Awolowo* V *Shagari* had generated in Nigeria and other parts of the world[24].

The Nigerian Draft Constitution has no provision comparable to s. 133 of the 1989 Nigerian Constitution. This therefore means that we are already back to the 1979 situation. So far, the government has been creating states which are divisible by three. A provision such as was contained in the 1989 Constitution seems ideal as it would cater for unforeseen contingencies as happend in the Supreme Court decision in *Awolowo* V *Shagari & ors*, 1979 discussed above.

Another innovation of the 1995 Constitutional Conference was the proposal that there shall be multiple vice-presidents "to reduce substantially the tension in our body politic since virtually every part of the country would be represented in the presidency"[25].

Whatever the merits in this recommendation, the suggestion is fraught with many problems. How does the president rank the vice-presidents? Won't there be unhealthy rivalry that can impede effective constitutional government if the vice-presidents start to engage in a power tussle? All these would create unnecessary distractions that can be a cog in the wheel of progress in the long run. This is why we should discard the recommendation. Rather, it should be accepted as the norm that anytime the president is from the North, the vice-president should be from the South and vice versa. Such an arrangement should also be practised in the states and local governments so that power is not unduly concentrated in one sector of the country or community.

The problem posed in the Second Republic by having deputies who were competing for power with their governors had not been properly addressed in the 1995 Draft Constitution. Under the 1979 Constitution, no specific responsibility is given to the the vice-president under s.136 (1) or the deputy governor in s.174 (1) of the 1979 Nigerian Constitution. This was indeed a great lacuna that had to be plugged since an over-ambitious president or governor may refuse to assign responsible duties to his deputy on the ostensible ground that his deputy would not handle these duties as efficiently as himself. Such alienation may eventually lead to disagreement and crisis.

S.145 (1) of the 1989 Nigerian Constitution had cured this defect by stipulating that the president shall assign to the vice-president specific responsibility for any business of the government of the federation. A similar provision is provided in s.191(1) of the 1989 Nigerian Constitution for the deputy governor and the state commissioner.

One is surprised that this important section has been deleted in ss.149 and 193 of the 1995 Nigerian Draft Constitution. Maybe, the members of the Constitutional Conference were not convinced of the usefulness of such a provision since a poor deputy handling sensitive schedules may constitute a serious embarrassment to a government. It must also have been felt that the president and the governor shall assign responsibilities as they deem fit. While this has its merit, it is still strongly felt that an assignment of certain responsibilities to the deputy would help reduce the load of the president and the governor so that they can have more valuable time devoted to serious policy issues. Moreover, this would at least give the deputies something to do since an idle mind is the devil's workshop. There was no doubt that most of the friction between the governors and their deputies in the Second Republic stemmed from the fact that many of them had little or nothing to do.

In a parliamentary system of government, ministers are appointed from the members of the legislature and as noted above, they sit and direct the affairs of government in the legislative houses. The practice in a presidential system of government is different. It is for the president and the governor[26] to establish the position of ministers and commissioners respectively.

In a parliamentary system of government, there is cabinet responsibility. This means that any member of the Cabinet must support all cabinet policies and he cannot be seen to disagree with any of the cabinet policies publicly. If he disagrees, and because of conscience, he cannot accept or abide by the cabinet decision, the most honourable course is to resign. In 1963, Ian Macleed and some cabinet members under Harold MacMillan resigned from the British cabinet when Sir Alec Home was appointed by Harold MacMillan to succeed him. A member of the cabinet can also be advised to resign honourably from the cabinet if his action could cause unnecessary embarrassment to the government as happened in Britain to George Brown in 1968.

But a presidential system of government does not operate on such basis. The ministers and commissioners are appointed by the president and the governors respectively but the president or the governor, as the case may be, is not strictly bound by their advice. In fact, under Art II s.2 cl.1 of the US Constitution, it is provided that the president "may require the opinion in writing of the principal officer in each of the executive departments, upon any subject relating to the duties of their respective offices".

As Ojo commented:

> there is no mention of any cabinet here. If the president decides to set one up, it is his own extra-constitutional arrangement. Secondly, the president is even not supposed to have meetings with all the ministers collectively but he is only required to have the opinions of the principal officers in writing and only with respect to the duties performed by the individual officers[27].

In fact, Dennis Brogan when commenting on the American president and his cabinet said that:

> there is in American theory and practice no question of *primus inter pares*. The famous story of Lincoln consulting his cabinet and announcing 'Noes seven, Ayes one, they ayes have it,' expresses perfectly the spirit of the American Constitution[28]

In *Lawal Kagoma* V *The Governor of Kaduna State and ors*,[29] 1981, the governor of Kaduna State appointed a Commission of Inquiry into the affairs of Kaduna Local Government Council purporting to act under s.2 Commissions of Inquiry law (Cap.25) laws of Kaduna State and s.98 of the Local Government Edict No.1 of 1977. The plaintiff, a supervisory councillor in the Local Government Council, challenged the governor's power by asking the Kaduna State High Court for a declaration that the inquiry was void because, as he contended, the inquiry into the affairs of the local government could only be made by the executive council and not the state governor under s.98[30] of the Local Government Law, 1977 and that the provision of that law overrides those of s.2 of the Commission of Inquiry Law, (Cap.25) of the laws of Kaduna State. He then asked for an injunction to stop the governor from carrying out the exercise.

At the high court, the claim was dismissed and he then appealed to the Federal Court of Appeal. The court of appeal held as follows; (1) that the only prescribed authority under s.98 of the local government law was the executive council and not the governor (2) that the executive council is one which the governor is obliged to set up under s.17A (5) of the Constitution and that since no executive council has been set up in Kaduna State because there were no commissioners, the governor had no power to institute an inquiry into the local government council without putting the matter before the members of the executive council (3) that even before the governor could set up a Commission of Inquiry under s.2 of the Commission of Inquiry Law, he is enjoined under s.174(2) of the Constitution to have the benefit of the advice of an executive council.

Mamman Nasir, the then president of the JCA, giving his judgement, said that:

> I am firmly of the view that the governor under our Constitution, is not intended to be a dictator. He is also in my opinion not as independent as the president of the United States as has been suggested in the exercise of his executive function... Sections 173 and 174 are intended to incorporate in the constitution a cabinet system of government in a modified form with a view to making it much more difficult for the Governor to assume the role of a dictator[31].

Ojo, criticising the cabinet system of government under the 1979, Nigerian Constitution, says that:

> the practice of the cabinet system of government under the British Constitution is different Secondly, the Constitution no where mentions any form of cabinet Government. It only asks the president to have regular meetings with the vice-president and all the ministers of the federal government for some purposes and not for all policy decisions[32].

Professor Nwabueze, in a similar vein, maintains that:

> the implication of this is that without an Executive Council, the political administration of the government by the president (or governor) alone is to a large extent unconstitutional."[33]

Members of Cabinet are appointed by the president or the governor after confirmation by Senate or by the House of Assembly as the case may be[34]. The problem with legislative screening under the 1979 Nigerian Constitution was that there was no limit to the number of times a minister or commissioner could be screened nor was there a limit also to the number of ministers or commissioners at the centre and the states. In essence, there was a proliferation of government ministers to create jobs `for the boys'[35].

The State Government (Basic Constitutional and Transitional Provisions) (Amendment) No. 3 Decree, 1992 provided in s.1(1) that the number of commissioners of the government of a state shall not be more than seven. But the 1995 Nigerian Draft Constitution has not limited the number of commissioners in a state[36]. All it has done is to provide in s.192(6) that any political party which wins not less than 10 per cent of the total number of seats in a House of Assembly shall be entitled to representation in the cabinet in proportion to the number of seats won by the political party in the Assembly.

It is hoped that this provision of the 1995 Nigerian Draft Constitution would not be used as an excuse to unreasonably enlarge the cabinet. It is strongly suggested that whatever proportion should be worked on, there should be a total number of seven commissioners in all for each state.

Another defect in the 1979 Nigerian Constitution was the screening of nominees for ministerial and commissioners' posts en bloc. This procedure did not allow Senate and the State Legislative House to evaluate the technical competence of each nominee for particular posts.

The government has abolished this procedure. Commissioners in the state governments are no longer to be approved by the state legislatures. The old system of legislative screening has been reinstated in the 1995 Nigerian Draft Constitution. Whatever advantage or benefit that might be gained from the earlier provision may be negated if the president or governor or the chairman of a local government decides to appoint people with questionable integrity into his cabinet. It is hoped that the president and the governor of a state will appoint people with high integrity and transparent honesty into the cabinet.

The 1979 Constitution stipulated that where a member of the National Assembly or of a House of Assembly is appointed a minister (or if in a state, a commissioner) he is deemed to have resigned his membership of the National Assembly or of the House of Assembly on his taking the oath of office as minister or as a commissioner in a state[37]. But the 1995 Nigerian Draft Constitution provides that any member appointed a minister under s.148(4) does not need to resign his membership of the National Assembly. This is quite different from s.192(3) of the 1995 Nigerian Draft Constitution which requires a person appointed as commissioner of the government of another state to resign his membership of the House of Assembly on taking the oath of office as commissioner. This means that if he is appointed a commissioner in his own state, he does not need to resign. These provisions are very untidy as this can blur the separation of powers doctrine. However, can a minister or commissioner perform as a member of the executive and the legislature? How will he be able to represent adequately the interests of his constitutency when he has to function in a dual capacity which are not mutually interchangeable? This mixed amalgam of presidential and parliamentary forms should be re-examined. Anyone appointed as minister, commissioner or supervisor under a local government structure should vacate his seat in parliament or local council as the case may be to allow for a replacement who will be able to perform the representative role properly.

Perhaps the 1995 Nigerian Draft Constitution envisages a situation where the country would return to the parliamentary system of government. If that happens, then the rigid separation of powers under a presidential system would be inapplicable in a parliamentary system.

One of the areas of contention is the executive and legislative relationship. Under s.63(1) of the 1979 Nigerian Constitution, the president may attend any joint meeting of the National Assembly or any meeting of either House of the National Assembly, either to deliver an address on national affairs including fiscal measures or to make such statement on the policy of government as he considers to be of national importance. Similarly, in s.63(2) of the 1979 Nigerian Constitution, a minister of the government of the federation shall attend a meeting of the National Assembly if invited to explain to the House the conduct of his ministry, and in particular when the affairs of that ministry are under discussion[38]. But s.19(1) of the State Government (Basic Constitutional and Transition Provisions) Decree, 1991 stipulates that the governor of a state shall address annually a meeting of the House of Assembly of the state on the state of affairs of a state. This is an innovation which was not in the 1979 Nigerian Constitution. This is like the situation in the United States where the president attends meetings of Congress to brief them on the affairs of the nation. Such occasions were full of fanfare and the people always received the president into the Chamber as the president of the United States and not one representing a party. This is the sort of spirit that could make constitutional government workable in the Third Republic. In the previous Nigerian Republics, there was a lot of political acrimony and issues were seen, on party lines rather than on national basis. But under s.70(1) of the 1995 Nigerian Draft Constitution, the president must address annually a joint meeting of the National Assembly on the state of affairs of the nation. Similarly, under s.111(1) of the 1995 Nigerian Draft Constitution, a governor of a state is under a duty to address annually a meeting of the House of Assembly on the state of affairs at the state. This is indeed an improvement over the 1979 and the 1989 Constitutions which never made this mandatory.

The president or the governor must assent to a bill within thirty days of the bill being presented to him. However, he could withhold assent but the veto could be overridden by two thirds majority of members of the House of the National Assembly or by two thirds majority of the members of the State House of Assembly[39].

Under s.6(1) of the 1979 Nigerian Constitution, the judicial powers of the federation are vested in the courts established for the federation while those of the states are vested under s.6(2) in the courts established for the state. This is well articulated in s.6(6)(b) that the judicial powers vested in accordance with the foregoing provisions shall extend to all matters between persons, or between government or authority and any person in Nigeria and to all actions and proceedings relating thereto for the determination of any question as to the civil rights and obligations of the person. There are similar provisions in s.6(1) (2) and s.6(6)(b) of the 1989 Constitution and the 1995 Nigerian Draft Constitution.

The cases of *Adegbenro* Vs. *Akintola*[40], 1963, *Awolowo* V. *Shagari, 1979*[41], *Shugaba Abdulrahman Darman* V *Federal Minister of Internal Affairs & ors*[42]. *Lakanmi & Anor* V *Attorney General of Western State*[43] 1970, *Governor of Ogun State & ors* V. *The President of Nigeria and ors*[44] have shown that courts of law have responsibility to determine cases between governments and individuals and between state and federal governments. The only cases which courts are reluctant to handle are political questions, which courts of law are ill-suited to determine.

This was read into *Balarabe Musa* V *Auta Hamza & ors*[45] by the court of appeal when it was considering the interpretation of s.170(10) which says that "No proceedings or determination of the committee (on impeachment) or of the House of Assembly or any matter relating thereto shall be entertained or questioned in any court." The Court held that:

> for the court to enter into the political thicket, as the invitation made to it clearly implies, would in my view be asking its gates and its walls to be painted with mud and the throne of justice from where the judgments are delivered with mire[46].

The decision has been severely criticised because not all the issues involved were political and some were justiciable[47].

Again under s.211(i) of the 1979 Nigerian Constitution, the Chief Justice of the federation's appointment is made by the president in his discretion subject to the confirmation of such an appointment by a simple majority of Senate. Similarly, the Chief Judge of a state court shall be appointed by the governor of the state on the advice of the state government subject to the approval of such appointment by a simple majority at the House of Assembly of the state[48].

But under s.231(1) of the 1995 Nigeria Draft Constitution, the appointment of a person to the office of a chief justice of Nigeria ``shall be made by the president on the advice of the National Judicial Council subject to the confirmation of such by the Senate." Similarly, the appointment of a person to the office of chief judge of a state" shall be made by the governor of the state on the advice of the National Judicial Court, subject to the confirmation of such appointment by the House of Assembly of the state". This is indeed a welcome departure from the former practice whereby judicial officers like the chief justice of the federation and the chief judge of the state were appointed at the discretion of the president and governor respectively. Being politicians, such appointment could be influenced by political considerations. In fact, the Constitutional Conference in its report on this issue maintained that:

> the National Judicial Council will enforce the independence and impartiality of the Judiciary especially during civilian regimes while justice and fairness will be assured to the citizens. It will maintain uniform standards and quality among judicial officers in the country through appropriate vetting and assessment of potential judicial appointees. The recommendations by the National Judicial Council .... will minimise the incursion of politics into the appointment of superior court judges and Kadis, in the state[49].

This is indeed a welcome departure from previous practice. It is hoped that the members of National Judicial Council would realise the sacred duty imposed on them by selecting people with high integrity and competence to occupy the highest seat of justice in the country.

The local government structure is also based partially on the separation of powers with the chairman and the supervisors forming the executive[50]. From the above, it is safe to conclude that even though we operate the presidential system of government, we have introduced some variants which differentiate it from the presidential system of the American type. Whether the system will be modified further to incorporate the French system of having a prime minister instead of the vice-president remains to be seen. The history of Nigeria since 1960 has shown that the country is adept in constitutional innovations and adaptations[51].

Notes and References

1. Ojo, J.D., *The Development of the Executive under the Nigerian Constitutions 1960-81.* Ibadan: University Press Ltd., 1985 at pp. 7-8
2. Azikiwe, N. Governor-General, "Call for a Republican State", *Daily Express,* Nov. 18, 20, 22, 23, 24, 25, 1961.
3. Ojo, J.D. "The Future of Parliamentary Democracy in Nigeria", *Viertal Jahres Berichte,* Nr. 60, June 1975 at p. 167.
4. See details in Ojo, J.D. *The Development of the Executive Under the Nigerian Constitutions 1960-81.* Ibadan: University Press Ltd. 1985 at pp 25-29.
5. Federal Republic of Nigeria, *Report of the Constitution Drafting Committee containing the Draft Constitution, vol. 1.* Lagos: Federal Ministry of Information, 1976 at p. xiii.
6. Federal Republic of Nigeria, *Proceedings of the Constituent Assembly, Official Report, vol., 1,* Lagos: Federal Ministry of Information 1978 cols. 496-497 at pp. 258-259.
7. *Ibid* col 635 at p. 328
8. *Ibid* col 771 at p. 396
9. *Ibid* col 1353 at p. 687
10. Wade and Phillips, *Constitutional Law* (ed). E.C.S. Wade and A.W. Bradley, 7th ed, 1965 at p. 23.
11. Madison, J. "The *Federalist* No. 45", The Federalist Papers; Hamilton Madison Jay (ed.) Clinton Rossiter, New York and Scarborgh, Ontario, New American, Library, 1961 at p. 301.
12. Wilson, Woodrow, *Constitutional Government in the United States,* 1908 at p.56
13. See Similar Provisions in ss. 4, 5 and 6 Nigerian Constitutions of 1989, and 1995 Nigerian Draft Constitutions and Arts I s(1), IIs(1) and IIIs(1) U.S. Constitution.
14. See ss.124-126 Nigerian Constitution, 1979 and s.164 Nigerian Constitution 1979 and ss. 130-133 and 176-179 Nigerian Constitution, 1989, ss.135-137 and ss. 179-181 Nigerian Draft Constitution, 1995.
15. See Similar Provisions in ss.140 and 186 Nigerian Constitution, 1989 and ss. 144 and 188 Nigerian Draft Constitution, 1995 ss.138 and 182.

16. 138(2), Nigerian Draft Constitution, 1995.
17. Federal Republic of Nigeria, *Report of the Constitutional Conference containing the Resolution and Recommendations* Vol.II, Abuja: National Assembly Press, 1995 at p.65.
18. *Ibid.* at p. 68
19. Ojo, J.D. ``The Rotational Axes Under the 1995 Nigerian Draft Constitution'' *Proceedings of the Conference on the Nigerian Draft Constitution 1995* (Forthcoming).
20. *Awolowo* v. *Shagari & ors* Suit No. SET/1/1979 delivered on 10 September, 1979 (unreported)
21. *Awolowo* v. *Shagari & ors* (1979) 6-9 S.C 51
22. *Ibid.* at p. 140
23. See a similar provision in s.179 with regard to the election of the state governor.
24. Ijalaiye, D.A. ``Differences between the Constitutions of the Federal Republic of Nigeria 1979 and 1989: How Fundamental'' *Faculty of Law, Ogun State University: Faculty Lectures* Ago Iwoye, Faculty of Law, Ogun State University, 1990 at p. 82.
25. *Report of the Constitutional Conference Containing the Resolution and Recommendations* Vol. II op.cit. at p. 66
26. S.135(1) and 173(1) Nigerian Constitution, 1979 see also a similar provision in s.144(1) and s.190(1) Nigerian Constitution, 1989.
27. Ojo, J.D. *The Development of the Executive op. cit.* p.100
28. Brogan, Sir Dennis, ``The Possibilities of the Presidential System in Developing Countries'', *Parliament as an Export* (ed) Burns, Sir Alan, London: George Allen and Unwin Ltd. 1966 at p. 195.
29. *Lawal Kogoma* V. *The Governor of Kaduna State & ors* (1981) 2 N C L R 529.
30. See S.98(2) Local Government Law 1976 Edict AC.1 1977, it is provided that ``Subject to the other provision of this sub section, the Executive Council may appoint in writing any person to conduct an inquiry and any person so appointed shall cause a notice of the time and place of the inquiry to be given to the local government and persons appearing to him to be interested''.
31. (1981) 2 N C L R 529 at pp. 546-547.

32. Ojo, J.D., *The Development of the Executive under the Nigerian Constitution 1960, 1981 op. cit* at p. 96.

33. Nwabueze, B.O., *Ideas and Facts in Constitution Making: The Morohundiya Lectures,* Faculty of Law, University of Ibadan, Ibadan: Spectrum Books Ltd., 1993 at pp 178-179.

34. SS.135(2) and 173(2), Nigerian Constitution 1979, See similiar provisions in ss.144(2) and 190(2) Nigerian Constitution 1989 and ss. 148(2) and 192(2) Nigerian Draft Constitution 1995.

35. Ojo, J.D., *The Development of the Executive, op.cit* at p.95

36. SS.148(1) and 192(1) for the federal and state governments respectively.

37. SS.135(4) and 173(3) Nigerian Constitution 1979, and 144(4) and 190(4) Nigerian Constitution, 1989.

38. See similar provisions with regard to the governor and the commissioner in s.102(1) and (2), Nigerian Constitution 1979. There is a similar provision with regard to the president and ministers and the governor and commissioners in ss.65(1)-(3) and 106 (1)-(3) Nigerian Constitution, 1989.

39. See SS.54 and 94 Nigerian Constitution, 1979, ss.56 and 98 Nigerian Constitution, 1989 and ss.61 and 103 Nigerian Draft Constitution, 1995.

40. *Adegbenro v. Akintola* (1963) A.C. 614.

41. *Awolowo v. Shagari & ors* (1979) 6-9 S.C. 51

42. *Shugaba Abdulrahaman Darman V Federal Minister of Internal Affairs & ors* (1981): N C L R 25 and (1981) 2 N C L R 459.

43. *Lakanmi & anor v. Att. Gen. of Western State,* (1971) 1 U.I.L.R. 201.

44. *Governor of Ogun State & ors v The President of Nigeria & ors* (1982) 3 N.C.L.R. 538.

45. *Balarabe Musa v. Auta Hamza & ors* (1982) 3 N.C.L.R. 229 and (1982) 3 N.C.L.R. 439.

46. (1982) 3 N.C.L.R. 229 at p. 247 per Ademola JCA

47. Ojo, J.D., *The Development of the Executive, op. cit* at pp. 117-118.

48. See similar provisions with respect to the federation and the states in ss.229(i) and 254(1) Nigerian Constitution, 1989.

49. Federal Republic of Nigeria, *Report of the Constitutional Conference Containing the Resolution and Recommendations* Vol. 11, Abuja: National Assembly Press, 1995 at p.95

50. The Local Government (Basic Constitutional and Transitional Provisions) Decree, 1989 and a similar provision in Sections 304-331 Nigerian Draft Constitution, 1995.

51. Ajayi J.F Ade and Ojo, J.D., "Federalism in Nigeria: Managing Instability in a Multi Ethnic State", *Politishe Studien* Sonderheft 1, 1990 at pp. 154-173.

CHAPTER 20

Bolade M. Eyinla

Prognosis for the Organisation of the Executive Arm of Government in Nigeria's Fourth Republic.

Introduction

In the speech to mark Nigeria's 35th independence anniversary on 1 October 1995, the Head of State and Commander-in-Chief of the Armed Forces, General Sani Abacha highlighted some of the main components of the 1995 Constitution. These components were those agreed upon by the Provisional Ruling Council, the country's highest ruling body. They were agreed upon by the body after a careful study of the report and recommendations of the Constitutional Conference which sat in Abuja from June 1994 to July 1995.

General Abacha made it known that the system of government decided upon for the Fourth Republic in the new constitution was the modified presidential system.[1] The system according to the General carries with it the inauguration of six national political offices. These offices consist of four executive and two legislative positions. The offices are to be zoned and rotated among six newly created geo-political zones within the country. The six executive and legislative positions to be so rotated are those of the president, vice-president, prime minister, deputy prime minister, Senate president and Speaker of the House of Representatives.[2] For the purpose of rotating these political offices, the country was divided into the following six geo-political zones; North-West, North-East, North-Central, South-West, South-East and Southern Minorities.[3]

This chapter attempts a critical analysis of the adopted modified presidential system of government with its multiplicity of executive political positions. In specific terms, the chapter will first look at the justification behind the adoption of this system of government. It will thereafter go on to examine the report and recommendation of the Constitutional Conference which served as the basis for the deliberation and decision of the Provisional Ruling Council.

In the speech earlier referred to, General Abacha took time not only to justify the adoption of the modified presidential system of government, but to also explain the reasons for the acceptance of the principle of zoning and rotational power-sharing formula. He stated that these options were agreed upon as a way of satisfying the fears of marginalisation by certain sections of the country.[4] They were also seen as a means of building a country where all segments of the society will be given a sense of belonging. In order to ensure that the decisions were rigidly enforced, they would be inserted in the constitution and will be practised at the federal level for an experimental period of at least thirty years.[5]

Evident in this justification was that the creation of the six executive positions was more of a balancing act, rather than a sound political decision, if viewed from the point of view of practicality. In other words, the positions were created in order to ensure that the six created geo-political zones have access to key executive or legislative positions without giving much thought on how the system will function.

Report of the Constitutional Conference on the Executive

According to the report of the Constitutional Conference Committee on the executive, five systems of government were considered for possible adoption in the new constitution.[6] First was the presidential system with cabinet members coming from the legislature. This was rejected on the grounds that it infringes on the principles of separation of powers between the executive and the legislature. The Committee agreed that this system will facilitate a smooth relationship and minimise friction between the executive and the legislature. However, it recognised that under the system, the ability of the president to bring in highly specialised professionals into his cabinet is circumscribed.[7]

Next to be considered was the other side of the first option, that is, presidential system with cabinet members coming from outside the legislature. This system was rejected as inadequate, although the Committee accepted that it could facilitate the principles of separation of power, with the inherent checks and balances in operation. In the opinion of the Committee, the system was grossly abused during the Second Republic when it was operated. The Committee blamed the failure of the system on both the legislature and the executive; the latter for appointing those who lost election into ministerial positions to the anger and envy of the former, and the former for constituting themselves into an institutionalised opposition to the latter.[8] However one fact that the Committee failed to acknowledge was the relative inexperience of the operators of the system, coupled with their intolerance and refusal to play the game according to the rules. The combination of these two factors led to the straining of relationship between the executive and the legislature.

While the executive made appointments on the basis of providing "job for the boys, instead of men for the jobs", the legislature resorted to obstruction and blackmail by blocking most of the legislative bills from the executive, thereby paralysing the workings of government.

The third option considered and rejected by the Committee was the combination of presidential and parliamentary systems. Under this system, a president elected by direct election, appoints a prime minister from parliament to head and run the day-to-day business of government. As a way of forestalling crisis and conflict within the system, specific functions will be assigned to both the president and the prime minister in the constitution. But in the opinion of the Committee, the system is too fraught with instability to be practised in a country like Nigeria given its diversity[9]

Also considered by the Committee was the parliamentary system of government which was deemed as inadequate due to its lack of stability. In this system, government is always formed based on coalitions which sometimes might involve parties with incompatible political agendas as was the case during the First Republic. This is due to the fact that no single political party in Nigeria can win enough vote to give it an outright majority in parliament. This meant that any prime minister that eventually emerges from the political horse-trading between two or more political parties that come together to form the government would hardly be a national leader acceptable to all sections of the country.[10]

Recommendation of the Constitutional Conference on the Executive

Having considered and rejected these four diverse and varied systems of government, the Committee went on to recommend a presidential system of government with cabinet from within and outside the legislature. This recommendation was made against the consideration that contest for the top political position in the country has always remained a source of political instability. The Committee believed that this system of government will satisfy the need of the country, secure and promote peace and stability and encourage all Nigerians to generally participate in government.[11]

However, in contrast to the American presidential system upon which this recommendation was based, the Constitutional Conference recommended a presidential system where the executive arm of government will consist of a president and three vice-presidents.[12] Evident in this recommendation is the fact that the organisation of the executive arm of government in the Fourth Republic will differ from what obtained under previous civilian dispensations. For example, the 1963, 1979 and the aborted 1989 Constitutions provided for only two executive political posi-

United States

As widely known, the American Constitution of 1787 provided for only two executive positions, those of the president and vice-president. The constitutional power and function of the American president is enshrined in Article II of the Constitution.[14] Section 1 of the Article vests executive power in the president as the chief executive officer of the federal government. Section 2 makes him the Commander-in-chief of the armed forces and gives him the authorisation to "require the opinion in writing of the principal officer in each executive department upon any subject relating to the duties of their respective offices".[15] It is also in this section that the power of the president to receive ambassadors and other public ministers is enshrined. Section 3 of the Article provides that the president shall nominate, and with the consent of the Senate, appoint Ambassadors and Consuls, Judges of the Supreme Court and other officers of the United States, "unless for inferior officers the Congress vests the appointment in the president alone, in the court of law, or in the heads of department".[16] Lastly, the Section empowers the president to make treaties, provided that two-third of the senators voting on them concur and to grant reprieves and pardons for offences committed against the United States, except for cases of impeachment.

The duties and functions of the second executive position, that of the vice-president, can be found in Article I of the American Constitution. It makes the vice-president the presiding officer of the Senate with a tie-breaking vote. His other identifiable constitutional role and function is to succeed to the presidency in the case that the incumbent president is not able to discharge the functions and duties of the office.[17]

France

The Constitution of the French fifth republic was inaugurated in October 1958. Opinions differ as to whether the constitution can actually be regarded as being in line with French republican traditions. While some critics refer to the document as quasi-monarchical and quasi-presidential, others see it as unworkable and the worst drafted in French constitutional history.[18] It is not necessary here to dwell on the imperfect nature of the constitution which was regarded by most Frenchmen as tailor-made for General Charles de Gaulle.[19] What is of concern to this chapter is the power and functions of the executive.

Like the American constitution, the French constitution provides for two executive positions, those of president and prime minister. The powers conferred on the president are quite wide and varied, but fall short of those of the American president. This is in spite of the intention of the authors of the constitution to systematically reinforce executive powers as a way of dealing with the limitations inherent in previous constitutions.[20] The executive powers of the president are enshrined in Title II of the constitution.[21] Article 5 gives him the power of "arbitration over the regular functioning of public authorities and continuity of the state". Article 8 empowers him to name the prime minister and also to appoint and dismiss other members of government, but at the request of the prime minister. His other powers can be found in Article 9 which makes him the presiding officer in the Council of ministers, Article 10 which gives him the power to promulgate laws passed by the parliament, and Article 12 which confers on him the power to dissolve the national assembly. His power to sign ordinances emanating from the council of ministers and to make appointments to certain civil and military positions is enshrined in Article 13, while by the provisions of Article 14, he has the power to receive and accredit ambassadors. By the provisions of article 15, he is the head of the army (but without authority of command) and the presiding officer in the higher councils and Committee of the judiciary and national defence.[22] The right of the president to grant pardon is in Article 17. In addition to these powers, Title IV, Article 52 gives him the power to negotiate and ratify treaties as well as the right to be informed of any international agreement that is not subject to his ratification.

The powers and functions of the prime minister are enshrined in Title III of the Constitution. Article 2 gives to the prime minister the general charge of the work of government, as he is responsible for national defence and execution of laws. It is also his duty to exercise rule-making powers and the prerogative of appointment into certain civil and military positions, including that of the higher council of the judiciary. The government which he heads has the power to decide and direct the policy of state and has at its disposal the administration of the armed forces.[23]

Germany

With her reputation for teutonic efficiency, it is hardly surprising that the German[24] *Grundgesetzt,* (Basic Law) has been described as one of the best functioning and most efficient working constitutions among the Western democracies.[25] Just like the Constitutions of the United States and France, the German Constitution provides for two executive positions, namely the federal president and federal chancellor. The duties and functions of the federal president are contained in Articles 59, 60, 63, and 64 of the Constitution. Article 59 gives the president the power of representation in matters concerning international law. He has the responsibility of concluding international treaties and of accrediting and receiving envoys.[26] Article 60(i) gives him power to appoint and dismiss federal judges and civil servants, while his power to exercise the right of pardon is contained in the provisions of Article 60(ii). The other duties and functions of the federal president can be found in Article 63, which gives him the right to propose the federal chancellor to the *Bundestag* and Article 64, by which he can appoint or dismiss federal ministers upon the advice of the federal chancellor.

The constitutional powers and functions of the federal chancellor are contained in Articles 65 and 69 of the Constitution. By the provisions of these articles, the federal chancellor, no doubt is chief executive of State and the central figure in the political system. He not only has the constitutional duty to determine and assume responsibility for general policy, it is on his shoulders that the conduct of the business of the federal government lies. Thus, Article 69 gives him full freedom to name and change his cabinet and to appoint a member of cabinet as the vice-chancellor[27]. Lastly in relation to the powers of the federal chancellor, it is important to note that under the provisions of the military constitution, he can only assume authority of command over the armed forces if the country is under the threat of external attack.[28] Otherwise, under normal circumstances, the authority of command of the armed forces (army, navy and air force) is in the hands of the defence minister.

From the foregoing examination of executive powers under the American, French and German constitutions, certain clear deductions can be made. First, common to the three constitutions is the existence of only two executive positions, but with varying degrees of executive powers. Secondly, each of the constitutions clearly spells out the duties and functions of the chief executive. The American President, the French President and the German Chancellor are undoubtedly the chief executive officers in their respective states. Real power lies in their hands and they are responsible for determining and directing state policies. The powers and functions of the other cadre of executive political position, that is the American vice-president, the French prime minister and the German president cannot in any way compare with theirs. For example, the American vice-president, apart from his limited constitutional role, holds his position at the behest and pleasure of the president. Even in the French system, where the prime minister is constitutionally head of government with the duty to determine and direct the policy of state, his power is severely circumscribed and curtailed by the president. This is a development that can be traced back to the presidency of General Charles de Gaulle, who utilised his immense personal legitimacy, prestige and charisma to undermine the position of the prime minister and build up that of the president.[29] His successors have continued to reinforce the position. In Germany, the president is no more than a political figure head with no real constitutional power, apart from his largely ceremonial functions.

The second point to note is that the organisation of the executive arm of government in these three countries can be described as a product of their socio-cultural history and political development. The constitution of the United States which favoured the position of a very strong and powerful presidency is a product of the confederal antecedents of the country. However, the working of the constitution is such that the power of the president is checked and balanced by the Congress. There is also the largely unquestionable independence of the judiciary in the system which also serves as a check on the possibility of a president assuming arbitrary power. In the case of France, the Constitution of 1958 was designed to put an end to political instability inherent in the previous republics due to parliamentary superiority. In order to put in place the principle of effective government, the constitution made a very bold attempt, unlike the preceding constitutions, to systematically reduce the power of Parliament and reinforce that of the executive. It was on this precept that General de Gaulle ascribed and arrogated to himself even powers that the constitution did not ascribe to the president. The German constitution was largely an American-created document in the aftermath of World War II. In the document, the Americans went to great lengths to ensure that all the provisions in the previous constitutions which proved auspicious for the rise of Nazism in the country were completely exterminated. This explains why decentralisation of power of the executive features very prominently in the document.

Prognosis

An attempt will now be made to address the adaptability of any one or all of these aforementioned comparative models for the organisation of the executive arm of government in Nigeria's Fourth Republic. But before this, it will be relevant to examine the systems that were operated during the First, Second and (aborted) Third Republics.

In the First Republic, there were two executive positions, namely, that of the governor-general (which was later transformed into the office of the president upon Nigeria's attainment of republican status in 1963) and that of the prime minister. Under this system, real power was in the hands of the prime minister who came from the largest party in Parliament. The roles and functions of the president were largely ceremonial. Although he was the Commander-in Chief of the armed forces, he lacked authority of command. Such authority was in the hands of the prime minister. Eventually when the political alliance between the two parties that formed the government broke down, the continued survival of the government was threatened.

It was in a bid to lessen the acrimonious relationship inherent in this system that the presidential system of government was adopted for the Second and Third Republics. The system provided for two executive positions, namely, the president and vice-president. The president was made the head of state, chief executive officer and Commander-in-Chief of the armed forces.[30] He may or may not in his discretion assign any duty of function to the vice-president who holds office at his pleasure and behest. The only constitutional requirement in his relationship with the vice-president is to hold regular meetings with the holder of the office and other ministers for the purpose of determining the general direction of domestic and foreign policies.[31]

These provisions of the 1978 and 1989 Constitutions were retained in the 1995 Draft Constitution, but with some variations. The most important variation is the inauguration of multiple vice-presidents for the purpose of wider distribution of power among the various sections of the country. According to the report of the Committee on Power Sharing, this decision was based on the principle of power-sharing which will lead to greater spread of power to all areas.[32] What the Committee however failed to do was to assign any specific constitutional role to the vice-presidents. Their duties and functions are to be determined by the president.[33]

Prescriptions

From the foregoing analysis, what is clear is that there is an urgent need to develop a workable, equitable and acceptable power-sharing formula especially between the various constituent power blocs within the Nigerian federation. The inauguration of four executive positions by the Provisional Ruling Council in the 1995 Draft Constitution can be described as a bold attempt to address this issue.

What is however problematic is the ability to dutifully assign specific constitutional role and duty to each of the executive political positions in a way that there will be no overlap of functions. Indeed there is already a public debate of sort going on as to the complications inherent in the adopted modified presidential system of government.[31] For example, questions are now being asked as to who will wield more power between the president and the prime minister? There is also the debate as to what will be the functions and duties of the four executive political officeholders. Beyond this is the issue of the mode of election for both the president and the prime minister. In other words, will they both be elected by direct popular vote or will only the president be thus elected, while the prime minister will be elected through the electoral college made up of members of the National Assembly. Though beyond the scope of this analysis, one other problem involves the question of the section of the country that will have the first shot at the political office which will wield the most power.

Available indications seem to be pointing to the fact that the duties and functions of the president and the prime minister in the 1995 Draft Constitution will be akin to those of the French System. For example, General Abacha is currently being canvassed by certain individuals and faceless organisations from different sections of the country to stand for election as a civilian president. If the General succumbs to such blandishments and decides to run for the presidency in a civilian dispensation, it is likely that the president in the Nigerian Fourth Republic will wield more power than the prime minister. Indeed, if this scenario eventually plays itself out, then it is certain that the duties and functions of the president will remain as they were in the 1979 and 1989 Constitutions. That is, the president will wield executive powers comparable to those of the American Chief Executive. It is also nearly certain that he will be elected by direct popular vote.

The position of the prime minister, on the other hand, will carry less power. He will no doubt be made responsible for the day to day functioning of government machinery, but he will be largely reduced to the status of pursuing and implementing state policies determined and formulated by the president. If logic is anything to guide us, then it is likely that the president will be given the constitutional power of appointing and dismissing a prime minister, as is currently the case in Pakistan.

It must however be pointed out that Nigeria is not France, and the French system if adopted, may well be the undoing of the forthcoming Constitution. As succinctly analysed by members of the Constitutional Conference, Nigeria presently lacks the capacity to develop and build the necessary institutional consensus within which such a system can be practised without the emergence of a dictatorship.[35] The inevitability of a dictatorship becomes real in a situation where the president not only rules, but reigns and the prime minister is no more than a powerless political figure head.

Perhaps one way of dealing with this problem will be to make the office of the president a ceremonial one, with all the powers ascribed to the office under the German Constitution. But he should be elected directly like the French president. In running for office, he should be allowed to select his own vice-presidential candidate who must come from a different geo-political zone from his own. This recommendation derives from the experience of party politics during the First Republic where the president was largely impotent in dealing with the prime minister both in the formulation and implementation of state policies. If he is elected through direct elections, this will no doubt enhance his national acceptance and broaden his power base. A popular mandate will give him a relatively strong power position in dealing with the prime minister.

Secondly, unlike the German system, the president should be the

Commander-in-Chief of the armed forces albeit, in a ceremonial position, as in the French system. He should also be given the constitutional power to make appointments into certain military positions. He should not however be given the authority of command. The authority of command over the armed forces should be given to the vice-president who should also be given the constitutional power of presiding over the meetings of the National Defence Council. Apart from this, the vice-president will naturally succeed the president whenever he is unable to carry out the functions of his office. But before assuming the office of the president in acting capacity, he should be made to relinquish his authority of command over the armed forces and chairmanship of the National Defence Council to the deputy prime minister.

Next is the position of the prime minister. This position should be occupied by the party that has the greatest majority of seats in the national assembly. Unlike in the French system where the prime minister does not emerge until after national assembly elections, the prime ministerial and deputy prime ministerial candidates of each of the political parties should be named before parliamentary elections. In other words, both the prime minister and the deputy prime minister must be elected members of the national assembly. To protect both positions from blackmail and intimidation from other members of the national assembly, their removal from office through a vote of no confidence should automatically lead to the dissolution of parliament and call for new elections. Also, it should be written in the constitution that the prime minister and his deputy can only be removed from office by a vote of no confidence in Parliament not by the president on trump-up charges as is common in Pakistan, and not by his political party as we have seen in the case of the United Kingdom. In observance of the principle of zoning, both the prime minister and the deputy prime minister should come from geo-political zones that are different from those of the president and vice-president. The duties and functions of the prime minister should roughly correspond to those of the federal chancellor under the German Constitution. He should have the power to name his cabinet, composed of people from both within and outside of Parliament. Nomination to cabinet position shall be subjected to the approval of the national assembly. Though empowered with the responsibility to initiate and pursue policies for the day-to-day administration of the state, such policies must be debated and agreed upon by the cabinet and Parliament. It should also be subjected to the approval of the president. As earlier stated, the deputy prime minister must not only be a member of Parliament, he should also be a member of cabinet and given the defence portfolio. His main responsibility would be to ensure civil control over the armed forces.

It would be noticed that in the allocation of duties and functions to the four executive political officeholders, specific attention was devoted to the issue of control over the armed forces. This is for obvious reasons. No one political office should be given the overall authority of command over such a sensitive and highly politicised national institution. Also evident in this prescription is the fact that a very bold attempt was made to disperse power, instead of concentrating it in the hands of only one executive political officeholder. The reason for this is quite obvious. As observed in the report of the Constitutional Conference, contest for the top political job in Nigeria is very contentious and acrimonious. The best way of attenuating this problem is to ensure that no one political office is made to wield more power than the others. Thirdly, it will be noticed that all the four executive political offices are made interdependent and given a clear stake in the functioning of government. In fact, no one office can ignore the other in carrying out its own duties and functions. In other words, the functioning of the four political offices was made highly mutually inclusive with the hope that it will lead to the development of an integrative approach to governance wherein all sections of the country will have a sense of belonging and participation in government. In this way, no one section of the country will be in a position to ignore or neglect the feelings and aspirations of the other sections.

The importance of proposing such an integrative approach to governance, wherein all sections of the country will wield one form of executive power or the other, derives from the experience of past civilian administrations. It would be recalled that the collapse of both the First and the Second Republics can be indirectly traced to the feeling of marginalisation and exclusion from the central government by a majority of mainstream politicians in the South-West. But with the six geo-political zones now fully represented in one executive or legislative position, it can safely be assumed that this will lessen the antagonism, promote political stability and thereby reduce the possibility of another military takeover.

By and large, two points need to be emphasised. First, no matter what system is adopted for the organisation of the executive arm of government in the Nigerian Fourth Republic, if the major geo-political power centres are not given a stake in governance, the ability of the government to survive will be highly jeopardised. Second is that there are socio-cultural and other differences from one country to the other. Thus any attempt to wholly export one model of governance from one country to another is bound to fail in the end. It is therefore important that a country's social and political development be taken into consideration in fashioning out its system of government. As we have seen, the parliamentary system, which still remains the bedrock of democracy in the United Kingdom, failed only after a period of six years in the First Nigerian

Republic. In order to solve some of the problems and imperfections inherent in the parliamentary system, the American presidential system of government was adopted for the Second Republic. But the system failed only after a period of four years. For the Fourth Republic, it is important that Nigeria adopts a system of governance that will engender political stability, entrench democracy, promote the rule of law and protect the fundamental human rights of the citizens.

Notes

1. Speech of the Head of State and Commander-in-Chief of the armed forces, General Sani Abacha, on the occasion of Nigeria's 35th independence anniversary. 1st October 1995.
2. *Ibid.*
3. *Ibid.*
4. *Ibid.*
5. *Ibid.*
6. Federal Republic of Nigeria, *Report of the Constitutional Conference containing the Resolutions and Recommendations.* Vol. II. Abuja: National Assembly Press, 1995 p.63
7. *Ibid.*
8. *Ibid.*
9. *Ibid.*
10. *Ibid.*
11. *Ibid.* p.64.
12. *Ibid.* p.66
13. Articles 133&147. Federal Republic of Nigeria. *Report of the Constitutional Conference containing the Draft Constitution.* Vol. 1: Abuja: National Assembly Press, 1995, pp.62 and 69
14. The Constitution of the United States of America. 1787.
15. *Ibid.*
16. *Ibid.*
17. *Ibid.*
18. D. Pickles, *The Fifth Republic.* London: Methuen, 1965, p. 26. Quoted by R. Capitant in the preface to, L. Hamon's *de Gaulle dans la Republique.* Plon, 1958

19. G. Carcassone, France (1958) The Fifth Republic after thirty years' in U. Bogdanor, *Constitution in Democratic Politics*. Aldershot: Gower, 1988, pp. 244-245.

20. S. Hoffman, 'Succession and Stability in France' in A. Lijphart (ed) *Politics in Europe: Comparison and Interpretation*. Englewood Cliffs, N.J: Prentice Hall, 1969 pp. 151-152.

21. The French Constitution of October 4th 1958.

22. *Ibid*.

23. *Ibid*.

24. Here reference is made to West Germany, whose Constitution was adopted upon the reunification of the two German states.

25. K. Sontheimer, 'The Federal Republic of Germany (1949): Restoring the *Rechtstaat* in V. Bogdenor, *Constitutions in Democratic Politics'*. p. 229.

26. The Constitution of the Federal Republic of Germany. Basic law of 23rd May 1949. Bonn: the Germany *Bundestag* Publications Section,1989.

27. *Ibid*.

28. See entry of the Federal Republic of Germany to Western European Union (W.E.U) and North Atlantic Treaty Organisation (N.A.T.O.), Paris Treaties of 23/10/94, and Ammendments to the Basic Law of 26/3/54 and 19/3/56.

29. Typical of this position is the declaration of General de Gaulle that: *The president is clearly the sole authority in the state... It must be clearly understood that the indivisible authority of the state is conferred entirely on the president by the people who elected him, that there exists no other source of authority, neither ministerial nor civil, nor military nor judicial, which is not conferred and maintained by him.*
Source: Press Conference of 31 January 1964.

30. Article 122(2). *The Constitution of the Federal Republic of Nigeria*. Lagos: Times Press Limited, 1978, p.49.

    Article 128(2) *Constitution of the Federal Republic of Nigeria*. Lagos: NERDC Press, 1989, p.55

31. Article 136 of 1978 Constitution. p.55.
    Article 145 of 1989 Constitution. p.57.

32. Federal Republic of Nigeria. *Report of the Constitutional Conference*. Vol.II p.144.

33. Federal Republic of Nigeria. *Report of the Constitutional Conference containing the Draft Constitution.* Vol I. p.69.
34. *The Guardian on Sunday*, Lagos, January 12, 1997.
35. Federal Republic of Nigeria. *Report of the Constitutional Conference containing the Draft Constitution.* Vol II. p.63

CONCLUSION

Conclusion

Rotimi T. Suberu and Adigun Agbaje

The Future of Nigeria's Federalism

Introduction

In this concluding chapter, we explore some of the `matters arising' from the various contributions to this volume. First, we examine the historical origins and development of Nigerian federalism, paying particular attention to the legacies of both British colonial hegemony and post-colonial military rule. Second, we outline the inherent limitations and palpable contradictions in current efforts to restructure Nigerian federalism under conditions of autocratic, personal rule. Third, and related to the preceding point, we criticise current proposals for executive power sharing as essentially misplaced, and unlikely to engender genuine changes in current trends and tendencies towards the centralisation, monopolisation and personalisation of political power. Fourth, we comment on the pervasive and corrosive impact of Nigeria's distributive politics on the country's federal culture and processes. Fifth and finally, we discuss the issue of alternative political futures and structures for Nigeria.

Origins and Legacies

The contemporary conditions and contradictions of the Nigerian federation have been heavily and directly shaped by the federation's colonial origins and the legacies of the country s successive post-independence military regimes. If we agree with Billy Dudley that `colonial rule was, for all practical purposes, military rule', then we may conclude that Nigerian federalism was not only instituted, but has developed and degenerated, under conditions of military autocracy[1]. Such heavy military influence is crucial to an understanding of the paradoxes, pathologies and irregularities that currently plague the Nigerian system of federalism.

In discussing the origins of federal systems, it is usual to make a distinction between aggregative or `coming together' federations and disaggregative, devolutionary or `holding together' federations[2]. Aggregative federalism reflects the classical method of federation-building in which a federal state is constituted through a compact or bargain to `bring together' previously sovereign entities in a new federation. The federal systems of the United States of America and Switzerland evolved in this manner.

The Nigerian federation, on the other hand, was established to 'hold together' the diverse ethnicities and nationalities that had been forcibly and arbitrarily incorporated into a Unitary Colonial State under British imperialism. As claimed by John P. Mackintosh,

> The Nigerian Federation has always had peculiar features, the most evident being that it was not created by the coming together of separate states but was the result of the subdivision of a country which had in theory been ruled as a single unit.[3]

Devolutionary federations like Nigeria tend to lack the integrative identities and the values of civic reciprocity and mutual respect associated with a voluntary compact or bargain to join a federal union. Rather, they tend to be besieged by the disruptive local loyalties that made the constitutional fragmentation or disaggregation of the state necessary in the first place. What is more, reflecting their unitary constitutional origins as well as the need to contain disruptive centrifugal pressures, devolutionary federations tend to develop relatively centralised constitutions and political institutions. In essence, 'holding together' federations like Nigeria tend to be more formally and institutionally centralised, but less politically integrated and structurally coherent, than 'coming together' federations.

The disaggregative and disintegrative impulses and pressures inherent in Nigerian federalism have been reinforced and compounded by a number of specific elements and developments associated both with British colonial domination and post-colonial military rule. The British colonial legacy in Nigeria was a paradoxical one of state-building and nation-destroying. As Larry Diamond puts it: 'While the British established over Nigeria a common political authority, transportation grid, and monetary system, they did not rule it as a single nation'.[4] Rather, the infamous British colonial project of divide-and-rule operated to deepen division, suspicion and recrimination among the diverse ethnic nationalities that had been capriciously consolidated into a single, culturally artificial state. Among the more perverse elements of this divide-and-rule policy were such measures as the active construction and reification of ethnic loyalty and consciousness, the separate development and modernisation of the northern and southern sections of the country, and the deliberate promotion of the interests of conservative, pro-British elements in Northern Nigeria.

Indeed, perhaps the most destructive political legacy of British colonial rule in Nigeria involved the decision, under the 1954 Lyttelton Constitution, to establish Nigeria as a three-region federation. This tripartite regional system not only institutionalised the political hegemony and demographic preeminence of the North over the two southern regions combined, but also effectively shortchanged the numerous ethnic minority groups located in the majority-dominated regions. Yet, the British colonial administration steadfastly resisted any further division of the existing three regions – rejecting minority group demands for the security of their own regions, and southern warning that a federal system in which one region had a population majority could not be stable'.[5]

It is broadly recognised that this politically flawed and structurally awkward three-region federal structure contributed enormously to the deluge of strains and tensions that culminated in the military's overthrow of the First Nigerian Republic, in 1966, and the outbreak of civil war during the following year. Despite its direct role, after the January 1966 coup, in contributing to the escalation of inter-regional tensions into large-scale inter-ethnic violence and civil war, however, the Nigerian military is often applauded for its historic feat in 1967 in reconstituting the unwieldy regional structure into a more balanced federal system.

There can be little doubt that the replacement of the old regions with twelve states in 1967 engendered numerous positive outcomes and consequences. These included the dilution of the hegemony of the North; the empowerment of some of the more prominent ethnic minority groups; the vitiation and ultimate nullification of the secessionist bid of the former Eastern region; the promotion of administrative and financial devolution; and the broad mediation and moderation of the disruptive, centrifugal tendencies inherent in Nigeria's ethnic fragmentation. Yet, particularly since the military coup that ended the Second Republic in 1983, the impact of military rule in Nigerian federalism has become progressively obnoxious and ruinous.

In essence, both historically and structurally, it is possible to speak of two distinct phases of post-colonial military rule in Nigeria, namely, the initial phase from 1966 to 1979, and a second phase from 1984 to date. The first phase of military rule was largely one of `hegemonic exchange.'[6] This was a period in which the country's military rulers allowed the military administrations in the states to exercise most of the powers assigned to the regions under the suspended democratic constitution; incorporated several credible and notable civilian politicians and ethnoregional elites into the structure of military rule; performed the aforementioned feat of creatively redesigning the structural architecture of Nigerian federalism; and initiated and implemented a fairly successful programme of redemocratisation which culminated in the inauguration of the Second Republic in October 1979.

Compared to the first phase, however, the second phase of military rule has been characterised by the excessive personalisation and concentration of state authority in the military head of state; an increasing reliance on hegemonic repression in managing state-ethnic and state-society **relations**; the wilful frustration and abortion of the country's democratic aspiration; and, most crucially, the near-total abrogation of the federal system through the imposition of crushing central controls on the subfederal units of government. The more prominent examples of such overcentralisation include: the complete subordination of constituent state governments to the unified military command system via the centre's appointment and frequent redeployment of relatively junior officers as state governors or administrators; the direct intervention of the central military government in the organisation and reorganisation of local government councils; the continued overwhelming, indeed near-total, dependence of the states and localities on central funding; the systematic (and apparently unchallengeable) manipulation of statutory intergovernmental revenue-sharing arrangements in a manner that has reinforced the financial hegemony of the centre and the fiscal emasculation of the states and localities; the complete erosion of the autonomy of the judiciary, which aberration has prevented this arm of government from playing its normal federalist role in arbitrating intergovernmental constitutional disputes; and the proliferation of new units of centrally-funded states and local governments as part of a strategy to consolidate the centre's hegemony, gratify sectional distributive pressures and promote the continuity and legitimacy of military rule.

The Paradoxes of Military Restructuring

The pathologies outlined so far in this concluding chapter are but intimations of the paradoxes etched into Nigeria's political history and contemporary reality by the dominance of the colonial regime and the postcolonial military in the architecturing and refurbishing of the political landscape. In fact, much of this book has brought into focus elements of this toxicity of autocratic (including military) rule for the health and vitality of federal practice in Nigeria even as opportunities lost and gained under such rule have equally been examined.

On the whole, however, the central argument of this collection has been that autocratic rule in all its forms is antithetical to the sustenance of genuinely federal practice, and for this reason a restructuring of federations initiated under the tight reign of repressive governments cannot but lead to a situation in which federalism is assaulted, abused and dismantled, reduced more or less to the status of false consciousness in the service of power – portraying a picture of divided power to hide the reality of monistic, undivided power.

The introduction to this volume has already broached the point, pursued further by the other chapters in their examination of the historical, political, economic and comparative dimensions of the Abacha regime's project of restructuring the Nigerian federation, that a prerequisite for federal architecturing and practice is a democratic or free political dispensation. The same point was made recently in an even more forceful manner by Alfred Stepan, endorsing Robert Dahl, to the effect that "in a strict sense, only a democracy can be a federal system" since federalism is

> a system in which some matters are exclusively within the competence of certain local units – cantons, states, provinces – and are constitutionally beyond the scope of the authority of the national government and where certain other matters are constitutionally outside the scope of the authority of the smaller units.[7]

While virtually all attempts to date to structure and restructure Nigerian federalism have been initiated by authoritarian regimes acting extra-constitutionally (occasionally without even a constitution to breach) and presiding over an illiberal political environment, the most recent initiative under General Sani Abacha is marked out by the increasingly personalist tone of rulership. This rise of a more unbridled form of personal rule, along with what we earlier described as increasing reliance on hegemonic repression, has brought out in bold relief the weaknesses of the strongman and the so-called strong state, increasingly strengthening the coercive elements of the state at the paradoxical cost of running down the bases of its authority and its stock of legitimising symbols and values.

These consequences have equally been reflected at the level of institutions and structures, where continued investment in and strengthening of institutions of coercion has, in the context of scarce resources, automatically translated into increasing divestment from and weakening of institutions and structure for effective and efficient governance.

In any event, increasing investment in personal rule in the Abacha years has generally further advanced the project of de-institutionalisation and capture of the state by private centres of power already noticeable in the preceding Babangida years.[8] The net effect for federal (and other forms of related) restructuring has been a weakening of formal structures along with the creation of what can at best be called the Real McCoys – shells of institutions emptied of much of their original, federalist, democratic content.

It is, therefore, not surprising that much of what has passed for political restructuring in recent times has in fact left Nigerian federalism bruised and traduced. Institutions, structures and framework for pluralist governance, at best weak or, worse still, deceptive imitations, have proved incapable of sustaining federal practice in the form in which the civilised world has come to know it, moreso since such structural ramparts have themselves been constructed or reconstructed in a context in which state managers have sought to weaken dissent in the belief that only in so doing can the state be strengthened. Effectively robbed of the required structures and value systems, Nigerian political practice has, perhaps ineluctably and understandably, in recent times continued to lead the Nigerian state down the path of self-destruction rather than in the direction of regeneration, undermining the state while seeking to preserve it by moving against autonomous forms of structural and attitudinal opposition to those in authority.[9]

The Limits of Consociationalism and Executive Power Sharing

As the essays in this volume have shown, attempting to introduce or strengthen executive power-sharing arrangements as part of a package of consociational practice for restructuring Nigerian federalism in the context that has been copiously described above cannot but have its limits. As the chapters in Section Two on Federal Character and Power Sharing have argued, the Nigerian terrain is toxic to consociational theory and practice. At the simple level of everyday experience one evidence of this toxicity is to be found in the argument that that which is monopolised, centralised and undivided can be dispersed or shared only in so far as the monopolistic, centralising and monistic tendencies are brought to an effective end. In other words, to propose to share is to be ready to give and take. If a proposal to share is unaccompanied by a willingness and move to give and to take, then such a proposal is at best an ideological one meant to create an impression of willingness to share power as veneer over the reality of power undivided.

If we interrogate Nigerian reality with this simple point, what do we come up with? We come up with a picture that increasingly portrays a nominally federal arrangement dominated, or perceived to be dominated, by favoured ethno-regional and religious groupings. We see an arrangement for making public appointments skewed in favour of the elite and working to entrench ethnonationalist, sectarian and regionalist sentiments rather than to cement loyalty to the Nigerian state. We see a federal structure dominated by the central government. We see even within that framework, a structure of government in which the executive arm in the three tiers of government (central, state, local) has emerged overdeveloped vis-a-vis the legislative and judicial arms, with the executive branch in the central government being the most overbearing and overdeveloped and that at the local government level the least developed.

This picture of concentrated power and privilege has been further compounded by developments since the Babangida era in which, as stated earlier, federal executive power has increasingly come to be concentrated in the person of the army General that heads the federal government.

In effect, the approporiate mix of autonomy, balance in territorial and hierarchical distribution of spheres of influence and power, as well as guarantees for minority rights required for consociational practice, have yet to be attained. Worse still, recent events which have exacerbated ethnoregional and religious tension and encouraged the deepening of even more unpredictable forms of personal rule appear to have led to the shrinking of the arena for peaceful, predictable political restructuring while increasing the volatile and episodic, not to talk of adversarial, dimensions of the interface of regime (and by extension state) and society, on the one hand, and of intra-regime and intra-society interactions, on the other.

The import of all this is that meaningful political restructuring of the Nigerian federation cannot be achieved in the present dispensation of personal repressive rule backed by military force, or in a succeeding dispensation of a pseudo-democratic regime. Such a restructuring would have to await the dawn of effective democratic transition and consolidation. Before then, however, the crisis engendered by the distributive nature of federal practice in Nigeria, which has defied regime change, needs to be contemplated, if not addressed.

The Crisis of Distributive Federalism

The primary pathology of Nigerian federalism involves the whole complex of motivations, orientations and actions associated with the country's 'cake-sharing' culture. Essentially, this culture is reflected in the domination of public discourse and praxis by individual and sectional competition for access to federally-controlled, oil-based revenues and resources. Although still somewhat undertheorised, the primacy of this cake-sharing syndrome in Nigeria's federal political culture is now broadly recognised by perceptive students or observers of the country's politics. Thus, according to Iyorchia Ayu:

> The first remark (to make) about Nigerian federalism is its preoccupation with revenue allocation or the distribution of rewards. Most people who have either written about or formulated policies for Nigeria have placed emphasis on distribution, or what is cynically referred to as the sharing of the national cake. Unfortunately, not much emphasis has been placed on the baking of the cake by every member and component part or segment of the Nigerian political community: inevitably distribution or sharing has completely overshadowed production and effective growth.[10]

Quite predictably, the issue of revenue allocation has provided the primary arena for intergovernmental or intersegmental distributive struggles in the Nigerian federation. The issue has involved at least four major axes of conflict. These are:

i. The conflict among the federal, state and local governments over what proportion of national revenues should be allocated to each of these three tiers of government;

ii. The tensions among the states and among the localities over the criteria to be used in sharing or distributing federal financial devolutions to these two subnational tiers of government;

iii The tensions between the oil-producing states on the one hand, and the federal government and many of the states which do not produce oil, on the other, over the proportion of federally-collected revenues that should be allocated to the former on the basis of the derivation principle and/or compensation for the ecological risks of oil production and;

iv. The general intergovernmental conflict over suspected irregularities or anomalies in the centre's administration of the Federation Account.

Theoretically, these revenue allocation conflicts should generate patterns of intergovernmental alliances that may crosscut and defuse, rather than simply reinforce or intensify, the federation's ethnic and regional fault lines. Furthermore, such purely distributive conflicts over revenue allocation should prove to be more negotiable or calculable, and therefore less intractable, than the symbolic or emotive sectional conflicts over `group-worth' and other intangible socio-psychological benefits.[11] Nevertheless, precisely because of the total dependence of all governments and regions on a single national source of revenue, revenue allocation conflicts in Nigeria have tended to be extremely intensive, explosive and disruptive in character. Quite logically, any effort to address or redress Nigeria's revenue allocation problems would involve policies that are designed both to reduce the centre's current stranglehold on national resources and induce the subnational governments to become relatively financially viable or develop some autonomous capacity for economic self-governance.

Beyond the issue of revenue allocation, Nigeria's distributive federalism has found expression in the politics of the `federal character', the struggles for new states and localities, and the politicisation of national population counts. As Peter Ekeh has argued, the `federal character' principle focuses

...exclusively on the sharing of the privileges and benefits that come with participation in government. It has no conception of the need for the units which will be the recognised beneficiaries from the operation of `federal character' to reciprocate by making contributions to the overall common good of the nation... Seen in these terms, `federal character' is... concerned with that age-long game of Nigerian politics: the sharing of the national cake.[12]

Indeed, by making ethno-territorial constituencies, rather than merit or other non-ascriptive criteria, the sole basis for representation in federal bureaucratic and political appointments, the `federal character' also tends to promote prebendalism which refers to those destructively familiar practices in Nigeria that are animated by the belief that officeholders could, and should, utilise their positions to aggrandise both personal and communal, as distinct from public or civic, interests.[13]

However, perhaps the most structurally disruptive aspects of Nigeria's `cake-sharing psychosis' involve the vociferous, popular, unrelenting and apparently implacable communal pressures for new units of state and local governments in the country. As argued in the chapter on `States' Creation and the Political Economy of Nigerian Federalism', these pressures are directly rooted in the struggles by ethno-territorial constituencies, and particularly the elites within those constituencies, for access to those federal revenues and resources that are disseminated or devolved through the states and localities. At the same time, the clamour for new sub-federal units is often exploited by the national military elite not only to promote the legitimacy of military rule or the political fortunes of the incumbent military dictator, but also to advance the military's centrist philosophy `of a pragmatic approach to Nigerian federalism' in which `the advantages of centralised military administration' are `used to strenghten the powers and status of the national government... and weaken the prospects of a confederation'.[14] In essence, the proliferation (and, therefore, emasculation) of the states and localities, by executive military fiat, may be seen as an important aspect of the military's historic project of creating `a unitary state in federal disguise', in Nigeria via the establishment and consolidation of an hegemonic central government. Ironically, far from working to prevent the `prospect of confederation' or the `dangers of disintegration', such centralisation is increasingly provoking much inter-ethnic dissatisfaction as well as ominous signs of state implosion and dismemberment.[15]

Finally, the distributive pressures associated with Nigerian federalism have found expression in the turbulent politics of national population counts in the country. All of Nigeria's post-independence censuses (in 1962, 1963, 1973, and 1991) have provoked intense controversies, not only because of the inter-regional (mainly North-South) pressures to manipulate such counts for politico-electoral purposes, but also because of popular local perceptions that population figures would determine the allocation of revenues and government distribution of public amenities like schools, roads, pipe-borne water and comparable facilities. In essence, lacking any autonomous capacity for resource generation and socio-economic development, subnational governments and segments have increasingly relied on `favourable' returns from national censuses to establish self-serving claims to the proportional distribution or redistribution of federally controlled resources. It seems obvious that no truly stable political system, nor viable national economic development strategy, can be promoted or sustained under such conditions of intensive, zero-sum, sectional pressures for distributive advantage.

Alternative Political Futures

The theme of this concluding essay has been the future of the contemporary Nigerian practice of federalism. If the country's current federal system is plagued by severe shortcomings or inadequacies, what alternative options or futures can be said to exist for the country? Although Nigerians have sometimes responded to this question in sharply conflicting ways, it is still possible to speak of a broad national consensus in the country in favour of a reformed, revitalised and truly decentralised and democratised federal system.

It seems obvious that the only two alternatives to a genuine system of federation in Nigeria, namely unitarism and confederalism, can only compound the country's current political problems. For instance, the brief attempt at a unitary system under General Aguiyi Ironsi in 1966 claimed the life of its chief protagonist (i.e. Ironsi) and accelerated the country's slide into chaos and civil war. Since then, the country's military rulers have found it expedient formally to maintain the federal character of the country, even while introducing or promoting extreme centralising measures or policies. As already indicated, however, such overcentralisation is largely responsible for the profound, pervasive and palpable sense of disaffection and disillusionment in Nigeria today with the operation of the country's federal system.

Similarly, a confederal arrangement appears to be a problematic and unworkable proposition in the Nigerian context. In the first place, as suggested by William Zartman, a confederation inherently is such an elusive and amorphous constitutional formula that it ultimately amounts to more of the figment of a legal imagination, than a practical or feasible political solution. According to Zartman, `the stark necessity of locating sovereignty somewhere and respecting its overwhelming exercise means that a confederation is really a federation, as in Switzerland, or else it is only an alliance of sovereign states, as in Senegambia'.[16] Thus, the attempt to evolve a confederal solution for Nigeria under the post-Ironsi Aburi Accords engendered enormous legal controversy and political confusion, which impasse was ultimately resolved through the victory of the federal forces in the civil war.

Second, and related to the above, a confederal arrangement can only mean the dissolution or dismemberment of Nigeria into two or more separate sovereign or quasi-sovereign states. Yet, given the complexity of Nigeria's ethnic heterogeneity and the absence of any significant consensus on the modalities for the fragmentation of the country, such dissolution is highly unlikely to solve Nigeria's ethnic problems or to be consummated in a peaceable or non-violent manner.

Third, and most importantly, it seems obvious that much of the agitation for the confederalisation or dissolution of Nigeria is inspired not by a disbelief in the viability or legitimacy of a single Nigerian state *per se,* but by the dissatisfaction or frustration with the inequities and anomalies that characterise the current practice of federalism in Nigeria. It, therefore, seems that the country's confederalists or separatists can be significantly pacified by the refederalisation of the country. This returns us to the important issue of the prospects and problems of federal reform in the country.

While unitarism, confederalism and the current pseudo-federalism do not appear to be viable options for Nigeria, the option of federal reform poses or imposes significant challenges or difficulties of its own. A fundamental problem is the likely opposition of entrenched and dominant interests within and outside the military to the emergence of a federal democratic system that may rob them of the powers and privileges they currently enjoy under the present centralised political framework. But such interests must ultimately yield to the greater interests of the majority of Nigerians and to the imperatives of the country's continued corporate unity. An equally fundamental problem appears to be the apparent absence of a strong national consensus regarding the precise mix or choice of policies or institutions for reforming the federal system. Among the several contested issues or questions regarding federal reform in Nigeria can be numbered the following:

1. Should Nigeria be a presidential federation, a parliamentary federation or a mixed presidential-parliamentary federation? It should be noted that the shift from the parliamentary federalism of the First Republic to the presidential federalism of the Second and (still-born) Third Republics was virtually imposed by military fiat. Although a few Nigerians had in 1993 canvassed for a French-style presidential-parliamentary system for the country, the decision to experiment with this system under the proposed Fourth Republic was also

unilaterally imposed by the Head of State, General Sani Abacha. Yet, a presidential system in the Nigerian setting appears to invite a zero-sum, ethnoregional competition for the all-powerful office of the presidency, while a presidential-parliamentary system harbours the real risk of a potentially debilitating confrontation between the president and the prime minister.

ii. What should be the respective constitutional responsibilities or functions of the federal, state and local governments, especially in such contested areas as education, agriculture, housing, domestic security and roads? In short, how can Nigeria achieve an economically and politically optimal allocation of constitutional responsibilities between the tiers of government?

iii The issue of revenue allocation reform is also a thorny one. Granted that there is an urgent need for resource devolution in Nigeria, how can such decentralisation be achieved? Should it involve the reallocation of tax jurisdictions or the redistribution of tax revenues? Which level of government should benefit more from financial devolution: the states or the localities? What would be the most appropriate formulae or criteria for the vertical and horizontal sharing of centrally collected revenues? How can the Federation Account be administered in a manner that ensures transparency and minimises intergovernmental distrust? Finally, and most crucially, what proportions of oil revenues should be allocated to the oil-bearing sections on the basis of derivation, or compensation for the ecological risks of oil production?

iv. Are the current Nigerian states too many or too few? If the states are too many, how can the state-structure be streamlined? If the states are too few, how may additional states be created? In short, what principles or rules should guide the internal territorial restructuring of the Nigerian federation?

v. What should be the relative roles of the federal and state governments, as well as the affected local communities themselves, in the reform, organisation and reorganisation of the local government system?

vi. How can the `federal character' principle, and the related power-sharing practices, be redefined to ensure that they promote genuine inter-sectional equity and amity, without destroying democratic equality and bureaucratic or governmental efficacy?

These constitute only a sample of the thorny issues on the agenda of federal reform in Nigeria. There are several other contested items, including the position of the federal capital territory, the status of Shari'a law, the issue of minority language rights, the federalisation of the party system, etc. Although the 1994-95 National Constitutional Conference (NCC) did make some effort to address a number of these issues, the controversial political circumstances surrounding its inauguration, deliberations and resolutions cannot give its work much transparency, credibility, legitimacy or viability. Only a federal constitutional arrangement that is freely and fairly agreed to by the genuine representatives of the Nigerian people can possess such desirable qualities. This leads us to a restatement of what we consider to be the irreducible requirement for true federalism and federal reform in Nigeria: the genuine democratisation of the Nigerian political space, and the abandonment by the military of its self-appointed role as Nigeria's political hegemon.

Conclusion

In essence, a united federal democratic constitution remains the best and most promising political option for Nigeria. Unfortunately, this conclusion has been misinterpreted by some to mean that the country's continued unity can be taken for granted. Yet, although we strongly believe that Nigeria should and ought not to disintegrate, we realise that this does not mean that the country cannot or will not disintegrate. Indeed, as already indicated, recent political conflicts and developments have engendered deep cynicism and scepticism about Nigeria's federation. The experiences of the civil war, and other subsequent challenges to Nigeria's unity (as, for example, in Gideon Orkar's coup of April 1990), should sound cautionary notes to those ideologues of Nigeria's unconditional or inexorable unity, who may be insensitive or blinded to the development of deep resentments and restiveness in the federation. To reiterate, therefore, Nigeria's unity should not be taken for granted; rather, it ought to be consciously and tenderly nurtured through truly federal democratic institutions and processes.

Endnotes

1. Billy Dudley, *Instability and Political Order: Politics and Crises in Nigeria*. Ibadan: Ibadan University Press, 1973, p.25
2. See Alfred Stepan, `Towards a New Comparative Analysis for the Democracy and Federalism', (Background Paper for the Conference on Democracy and Federalism, Oxford University, June 5-8 1997), p.4; Juan Linz, `Democracy, Multinationalism and Federalism', (Paper for the Conference on Democracy and Federalism, Oxford University, June 5-8 1997), pp. 7-8; and Ronald Watts, *New Federations: Experiments in the Commonwealth'* London: Oxford University Press, 1966, pp.115-119.
3. John P. Mackintosh, `Federalism in Nigeria, `*Political Studies,* 10, 3 (1962), p. 223.
4. Larry Diamond, *Class, Ethnicity and Democracy in Nigeria: The Failure of the First Republic*. London: Macmillan Press, 1988, p.26
5. Diamond, *Class, Ethnicity and Democracy*. p.29.
6. Donald Rotchild, `State-Ethnic Relations in Middle Africa,' in Gwendolen M. Carter and Patrick O' Meara, eds. *African Independence: the first twenty-five years*. Bloomington, IN: Indiana University Press, 1985, pp. 71-96.
7. See Stepan, ``Towards a New Comparative Analysis of Democracy and Federalism", p.3
8. On this, see Larry Diamond and Oyeleye Oyediran, ``Military Authoritarianism and Democratic Transition in Nigeria", *The National Political Science Review 4* (1994), pp.221-244, esp. p.233.
9. On the philosophical basis of this phenomenon, see Billy J. Dudley, ``Scepticism and Political Virtue", *Inaugural Lecture,* University of Ibadan, 1975, p.21
10. Iyorchia Ayu, `Reflections on Federalism and National Assembly Politics in Nigeria', in J. Isawa Elaigwu, P.C. Logams and H.S. Galadima (eds) *Federalism and Nation Building in Nigeria: The Challenges of the 21st Century*. Abuja: National Council on Intergovernmental Relations, 1994, p. 131.
11. See Larry Diamond, `Ethnicity and Ethnic Conflict', *The Journal of Modern African Studies*. 25, 1(1987), pp. 117-128.
12. Peter Ekeh, `The Structure and Meaning of Federal Character in the Nigerian Political System', in Peter Ekeh and E.E. Osaghae (eds), *Federal Character and Federalism in Nigeria*. Ibadan: Heinemann

1989, pp.32,36.

13. Richard Joseph, *Democracy and Prebendal Politics in Nigeria: The Rise and Fall of The Second Republic*. Ibadan: Spectrum Books, 1991.

14. A.A. Aikhomu, `Federal-State Relations Under Military Government, 1985-1992', in Elaigwu, *et al* (eds) *Federalism and Nation-Building*, p.45.

15. Aikhomu, `Federal-State Relations', p.45

16. William Zartman, `Negotiations and Prenegotiations in Ethnic Conflict: The Beginning, The Middle, and the Ends', in J.V. Montville (eds.), *Conflict and Peace-making in Multiethnic Societies*. Lexington: Lexington Books, 1989, p.529.

Index

Abacha administration/government/ 125,132,136,140-142,241-242
Abacha military junta (child of necessity) 7-8, 71-72,77,79,82,90,92
Abacha regime 160,169,172,180
Abacha, Sani 71-72,77,80-81,83,85-86, 88-91,106,123,125,127,130,147,172, 276,286-287,289,292,316-317,326,339,346
Abiola, Kudirat 89
Abiola, M.K.O. 7,71,82,88-90,92-93,169,303
Aboyade, Ojetunji 236
Aboyade Technical Committee on Revenue Allocation 213-214,222,234-236,238,250,256
Aburi Accords in Ghana 180,345
Abuse of State Character 208
Academic Staff Union of Universities (ASUU) 73
Action Group (AG) 40,42,51,53-54,103, 179,281-282
Adebayo, Cornelius 66
Adebo, Chief 301
Adedeji, Adebayo 236-237
Adedoyin, Adeleke 38,40
Adesanya, Abraham 89
Adeusi, Joseph 242
Adisa, Abdulkareem 67
Affirmative action 194-195,197
African politics 52
Afrocracy system 125
Aggregative federalism 335
Ajasin, Michael 86,89
Aka-Bashorun, Alao 85
Ake, Claude 86,130
Akilu, Ali 60
Akinrinade, Alani 66,89
Akinyemi, Bolaji 66
Alhaji, Abubakar 241
Allen, Christopher S. 4
Allocation and Fiscal Commission 24

American Constitution 301-302,306,321
Amalgamation (1914) 23,26,170,178,263
— arrangements (1898-1914) 16
Anglo-Saxon model 113
Annulment of June 12, 1993 Presidential election 7,65,71-72,85,87,141,143,147,164, 170
Anti-June 12 sentiments 91
Aristocratic feudalism 61
Armed Forces Ruling Council (AFRC) 215
Asiodu, Philip 282
Association of Mineral Oil States (AMOS) 270
Attah, Abdulaziz 282
Authoritarian regimes 4
Autonomous Foreign Exchange Market (AFEM) 242
Awolowo, Obafemi 33,52,77,88,102,179, 198,304
Awolowo vs. Shagari 304,310
Ayida, Allison 282
Ayu, Iyorchia 341
Azikiwe, Nnamdi 38-41,43,51-52,179, 299-300

Babangida, Ibrahim 71,88,91-93,105,129, 147,197,241,276,279,284-285,289,291,303
Babangida, Maryam 158
Bako, Sabo 117
Bala, Usman Yusufu 186
Balewa, Abubakar Tafawa 37,52,180,300
Balewa-led federal government 77
Barrack revolts or coup d'etat 45
Bayero, Yusuf 59
Beijing Conference 148
Beijing Declaration 152,157
Bello, Ahmadu (Sultan of Sokoto) 42, 54-55,59,76,78,93,104,130,196
Berlin wall 4

Index

Better Life for Rural Women Programme (BLP) 148,154,158,160
Biafra Movement 16,30
Biafra propaganda 112
Binn's Commission of 1964 234
Borno Youth Movement (BYM) 78
Bourdillon Act of 1939 102
Bourdillon effect 103
British Administration 52
British colonialism and imperialism 73
British hegemony 164
British imperialism 336
British Policy Makers 15
Budgetary allocations 227
Bugaje, Usman 84

Cabinet Responsibility 26
Cake-sharing syndrome 45,341
Calabar-Ogoja-Rivers (COR) State Movement 44
Campaign for Democracy (CD) 73,82
Capital grains tax 252
Census controversy 1962 300
Charles de Gaulle 321,323-324
Chick Commission of 1953 233,264
Child abuse 155
Child marriage and teenage pregnancy 154-155
Child neglect 155
Civil Liberties Organisation 153
Civil War 30,45,69,77,104,166,170,180-181, 203,206,233-234,263,265,269,337,344-345, 347
Citizenship rights 108
Clifford Constitution of 1922 178,203
Clifford, Hugh 37,109
Colonial administration 102
Colony and Protectorate of Lagos 15,101
Communal groupings 71
Communal violence 291
Community Development Associations 206
Company income tax 254
Competitive federalism 43-45
Conflict-resolution 13
Consociational democracy 122,128,169,202
Constituent Assembly (CA) 106,137,153, 157,301
Constitution
— Drafting Committee (CDC) 107-109,112,166,181-182,300
—, 1848   13

— 1951   39,41-43
—, 1954   34,43,179,264
—, 1963   319
—, 1979   17-18,27,105,108,114, 125-126,164-165,167,169,181-182, 192,198,205,252,254,256, 302-303,305,307-310,319,326
—, 1989   17,126,182,304-305, 310,318-319,326
—, 1992   205
—, 1998   241,243
Constitutional arrangements 29,37
Constitutional assignment of powers and function 46
Constitutional
— Conference 7,14,16,79,84,88,117, 127,130,137,140-144,152-154,157, 161,172,303,305,311,316,318-319, 326,328
— report on the Executive 317-318
— recommendations on the Executive 318-319
— Commission 7,85
— in London 43
— Development 17
— government 26
— provisions 19
— reforms 40
Constitutions
—, 1922-54 era (Clifford, Richards Macpherson, Lyttleton) 16
—, 1960 and 1963   17,29
— post independence 19,34
Cooperative federalism 28
Cooperative governments 14,17
Coups d'etat 19,30,129
Cultural
— affinity 40
— beliefs and practices 156
— diversity 13,21,40
— pluralism 232
Customs Union 14

Danjuma, T.Y. 240
Dantata, Ahmadu 58-59
Dasuki, Ibrahim 60,93
Decade for Women (1975-1985) 148
Decrees and edicts 19

Dedicated Accounts 225,255,278
Democractic
    — culture 68
    — ethos 68
    — idea 4-6
    — practice 5-6,68
    — process 45
    — society 156
    — stability 164-176
    — transition programme 66,68
Derivation principle (for revenue allocation) 25,213-214,231,250,256,259,264 342
Devolutionary federations 336
Diamond, Larry 68-69,130,280,336
Dikko, Umaru 85.
Dina
    — Commission 235,238,265
    — Committe (1969) 256
    , I.O. 235
Distributive Pool Account (DPA) 264-265, 268
Distributive Federalism 341-344
    — crisis of 341-344
Diya, Oladipo 83,93
Draft Constitution 1995 18,26-29,105,126, 153-154,182,302,304,308-311,316,319, 325-326
Dudley 53

Eastern States Interim Assets and Liabilities Agency (ESIALA) 104
Ebong, Eme 282
Economic
    — reform programme 225
    — statism 276
Economics of Federalism 23-25
Educational disparities 196
Egbe Omo Oduduwa 40
Egerton, Walter 36
Ekekwe, Eme 280
Ekukinam, A.E. 236
Elaigwu, J. Isawa 16
Electoral
    — malpractices 300
    — politics 73
    — process 29
    — rigging and violence 29
    — verdict 29,89
Elite factionalism 7

El-kanemi, Mustapha (Shehu of Borno) 86
Emirs-traditional rulers 51
Enahoro, Anthony 42,54,66,84,86,90
Enahoro motion 104,110
Entertainment tax 252
Equity principle 201-209,223
Eso, Kayode 304
Ethnic
    — balancing 183,191-200
    — chauvinism 132
    — classification 40
    — cleavages 129
    — conflicts 50-51,116,247
    — differentiation 104,109-110
    — federalism 179
    — fragmentation 337
    — groups 50-51,107,115,117,129, 132,165-167,177-178,180,184,186 -187,191-192,198,235,239,263, 282,303
    — hegemonists 91
    — heterogeneity 277
    — minority groups 337
    — Minority Organisation of Africa (EMIROAF) 269
    — origin 109
    — particularism 92,110
    — pluralism 13,21,82,277
    — politics 22,51,233
    — sectionalism 23
Ethno
    — linguistic groups 277
    — moral debate 109
    — regional competition 82
        — elites 337
        — groups 166
        — hegemony 75
Executive presidential system 299-300
Ezeife, Chukwuemeka 88

Family and Child Welfare issues 156
Family Support Programme (FSP) 148,154
Fatayi-Williams, Atanda 13-14
Fawehinmi, Gani 67
Federal
    — Character 22-23,105-120,126-127, 133,154,164-176,279,301,340,342 -343

— Commission (FCC) 117,124,126,169,173,182,205, 279-280
and Social Justice 195-198
— principle 22-23,79,122,155,164-192,195-198,201-209,279,342,346
— problems and prospects 183-186
— recommendations and suggestions 186-187
— constitutions 5,14,30,44
— Council of Traditional Rulers 18
— Public Service Commission 185
— system 3-5,45,46,78,91-92,104, 122,166,179,183,247,267,276-277, 335-339,344-345
Federalism
— definition of 13
— attributes of 4
Federation Account 24,214-216,220-221, 226,236,238-239,247,249,254-259,268,278 -279,290,342,346
Femocracy 157
5th National Yoruba Convention 8
Fika, Adamu 118
Fiscal discipline 222
Fiscal equity 24-25
Fiscal Regime (1994-97) 241-243
First
— home-made Revenue Allocation Commission 234
— Ladies 157-158,160-161
— Republic (1960-1968) 8,45,64, 77-78,130,140,150,166,170,205, 234,281,318,324,326,328,337,345
Formal federation (1946-1966) 50
Forrest, Tom 277
Fourth Republic 91,121-122,127,132-133, 153,155,169,262,289,316,318-320,324,326, 329,345
Frankel, Max 3
Freedom Charter of NCNC 40
French Constitution 321
French Constitutional History 321
Fundamental human rights 329

Gender
— balanced Nigerian Political System 153
— balanced power structure 150

— bias 153
— conflicts 5
— equality campaign 149,153,156, 160-161
— equity 149,152-154,157
— neutral recommendation 153
— oppression 157
— participation in proposed 4th Republic 153
— profile 153
— question 155
— relations 156
General Conference at Ibadan 16
General Constitutional Conference 1950 39-41
Genocidal Conflicts 68
German Constitution 322,324,326-327
German politics 4
Global communication satellites 31
Gowon era 64
Gowon, Yakubu 77,104,166,180,234,276, 282,284
Gwarzo, Ismaila 86

Hegemonic exchange 337
Hicks-Phillipson Commission 233,264
Human Development Report (1993) 157

Ibadan Constitution Conference 104
Idiagbon 83
Ige, Bola 73-74,76
Ijaw Ethnic Minority Rights Protection Organisation 269
Ikime, Obaro 41,196
Ikoku, S.G. 88
Illiteracy 155-156
Imperial policy 15
Independence Constitution, 1960   140
Indian Constitution 5
India's Republican Constitution (1949) 13,17,28
Indigene Syndrome 187
Indigenisation policy 187
Indirect Administration 17
Indirect rule 17,51,165-166
Industrialisation and democracy 4
Informal federation (1900-1946) 50,166
Institutional reforms 6
Inter-class political competition 80
Inter-ethnic harmony 22
Inter-ethnic rivalry 192

Index

Intergovernmental resources transfer 247
Interim Common Service Agency (ICSA) 104
Interim Revenue Allocation Review Committee (IRARC) 235
Internally generated revenue 252
International community 93
Intra-communal crisis 89
Intra-elite political contestation 80
Irikefe led Commission 282,284
Ironsi, Aguiyi 77,170,180-181,344
Islamic influence 53
Ita, Eyo 40
Iyam, Baba 66

Joseph, Richard 130,167,203
June-12 1993 Presidential election 137,141

Kaduna Mafia 76-78
Kano, Aminu 62
Kerekou Coup 133
Komo, Dauda Musa 66-67
Kontagora, Mamman 68
Kukah, M.H. 84

Lamido of Adamawa 51
Leaders of Women (Iyalode Efunsetan) 149
Legislative Council for Lagos 178
Leton, G.B. 236
Lewis, Peter 277,285

Macpherson Constitution of 1951 14,41,140,179,233
Macpherson, John 38
Male domination 161
Marginalised groups 197
Marketing Boards 251
Mbanefo, Arthur 287
Meritocracy 207
Militarised transition programme 90
Military
— autocracy 335
— autocrats 65
— constitutionalism 80
— courts 65,67
— driven constitutionalism 79
— federalism 16
— government 64,76,78
— logic 64
— oligarchs in power 65
— parity 112
— presidency 29,67
— regime 65,68
— strategies 64
Mineral producing states 215,221,227,238, 240,269-270
Misleading federation 198
Mohammed, Murtala 300
Momoh, K.S.Y. 44
Morel, E.D. 36
Motion of Destiny 42
Movement for the Survival of Ogoni People (MOSOP) 170,269,271
Multi-party arrangements 29
Multi-party system 152,203
Murtala/Obasanjo regime (1975-79) 78, 105,166,180,276,284
Musa, Balarabe 302
Mustapha, Hamza 86
Mu'azu, Yakubu 90

NADECO 86,88-90
Nas, Wada 88
Nasir, Mamman 88
Nation building 45
Native Authority 21
National
— Assembly 125,302,308-310,325, 327
— cake 166-167,169,171,177,292,343
— Commission for Women 148,198
— Conference 17,92
— Congress of British West Africa (NCBWA) 204
— Consensus 80-81,345
— Constitutional Conference 21-22,26-27,80,83,123,147,152-153 286,347,
— inaugural address 83
— Commission 153
— Council for Women's Societies 153,158
— Council of Nigeria and the Cameroons (NCNC) 40,51-53,103, 179,281
— Defence Council 327
— Development Plans 214
— Electoral Commission of Nigeria (NECON) 92

— Integration 22-23,31,34-35,42-46 71,108-110,114,116,123-124,132-133,164,166-170,177-190,202,205, 209,247,250,256,258-259
— Judicial Council 311
— Legislative Assembly 51
— Party of Nigeria (NPN) 75,168-169,173
— Planning Commission 117
— politics 24,77,79,87
— Population Census 285
— question 45-46,71,78,84,164,166, 170-174,177,181,270
— Reconciliation Commission (NARECOM) 86
— Reconstruction 262,271
— Republican Convention (NRC) 285
— Republican Party 302
— Revenue Mobilisation 24
— Revenue Mobilisation, Allocation and Fiscal Commission (NRMAFC) 215,240-242
— Unity 37,71,108-109,114-115,124
Nationalist struggle 55
Ndem, U.O. 44
Niger Coast Protectorate 101
Niger or Selborne Committee of 1898 101
Niger territories 15
Niger Committee (1898) 15
Nigeria Country Report 152
Nigeria Police Force 21
Nigerian
    — Civil War 137,140
    — factor 23
    — Legislative Council 37
    — National Alliance (NNA) 300
    — Political Science Association (NPSA) Ilorin 8
    — politics 164,171,203,276
    — Youth Movement 40
Nigerianisation 52
    — policy of 1956   204
Nigeria's Constitution, 1960 29
Nigeria's fiscal federalism 213-214,223, 226,261-265
Nigeria's political future 15
Nigeria's traditional rulers 17
1953 London Conference 56
1953 riots 56
1981 Revenue Act 214
1995 Constitutional Conference 214,225, 241
Nnoli, Okwudiba 22,280
Non-governmental agencies (NGOs) 147-148,152,161-162
Non-Northern Nigerians 57
Non-oil producing states 222,266,270
Non-Statutory allocation 215
North/South Dichotomy 37,166
Northern
    — Amalgamated Merchants Union 58
    — Elders Forum 127
    — Elements Progressive Union (NEPU) 62,78,103
    — hegemonists 78,83,89-91
    — House of Assembly 42
    — House of Chiefs 42
    — Nigerian Contractors Association 58
    — Peoples Congress (NPC) 40,42, 51,53-55,57,61-62,77-78,111,178 -180,281
    — Protectorate 51
    — Public Service 57,111-112
    —/Southern Protectorate 165
    — Transporters and Contractors Company 58
Northernisation Implementation Committee 58
Northernisation Policy 50,54,57-62,76,111
    — critique of 60-62
Nyiam 90

Obasanjo, Olusegun 187
Obasanjo regime 235
Odili, Peter 286
Odu'a States 104
Ofonagoro, Walter 87-88
Ogoni nine 65,86
Ogundimu, Olu 67
Oil boom 267
Oil Mineral Producing Areas Development Council (OMPADEC) 269-270
Oil Minorities Vs Oil Multinationals 271
Oil Pollution 225,255,270
Oil Producing States 215,221-225,227,266, 268,270,342

Oil-revenue allocation 263
Oil Rivers (later Niger Coast) Protectorate 15
Ojike, Mbonu 40
Ojo, J.D. 26
Ojukwu, Odumegwu 92,180
Okadigbo, Chuba 105
Okigbo Commission 214,236,238,250,256
Okigbo Pius 235,237
Okigbo Revenue Allocation Commission (1981) 213-214,222,235,238-239
Olanrewaju, T. 67
Olorun-Nimbe, I. 40
Olukoshi, Adebayo 77-78,91
Omoruyi 105
Onagoruwa, Olu 84
One North One People 53,62
Order-in-Council of the British Crown 18
Osoba, Segun 241
Otedola, Sir 241
Otite, Onigu 21-22
Oyegun, John 66
Oyinlola, Olagunsoye 66
Oyovbaire, S.E. 8

Palace Women (Idia)149
Parliamentary System 125,300-302,306,309, 318,328-329,345
Party Political leaders 16
Party system 65
Peoples Redemption Party 302
Personal Income tax 218,251-252,257
Petroleum profits tax 254
Petroleum Trust Fund (PTF) 117,225-227, 242,255,278
Phillips, Dotun 236-237
Phillipson Commission recommendation 264
Phillipson Fiscal Commission of 1942 222,233
Political
— action 43,200
— administration 307
— agenda 148
— agitation 42
— alliance 324
— ambition 89
— arrangement 147,149,152,161, 201-202
— ascendancy 110,112,282
— associations 29,150

— assumptions 238
— authority 83,183,336
— bargaining 6
— behaviour 84
— behavioural traits 77
— beliefs 113
— Bureau 106,108,129,152
— culture 341
— character 132,264
— chicanery 65
— class 44-45,87,165,167-168,170, 173,281,289
— climate 112
— cloning 101
— clout 102
— cohesion 183
— community 184,202
— competition 44,168
— consideration 14
— contestants 103
— contests 140
— context 73
— contradictions 179
— control 179,204
— course 80
— crises/crisis 35,42-43,68,81,86,92 ,141
— culture 41,46,122,147,265
— debate 152,277
— demand 21
— dialogues 102
— discourse 72
— dispensation 60
— diversities 178
— domination 205
— dynamite 29
— Economy 87-88,90,261-262,**272**, 276-295,343
— elites 233,292,320
— emancipation 61
— environment 339
— factors 281,290
— force 14,104,106
— formula 192
— framework 179
— future 30,37
— goals 54
— groups 79,142

— history 42,64,71,101,133,338
— horizon 6,15
— humiliation 76
— identity 17
— impasse 8
— implications 38
— incompatibles 82
— independence 164,191
— infiltration 103
— instability 29,137,318
— institutions 4,6,69,149,336
— interest 53,93
— intrigue and bloodshed 45
— landscape 72,133,338
— leaders 5,35,51,53,60,169-170,179
— lexicon 166
— loyalties 122
— machinery 180
— manoeuvrings 7
— market 7
— merchants 90
— minority 102
— movement 22
— objective 42,79
— office 65
— opinion 81
— order 18,34,79
— outlook 43
— patronage 58,61
— parties/party 29,40-41,43-44,67, 152,179,300,303,318,327
— power 22,40,51,53,69,81,86,77,90 -91,104,110,112,114,116,124,126, 147,149-150,155,157,180,183,223, 335
— pluralism 202
— practice 41,169
— praxis 72
— protection 171
— reconstruction 69
— reform 68
— relationships 122
— rendition 72
— representation 170
— Restructuring 34
    — essence of 6
        — Nigerian example 7-9
— situation (post independence) 35

— society 65,68,70
— sophistication 52
— space 6
— sphere 45
— stability 26-27,29-30,164-165,169, 174,177
— stalemate 102
— statements 51
— structure 36
— symmetry 112
— system 44-55,75,91,105,121,147, 154,187,323
— tensions 6
— thuggery 168
— transition 63
    — programme 140
    — timetables 65
— trespassers 103
— turmoil 300
— units 36,46
— uproar 137
— viability 86
— victory 103
— war 113
— world-view 85
    — zones 138
Politico-military acolytes 8
Politico-moral balance 109
Politico-structural imbalance 281
Politics of deception 90
— of domination 122
— of group equality 122
Pollution 224-225
Pope, Alexander 20
Post cold war era 4,9
Post-Gaullist France 28
Post-Gorbachev reforms 9
Post Independence Revenue Allocation Commissions 232,235-238
Post-military civilian restoration regime 8
Power Sharing 21-22,25,121-136,152-155
Prebendal 157-162,164,170,172-173,340
— politics 203
— system 167
Prebendalism 343
Presidential
— dictatorship 26
— elections 143
— Liaison Officers 168
Pro-democracy and human rights group 7

Produce Sales Tax 251
Progressive or revolutionary regime 22
Progressive politicians 71
Property tax 254
Property taxation 257
Proportional Representation (PR) 27-29
Protectorate of Northern Nigeria 101
Protectorate of Southern Nigeria 101
Provisional Ruling Council 148,153,155, 172,316,319,325
Provincial Tender Boards of Northern Nigeria 58
Pseudo-federal 16

Quasi-federal 16
Quota system 128,152,172,174,181,185, 192,197-198,205

Racial discrimination 204
Radical insurgency 91
Raisman Commission, 1958 233
Raisman and Tress Commission 264-265
Ramphal, Shridath 201
Ransome-Kuti, Beko 90
Rasaq, Abdul 57
Rawls, John 193
Regional jingoism 132
Regional Public Service Commission 57
Religious bigotry 132
Religious outcasts 53
Religious symbolism 53
Representative Bureaucracy 111-117
Republican variant 1968   17
Residency rights 108,187
Resource allocation and distribution   164, 171
Revenue
— Allocation 23-25,181,213-247, 249,262-263,342, 346
— criteria for 213
— historical background 263-266,268
— politics of 234-235
— Allocation Act of 1981 238-239
— Formula 136,214,222,232, 238-239,241-242,255-257, 259,267
— Reform 346
— Scheme 222

— System 261-265,267,270, 272
— Sharing Formula 214-215,279
Reverse discrimination 194-195,197
Rewane, Alfred 89
Richard, Arthur 191
Richards Constitution of 1946 38-39,51,102,166,178,233,264
Rights of widows, single parent and single women 156
Rotational power sharing and zoning of offices 172,174
Rotational presidency 21,26,85,92,124, 131,137-146
Royal Niger Company 15,101
Rule of Law 19,66-67,74,329
Rulers of (Queen Amina of Zaria) 149
Ruling Class 184.261-262,267
Rural and urban power majority 22
Rural women 160

Saro-Wiwa, Ken 65,67,89,170,183
Secession threats 30
Second Republic (1979-83) 45,64,79,85, 140,150,165,167-169,173,272,284,302, 305,317,324-325,328-329,337,345
Secondary coup 90
Secret ballot 29
Secret cults 66
Selbourne Lord 15
Selbourne Committee (1898) 15
Self-government 15,37-38,41-42,44,55,104,110
Sense of national identity 186
Shagari, Shehu 75,164-165,168,214,235, 286,304
Sharia Law 347
Shettima, Bargudu 185
Shonekan, Ernest 82,90
Social and political engineering 180
Social
— diversity 46
— Democratic Party (SDP) 82,285
— engineering 45
— harmony 183
— justice and Reverse Discrimination 193-195
— Welfare 155-157
Socio-political ladder 14
Socio-political landscape 65-66

Sokoto Caliphate 51,86
Southern Minorities Movement 269
Southern Protectorates 51
Soyinka, Wole 66,89
Special Fund 258
Stabilisation Fund 225,278
— Account 252,255
State
— creation exercise 180,183,186, 269-275,343
— and revenue allocation 219,235
— Electoral Commission 125
— Security Service (SSS) 68
Structural adjustment programme (SAP) 240,251,269-270,285
Sub-national forums 71
Sule, Maitama 75,78
Suleiman, Dan 108
Sultan of Sokoto 51,53
Supreme law 19

Tahir, Ibrahim 85,110
Talib, Ahmed 109,236
Temple, C.L. 36
Teriba, R.O. 236
Territorial configuration 276
Third Republic 45,66,87,150,153,161,284, 309,324-325,345
Tinubu, Bola 66
Tofa, Alhaji 303
Traditional northern ruling oligarchies 61
Transition agencies 86
Transition Implementation Committee (TIC) 88
Transitional Committee on Devolution of Powers 241-242
Treason trial 1963   300
Tribal war 87

Unification Decree Number 34   77
Unitary Colonial State   336
Unitary Constitution   42
United Middle Belt Congress (UMBC) 61-62,78,103
United Progressive Grand Alliance (UPGA) 300
Unongo, Paul 286
US-based Congress for Racial Equity

(CORC) 92
Usman, Ahmed 66
Usman, Bala 22

Value-Added Tax 242,251-252,254,**256**, 273,278

Wada, Inuwa 55
Wage policies and structures 24
Water-borne diseases 224
Water contamination 224
WAZOBIA 29
Western education 51-52,54,196
Western liberal democracies 70
Westminster model 21,27,301
Westminster system 140,205
Wheare, K.C. 13-14,16,247
Willink Commission (1957) 19,21,44,281
Wilson, Woodrow 302
Women
— advancement 148
— and development 155
— future of Power Sharing 152-155
— and political arrangement 148-151
— Education Unit 158
— in Agriculture Unit 158
— in Development 158
— in Nigeria (WIN) 152
Women's
— associations and professional groups 148
— development advocacy 148
— disenfranchisement 150
— empowerment 149
— issues (in Social Welfare) 155-157
World War II 15

Yoruba leadership 78
Yoruba nation 8

Zero-party municipal election 92
Zoning system 21-22,164,172,174

IFRA
IBADAN

List of Publications

Adediran, A.O., 1994. *The Frontier States of Western Yorubaland, ca 1600-1889: State Formation and Political Growth in an Ethnic Frontier Zone.* Ibadan: IFRA, 304 p. *ISBN 978 2015 25 3.*

Adesanmi, P., 1997. *Youth, Street Culture and Urban Violence in Africa* Report on the International Symposium held in Abidjan, 5-7 May, 1997. Ibadan: IFRA, iv + 40 p., *ISBN 978 2015 53 9.*

Adeyemo, R., 1994. *Access to Shelter by the Poor through Community Participation.* Ibadan: IFRA, 16p., *ISBN 978 2015 29 6*

Adisa, J., 1996. *The Comfort of Strangers. The Impact of Rwanda Refugees in Neighbouring Countries.* Ibadan: IFRA, xii + 101 p., *ISBN 978 2015 41 5.*

Adisa, J., I.O. Albert and G. Hérault, 1995. *Report on the International Symposium on Urban Management and Urban Violence in Africa.* Ibadan: IFRA, 82p., *ISBN 978 2015 36 9.*

Agbaje-Williams, B., 1995. *Archaeological Investigation of Itagunmodi Potsherd Pavement Site, Ijesaland, Osun State, Nigeria (1991-92 Season).* Ibadan: IFRA, 34 p., *ISBN 978 2015 32 6.*

Agboola, T., 1997. *The Architecture of Fear. Urban Design and Construction Reaction to Urban Violence in Lagos, Nigeria.* Ibadan: IFRA, 138 p., *ISBN 978 2015 57 1.*

Ake, C., 1992. *The Feasibility of Democracy in Africa*, Ibadan: CREDU, 10 p. *ISBN 978 2015 15 6.*

Akinyele, I.O. and I.O. Onifade, 1996. *Trends & Social Behaviour among Secondary School Adolescents in Ibadan.* Ibadan: IFRA, 38 p., *ISBN 978 2015 40 7.*

Albert, I.O., 1993. *Inter-Ethnic Relations in a Nigerian City: The Historical Perspective of the Hausa-Igbo Conflicts in Kano, 1953-1991.* Ibadan: IFRA, 19 p., *ISBN 978 2015 24 5* (second printing).

Albert, I.O., 1996. *Women and Urban Violence in Kano, Nigeria.* Ibadan: Spectrum Books Ltd and IFRA, xii + 120 p., *ISBN 978 246 287 X.*

Albert I.O., J. Adisa, T. Agboola and G. Hérault (eds), 1994. *Urban Management and Urban Violence in Africa.* Proceedings of the International Symposium held at Ibadan, Nigeria, 7-11 November 1994. Ibadan: *IFRA*, 2 vol., 850 p., *ISBN 978 2015 31 8 and ISBN 978 2015 33 4*.

Albert I.O., T. Awe, G. Hérault and W. Omitoogun, 1995. *Informal Channels for Conflict Resolution in Ibadan, Nigeria*. Ibadan: IFRA, viii+107 p., *ISBN 978 2015 39 3*.

Bello-Imam, I.B., 1996. *Local Government in Nigeria: Evolving a Third Tier of Government*. Ibadan: Heinemann and IFRA, xvi + 218 p., *ISBN 978 246 287 X*.

Caron, Bernard, A. Gboyega and E. Osaghae (eds), 1992. *Democratic Transition in Africa*. Ibadan: CREDU, 436 p., *ISBN 978 2015 13 X*.

Chouin, Gérard, 1996. *Ecrits d'entre-deux Mondes. Index Analytique des sources Manuscrites de l'histoire des Etats de la Côte de l'Or (Côte d'Ivoire, Ghana) dans les fonds de la Bibliothèque Nationale et des Archives Nationales de France (1634-1710)*. Madison: University of Wisconsin and IFRA, 62 p., *ISBN 0 9 42615 30 1*.

Dawha, E.M.K., 1996. *Yan Daba, 'Yan Banga and 'Yan Daukar Amarya, A Study of Criminal Gangs in Northern Nigeria*. Ibadan: IFRA, v + 30 p., *ISBN 978 2015 47 4*.

Deffontaine, Y., 1993. *Guerre et Société au Royaume de Fetu (Efutu): Des Débuts du Commerce Atlantique à la Constitution de la Fédération Fanti (Ghana, Côte l'Or, 1471-1720)*. Ibadan/Paris: IFRA-KARTHALA, xiii + 280 p., *ISBN 978 2015 23 7*.

Enwerem, I.M., 1995. *A Dangerous Awakening. The Politicization of Religion in Nigeria*. Ibadan: IFRA, xiv + 252 p., *ISBN 978 2015 34 2*.

Hérault, G. and P. Adesanmi (eds), 1997. *Jeunes, Culture de la rue et Violence Urbaine en Afrique, Actes du Symposium International d'Abidjan, 5-7 mai 1997 / Youth, Street Culture and Urban Violence in Africa*. Proceedings of the International Symposium held in Abidjan. 5-7 May, 1997. Ibadan: IFRA, vii + 417 p., *ISBN 978 2015 58 X*.

Ihimodu, I.I. 1996. *The Impact of the Better Life Programme on the Economic Status of Women*. Ibadan: IFRA, v + 45 p., *ISBN 978 2015 46 6*.

Jacob, Haruna H. and Massoud Omar (eds), 1992. *France and Nigeria: Issues in Comparative Studies*. Ibadan: CREDU, 180 p., *ISBN 978 2015 16 4*.

Joubert, H., 1995. *Les musées du Nigeria, (rapport d'enquêtes)*, Ibadan: IFRA, 75 p., *mimeo*.

de Montclos, M-C., 1994. *Le Nigeria*. Paris: Karthala - IFRA (collection Méridiens), 323 p., *ISBN 2 86537 466 1*.

Nwokedi, E. and J-P. Daloz (eds), 1990. *French Revolution: A Nigerian Perspective*. Ibadan / Lagos: Macmillan Nigeria Publishers Ltd, 235 p., ISBN 978 132 941 6.

Ojo, J.D., 1995. *Students' Unrest in Nigerian Universities: A Legal and Historical Approach*. Ibadan: Spectrum Books Ltd and IFRA, xx + 110p., ISBN 978 246 261 6.

Omitoogun, W. and K. Onigu-Otite, 1996. *National Conference as a Model for Democratic Transition: Nigeria and Benin*. Ibadan; IFRA, 43 p., ISBN 978 2015 44 X.

Omojola, B., 1995. *Nigerian Art Music (with an Introductory Study on Ghanaian Art Music)*. Ibadan: IFRA, x + 186 p. ilus., ISBN 978 2015 38 5.

Onibokun, A.G. and A. Faniran, 1995. *Urban Research in Nigeria*. Ibadan: IFRA, v + 191 p., ISBN 978 2015 37 7.

₦420, FF 100, US $ 20

Osaghae, E.E., 1994. *Trends of Migrant Political Organisation in Nigeria: The Igbo in Kano*. Ibadan: IFRA, 112p., ISBN 978 2015 27 X.

Osaghae, E.E., I. Touré, N. Kouamé, I.O. Albert and J. Adisa, 1994. *Urban Violence in Africa: Pilot Studies (South Africa, Côte-d'Ivoire, Nigeria)*. Ibadan: IFRA, 140 p., ISBN 978 2015 30 X.

Owolabi, K.A., 1996. *Because of Our Future. The Imperative of Environmental Ethics for Nigeria*. Ibadan: IFRA, 47 p., ISBN 978 2015 45 8.

Sani, A.A., J. Ibrahim and E. Babatunde Omobowale, 1997. *Creative Writing, Writers and Publishing in Northern Nigeria*. Ibadan: IFRA, iv + 51 p., ISBN 978 2015 50 4.

Smah, S.O. 1997. *Juvenile Delinquency and Juvenile Violence in Jos, Nigeria*. Ibadan: IFRA, vii + 67 p., ISBN 978 2015 48 2.

Suberu, R.T., 1994. *The 1991 State and Local Government Reorganizations in Nigeria*. Ibadan and Bordeaux: IFRA / CEAN (*Travaux et Documents* No. 41), 40 p., ISSN 0298-8879, ISBN 2 908065 24 Y.

Universal Declaration of Human Rights: English, French, Hausa, Igbo and Yoruba. Foreword by Wole Soyinka, 1993. Ibadan: IFRA, 56 p.,1993, ISBN 978 2015 26 1.

Institut Français de Recherche en Afrique/French Institute for Research in Africa
U.I. P.O. Box 21540 Ibadan, Oyo State, Nigeria
Tel/Fax: 234 2 810 40 77   E-mail: ifra @infoweb.abs.net